YOUR COLLEGE EXPERIENCE

STRATEGIES FOR SUCCESS

AT THE CITY COLLEGES OF CHICAGO

NINTH EDITION

YOUR COLLEGE EXPERIENCE

STRATEGIES FOR SUCCESS

AT THE CITY COLLEGES OF CHICAGO

CITY COLLEGES
of CHICAGO
Education that Works

JOHN N. GARDNER

A. JEROME JEWLER

BETSY O. BAREFOOT

BEDFORD/ST. MARTIN'S
BOSTON · NEW YORK

Manufactured in the United States of America.

6 5 4 3 2 1
f e d c b a

For information, write: Bedford/St. Martin's, 75 Arlington Street, Boston, MA 02116 (617-399-4000)

ISBN: 978-1-4576-0722-6

HISTORY OF THE CITY COLLEGES OF CHICAGO

Community college education has existed in Chicago since 1911, when Crane Technical High School opened its doors to 28 adults seeking higher education. This led to the establishment of Crane Junior College (now Malcolm X College). From this modest beginning, the City Colleges of Chicago (CCC) has grown to a system of 7 individually accredited colleges and 7 satellite centers.

Clarence Darrow, the renowned Chicago lawyer, argued in the defense of the City Colleges of Chicago when, during the Depression, its existence was threatened by a financially strapped Board of Education. Darrow stated that higher education in the form of the then "junior college, had to endure" because the City Colleges of Chicago were "for the people."

As a result of state legislative action in the late 1960s, the City Colleges of Chicago's status as a junior college changed to that of a comprehensive community college.

The City Colleges of Chicago, Community College District 508, today reaches more than 200,000 people annually, through the 14 facilities of the City College system; programs conducted in local community centers, public and parochial high schools, social service centers; and branches of the Chicago Public Library. Students can also take Internet-based courses via television through CCC's Public Broadcast Station, WYCC-TV Channel 20, and the Center for Distance Learning.

The district offers a variety of Associate Degree Programs that prepare students for transfer with junior-level standing to four-year institutions. A comprehensive offering of certificate programs also prepares students for immediate entry into their chosen careers.

City Colleges of Chicago provides specialized training for many workforce development programs, and tuition-free Adult Education courses including English as a Second Language (ESL), Adult Basic Education (ABE), and General Education Equivalency (GED), as well as Continuing Education (CE) programs that add value to the quality of life.

City Colleges of Chicago continues to serve its community, offering highly qualified faculty, a sustained commitment to affordable tuition, and excellence in higher education for all citizens of Chicago. Please visit the City Colleges of Chicago at **www.ccc.edu** for additional information.

ABOUT RICHARD J. DALEY COLLEGE

Richard J. Daley College was first established as the Southwest Side College in 1960 on the Bogan High School campus. The program enrolled mostly part-time evening students and evidenced rapid growth. In 1970, the Southwest College opened its doors in a set of pre-fabricated buildings and trailers designed to accommodate 1,000 students. The current College site was purchased by the City of Chicago and opened in 1981. It was named after Richard J. Daley, the former Mayor of the City of Chicago. The College has expanded its sites to meet the increased needs of the population in the service area. In 1997, it opened a technical training center, the West Side Technical Institute on Western Avenue and 28th Street, which was renamed the Arturo Velasquez Institute in 2009.

Daley College Locations
The Daley College campus is located on the Southwest Side on South Pulaski Road. The Arturo Velasquez Institute in located at 2800 South Western Avenue. The College also offers courses at the Cantu Center, the Orozco School, the Perez School, the Reyes Center, and Piotrowski Park.

Mission Statement
Richard J. Daley College provides a broad educational experience that reflects a 100-year commitment to the Chicago community for fostering lifelong learning. The College's hallmark is creating an academic environment encouraging the development of values, technological understanding, critical thinking, and cultural awareness that helps students to think clearly, communicate effectively, and analyze carefully everyday issues associated with local, national, and global life.

HISTORY OF THE CITY COLLEGES OF CHICAGO

ABOUT KENNEDY-KING COLLEGE

Kennedy-King College, formerly known as Woodrow Wilson Junior College, was established in the fall of 1935 at 6800 South Stewart Street. In 1966, the College's status was changed from that of a junior college to that of a comprehensive community college. In July 1969, the name was officially changed from Woodrow Wilson Junior College to Kennedy-King College in honor of Robert F. Kennedy and Martin Luther King Jr.

Situated on 30 acres, the new Kennedy-King College campus facility was completed in 2007. Kennedy-King College's new multi-building educational complex includes state-of-the-art classrooms, a natatorium with balcony seating, a day care center, a 300-seat theatre, banquet and catering accommodations, WYCC Television studio, WKKC FM radio station, a restaurant and bakery, and a world-class chef's kitchen and baking facility.

Kennedy-King College Locations
The Kennedy-King College campus is located at the corner of Halsted and 63rd Streets. Courses are also offered at Dawson Technical Institute at 3901 South State Street, Washburne Culinary Institute at 740 West 63rd Street, the Parrot Cage Restaurant at the South Shore Cultural Center, the French Pastry School at 226 West Jackson, Sikia Restaurant at 740 West 63rd Street, and the Child Development Lab School at 710 West 65th Street.

Mission Statement
Kennedy-King College is dedicated to providing high quality, comprehensive, accessible education and training opportunities that respond to changing community needs and that enable individuals to reach their full potential and successfully complete in the global marketplace.

ABOUT MALCOLM X COLLEGE

The first of the City Colleges of Chicago, Malcolm X College was founded as Crane Junior College in 1911. Initially, the College was housed in and served the graduates of Crane High School. In 1933 the College was closed due to the Great Depression. As a consequence of the advocacy of Hull House founder Jane Addams and noted attorney Clarence Darrow, the College reopened the following year. At the request of students and the community, in 1969, the College was renamed in honor of civil rights advocate and orator Malcolm X, also known as El-Hajj Malik El-Shabazz.

Malcolm X College is a major provider of training for allied health care professionals in Chicago, offering the largest selection of Health Science Degrees and Certificate programs in Cook County. Adjacent to one of the nation's largest medical centers, the College offers students a unique opportunity for clinical affiliations.

Malcolm X College Locations
Malcolm X College is located on the West Side on 20 acres on West Van Buren Street. The four-story building houses a modern Academic Support Center; a 430-seat, acoustically perfect Bruce K. Hayden Performing Arts Center; the newly renovated Carter G. Woodson Library; and a large physical education center with a gymnasium, swimming pool, dance studios, and weight-training center.

Mission Statement
Malcolm X College, a learning and assessment-centered community college, empowers students of diverse backgrounds and abilities to achieve academic, career, and personal success.

ABOUT OLIVE-HARVEY COLLEGE

Olive-Harvey College began its service to residents of the South Side in the late 1950s with the opening of the Fenger and Southeast campuses of the City Colleges of Chicago. These two campuses were consolidated and renamed Olive-Harvey College in 1970. The main campus of Olive-Harvey College was completed with the opening of a four-level building at 101St Street and Woodlawn Avenue in 1981. The building houses special instructional areas, new state-of-the-art laboratories and computer labs, and a Learning Resource Center, which contains the College's largest open computer laboratory. Physical education facilities include an indoor swimming pool and gymnasium, weight and exercise room, and a newly constructed baseball field, all located on a landscaped campus.

The College is named in honor of Private First Class Milton Lee Olive, III (1946-1965), who was posthumously awarded the Congressional Medal of Honor by President Lyndon Johnson, and Specialist Four Carmel Bernon Harvey Jr.

(1946-1967), who was awarded the Congressional Medal of Honor by President Richard Nixon. Both Olive and Harvey exhibited exceptional valor during combat in Vietnam.

Olive-Harvey College Locations
The Olive-Harvey College campus is on 67 acres at 10001 South Woodlawn Avenue. Courses are also offered at the South Chicago Learning Center, which is located at 3055 East 92nd Street.

Mission Statement
Olive-Harvey College provides high quality educational programs and support services and is dedicated to student learning and academic and career success through instructional excellence and responsiveness to student, business, and community needs.

ABOUT HARRY S. TRUMAN COLLEGE

In 2011, Truman College celebrates its 55th anniversary. The College began in 1956 as an unnamed "evening college" at Amundsen High School on the northwest side of Chicago. In 1961, it moved to its own building, a former elementary school, and was named Mayfair College after the school and the surrounding neighborhood. In 1976, the College moved to its current Uptown location and was going to be called Northeast Community College until Frank Sullivan, Mayor Richard J. Daley's press secretary, suggested naming it after the 33rd president, whose 1947 Commission on Higher Education greatly expanded the concept of the community college. Local residents, afraid the College would attract outsiders and offer them nothing, painted a mural on the wall of the "L" station facing the College. It depicts an array of faces from all races and includes the words: "This College must be for everyone." Those words guide the College to this day.

In the fall of 2010, the College completed construction on the new Larry McKeon Administrative Building. It includes a new Student Services Center, which is energy efficient, and a new nine-level Parking Deck, which will accommodate 1,100 parking spaces.

Harry S. Truman College Locations
The Truman College campus is located at 1145 West Wilson Avenue. Courses and programs are also offered at the Truman Technical Center, the Lakeview Learning Center, and the Truman Middle College Alternative High School.

Mission Statement
Truman College is dedicated to delivering high quality, innovative, affordable, and accessible educational opportunities and services that prepare students for a rapidly changing and diverse global economy.

ABOUT HAROLD WASHINGTON COLLEGE

Harold Washington College was first established as Loop College in fall 1962. It was located on East Lake on the 11th floor of the former University of Chicago/DePaul Center and opened its doors to 250 students. In January 1983, the College obtained its own building at the Wabash and Lake site. Constructed with local funds, the new building served as the home of the City Colleges of Chicago's District Office, the Chicago City-Wide College, and Loop College for many years.

Loop College was renamed Harold Washington College in 1987 to honor Chicago's first African-American mayor, Harold Washington. On April 19, 1988, the College was officially dedicated in memory of Mayor Harold Washington. Mayor Washington was a City Colleges of Chicago alumnus and was a strong advocate of the importance of community. That advocacy was illustrated in his commencement address at Loop College on May 10, 1984: "It is from the diversity of city life and the variety of cultures and backgrounds it offers, that we find the common threads that bring us together to form a college community." A major renovation of the building in 2003-2005 provided 11 floors of space for state-of-the art classrooms, community rooms, and science and computer labs to accommodate Harold Washington College's enrollment of over 19,000 students.

Harold Washington College Locations
Harold Washington College is located in the heart of Chicago's downtown loop between State and Wabash at 30 East Lake Street. It is accessible by bus and all CTA trains.

HISTORY OF THE CITY COLLEGES OF CHICAGO

Mission Statement

Harold Washington College is a learning-centered urban institution of higher education offering accessible and affordable opportunities for academic advancement, career development, and personal enrichment. The College is committed to upholding high institutional and academic standards and to understanding and improving student learning.

ABOUT WILBUR WRIGHT COLLEGE

Wilbur Wright College was established in 1934 at 3400 North Austin and moved to its present location at North Narragansett in 1993. Wright's 22-acre, park-like campus features five architecturally significant, interconnected buildings designed by Bertrand Goldberg, an award-winning architect whose work includes the Marina Towers in downtown Chicago.

The College is named for Wilbur Wright who "along with his brother Orville, launched into both history books and legend with the first ever manned powered flight… in 1903. In 1965 he was selected for the Hall of Fame for Great Americans" (**wright.nasa.gov/wilbur.htm**).

Wilbur Wright College Locations

Located on Chicago's Northwest Side, Wilbur Wright College is located at 4300 Narragansett Avenue at the corner of Montrose Avenue and Narragansett Street. Since 1995, Wright College's Humboldt Park Vocational Education Center, which is located at 1645 North California Street, has offered job training and educational programs for the Humboldt Park and West Town communities.

Mission Statement

Wilbur Wright College is learning-centered multi-campus institution of higher education offering students of diverse backgrounds, talents, and abilities a quality education leading to baccalaureate transfer, career advancement, and personal development.

City Colleges of Chicago – College Credit Academic Calendar 2011[1]

SPRING 2011 TERM	REGULAR 16 WEEK SESSION	12 WEEK SESSION[2]	8 WEEK SESSION[2]
Early online registration[3,4]	---------- November 8, 2010 ----------		
Early on campus registration[3,4]	---------- November 22, 2010 ----------		
Open registration	Jan 3	Jan 31	Feb 28
Martin Luther King Holiday	---------- January 17, 2011 ----------		
First day of class	Jan 18	Feb 14	Mar 14
President's Day Holiday	---------- February 21, 2011 ----------		
Complete financial aid appication for next academic year[5]	---------- NO LATER THAN March 1, 2011 ----------		
Spring Break	---------- April 18-24, 2011 ----------		
Last day for student initiated withdrawals	Apr 25	Apr 25	Apr 29
Spring 2011 session ends	---------- May 14, 2011 ----------		

SUMMER 2011 TERM	REGULAR SESSION	MINI SESSION[2]
Early online registration[2,3]	---------- April 4, 2011 ----------	
Early on campus registration [3,4]	---------- April 25, 2011 ----------	
Open registration	---------- June 6, 2011 ----------	
First day of class	---------- June 8, 2011 ----------	
Independence Day Holiday	---------- July 4, 2011 ----------	
Last day for student initiated withdrawal	Jul 18	July 6
Summer 2011 session ends	July 30	July 16

FALL 2011 TERM	REGULAR 16 WEEK SESSION	12 WEEK SESSION[2]	8 WEEK SESSION[2]
Early online registration[3,4]	---------- April 4, 2011 ----------		
Early on campus registration[3,4]	---------- April 25, 2011 ----------		
Open registration	Aug 8	Sept 6	Oct 3
First day of class	Aug 22	Sept 19	Oct 17
Labor Day Holiday	---------- September 5, 2011 ----------		
Last day for student initiated withdrawals	Nov 14	Nov 21	Nov 28
Thanksgiving Holiday (Thursday & Friday)	---------- November 24-25, 2011 ----------		
Fall 2011 session ends	---------- December 10, 2011 ----------		

NOTES:

1. *College Credit Academic Calendar is subject to change. Please contact the college for details.*

2. **Sessions and course offerings:** *not all courses are offered each session, nor are all sessions offered at each college. Please contact the college for details.*

3. **New Students:** *all new students are strongly encouraged to complete the registration process as early as possible, preferably prior to end of summer for fall entering students. The registration process for new students includes placement testing, college orientation, financial aid processing, career advising and academic program selection, and initial course selection. Please see your College Advisor to begin.*

4. **Continuing Students:** *continuing students are strongly encouraged to complete the registration process as early as possible to ensure the best course and schedule availability. Please see your College Advisor prior to registering to discuss your career and education goals, academic program, graduation requirements and your progress toward graduation, course selection, and, if applicable, transfer.*

5. **Financial aid:** *students are strongly urged to apply for financial aid (www.fafsa.gov) as early as possible (preferably by March 1st) for the academic year beginning in the fall. Please contact the financial aid office for details.*

STUDENT SERVICES

The Student Services team at your college is committed to providing our diverse student population with a broad range of quality services to address students' academic, financial, career, and life goals. Your Student Services team can also refer students to external support agencies when needed. Some of the many services offered by your Student Services team are listed below, and are subject to change.

ACADEMIC SUPPORT SERVICES

Tutoring
Tutoring Centers offer one-on-one tutoring, study groups, and computerized tutorial sessions. Students can attend workshops to learn how to improve study skills, time management, test taking, or note taking.

College Advising
Every City College provides a cadre of professional College Advisors available and eager to assist students in exploring their career interests, setting clear educational and career goals, and enrolling in appropriate courses to ensure they meet their chosen program of study leading to successful program completion and graduation. College Advisors are available to guide students in accessing necessary support services at the college or in the surrounding community to support their academic success.

CTA U-Pass
Through a partnership with the Chicago Transit Authority (CTA), the City Colleges offers full time enrolled credit students the U-Pass, which enables unlimited ridership on the CTA for the duration of the semester in which they are enrolled full time. Students MUST maintain full time enrollment status in order to retain their U-Pass privileges. Contact the Office of Dean of Students at the college for more information.

Credit for Prior Learning or Life Experiences
College credit may be granted for specialized courses, general education courses, or elective courses through the evaluation and/or assessment of appropriate prior learning or life experiences. The City Colleges of Chicago may grant credit for college-level knowledge or skills acquired outside the classroom through Credit by Examination or Credit by Evaluation. Grades will not be awarded and credit earned will not factor into Grade Point Average (GPA). For more information, see your College Academic Advisor or refer to the Student Policy Manual:
http://www.ccc.edu/Files/studentpolicymanual.pdf.

Disabilities
Disability Access Centers (DAC) at the City Colleges of Chicago are dedicated to meeting the special needs of students with disabilities and assisting them in their academic pursuits.

No qualified individual with a disability shall, by reason of such disability, be excluded from participation in or be denied the benefits of DAC services, programs or activities, or be subjected to discrimination. City Colleges of Chicago's goal is to promote equality of opportunity and full participation in our services, programs and activities. We will endeavor to provide reasonable modifications and/or accommodations to qualified individuals in accordance with the Americans with Disabilities Act (ADA) of 1990, Section 504 of the Rehabilitation Act of 1973, the ADA Amendment Act of 2008, and all pertinent federal, state and local anti-discrimination laws.

Students who have a need for disability accommodations or modifications are responsible for requesting such accommodation or modification, and are responsible for providing all requisite documentation to verify eligibility to the Disability Access Centers. DAC will make every effort to accommodate qualified students with disabilities as required by law.

Disability Access Centers:
Daley College: 773-828-7578
Harold Washington College: 312-553-6096
Kennedy-King College: 773-602-5278
Malcolm X College: 312-850-7088
Olive-Harvey College: 773-291-6345
Truman College: 773-907-4725
Wright College: 773-481-8015

FINANCIAL AID
The purpose of the financial aid program at the City Colleges of Chicago is to provide financial assistance to students as they pursue their educational goals. The program is committed to the philosophy that eligible students should not be denied access to higher education because of a lack of financial resources.

City Colleges of Chicago offers a variety of financial aid to assist students in meeting the costs of their education. Students are encouraged to stop by the Financial Aid Office to obtain information on eligibility requirements and necessary application forms.

Apply for Financial Assistance:
Students are required to complete the Free Application for Federal Student Aid (FAFSA) online. http://www.fafsa.ed.gov/. Filing online is fast and convenient. Any errors are revealed and highlighted for correction before your FAFSA is submitted, which leads to easier processing and reduced need to submit additional documentation.

Grant Assistance for Students:
The FAFSA is the application for all need-based grant programs at the City Colleges of Chicago. The City Colleges of Chicago offers grants, which are not subject to repayment such as: the Federal Pell Grant. The Pell Grant program is funded and administered by the U.S. Department of Education. To qualify for a Pell Grant, students must demonstrate significant financial need. The U.S. Department of Education determines students' eligibility for the Pell Grant, based on the information indicated on their FAFSA.

Supplemental Educational Opportunity Grant (SEOG)
The Federal SEOG is a campus-based program. Students with exceptional financial need are given priority for these limited funds. SEOG is awarded to students who qualify for a Federal Pell Grant.

State of Illinois Monetary Award Program (MAP) Grant
MAP grants are awarded to Illinois residents attending in-state colleges. Illinois residents apply for the MAP grant by submitting a FAFSA. The award is restricted to tuition and mandatory fees. Students are encouraged to apply early to increase eligibility to receive these funds.

Student Employment Program
The Federal Work Study (FWS) program is a federally funded, campus-based program offering employment to students demonstrating financial need. FWS employees are paid at least the current federal minimum wage and receive a paycheck every two weeks.

Federal Loan Program
As a part of the Health Care and Education Affordability Reconciliation Act of 2010, City Colleges of Chicago is now a participant in the William D. Ford Federal Direct Student Loan (Direct Loan) Program.

Direct Loans are low-interest loans for students and parents to help finance the cost of education at the post-secondary level. Under the Direct Loan Program, students will work with the Financial Aid Office to obtain Federal Stafford Loans or PLUS Loans from the U.S. Department of Education, rather than from private banks and credit unions.

If a financial need is demonstrated, the government will pay the interest on a student's subsidized loan. Students who do not demonstrate a financial need will be responsible for interest from the day the unsubsidized loan is disbursed. Both the subsidized and unsubsidized loans are eligible for deferred payment while the student is enrolled at least half-time.

Students are **strongly encouraged** to consult with a Financial Aid Advisor. The Financial Aid Office staff will help coordinate scholarships that are available to students based on academic excellence and other criteria to ensure that students are maximizing their financial assistance.

Scholarships
A wide variety of scholarhships are available by visiting www.ccc.edu/scholarships.

ACADEMIC POLICIES

Grade Designations
Grades are issued to degree-seeking students to apply towards graduation and are recorded on students' permanent academic record, or transcript, and are used to calculate students' grade point average (GPA). Grades awarded by the City Colleges of Chicago for Credit and Skills courses are: A=Excellent; B=Good; C=Average; D=Minimum Passing; F=Failure.

Grading for Foundational Studies and Continuing Education courses are: S=Satisfactory and F=Failure. Grading for Adult Education is: P=Completed all course and level requirements and can take next course at next level; R=Completed all course requirements; however more work is need at this level; F=Failed to meet the requirements of the course.

Graduation Requirements
To be eligible for graduation in all credit degree and certificate programs, students must earn a grade of "C" or better in all courses used to satisfy core curriculum and/or general education requirements and hold a minimum cumulative GPA of 2.0. Elective courses with a "D" final grade may count towards graduation. This policy is effective for all students entering or returning to the City Colleges of Chicago after May 1, 1998 (Board Report #20582, adopted 5-9-98).

Human Diversity Requirement
At least one course must meet the State of Illinois' Human Diversity requirement. Students should meet with a college Academic Advisor for course selection.

Residency Requirement
All students must complete 21 credit hours of residency at the City Colleges of Chicago. (Special consideration may be given on a case by case basis by the College President.) The student's degree will be awarded by the college where 15 of the last 21 credit hours were earned.

Foreign Language Requirement
EFFECTIVE FALL 2009: All students entering, or returning to the City Colleges of Chicago after a two (2) year break from taking courses, seeking an Associate of Arts (A.A.) degree are required to demonstrate proficiency in a language that has a recognized literature or culture and that is offered by the City Colleges of Chicago. The level of proficiency must be equivalent to that of successful completion of a second semester language course.

STUDENT SERVICES

INTERNATIONAL STUDENTS

International students are warmly welcomed to continue their studies at the City Colleges of Chicago. Whether you decide to seek a Liberal Arts Education or pursue a career program to acquire work skills, the City Colleges of Chicago can meet your educational needs.

In addition to completing an application to City Colleges of Chicago and providing required transcripts or test scores, International students must also submit the necessary documents for the U.S. Citizenship & Immigration Services (USCIS).

Please note: the application review and processing take time, so it is essential that students apply early. Please allow a minimum of 30 days for review/evaluation.

International (F-1 holders) must identify themselves early in the application process for proper advisement of the Immigration & Naturalization Services transfer procedures. To complete the transfer procedure an International student must provide:

- $100.00 non-refundable charge for I-20 application processing for regular college-level enrollments. (Upon registration, $50.00 will be credited toward tuition.)

- TOEFL SCORE 61 (internet-based), 173 (computer-based), 500 (paper based). (If you are already in the United States, you can take a placement exam at the City Colleges in place of the TOEFL.)

- A transfer permission letter from the last school attended in the U.S. (If applicable)

- An Affidavit of Support (Form I-134) from sponsor, guardian or parent.

- Bank and tax documents proving availability of funds.

- Passport and recent photo

- I-94 departure record

- Student Visa

- Proof of Medical Insurance (required each semester)

- Provide a copy of I-20 that Homeland Security stamped and approved, if applicable

For more information contact the Office of Student Affairs - International Students: 312-553-3441 or visit our website at: http://ccc.edu/isa/index.shtml.

PLACEMENT EXAMINATIONS

City Colleges of Chicago utilizes the computerized COMPASS exams (reading, writing, math & e-Write), paper & pencil ASSET, and ACT scores for appropriate placement into courses to support students' academic success. All students new to the City Colleges are required to take the complete battery of placement exams, unless they show proof of having successfully completed appropriate college level courses, or opt to use ACT scores that are less than two years old.

STUDENT ACTIVITIES

Many opportunities for students to become engaged in college life are available at each college, including involvement in honor societies such as: Phi Theta Kappa, Psi Beta, and Sigma Kappa Delta. Students are encouraged to seek out student organizations to enhance their college experience.

Student Government Association

Student Government Association (SGA) is the main vehicle for student input regarding activities of the college and in policies affecting student life. The purpose of the SGA members (officers, senators, and appointed representatives) is to represent themselves and the City Colleges of Chicago student body in the most positive and professional manner possible, recognizing that they are always working in the best interest of the City Colleges of Chicago community.

Student government officers and members are elected in the spring of each year and will remain in office for one year (May 31 – May 30), provided they are enrolled for a minimum of six (6) credit hours each semester and maintain a 2.3 cumulative grade point average. A student may be a candidate for, and elected to, a student government office in consecutive years, provided the student meets the eligibility criteria.

In order to provide complete representation of all CCC student governments, each student government president should attend all regularly scheduled and special SGA meetings called by the CCC District SGA Council (DSGAC) chairperson. All student government officers and members are welcome to attend the DSGAC meeting; however, only the President or their proxy are eligible to vote.

TEXTBOOK RENTAL

City Colleges of Chicago has an agreement with Follett and Beck's bookstores to offer rental textbook programs to assist students with offsetting the costs of textbooks. For more information, students should contact the Office of Student Services.

VETERANS SERVICES

City Colleges has a long history of providing education to veterans who are seeking to gain new skills and transform skills learned in the military for use in the civilian world. City Colleges are committed to making the college educational experience rewarding for our veterans. *Special thanks to all who served our country to protect our cherished freedoms.*

If you are a Veteran and/or dependant of a Veteran, you may be eligible for grants and/or scholarships, such as the Illinois Veteran Grant, Illinois National Guard, Missing in Action/Prison of War (MIA/POW) Scholarship and many other educational benefits. Consult with your Financial Aid staff.

RESIDENCY

Enrollment of students is classified, for the purpose of determining fees and tuition, as in-district, out-of-district, out-of-state, or international students. Preferred documents which can be used for residency verification include:

- Driver's License
- Voter Registration Card
- Copy of Lease
- Utility or Home Telephone Bill
- State of Illinois Identification Card
- Mexican Consular ID
- Official ISIR

Dependent Registrants may present the following:

- State of Illinois Identification Card
- Utility or Home Telephone Bill
- Copy of Lease in Parents' Name(s) at Student's Address

In-District Students

To qualify as in-district, students must reside within the City of Chicago for at least 30 days immediately prior to the date established by the District for classes to begin for the term.

Out-of-District Students

Students who reside in Illinois but outside Chicago for at least 30 days prior to the date established by the District for classes to begin, are considered out-of-district students. Students will be required to furnish legal evidence proving residence.

Out-of-district students, who want to obtain a degree or certificate offered by one of the City Colleges of Chicago, but not their own district community college, should refer to the Tuition Chargeback policy below and at: http://www.ccc.edu/files/studentpolicymanual.pdf.

Out-of-State Students

Students who legally reside outside of Illinois are considered out-of-state students.

FEES AND CHARGES

1. **Miscellaneous Fees** - Fees that are assessed to students are determined by each college.
2. **Required Fees** The following fees associated with course registration are required. They include, but are not limited to:
   - Registration Fees
   - Activity Fees
   - Partial Payment Fees
   - CDL Licensing Fees
   - Lab Fees
3. **Non-Refundable Fees** The following fees associated with course registration are non-refundable. They include, but are not limited to:
   - Registration Fees
   - Partial Payment Fees
   - Activity Fees (activity fees may be refunded if courses are dropped before the term begins)

Financial Obligation

Students are expected to pay when enrolling. Acceptable payment includes cash, check, credit/debit cards, or enrollment in NBS e-Cashier or a Financial Aid Deferment. Failure to make appropriate payment arrangements within two business days of enrollment will result in the initiation of drop processing of all enrolled classes. Whenever possible, students dropped for non-payment will be notified by email or by phone.

Transcript Charges

- First transcript requested is complimentary, unless same day service is requested.
- $10.00 per transcript for same day service.
- $5.00 charge for each transcript issued after first transcript, including Continuing Education transcripts.

Other Charges

- $100.00 non-refundable charge for I-20 application processing for regular college-level enrollments.
- $40.00 per check returned for non-sufficient funds.
- $5.00 for student I.D. card replacement.

Tuition and fees are subject to change. Please refer to http://www.ccc.edu/student/Tuition.asp for the most current tuition and fee information.

STUDENT SERVICES

Tuition Chargeback

Chicago residents who wish to enroll in a degree program not available at any of the City Colleges of Chicago may apply for tuition assistance to attend another public community college in Illinois where the desired certificate or degree program is offered. Applications are available online, please refer to http://www.ccc.edu/student/files/chargeback_application628.pdf. Applications must be received by the City Colleges of Chicago 30 days prior to the beginning date of the semester or term of enrollment at the college the student plans to attend.

Non-Chicago residents who plan to enroll in a college program at the City Colleges of Chicago which is not available at a community college in their district, should apply for tuition assistance at their local community college. If no community college exists in their district, residents should go to their high school district to apply.

Tuition Waivers

Senior Citizens (65 years of age or older) - Senior Citizens may be eligible for a tuition waiver for the first six regular college credits during open registration, if seats are available. Proof of senior citizen status is a birth certificate, driver's license, or RTA Special Users' Pass, and must be presented at time of registration. All hours above six will be paid by the enrolled senior citizen student at the regular tuition rate per semester/term.

Public Aid Recipients

Public Aid recipients [categories beginning with (0)] may apply for tuition waivers only after they apply for Financial Aid and have been determined as Financial Aid ineligible. Public Aid recipients may be eligible for a tuition waiver of up to six credit hours. All hours above six will be paid by the enrolled public aid recipient at the regular tuition rate per semester/term.

WITHDRAWALS AND REFUNDS

Refunds for Dropped Classes Within First Seven Days

Students may drop courses during the first seven days from the start date of class for regular sessions (or equitable time period for special sessions) without incurring a penalty. If processed during the first seven days from the start of class in a regular session during the fall and spring terms, drop refunds for student-initiated withdrawals (WTH) are available at one hundred percent of tuition and applicable fees only. (100% REFUND WITHIN FIRST 7 DAYS OF A REGULAR SESSION.)

THERE WILL BE NO REFUNDS ALLOWED AFTER THE FIRST SEVEN DAYS OF THE START OF CLASSES FOR A REGULAR SESSION.

Failure to withdraw may result in mandatory payment of tuition/fees and/or a failing grade.

Refunds – No-Show Withdrawal (NSW)

Students who do not attend the first two class sessions will be withdrawn from the class by the instructor and issued a No-Show Withdrawals (NSW). No refunds of tuition and/or fees will be issued for classes with (NSW). Students will be held accountable for the payment of tuition and fees of NSW courses. Federal financial aid cannot be used to cover the cost of NSW classes.

Students who do not attend the first class session of a course which meets only once per week will be considered a No-Show (NSW).

Refunds – Center for Distance Learning Online with Video Component Courses (TW)

Center for Distance Learning (CDL) courses combine Internet-based instruction with video and are accessed on WYCC-TV Channel 20. Refunds will not be issued for lack of access to WYCC Channel 20.

NOTE: Some areas of Chicago and surrounding suburbs DO NOT have access to WYCC Channel 20.

Please refer to http://www.ccc.edu/student/Tuition.asp for the most current refund policies prior to enrolling in CDL/WYCC courses.

BACCALAUREATE/TRANSFER & GENERAL STUDIES										
#	PROGRAM/PLAN	AWARD	HRS.	DA	HW	KK	MX	OH	TR	WR
0210	Associate in Arts	AA	62	x	x	x	x	x	x	x
0211	Associate in Science	AS	64	x	x	x	x	x	x	x
0100	Associate in Engineering Science	AES	64	x	x				x	x
0217	Associate in Fine Arts-Art (Education)	AFA	60		x					
0216	Associate in Fine Arts-Art (Studio)	AFA	61		x				x	
0208	Associate in Fine Arts - Music Education	AFA	63		x					
0205	Associate in Fine Arts - Music Performance	AFA	68		x					x
0209	Associate of Arts in Teaching - Early Childhood Education	AAT	63		x					
0212	Associate of Arts in Teaching - Secondary Math	AAT	62						x	
0203	Associate in General Studies	AGS	60	x	x	x	x	x	x	x

AGRICULTURE, FOOD & NATURAL RESOURCES										
#	PROGRAM/PLAN	AWARD	HRS.	DA	HW	KK	MX	OH	TR	WR
0160	Environmental Technology	AAS	68							x
0161	Environmental Technology	BC	18							x
0241	Horticulture	AAS	63		x					
0320	Horticulture	BC	18		x					
0828	Horticulture (Sustainable Urban)	AC	31	x						

ARCHITECTURE & CONSTRUCTION										
#	PROGRAM/PLAN	AWARD	HRS.	DA	HW	KK	MX	OH	TR	WR
0117	Air Conditioning & Refrigeration	AAS	62			x				
0118	Air Conditioning & Refrigeration	AC	36			x				
0153	Air Conditioning - Commercial Refrigeration	BC	17			x				
0177	Air Conditioning - Domestic Refrigeration	BC	17			x				
0178	Air Conditioning - Heating	BC	18			x				
0132	Architectural CAD	BC	9							x
0122	Architectural Drafting	AAS	63		x					x
0124	Architectural Drafting	BC	16		x					x
0760	Bricklayer	BC	16			x				
0159	Building Energy Technologies	BC	21							x
0144	CAD Technology	AAS	60						x	
0138	CAD Technology	AC	34						x	
0139	CAD Technology	BC	16						x	
0780	Carpentry	AC	37			x				
0750	Communications Technology	AAS	65	x						
0759	Concrete Masonry	BC	16			x				
0775	Construction Carpentry	BC	16			x				
0375	Construction Management	AAS	65			x				
0768	Construction Painter	BC	16			x				
0752	Electrical Construction Technology	AAS	65	x						
0766	Electrical Line Worker (Overhead)	AC	30			x				
0163	Mechanical Technology CAD	BC	9							x
0753	Plumbing & Fire Protection	BC	16			x				
0758	Welder (Combination)	BC	16			x				
0827	Welding (Industrial Technology)	BC	13	x						

DA=RICHARD J. DALEY, HW=HAROLD WASHINGTON, KK=KENNEDY-KING, MX=MALCOLM X, OH=OLIVE-HARVEY, TR=HARRY S. TRUMAN, WR=WILBUR WRIGHT

CCC-11

PROGRAMS OF STUDY
PROGRAM/PLANS BY CLUSTER A.A.S. (ASSOCIATE APPLIED SCIENCE) A.C. (ADVANCED CERTIFICATE) B.C. (BASIC CERTIFICATE)

#	PROGRAM/PLAN	AWARD	HRS.	DA	HW	KK	MX	OH	TR	WR
ARTS, A/V TECHNOLOGY & COMMUNICATIONS										
0350	Digital Multimedia Design	AAS	67		x					
0351	Digital Multimedia Design	AC	36		x					
0352	Digital Multimedia - Video & Sound	BC	18		x					
0353	Digital Multimedia - 3D Graphics	BC	21		x					
0354	Digital Multimedia - Interactive Media	BC	18		x					
0083	Media Communications	AAS	63			x				
0093	Music Business	BC	21		x					
0094	Music Technology	BC	26		x					
0085	Theater Arts	AAS	62			x				
0086	Theater Technology	AC	35			x				
0165	Visual Media Communications	AAS	60			x				
0166	Visual Media Communications	AC	30			x				
0194	Vis Med Com-Animation	BC	15			x				
0192	Vis Med Com-Page Layout	BC	15			x				
0193	Vis Med Com-Web Page Design	BC	15			x				
BUSINESS, MANAGEMENT, ADMINISTRATION & FINANCE										
0001	Accounting	AAS	60	x	x	x		x	x	x
0002	Accounting	BC	17	x	x	x		x	x	x
0003	Accounting	AC	30	x	x	x		x	x	x
0861	Bank Teller (Professional)	BC	17							x
0042	Business Admin - General Business	AC	30	x				x		
0388	Finance	AC	31							x
0303	Library Technical Assistant	AAS	60							x
0330	Library Technical Assistant	BC	12							x
0021	Management/Marketing	AAS	62	x	x	x		x	x	x
0022	Management/Marketing	AC	35	x	x	x		x	x	x
0023	Management/Marketing	BC	18	x	x	x		x	x	x
0883	Office Specialist	BC	20	x						
0882	Real Estate Broker	BC	5	x						
0812	Real Estate Sales	BC	2.5						x	

DA=RICHARD J. DALEY, HW=HAROLD WASHINGTON, KK=KENNEDY-KING, MX=MALCOLM X, OH=OLIVE-HARVEY, TR=HARRY S. TRUMAN, WR=WILBUR WRIGHT

A.A.S. (ASSOCIATE APPLIED SCIENCE) A.C. (ADVANCED CERTIFICATE) B.C. (BASIC CERTIFICATE)

#	PROGRAM/PLAN	AWARD	HRS.	DA	HW	KK	MX	OH	TR	WR
	EDUCATION & TRAINING									
0276	Child Development - Bilingual Teacher Aide	AAS	61		x					
0280	Child Development - Elementary Education	AAS	61		x	x				
0284	Child Development - Elementary Education	AC	34		x	x				
0300	Child Development - IDC Level I	AC	41	x						
0331	Child Development - Infant Toddler Care	AAS	62				x			
0332	Child Development - Infant Toddler Care	AC	32				x			
0278	Child Development - Pre-School Education	AAS	62	x	x	x	x	x	x	
0282	Child Development - Pre-School Education	AC	32	x	x	x	x	x	x	
0277	Child Development - Pre-School Education	BC	10					x	x	
0286	Child Development - Pre-School Educ/Infant Toddler	AC	32		x					
0275	Child Development - School Age Child Care	AAS	61		x					
0281	Child Development - Special Education	AAS	63			x				
0285	Child Development - Special Education	AC	33			x				
0831	Family Child Care Business	BC	1.5						x	
0055	Teaching, Leadership & Support Professionals	AAS	63		x					
0057	Teaching, Leadership & Support Professionals	AC	35	x						
	ALSO SEE BACCALAUREATE/TRANSFER A.A.T. - Early Childhood Education									
	HEALTH SCIENCE									
#	PROGRAM/PLAN	AWARD	HRS.	DA	HW	KK	MX	OH	TR	WR
0215	Biotechnology	AAS	67						x	
0868	Dental Assistant	BC	4							x
0810	Dental Assisting	BC	3.5						x	
0222	Dental Hygiene	AAS	72			x				
0808	Dialysis Technician	AC	3						x	
0830	EKG Technician	BC	2						x	
0867	Emergency Medical Technician (EMT)	BC	9					x		x
0252	Emergency Medical Technician - Basic	BC	6		x		x	x		x
0265	EMT II Paramedic	AC	34				x			
0263	EMT II Paramedic	AAS	61				x			
0809	Medical Administrative Assistant	BC	3						x	
0359	Medical Assistant (Basic)	AC	33							x
0386	Medical Assisting	AC	26						x	
0862	Medical Billing/Coding (Computerized)	BC	15	x	x	x	x	x	x	x
0870	Medical Secretary	BC	20.5				x			x
0257	Mortuary Science	AAS	62				x			
0247	Nephrology/Renal Technology	AAS	65				x			
0239	Nursing	AAS	69	x			x		x	
0801	Nursing Assistant (Basic)	BC	10	x	x	x	x	x	x	x
0240	Nursing - Practical	AC	40	x		x	x	x		x
0381	Nursing (RN Completion)	AAS	70				x			x
0221	Obstetrics & Gynecologic Technology	BC	11				x			
0259	Occupational Therapy Assistant (OTA)	AAS	75							x
0382	Ophthalmic Technology	AAS	65					x		
0802	Pharmacy Technician	BC	8.5	x	x	x		x	x	x

DA=RICHARD J. DALEY, HW=HAROLD WASHINGTON, KK=KENNEDY-KING, MX=MALCOLM X, OH=OLIVE-HARVEY, TR=HARRY S. TRUMAN, WR=WILBUR WRIGHT

CCC-13

PROGRAMS OF STUDY
PROGRAM/PLANS BY CLUSTER A.A.S. (ASSOCIATE APPLIED SCIENCE) A.C. (ADVANCED CERTIFICATE) B.C. (BASIC CERTIFICATE)

HEALTH SCIENCE (CONTINUED)

#	PROGRAM/PLAN	AWARD	HRS.	DA	HW	KK	MX	OH	TR	WR
0254	Pharmacy Technology	AC	33				x			
0219	Phlebotomy	BC	11				x			
0866	Phlebotomy (Accelerated)	BC	15							x
0262	Physician Assistant	AAS	78				x			
0246	Radiography	AAS	75				x			x
0248	Renal Dialysis Technology	AC	36				x			
0234	Respiratory Care	AAS	71				x			
0269	Sterile Processing Clinical	BC	11				x			
0267	Surgical Technology	AAS	61				x			

HOSPITALITY & CULINARY

#	PROGRAM/PLAN	AWARD	HRS.	DA	HW	KK	MX	OH	TR	WR
0365	Baking & Pastry Arts	AAS	62			x				
0366	Baking & Pastry Arts	AC	38			x				
0367	Baking & Pastry Arts	BC	15			x				
0392	Cake Decorating & Baking (L'Art Du Gateau)	BC	16			x				
0362	Culinary Arts	AAS	63			x				
0363	Culinary Arts	AC	41			x				
0364	Culinary Arts	BC	13			x				
0253	Food Sanitation	BC	2		x	x	x		x	
0891	Food Service Sanitation - Recertification	BC	1		x		x		x	
0061	Hospitality	AAS	63		x					
0062	Hospitality Front Office	AC	32		x					
0746	Pastry & Baking (L'Art de la Patisserie)	BC	24			x				

HUMAN SERVICES

#	PROGRAM/PLAN	AWARD	HRS.	DA	HW	KK	MX	OH	TR	WR
0344	Addictions Studies	AAS	64		x	x				
0343	Addictions Studies	AC	37		x	x				
0345	Addictions Studies	BC	18		x	x				x
0349	Cosmetology	AC	36						x	
0339	Gerontology Aide	BC	12							x
0340	Gerontology Specialist	AAS	61							x
0195	HIV/STI Prevention Education	BC	24							x
0895	Homemaker/Homehealth Aide	BC	4.5				x			
0391	Human Development & Familly Studies	AAS	60					x		
0387	Human Resource Management	AC	30							x
0341	Nursing Home Administration	BC	12							x
0896	Personal Trainer	BC	1.5			x	x			
0368	Property Management/Desk Clerk	BC	12							x
0369	Property Management/Leasing Specialist	BC	12							x
0258	Psychiatric Rehabilitation	BC	14							x
0313	Social Work - Generalist	AAS	66		x	x				
0317	Social Work - Generalist	AC	37		x					
0370	Social Work-Youth Work	AAS	63		x					
0371	Social Work-Youth Work	AC	31		x					
0372	Social Work-Youth Work	BC	15		x					

DA=RICHARD J. DALEY, HW=HAROLD WASHINGTON, KK=KENNEDY-KING, MX=MALCOLM X, OH=OLIVE-HARVEY, TR=HARRY S. TRUMAN, WR=WILBUR WRIGHT

INFORMATION TECHNOLOGY

#	PROGRAM/PLAN	AWARD	HRS.	DA	HW	KK	MX	OH	TR	WR
0806	A+ Certified Computer Technician	BC	6	x			x			x
0011	Computer Information Systems	AAS	60	x	x	x	x	x	x	x
0012	Computer Information Systems	BC	12	x	x	x	x	x	x	x
0013	Computer Information Systems	AC	30	x	x	x	x	x	x	x
0852	Computer Literacy	BC	7							x
0297	Computer Security & Forensic Investigation	BC	20							x
0264	Environmental (GIS) Geographic Information Systems	BC	21		x					
0719	Information Processing	AC	26							x
0384	Network Security & Forensics	AC	31		x					
0383	Network Security & Forensics	BC	18		x					
0141	Networking Systems & Technologies	AAS	60	x					x	
0142	Networking Systems & Technologies	AC	30	x					x	
0143	Networking Systems & Technologies	BC	18	x					x	
0811	Web Design	BC	5						x	
0155	Web Development	AC	31						x	
0152	Web Development	BC	16						x	

LAW, PUBLIC SAFETY, CORRECTIONS & SECURITY

#	PROGRAM/PLAN	AWARD	HRS.	DA	HW	KK	MX	OH	TR	WR
0319	Criminal Justice - Private Police Services	AC	30	x						
0326	Criminal Justice - Private Police Services	BC	18	x						
0294	Criminal Justice - Public Police Services	AAS	60	x	x	x		x	x	x
0295	Criminal Justice - Public Police Services	AC	30	x	x	x		x	x	x
0296	Criminal Justice - Public Police Services	BC	15	x	x	x		x	x	x
0897	Emergency Dispatch (911)	BC	2.5			x	x			
0355	Emergency Management	AAS	64					x		x
0358	Emergency Preparedness	BC	18					x		x
0336	Fire Science & Technology	AAS	60		x					
0356	Homeland Security	BC	18					x		x
0357	Incident Command	BC	18					x		x
0304	Paralegal	AAS	63							x
0829	Paralegal	BC	11.5						x	
0898	Unarmed Security Guard	BC	2	x						

MANUFACTURING

#	PROGRAM/PLAN	AWARD	HRS.	DA	HW	KK	MX	OH	TR	WR
0826	Computer Numeric Control Technician	BC	15	x						
0748	Computerized Numerical Control (CNC)	AC	41							x
0790	Industrial Maintenance	AC	36	x						x
0825	Manufacturing (Basic)	BC	14.5	x						
0770	Manufacturing Tech - Maintenance Mechanic	AAS	62	x						
0771	Manufacturing Tech - Maintenance Mechanic	AC	34	x						
0789	Process Technology	AAS	63					x		
0754	Process Technology	AC	38					x		

DA=RICHARD J. DALEY, HW=HAROLD WASHINGTON, KK=KENNEDY-KING, MX=MALCOLM X, OH=OLIVE-HARVEY, TR=HARRY S. TRUMAN, WR=WILBUR WRIGHT

CCC-15

PROGRAMS OF STUDY
PROGRAM/PLANS BY CLUSTER A.A.S. (ASSOCIATE APPLIED SCIENCE) A.C. (ADVANCED CERTIFICATE) B.C. (BASIC CERTIFICATE)

#	PROGRAM/PLAN	AWARD	HRS.	DA	HW	KK	MX	OH	TR	WR
	SCIENCE, TECHNOLOGY, ENGINEERING & MATHEMATICS									
0389	Agricultural Biotechnology	AC	31		x					
0137	Chemical Laboratory Technology	AAS	62						x	
	TRANSPORTATION, DISTRIBUTION & LOGISTICS									
0125	Automotive Technology	AAS	66			x			x	
0130	Automotive Technology	AC	46			x			x	
0116	Automotive Technology	BC	20						x	
0112	Auto Body Reconstruction Technology	BC	25			x				
0111	Auto Body Repainting Technology	BC	26			x				
0134	Automotive Chassis Maintenance	BC	19			x				
0133	Automotive Collision Technology	AC	44			x				
0136	Automotive Fuel Management Technology	BC	27			x				
0128	Automotive Maintenance	BC	27			x				
0185	Automotive Parts Specialists	BC	21			x				
0876	Commercial Driver Training	BC	12					x		
0875	Commercial Passenger Driver - Class B	BC	9					x		
0890	Defensive Driving - Attitudinal	BC	1		x					
0848	Forklift Operation & Safety	BC	2					x		
0889	Limousine - Residential Chauffeur Training	BC	1		x					
0713	Logistics/Transportation/Distribution	AAS	63	x						
0712	Logistics/Transportation/Distribution	AC	36	x						
0715	Public Passenger Vehicle Training - Taxi	BC	6		x					
0832	Supply Chain Management (Fundamentals of)	BC	4		x			x		x
0385	Supply Chain Management (SCM)	BC	16		x	x		x		

ILLINOIS ARTICULATION INITIATIVE (IAI)

**Models for CCC Associate in Arts (A.A.) and Associate in Science (A.S.)
Transfer Degrees and General Education**

City Colleges of Chicago participates in the Illinois Articulation Initiative (IAI), which is a comprehensive statewide effort among more than 100 colleges and universities in Illinois to facilitate the transfer of students. IAI became effective for students entering a participating college or university as first-time, first-year students the summer of 1998. Benefits for students are as follows:

- Students who complete the A.A. or A.S. degree at the City Colleges of Chicago, and who meet the admission requirements of the IAI participating baccalaureate degree granting institution to which they transfer, will have completed the lower-division general education requirements for an associate or baccalaureate degree in lieu of the receiving institution's general education requirements.

- Students who complete the IAI General Education Core Curriculum (GECC) at City Colleges of Chicago and transfer to participating institutions have the assurance that lower-division general education requirements for an associate or baccalaureate degree have been satisfied and the GECC will transfer.

A participating/receiving institution may require transfer students to complete an institution-wide and/or mission-related graduation requirement beyond the scope of the Illinois General Education Core Curriculum.

The IAI Website http://www.itransfer.org/newwebsite includes information on requirements for general education and specific majors, course descriptions, and a student planning worksheet. (See IAI equivalency course grids in this section for general education and majors.)

Due to the increasing number of students fulfilling degree requirements at more than one City College, district-wide models for A.A. and A.S. Transfer Degrees showing minimum general education requirements have been designed. The models facilitate the need for a smooth transition for the student's path to degree completion.

The CCC degree models for both the Associate in Arts and Associate in Science programs, indicate general education minimum requirements as well as the State of Illinois Human Diversity requirement which follow the IAI course equivalency grids.

PROGRAMS OF STUDY
BACCALAUREATE TRANSFER – IAI GENERAL EDUCATION

IAI APPROVED GRIDS FOR GENERAL EDUCATION COURSES											
SUBJECT	NO	COURSE DESCRIPTION	IAI NO.	CREDIT	DA	HW	KK	MX	OH	TR	WR
AFRICAN AMERICAN STUDIES (0117)											
AFRO AM	101	Intro to African-Amer Stds	HF 906D	3					x		
ANTHROPOLOGY (0081)											
ANTHRO	201	Intro, Biol & Cult Evol-Human	S1 900N	3	x		x	x		x	x
ANTHRO	202	Cultural Anthropology	S1 901N	3	x	x	x	x	x	x	x
ART (0010)											
ART	103	Art Appreciation	F2 900	3	x	x			x	x	x
ASTRONOMY (0071)											
ASTROMY	201	Descriptive Astronomy	P1 906	3	x	x		x		x	x
BIOLOGY (0023)											
BIOLOGY	107	Nutrition-Consumer Education	L1 904	3				x			
BIOLOGY	109	Human Genetics and Evolution	L1 907	3		x					
BIOLOGY	114	General Education Biology	L1 900L	4	x	x	x	x	x	x	x
BIOLOGY	115	Human Biology	L1 904L	4	x	x	x	x	x	x	x
BIOLOGY	116	Anatomy and Physiology	L1 904L	4				x			
BIOLOGY	119	Environmental Biology	L1 905L	4							x
BIOLOGY	242-1	Evolution	L1 907	3	x		x				
BOTANY (0025)											
BOTANY	201	General Botany I	L1 901L	4	x					x	x
CHEMISTRY (0073)											
CHEM	121	Basic Chemistry I	P1 902L	4	x	x	x	x	x	x	x
CHEM	201	General Chemistry I	P1 902L	5	x	x	x	x	x	x	x
COMMUNICATION MEDIA (0004)											
CMMEDIA	163	Film Rhetoric	F2 905	3					x		
ECONOMICS (0082)											
ECON	201	Principles of Economics I	S3 901	3	x	x	x	x	x	x	x
ECON	202	Principles of Economics II	S3 902	3	x	x	x	x	x	x	x
ENGLISH (0035)											
ENGLISH	101	Composition	C1 900	3	x	x	x	x	x	x	x
ENGLISH	102	Composition	C1 901R	3	x	x	x	x	x	x	x
ENVIRONMENTAL TECHNOLOGY (0027)											
ENVR TC	105	Introduction to Atmospheric Sciences	P1 905	3							x
FINE ARTS (0042)											
FIN ART	104	The World of the Cinema	F2 908	3		x		x		x	
FIN ART	105	History of Paint Sculp Arc	F2 900	3	x	x				x	
FIN ART	107	Hist of Arch Paint Sculp I	F2 901	3	x	x	x	x		x	x
FIN ART	108	Hist of Arch Paint Sculp II	F2 902	3	x	x	x	x		x	x
FIN ART	109	History of Cinema	F2 909	3		x					
FIN ART	110	Opera and the Humanities	F1 910	3		x				x	
FRENCH (0051)											
FRENCH	104	Fourth Course French	H1 900	4		x				x	x
FRENCH	213	Intro to Moder Lit French	H3 916	3		x					
FRENCH	214	Readings in Lit French	H3 916	3		x				x	

IAI APPROVED GRIDS FOR GENERAL EDUCATION COURSES

SUBJECT	NO	COURSE DESCRIPTION	IAI NO.	CREDIT	DA	HW	KK	MX	OH	TR	WR
GEOGRAPHY (0084)											
GEOG	101	World Geography	S4 900N	3	x	x	x	x		x	x
GEOG	102	Economic Geography	S4 903N	3		x	x				x
GEOG	201	Physical Geography	P1 909	3	x						
GEOLOGY (0075)											
GEOLOGY	201	Physical Geology	P1 907L	3	x	x				x	
HISTORY (0085)											
HISTORY	111	Hist Amer People to 1865	S2 900	3	x	x	x	x	x	x	x
HISTORY	112	Hist Amer People From 1865	S2 901	3	x	x	x	x	x	x	x
HISTORY	141	Hist World Civilization to 1500	S2 912N	3	x	x	x	x	x	x	x
HISTORY	142	Hist World Civilization From 1500	S2 913N	3	x	x	x	x	x	x	x
HISTORY	215	History of Latin America	S2 910N	3	x	x	x			x	x
HISTORY	225	Modern Middle East History	S2 919N	3		x					
HISTORY	243	Far East in the Modern World	S2 909N	3			x			x	x
HISTORY	247	African Hist to Col Period	S2 906N	3	x	x		x	x	x	x
HISTORY	248	African Hist - Modern World	S2 907N	3		x	x	x			
HUMANITIES (0041)											
HUM	123	Intro to Arts and Ideas	HF 900	3	x	x					x
HUM	143	Intro to Latin American/Latino	HF 906D	3		x					
HUM	201	General Course I Hum	HF 900	3	x	x	x	x	x	x	x
HUM	202	General Course II Hum	HF 901	3	x	x	x	x	x	x	x
HUM	203	Arts of Cont America	HF 900	3		x					
HUM	205	World Literature I	H3 906	3	x	x	x	x	x	x	x
HUM	207	The Great Books	H3 907	3	x	x	x	x			
HUM	208	Women in Creative and Performing Arts	HF 907D	3		x					x
HUM	210	Comparative Mythology	H9 901	3		x	x	x		x	x
HUM	212	Non-Western Humanities	HF 904N	3		x	x	x		x	x
HUM	215	Art & Phil of African Cont	HF 904N	3		x			x		
ITALIAN (0052)											
ITALIAN	104	Fourth Course Italian	H1 900	4		x					
JAPANESE (0054)											
JAPANES	104	Fourth Course Japanese	H1 900	4		x					

PROGRAMS OF STUDY
BACCALAUREATE TRANSFER – IAI GENERAL EDUCATION

SUBJECT	NO	COURSE DESCRIPTION	IAI NO.	CREDIT	DA	HW	KK	MX	OH	TR	WR
		IAI APPROVED GRIDS FOR GENERAL EDUCATION COURSES									

IAI APPROVED GRIDS FOR GENERAL EDUCATION COURSES

SUBJECT	NO	COURSE DESCRIPTION	IAI NO.	CREDIT	DA	HW	KK	MX	OH	TR	WR
LITERATURE (0036)												
LIT	110	Introduction to Literature	H3 900	3	x	x	x	x	x	x	x
LIT	111	Poetry	H3 903	3	x	x	x	x	x	x	x
LIT	112	Drama	H3 902	3	x	x	x	x	x	x	x
LIT	113	Fiction	H3 901	3	x	x	x	x	x	x	x
LIT	114	Ideas in Prose	H3 904	3	x			x			
LIT	116	Amer Lit Col Days-Civil War	H3 914	3		x	x	x			x
LIT	117	Amer Lit Civ War-20th Cent	H3 915	3	x	x	x			x	x
LIT	118	English Lit Begin to Johnson	H3 912	3		x					x
LIT	119	English Literature Rom Rev-20th Cent	H3 913	3		x	x	x			x
LIT	121	Contemporary Afro-American Literature	H3 910D	3		x	x	x	x		x
LIT	122	Perspectives in Black Lit	H3 910D	3		x		x			
LIT	123	Lit/ US from Civil War to Present	H3 915	3					x		
LIT	126	Contemporary American Literature	H3 915	3							x
LIT	127	Contemporary British Literature	H3 913	3							x
LIT	128	Latin American Literature	H3 908N	3		x		x		x	x
LIT	129	U.S. Latino (A) Literature	H3 910D	3		x					
LIT	131	Survey of Afro-Amer Poetry	H3 910D	3		x		x			
LIT	133	African American Fiction	H3 910D	3				x			
LIT	150	Women's Literature	H3 911D	3	X	x	x	x	x	x	x
LIT	155	Literature and Film	F2 905	3						x	x
LIT	156	Creative Nonfiction	H3 904	3							x
LIT	211	Shakespeare	H3 905	3	x	x	x	x		x	x
LIT	220	World Literature	H3 906	3	x						
LIT	221	Topics in Literature: Romanticism in British and Am Lit	H3 907	3	x						
MATH (0045)												
MATH	118	General Education Math	M1 904	4	x	x	x	x	x	x	x
MATH	122	Math for Elementary Teachers I	M1 903	4	x	x	x	x	x	x	x
MATH	125-1	Introductory Statistics	M1 902	4	x	x	x	x	x	x	x
MATH	144	Finite Mathematics	M1 906	4	x	x	x	x		x	x
MATH	146	Discrete Mathematics	M1 905	4	x	x					
MATH	204-1	Calculus for Business and Social Science	M1 900-B	5	x	x	x	x	x	x	x
MATH	207	Calculus and Analytic Geometry I	M1 900-1	5	x	x	x	x	x	x	x
MATH	208	Calculus and Analytic Geometry II	M1 900-2	5	x	x	x	x	x	x	x
MATH	209	Calculus and Analytic Geometry III	M1 900-3	5	x	x	x	x	x	x	x
MUSIC (0060)												
MUSIC	121	Introduction to Music	F1 900	3	x	x	x	x	x	x	x
MUSIC	124	Trends in Modern American Music	F1 904	3		x					
MUSIC	183	World Music	F1 903N	3		x					
MUSIC	221	Music Literature and History	F1 901	3		x					
MUSIC	223	Music History to 1750	F1 901	3			x	x		x	
OCEANOGRAPHY (0070)												
OCEAN	101	Introduction Oceanography	P1 905	3						x	

IAI APPROVED GRIDS FOR GENERAL EDUCATION COURSES

SUBJECT	NO	COURSE DESCRIPTION	IAI NO.	CREDIT	DA	HW	KK	MX	OH	TR	WR
		PHILOSOPHY (0043)									
PHIL	105	Logic	H4 906	3	x	x	x	x	x	x	x
PHIL	106	Introduction to Philosophy	H4 900	3	x	x	x	x	x	x	x
PHIL	107	Ethics	H4 904	3	x	x	x	x	x	x	x
PHIL	108	Philosophy of Religion	H4 905	3	x	x	x	x		x	x
PHIL	201	Greek Philosophy to Renaissance	H4 901	3		x					
PHIL	202	Enlightenment to Present	H4 902	3		x					
PHIL	215	Problems in Philosophy	H4 900	3						x	
PHIL	216	Critical Thinking	H4 906	3	x						
		PHYSICAL SCIENCE (0076)									
PHY SCI	101	General Course Phy Sci	P9 900	3	x		x	x		x	x
PHY SCI	102	General Course Phy Sci	P9 900	3	x			x		x	x
PHY SCI	107	Current Public Issues in Phy Sci	P9 900	3		x			x	x	
PHY SCI	111	General Course I w/Lab Phy Sci	P9 900L	4			x	x	x	x	x
PHY SCI	111	General Course I w/Lab Phy Sci	P1 905L	4		x					
PHY SCI	112	General Course II w/Lab Phy Sci	P9 900L	4			x	x	x	x	x
PHY SCI	118	Introduction to Meteorology	P1 905L	4		x					
		PHYSICS (0077)									
PHYSICS	220	Physics Calculation and Practice	P1 900L	2						x	
PHYSICS	221	Mechanics and Heat	P1 900L	4	x	x		x			x
PHYSICS	231	General Physics I: Mechanics and Wave Motion	P1 900L	4						x	
		POLITICAL SCIENCE (0086)									
POL SCI	200	Principles of Political Science	S5 903	3	x						
POL SCI	201	The National Government	S5 900	3	x	x	x	x	x	x	x
POL SCI	203	Comparative Government	S5 905	3	x		x	x		x	x
POL SCI	204	International Relations	S5 904N	3	x		x	x		x	x
POL SCI	207	U.S. State and Local Government	S5 902	3	x	x	x	x		x	
		POLISH (0046)									
POLISH	104	Fourth Course Polish	H1 900	4							x
POLISH	214	Readings in Literature Polish	H3 916	3							x
		PSYCHOLOGY (0087)									
PSYCH	201	General Psychology	S6 900	3	x	x	x	x	x	x	x
PSYCH	207	Child Psychology	S6 903	3	x	x	x	x	x	x	x
PSYCH	211	Social Psychology	S8 900	3	x		x			x	x
PSYCH	214	Adolescent Psychology	S6 904	3				x			x
PSYCH	222	Adult Development and Aging	S6 905	3				x		x	x
PSYCH	224	Life Span Developmental Psychology	S6 902	3							x

PROGRAMS OF STUDY
BACCALAUREATE TRANSFER – IAI GENERAL EDUCATION

SUBJECT	NO	COURSE DESCRIPTION	IAI NO.	CREDIT	DA	HW	KK	MX	OH	TR	WR
		IAI APPROVED GRIDS FOR GENERAL EDUCATION COURSES									
		COMPARATIVE RELIGION (0133)									
RELIGN	101	Introduction to Religion	H5 900	3			x			x	
RELIGN	102	The Bible - Hebrew Old Testament	H5 901	3			x			x	
RELIGN	103	The Bible - New Testament	H5 901	3			x			x	
RELIGN	106	Comparative Religion I / Eastern Religion	H5 904N	3	x		x	x		x	x
RELIGN	107	Comparative Religion II / Western Religion	H5 904N	3			x			x	
		SOCIOLOGY (0089)									
SOC	201	Introduction to Study of Society	S7 900	3	x	x	x	x	x	x	x
SOC	203	Marriage and the Family	S7 902	3	x	x	x	x	x	x	x
SOC	205	Social Problems	S7 901	3	x	x	x			x	x
SOC	207	The Sociology of Sex and Gender	S7 904D	3	x						
SOC	211	Race and Ethnic Relations	S7 903D	3							x
		SOCIAL SCIENCE (0088)									
SOC SCI	101	General Course I Soc Sci	S9 900	3	x	x	x	x	x	x	x
SOC SCI	102	General Course II Soc Sci	S9 901	3	x	x	x	x	x	x	x
		SPANISH (0057)									
SPANISH	104	Fourth Course Spanish	H1 900	4	x	x	x		x	x	x
SPANISH	111	Spanish for Hispanos	H1 900	3	x						
SPANISH	210	Modern Civilization and Culture Spanish	H1 900	3	x						
SPANISH	213	Introduction to Mod Lit Spanish	H3 916	3		x					
SPANISH	214	Readings in Literature Spanish	H3 916	3	x	x					x
		SPEECH (0095)									
SPEECH	101-1	Fundamentals of Speech Communication	C2 900	3	x	x	x	x	x	x	x
SPEECH	131	Introduction to the Theatre	F1 907	3							x
		THEATER ART (0099)									
THR ART	131	Introduction to Theatre	F1 907	3			x				
THR ART	134	Theater in Modern World	F1 907	3	x	x	x			x	x
		ZOOLOGY (0029)									
ZOOLOGY	211	General Zoology	L1 902L	4	x					x	x

IAI APPROVED GRIDS FOR MAJOR COURSES

SUBJECT	NO	COURSE DESCRIPTION	IAI NO.	CREDIT	DA	HW	KK	MX	OH	TR	WR
ENGINEERING & INDUSTRIAL (0332)											
332ENGR	300	Introduction to Computer Aided Design	IND911	3							x
		Biology (0023)									
BIOLOGY	121	Biology I	BIO910	5	x	x	x	x	x	x	x
BIOLOGY	122	Biology II	BIO910	5	x	x	x	x	x	x	x
BUSINESS (0030)											
BUSINES	181	Financial Accounting	BUS903	4	x	x	x	x	x	x	x
BUSINES	182	Managerial Accounting	BUS904	4	x	x	x	x	x	x	x
BUSINES	236	Advertising	MC912	3		x					
CHEMISTRY (0073)											
CHEM	201	General Chemistry I	CHM911	5		x	x	x	x	x	x
CHEM	203	General Chemistry II	CHM912	5		x	x	x	x	x	x
CHEM	205	Organic Chemistry I	CHM913	6	x	x	x	x	x	x	x
CHEM	207	Organic Chemistry II	CHM914	6	x	x	x	x	x	x	x
COMPUTER INFORMATION SYSTEMS (0032)											
CIS	120	Introduction to Microcomputers	BUS902	3	x	x	x	x	x	x	x
CIS	142	Introduction to C or C++ Language	CS911	3	x	x	x		x	x	x
CIS	144	Introduction to JAVA Programming Lang	CS911	3	x	x	x	x	x		x
CIS	242	Advanced C or C++ Language	CS912	3	x	x	x	x		x	
CIS	244	Advanced Java Programming Language	CS912	3	x	x	x	x	x		x
CRIMINAL JUSTICE (0080)											
CRM JUS	102	Administration Criminal Justice	CRJ901	3	x	x	x	x	x	x	x
CRM JUS	114	Administration Juvenile Justice	CRJ914	3	x	x	x	x	x	x	x
CRM JUS	155	Introduction to Corrections	CRJ911	3	x	x				x	x
CRM JUS	250	Introduction to Criminology	CRJ912	3	x	x	x			x	x
DIGITAL MULTIMEDIA (0138)											
DMD	105	Animation	MC924	3		x					
DMD	131	Multimedia I	MC923	3		x					
ELECTRONICS (0033)											
ELECTRN	206	Digital Circuits and Systems	EGR932L	5	x	x				x	x
ENGINEERING (0034)											
ENGR	215	Electrical Circuit Analysis	EGR93IL	5	x	x				x	x
ENGLISH (0035)											
ENGLISH	151	News Reporting and Writing	MC919	3							x
ENGLISH	152	Introduction to Mass Communication	MC911	3		x					x
MATH (0045)											
MATH	125	Introductory Statistics	BUS901	4	x	x	x	x	x	x	x
MATH	146	Discrete Mathematics	CS915	4	x	x				x	x
MATH	207	Calculus & Analytic Geometry I	MTH901	5	x			x	x	x	x
MATH	208	Calculus & Analytic Geometry II	MTH902	5	x			x	x	x	x
MATH	209	Calculus & Analytic Geometry III	MTH903	5	x			x	x	x	x
MATH	210	Differential Equations	MTH911	3	x				x	x	x
MATH	212	Linear Algebra	MTH911	3	x					x	x
MATH	216	Statistics for Business	BUS901	4	x	x	x		x	x	x

IAI APPROVED GRIDS FOR MAJOR COURSES

SUBJECT	NO	COURSE DESCRIPTION	IAI NO.	CREDIT	DA	HW	KK	MX	OH	TR	WR
MEDIA COMMUNICATION (0011)											
MEDIACM	102	Announcing	MC918	3			x				
MEDIACM	203	Media Writing	MC917	3			x				
MEDIACM	221	Radio Production I	MC915	3			x				
MEDIACM	231	TV Production I	MC916	3			x				
PHILOSOPHY (0043)											
PHIL	110	Social & Political Philosophy	PLS913								x
PHYSICS (0077)											
PHYSICS	215	Statics	EGR942	3	x	x				x	x
PHYSICS	216	Dynamics	EGR943	3	x	x				x	x
PHYSICS	217	Mechanics of Materials	EGR945	3	x	x				x	x
PSYCHOLOGY (0087)											
PSYCH	206	Business and Industrial Psychology	PSY906	3	x					x	x
PSYCH	210	Principles of Supervisory Psychology	PSY906	3	x		x				
PSYCH	213	Abnormal Psychology	PSY905	3	x			x		x	x
PSYCH	215	Psychology of Personality	PSY907	3	x	x				x	x
SPEECH (0095)											
SPEECH	144	Oral Reading and Interpretation	TA916	3			x				x
THEATER ART (0099)											
THR ART	130	Stagecraft	TA911	3			x				x
THR ART	133	Acting	TA914	3		x		x	x	x	x

The Associate in Arts (A.A.) degree is intended for students planning to transfer to a four-year college or university to complete a baccalaureate degree. The 62 credit hour degree comprises a minimum of 38 credit hours in general education, 16 elective credit hours, and 8 credit hours in a foreign language and is designed so that students may choose from a broad selection of liberal arts courses.* Completion of the A.A. degree prepares students to transfer with junior standing.

Illinois Articulation Initiative (IAI)
City Colleges of Chicago (CCC) participates in the Illinois Articulation Initiative (IAI) which is a comprehensive statewide effort among more than 100 colleges and universities in Illinois to facilitate the transfer of students. Benefits for students include:

- Students who complete the A.A. degree at the CCC, and who meet the admission requirements of the IAI participating baccalaureate degree granting institution to which they transfer, will have completed the lower-division general education requirements for an associate or baccalaureate degree in lieu of the receiving institutions general education requirements.

- Students who complete the IAI General Education Core Curriculum (GECC) at the CCC and transfer to participating institutions have the assurance that lower-division general education requirements for an associate or baccalaureate degree have been satisfied and the GECC will transfer.

The IAI website http://www.itransfer.org/newwebsite includes information on requirements for general education and specific majors, course descriptions, and a student planning worksheet. Also, see CCC general education and majors IAI equivalency charts on pages 31 - 37.

Foreign Language Requirement for the Associate in Arts Degree
Effective fall 2009, all incoming students to the CCC seeking an Associate in Arts degree are required to successfully complete eight (8) semester hours of credit in a foreign language, which is equivalent to completion of a 102 foreign language course.

*Students intending to major in communications, humanities, social sciences, or other related professional fields should pursue the A.A. degree. Within the A.A. degree, students can choose from among various concentration areas listed below. **However, the concentration areas offered for the A.A. degree are not separate degrees and will not show on transcripts as the specific concentration, but simply as the Associate in Arts degree.** Specific course requirements within each concentration will be determined by the individual college during student advisement. Students are encouraged to select courses that will transfer to the baccalaureate degree granting institution they plan to attend: either IAI approved courses, or when applicable, courses that have signed form 13 articulation agreements on file, or satisfy course equivalency status. (See A.A. 210 degree model in this section which provides transfer definitions in end notes.)

Concentration Areas
See IAI approved majors in Business, Criminal Justice, English, History, Mass Communications, Political Science, Psychology, Sociology, and Theater Arts – see IAI Majors Grid, or visit the IAI website at http://www.itransfer.org/iai/majors/default.aspx?file=iai&section=students.

Additionally, other areas of concentrations include: Addiction Studies, Afro-American Studies, Child Development, Cinema/Media Studies, Diversity/Ethnic Studies, Entrepreneurship, Foreign Language, Humanities, Information Systems, Journalism, Latin American/Latino Studies, Law (pre), Literature, Philosophy, Physical Education, Public Safety, Religion, Social Science, Social Work, Speech, Women's Studies, and Youth Work.

Note: For either IAI approved majors or other areas of concentration, students should meet with a CCC Academic Advisor early to create an interdisciplinary plan that will best suit their needs. For a course(s) that is not part of an IAI-approved major, students should immediately consult both a CCC Academic Advisor and an Admissions Representative at the four-year institution to which they will transfer regarding the transferability of the course(s).

PROGRAMS OF STUDY
BACCALAUREATE TRANSFER – ASSOCIATE IN ARTS

ASSOCIATE IN ARTS DEGREE (A.A.) 210

minimum 62 CH

I. GENERAL EDUCATION APPROVED CORE* 38 CH

A. COMMUNICATIONS 9 CH
English 101, English 102, Speech 101

B. MATHEMATICS 4 CH
Mathematics 118 – or above

C. PHYSICAL/LIFE SCIENCES** 7 CH
Minimum of <u>one</u> course each in
Physical Science & Life Sciences (Group A & B)
One of the courses from Group A or B must be a lab.

<u>Group A (Physical Sciences)</u>:
Astronomy 201 *(no lab)*
Chemistry
Geology 201
Physical Sciences
Physics

<u>Group B (Life Sciences)</u>:
Biology
Botany 201
Oceanography 101 *(no lab)*
Zoology 211

D. HUMANITIES/FINE ARTS** 9 CH
Minimum of <u>one</u> course each in
Humanities & Fine Arts (Group A & B)

<u>Group A (Humanities)</u>:
Afro American Studies 101
Humanities
Literature
Philosophy
Religion

<u>Group A (continued)</u>:
Foreign Languages *(104 or above)*

Arabic	French	Japanese	Polish
Chinese	Italian	Latin	Spanish

<u>Group B (Fine Arts)</u>:

Art 103	Music
Fine Arts	Theater Art

E. SOCIAL/BEHAVIORAL SCIENCES** 9 CH

Anthropology 201, 202	Political Science
Economics 201, 202	Psychology
Geography	Social Science 101, 102
History	Sociology

<u>Human Diversity Requirement</u>: At least one course must meet the State of Illinois' Human Diversity requirement. The course descriptions on the IAI website shown below for Humanities, Fine Arts, and the Social and Behavioral Sciences include the designations "D" or "N".

The "D" designation represents courses designed specifically to examine aspects of human diversity within the United States;

The "N" designated courses are designed specifically to examine aspects of human diversity from a non-U.S./non-European perspective, or courses designed specifically to examine aspects of human diversity from a non-Western perspective.

http://itransfer.org/iai/gened/Defaultaspx?section=students&p=h

http://itransfer.org/iai/gened/Default.aspx?section=students&p=s

Students should meet with a college Academic Advisor for course selection from the general education core courses shown on the A.A. model under Humanities/Fine Arts, and Social/Behavioral Sciences.

II. ADDITIONAL COLLEGE AA REQUIREMENTS** ***

A. ELECTIVES 16 CH

B. FOREIGN LANGUAGE**** 8 CH
Foreign language which is equivalent to completion of a 102 foreign language course.

* All courses shown in the General Education core must be IAI approved and are listed in the IAI general education equivalency chart of the catalog or, when applicable, have signed Illinois Community College Board (ICCB) form 13 articulation agreements on file indicating by the receiving institution that the course is accepted for transfer under general education.

"The IAI General Education core transfers as a 'package' to all colleges and universities participating in the IAI. Course-to-course transfer is not guaranteed."

** Some courses may not be offered every semester. Thus, students should select their courses with consultation from a college Academic Advisor or Department Chairperson. Students should also obtain the course schedule published each academic term or semester for the CCC College from where the student will take courses. The course schedule can also be downloaded from the CCC website at *http://www.ccc.edu*.

*** Courses in the category of Additional College A.A. Requirements and Electives must be either IAI approved or, when applicable, have signed form 13 articulation agreements on file, or satisfy equivalency status in compliance with ICCB guidelines.

[Equivalency is defined as: A "Transfer Guide" from X University that demonstrates that Y course from one of the City Colleges of Chicago (CCC) is comparable to a course taught at X University and that the "Transfer Guide" from that University will suffice in lieu of IAI approval or signed form 13 articulation agreements on file at the College and at the CCC District Office of Academic and Occupational Programs.]

**** Effective Fall 2009

The Associate in Science (A.S.) degree is intended for students planning to transfer to a four-year college or university to complete a baccalaureate degree. The 64 credit hour degree comprises a minimum of 39 credit hours in general education, 14 additional credit hours in Mathematics and Physical/Life Sciences, and 11 elective credit hours and is designed so that students may choose from a broad selection of science courses.* Completion of the A.S. degree prepares students to transfer with junior standing.

Illinois Articulation Initiative (IAI)

City Colleges of Chicago (CCC) participates in the Illinois Articulation Initiative (IAI) which is a comprehensive statewide effort among more than 100 colleges and universities in Illinois to facilitate the transfer of students. Benefits for students include:

- Students who complete the A.S. degree at the CCC, and who meet the admission requirements of the IAI participating baccalaureate degree granting institution to which they transfer, will have completed the lower-division general education requirements for an associate or baccalaureate degree in lieu of the receiving institutions general education requirements.

- Students who complete the IAI General Education Core Curriculum (GECC) at the CCC and transfer to participating institutions have the assurance that lower-division general education requirements for an associate or baccalaureate degree have been satisfied and the GECC will transfer.

The IAI website *http://www.itransfer.org/newwebsite* includes information on requirements for general education and specific majors, course descriptions, and a student planning worksheet. Also, see CCC general education and majors IAI equivalency charts on pages 31 - 37.

*Students intending to major in mathematics, science, or other related professional fields should pursue the A.S. degree. Within the A.S. degree, students can choose from among various concentration areas listed below. **However, the concentration areas offered for the A.S. degree are not separate degrees and will not show on transcripts as the specific concentration, but simply as the Associate in Science degree.** Specific course requirements within each concentration will be determined by the individual college during student advisement. Students are encouraged to select courses that will transfer to the baccalaureate degree granting institution they plan to attend: either IAI approved courses, or when applicable, courses that have signed form 13 articulation agreements on file, or satisfy course equivalency status. (See A.S. 211 degree model in this section which provides transfer definitions in end notes.)

Concentration Areas
See IAI approved majors in Agriculture, Biological Sciences, Chemistry, Computer Science, Engineering, Industrial Technology, Mathematics, and Physics – see IAI Majors Grid, or visit the IAI website at:
http://www.itransfer.org/iai/majors/default.aspx?file=iai&section=students

Additionally, other areas of concentrations include: Earth Sciences, Environmental Science, Health Sciences, Natural Science, Physical Science, Science/Pre-Professional (Architecture, Dentistry, Engineering, Medicine, Optometry, and Pharmacy).

Note: For either IAI approved majors or other areas of concentration, students should meet with a CCC College Academic Advisor early to create an interdisciplinary plan that will best suit their needs. For a course(s) that is not part of an IAI-approved major, students should immediately consult both a CCC Academic Advisor and an Admissions Representative at the four-year institution to which they will transfer regarding the transferability of the course(s).

PROGRAMS OF STUDY
BACCALAUREATE TRANSFER – ASSOCIATE IN SCIENCE

ASSOCIATE IN SCIENCE DEGREE (A.S.) 211
minimum 64 CH

I. GENERAL EDUCATION   **39 CH**
APPROVED CORE*

A. COMMUNICATIONS   **9 CH**
English 101, English 102, Speech 101

B. MATHEMATICS   **5 CH**
Mathematics 207 – or above

C. PHYSICAL/LIFE SCIENCES**   **7 CH**
Minimum of <u>one</u> course each in
Physical Science & Life Sciences (Group A & B)
One of the courses from Group A or B must be a lab.

Group A (Physical Sciences):
Astronomy 201 (no lab)
Chemistry
Geology 201
Physical Sciences
Physics

Group B (Life Sciences):
Biology
Botany 201
Oceanography 101 (no lab)
Zoology 211

D. HUMANITIES/FINE ARTS**   **9 CH**
Minimum of <u>one</u> course each in
Humanities & Fine Arts (Group A & B)

Group A (Humanities):
Afro American Studies 101
Humanities
Literature
Philosophy
Religion

Group A (continued):
Foreign Languages (104 or above)

Arabic	French	Japanese	Polish
Chinese	Italian	Latin	Spanish

Group B (Fine Arts):

Art 103	Music
Fine Arts	Theater Art

E. SOCIAL/BEHAVIORAL SCIENCES**   **9 CH**

Anthropology 201, 202	Political Science
Economics 201, 202	Psychology
Geography	Social Science 101, 102
History	Sociology

Human Diversity Requirement: At least one course must meet the State of Illinois' Human Diversity requirement. The course descriptions on the IAI website shown below for Humanities, Fine Arts, and Social and Behavioral Sciences include the designations "D" or "N".

The "D" designation represents courses designed specifically to examine aspects of human diversity within the United States;

The "N" designated courses are designed specifically to examine aspects of human diversity from a non-U.S./non-European perspective, or courses designed specifically to examine aspects of human diversity from a non-Western perspective.

http://itransfer.org/iai/gened/Defaultaspx?section=students&p=h

http://itransfer.org/iai/gened/Default.aspx?section=students&p=s

Students should meet with a college Academic Advisor for course selection from the general education core courses shown on the A.S. model under Humanities/Fine Arts, and Social/Behavioral Sciences.

II. ADDITIONAL HOURS IN MATHEMATICS   **14 CH**
    AND PHYSICAL/LIFE SCIENCES   **(minimum)**
    REQUIREMENTS ** ***

Astronomy 201	Mathematics 208, 209, 210
Biology	Oceanography 101
Botany 201	Physical Sciences
Chemistry	Physics
Geology 201	Zoology 211

III. ELECTIVES ** ***   **(minimum) 11 CH**

* All courses shown in the General Education core must be IAI approved and are listed in the IAI general education equivalency chart of the catalog or, when applicable, have signed Illinois Community College Board (ICCB) form 13 articulation agreements on file indicating by the receiving institution that the course is accepted for transfer under general education.

"The IAI General Education core transfers as a 'package' to all colleges and universities participating in the IAI. Course to-course transfer is not guaranteed."

** Some courses may not be offered every semester. Thus, students should select their courses with consultation from a college Academic Advisor or Department Chairperson. Students should also obtain the course schedule published each academic term or semester for the CCC College from where the student will take courses. The course schedule can also be downloaded from the CCC website at http://www.ccc.edu.

*** Courses in the category of Additional Hours in Mathematics and Physical/Life Sciences and Electives must be either IAI approved or, when applicable, have signed form 13 articulation agreements on file, or satisfy equivalency status in compliance with ICCB guidelines.

[Equivalency is defined as: A "Transfer Guide" from X University that demonstrates that Y course from one of the City Colleges of Chicago (CCC) is comparable to a course taught at X University and that the "Transfer Guide" from that University will suffice in lieu of IAI approval or signed form 13 articulation agreements on file at the College and at the CCC District Office of Academic and Occupational Programs.]

ASSOCIATE IN ENGINEERING SCIENCE 100 (A.E.S.)
64 Credit Hours (CH)

The Associate in Engineering Science (A.E.S.) degree offers courses required for transfer to a four-year college or university for students majoring in engineering sciences. Completion of the A.E.S. degree does **not** fulfill the requirements of the Illinois Transferable General Education Core Curriculum (IAI GECC). A student must complete the general education requirements of the college or university to which she/he transfers.

I. GENERAL EDUCATION*   (minimum) 20 CH

A. COMMUNICATIONS   3 CH
English 101: Composition I

B. FINE ARTS AND HUMANITIES ** ***   6 CH
Select any two courses from the following disciplines:
Afro-American Studies, Art, Fine Arts, Foreign Language, Humanities, Literature, Music, Philosophy, Religion, Theater Art

C. MATHEMATICS AND SCIENCE*   6 - 8 CH
Select any two courses from the following disciplines:
Astronomy, Biology, Botany, Chemistry, Geology, Mathematics, Oceanography, Physical Science, Physics, Zoology

D. SOCIAL AND BEHAVIORAL SCIENCES ** ***   6 CH
Select any two courses from the following disciplines:
Anthropology, Economics, Geography, History, Political Science, Psychology, Social Science, Sociology

II. REQUIRED PROGRAM CORE***   44 CH

Chemistry (073)	
201 General Chemistry I	5
Engineering (034)	
190 Computer Applications in Engineering	3
Mathematics (045)	
207, 208, and 209 Calculus and Analytical Geometry I, II, III	15
210 Differential Equations	3
Physics (077)	
215 Statics	3
216 Dynamics	3
235 Engineering Physics I Mechanics & Wave Motion	4
236 Engineering Physics II Electricity & Magnetism	4
237 Engineering Physics III Heat Light & Modern Physics	4

TOTAL PROGRAM MINIMUM CREDIT HOURS   64 CH

III. ELECTIVES***
(Additional courses recommended for various fields of engineering.)

CAD Technology (049)
170 Computer Aided Design I (CAD) (3)
Chemistry (073)
203 General Chemistry II (5)
Engineering (034)
111 Introduction to Engineering Profession (2)
131 Engineering Graphics & Introduction to Design (3)
Physics (077)
217 Mechanics of Materials (3)
224 Physics Calculations and Practice (2)

* The courses listed under General Education are transferable courses either through IAI approval, signed form 13 articulation agreements, or they satisfy equivalency status in compliance with ICCB guidelines.

**Human Diversity Requirement: At least one course must meet the State of Illinois' Human Diversity requirement. The course descriptions on the IAI website shown below for Humanities, Fine Arts, and Social and Behavioral Sciences include the designations "D" or "N".

The "D" designation represents courses designed specifically to examine aspects of human diversity within the United States;

The "N" designated courses are designed specifically to examine aspects of human diversity from a non-U.S./non-European perspective, or courses designed specifically to examine aspects of human diversity from a non-Western perspective.

http://itransfer.org/iai/gened/Defaultaspx?section=students&p=h

http://itransfer.org/iai/gened/Default.aspx?section=students&p=s

Students should meet with a college Academic Advisor for course selection from the general education core courses shown on the A.E.S. model under Humanities/Fine Arts, and Social/Behavioral Sciences.

*** Some courses may not be offered every semester. Thus, students should select their courses with consultation from an Academic Advisor or Department Chairperson. Students should also obtain the course schedule published each academic term or semester for the CCC College from where the student will take courses. The course schedule can also be downloaded from the CCC website at http://www.ccc.edu.

PROGRAMS OF STUDY
BACCALAUREATE TRANSFER – ASSOCIATE IN FINE ARTS

ASSOCIATE IN FINE ARTS (A.F.A.)
60-68 Credit Hours (CH)

**Art (Studio) 216; Art Education 217 and
Music Performance 205; Music Education 208**

The Associate in Fine Arts (A.F.A.) degree offers courses required for transfer to a four-year college or university for students majoring in art (studio), art education, music education, or music performance. Completion of the A.F.A. degree does **not** fulfill the requirements of the Illinois Transferable General Education Core Curriculum (IAI GECC). A student must complete the general education requirements of the college or university to which she/he transfers.

REQUIRED PROGRAM A.F.A. DEGREE
                                   Range from 60 - 68 CH

I. GENERAL EDUCATION*   **(minimum) 29 - 35 CH**

A. COMMUNICATIONS
English (035)
101 Composition I   3
102 Composition II   3
Speech (095)
101 Fundamentals of Speech Communication   3

B. FINE ARTS AND HUMANITIES by MAJOR** ***
Art (Studio) (216) - select two courses   6
Art Education (217) - select three courses   9
Music Education (208) - select two courses   6
Music Performance (205) - select two courses   6

Select any <u>two</u> or <u>three</u> courses from the following disciplines:
Afro-American Studies, Art, Fine Arts,
Foreign Language, Humanities, Literature,
Music, Philosophy, Religion, Theater Art

C. MATHEMATICS
118 General Education Math or   4
125 Introductory Statistics

D. PHYSICAL AND LIFE SCIENCES***   7 - 8 CH
Select any <u>two</u> courses from the following disciplines;
at least one course must be a lab course:
Astronomy, Biology, Botany, Chemistry,
Geology, Mathematics, Oceanography,
Physical Science, Physics, Zoology

E. SOCIAL AND BEHAVIORAL SCIENCES by MAJOR** ***
Art (Studio) (216) - select two courses   6
Art Education (217) - select two courses   6
Music Education (208) - select three courses   9
Music Performance (205) - select one course   3

Select any <u>one</u> to <u>three</u> courses from the following disciplines:
Anthropology, Economics, Geography,
History, Political Science, Psychology,
Social Science, Sociology

II. Required Credit Hours for Core by MAJOR
Art (Studio) (216)   30
Art Education (217)   12
Music Education (208)   26
Music Performance (205)   35

Consult with a college Academic Advisor for selection of required core courses by Major.

III. Required Elective Credit Hours by MAJOR
Art Education (217)   13
Music Education (208)   2
Music Performance (205)   4

Consult with a college Academic Advisor for selection of required elective courses.

* The courses listed under General Education are transferable courses either through Illinois Articulation Initiative (IAI) approval, signed form 13 articulation agreements, or they satisfy equivalency status in compliance with ICCB guidelines. The number of required General Education credit hours varies by major.

**<u>Human Diversity Requirement</u>: At least one course must meet the State of Illinois' Human Diversity requirement. The course descriptions on the IAI website shown below for Humanities, Fine Arts, and Social and Behavioral Sciences include the designations "D" or "N".

The "D" designation represents courses designed specifically to examine aspects of human diversity within the United States;

The "N" designated courses are designed specifically to examine aspects of human diversity from a non-U.S./non-European perspective, or courses designed specifically to examine aspects of human diversity from a non-Western perspective.

http://itransfer.org/iai/gened/Defaultaspx?section=students&p=h

http://itransfer.org/iai/gened/Default.aspx?section=students&p=s

Students should meet with a college Academic Advisor for course selection from the general education core courses shown on the A.F.A. model under Humanities/Fine Arts, and Social/Behavioral Sciences.

*** Some of these courses may not be offered every semester. Thus, students should select their courses with consultation from a college Academic Advisor or Department Chairperson. Students should also obtain the course schedule published each academic term or semester for the CCC College from where the student will take courses. The course schedule can also be downloaded from the CCC website http://www.ccc.edu.

ASSOCIATE OF ARTS IN TEACHING (A.A.T.)
61 - 63 Credit Hours (CH)

Early Childhood Education 209 *and* Secondary Mathematics 212

The Associate of Arts in Teaching (A.A.T.) degree offers courses required for transfer to a four-year college or university for students majoring in teaching secondary mathematics or early-childhood education. The A.A.T. degree is based on the Illinois Professional Teaching Standards and includes the IAI General Education Core Curriculum (IAI GECC). Degree requirements include a 2.5 GPA, successful completion of the Illinois Test of Basic Skills, initiation of standards-based professional portfolio and evidence of appropriate professional dispositions. The general principles of the A.A.T. majors can be found on the ICCB website *http://www.iccb.org/index.html*

REQUIRED PROGRAM A.A.T. DEGREE
Range from 61 - 63 CH

I. GENERAL EDUCATION REQUIREMENTS* 39 – 42 CH

A. COMMUNICATIONS
English (035)
101 Composition I   3
102 Composition II   3
Speech (095)
Speech 101: Fundamentals of Speech Communication   3

B. FINE ARTS AND HUMANITIES**   9 CH
Select at least <u>one</u> course from Humanities and at least <u>one</u> course from Fine Arts.

C. PHYSICAL AND LIFE SCIENCES   7 - 9 CH
Select <u>one</u> course from Life Sciences and one course from Physical Sciences. At least <u>one</u> of the courses must be a laboratory course.

D. SOCIAL AND BEHAVIORAL SCIENCES** ***   9
Select <u>three</u> courses from at least <u>two</u> different disciplines:
Anthropology, Economics, Geography, History, Political Science, Psychology, Social Science, Sociology

E. MATHEMATICS by Major***
Secondary Mathematics (212)
Mathematics (045)
207 Calculus I   5

Early-Childhood Education (209)
121 Mathematics for Elementary Teachers I <u>and</u>   4
122 Mathematics for Elementary Teachers II   4

II. PROFESSIONAL EDUCATION COMPONENT by MAJOR***
Secondary Mathematics (212)
Education (083)
101 Introduction to Education   3
(includes at least 15 contact hours of field experience)

Select at least <u>two</u> courses from among the following:
Education (083)
102 Technology in the Classroom (3)
103 Students with Disabilities (3)
Psychology (087)
203 Educational Psychology (3)
207 Child Psychology (3)

Early-Childhood Education (209)
Education (083)
101 Introduction to Education (3)
(includes at least 15 contact hours of field experience) <u>and</u>
Child Development (090)
101 Human Growth & Development I <u>OR</u>   3
Psychology (087)
207 Child Psychology (3)

Select at least <u>one</u> course from among the following:
Education (083)
102 Technology in the Classroom (3)
103 Students with Disabilities (3)
Psychology (087)
203 Educational Psychology (3)
Speech (095)
243 Speech for Teachers (3)

III. REQUIRED AREA OF CONCENTRATION HOURS by MAJOR***
Secondary Mathematics (212)
Mathematics (045)
208 Calculus II <u>and</u>   5
209 Calculus III <u>and</u>   5
212 Linear Algebra   3

Early-Childhood Education (209)
Education (083)
120 Introduction to Early Childhood Education
(Must include contact hours in field experience) <u>and</u>   3
Child Development (090)
107 Health, Safety, Nutrition <u>and</u>   3
149 Creative Activities for Young Children <u>and</u>   3
262 Child, Family & Community   3

* The courses listed in Section I, General Education Requirements, are transferable courses either through Illinois Articulation Initiative (IAI) approval, signed form 13 articulation agreements, or they satisfy equivalency status in compliance with ICCB guidelines. The number of required General Education credit hours varies by major.

**Human Diversity Requirement: At least one course must meet the State of Illinois' Human Diversity requirement. The course descriptions on the IAI website shown below for Humanities, Fine Arts, and Social and Behavioral Sciences include the designations "D" or "N".

The "D" designation represents courses designed specifically to examine aspects of human diversity within the United States;

The "N" designated courses are designed specifically to examine aspects of human diversity from a non-U.S./non-European perspective, or courses designed specifically to examine aspects of human diversity from a non-Western perspective.

http://itransfer.org/iai/gened/Defaultaspx?section=students&p=h

http://itransfer.org/iai/gened/Default.aspx?section=students&p=s

Students should meet with a college Academic Advisor for course selection from the general education core courses shown on the A.A.T. model under Humanities/Fine Arts, and Social/Behavioral Sciences.

*** Some courses may not be offered every semester. Thus, students should select their courses with consultation from an Academic Advisor or Department Chairperson. Students should also obtain the course schedule published each academic term or semester for the CCC College from where the student will take courses. The course schedule can also be downloaded from the CCC website at http://www.ccc.edu.

NINTH EDITION

YOUR COLLEGE EXPERIENCE

Strategies for Success

John N. Gardner

President, John N. Gardner Institute for Excellence in Undergraduate Education

Distinguished Professor Emeritus, Library and Information Science
Senior Fellow, National Resource Center for The First-Year Experience and
Students in Transition
University of South Carolina, Columbia

A. Jerome Jewler

Distinguished Professor Emeritus, School of Journalism and
Mass Communications, College of Mass Communications
and Information Studies
University of South Carolina, Columbia

Betsy O. Barefoot

Vice President and Senior Scholar

John N. Gardner Institute for Excellence
in Undergraduate Education
Brevard, North Carolina

Bedford / St. Martin's
Boston ◆ New York

For Bedford/St. Martin's

Executive Editor: Carrie Brandon
Developmental Editor: Julie Kelly
Production Editor: Kerri A. Cardone
Senior Production Supervisor: Nancy Myers
Marketing Manager: Casey Carroll
Editorial Assistant: Nicholas Murphy
Copyeditor: Barbara Willette
Senior Art Director: Anna Palchik
Text Design: Jerilyn Bockorick
Cover Art and Design: Billy Boardman
Composition: Nesbitt Graphics, Inc.
Printing and Binding: RR Donnelley and Sons

President: Joan E. Feinberg
Editorial Director: Denise B. Wydra
Editor in Chief: Karen S. Henry
Director of Marketing: Karen R. Soeltz
Director of Editing, Design, and Production: Marcia Cohen
Assistant Director of Editing, Design, and Production: Elise S. Kaiser
Managing Editor: Elizabeth M. Schaaf

Library of Congress Control Number: 2009929004

Manufactured in the United States of America.

4 3 2 1
f   e   d   c

For information, write: Bedford/St. Martin's, 75 Arlington Street, Boston, MA 02116 (617-399-4000)

ISBN-10: 0-312-68774-5
ISBN-13: 978-0-312-68774-8

Acknowledgments

Dear Student,

When we were in our first year of college, first-year seminars were, by and large, non-existent. Colleges and universities just allowed new students to "sink or swim." As a result, some students made it through their first year successfully, some barely survived, and some dropped out.

Today, most colleges and universities offer college success courses to provide essential help to students in navigating their way through the first year. You are likely reading *Your College Experience* because you are enrolled in your institution's college success course. Although this book might seem different from your other textbooks, we believe that it could be the most important book you read this year because it's all about improving your chances for success in college and beyond. But before you start reading, you probably have some questions about the book and the course. Here are some of the most common questions we hear from students across the country.

- **Why should I take this course?** Research conducted by colleges and universities has found that first-year students are far more likely to be successful if they participate in courses and programs designed to teach them how to succeed in college. This course is designed to help you avoid some of the pitfalls—both academic and personal—that trip up many beginning students.

- **Aren't all the topics in this book common sense?** In college, issues such as relationships and personal health become even more important when you're living away from home. Even if you're living with your family or have a family of your own, college will challenge you to manage your time, feel comfortable interacting with professors, and study effectively. So while some of this may be common sense, this book will provide new insights and information to help you make decisions that will lead to success.

- **What am I going to get out of this course?** This course will provide a supportive environment in which you can share your successes and your frustrations, get to know others who are beginning college, develop a lasting relationship with your instructor, and begin making plans for life after college.

As college professors with many years of experience working with first-year students, we're well aware that starting college can be challenging. But we also know that if you apply the ideas in this book to your everyday life, you will be more likely to enjoy your time in college, graduate, and achieve your life goals. Welcome to college!

John N. Gardner
A. Jerome Jewler
Betsy O. Barefoot

John N. Gardner brings unparalleled experience to this authoritative text for first-year seminar courses. He is the recipient of his institution's highest award for teaching excellence. He has twenty-five years of experience directing and teaching in the most respected and most widely emulated first-year seminar in the country, the University 101 course at the University of South Carolina. He is recognized as one of the country's leading educators for his role in initiating and orchestrating an international reform movement to improve the beginning college experience. He is the founding executive director/president of three influential higher education centers that support campuses in their efforts to improve the learning and retention of beginning college students: the National Resource Center for The First-Year Experience and Students in Transition at the University of South Carolina (www.sc.edu/fye), the Policy Center on the First Year of College (www.fyfoundations.org), and most recently the John N. Gardner Institute for Excellence in Undergraduate Education (www.jngi.org); the latter two are based in Brevard, North Carolina. The experiential basis for all of his work is his own miserable first year of college on academic probation, an experience that he hopes to prevent for this book's readers. Today, as a much happier adult, John is married to fellow author of this book, Betsy Barefoot.

A. Jerome Jewler is a best-selling author, educator, and friend to students. As distinguished professor emeritus of the College of Mass Communications and Information Studies as well as codirector of the University 101 first-year seminar, including its faculty development component, at the University of South Carolina, Columbia, he has been a mentor to advertising students, has taught a doctoral seminar on teaching mass communication courses, and has helped hundreds of new students—as well as upperclass students—determine their academic and life goals. As University 101 codirector, he planned and conducted training workshops for first-year seminar instructors. He is a recipient of the Mortar Board award for teaching excellence, and he was recognized as USC Advisor of the Year and nationally as the Distinguished Advertising Educator in 2000. Like John Gardner, he also had a negative experience during his first year in college, vowing to drop out until he found redemption—and ultimate success—by joining the staff of the student newspaper. In retirement, he guides public school children on tours of natural history, cultural history, and science and technology at the South Carolina State Museum and volunteers at the information desk of the Richland County Public Library in Columbia, South Carolina.

Betsy O. Barefoot is a writer, researcher, and teacher whose special area of scholarship is the first year of college. During her tenure at the University of South Carolina from 1988 to 1999, she served as codirector for research and publications at the National Resource Center for The First-Year Experience and Students in Transition. She taught University 101, in addition to special-topics graduate courses on the first-year experience and the principles of college teaching. She conducts first-year seminar faculty training workshops around the United States and in other countries, and she is frequently called on to evaluate first-year seminar outcomes. She currently serves as codirector and senior scholar in the Policy Center on the First Year of College and as Vice President of the John N. Gardner Institute for Excellence in Undergraduate Education, in Brevard, North Carolina. In her Policy Center role she led a major national research project to identify institutions of excellence in the first college year. She currently works with both two- and four-year campuses in evaluating all components of the first year.

Icon KEY...

On the cover and throughout the text we've used icons to represent the different topic areas covered in this book. While the connections between some of the icons and their topic areas are likely to be obvious to you, you might find others a bit more obscure. Check out the following key to learn some interesting facts.

1 Exploring Your Purpose for Attending College

Named for its similarity in appearance to a tool used by bricklayers to hold mortar, the mortarboard is an item of academic headwear traditionally worn, in conjunction with a gown, by participants in ceremonies such as graduation.

2 Managing Your Time

The first mechanical alarm clock, capable of striking an alarm at any time specified by the user, was invented in 1559 by Taqi al-Din of the Ottoman Empire.

3 Understanding Emotional Intelligence

The two masks associated with drama are symbols of the ancient Greek Muses Thalia and Melpomene. Thalia was the Muse of comedy (the laughing face), and Melpomene was the Muse of tragedy (the weeping face).

4 Discovering How You Learn

Although Thomas Edison is often credited with the invention of the lightbulb, the first patent for an incandescent lightbulb was granted to Joseph Wilson Swan in 1878, about a year before Edison.

5 Thinking Critically: the Basis of a College Education

Created in 1974 by Hungarian sculptor and professor of architecture Ernő Rubik, the Rubik's Cube is considered the world's best-selling toy; as of January 2009, 350 million of them have been sold worldwide.

6 Being Engaged in Learning: Listening, Taking Notes, and Participating in Class

Because of their durability, composition notebooks are often used in long-term projects that involve peer review, journaling, or frequent editing by teachers.

7 Reading to Learn from College Textbooks

Books written specifically for educational purposes were used as early as ancient Greece. The modern textbook has its roots in the standardization made possible by the printing press, invented in the fifteenth century.

8 Learning to Study, Comprehend, and Remember

The common folk wisdom that an elephant never forgets is based on observations that elephants follow the same paths and even hand down memories of directions and places across generations.

Brief
CONTENTS

CONTENTS

PART 1

Preparing for SUCCESS   1

1 Exploring Your Purpose for Attending College   3

2 Managing Your Time   19

Preparing to STUDY 75

5 Thinking Critically: The Basis of a College Education 77

6 Being Engaged in Learning: Listening, Taking Notes, and Participating in Class 93

11 Developing Library, Research, and Information Literacy Skills   191

Preparing for LIFE 213

12 Making the Right Choice for Majors and Careers 215

PREFACE

Anyone who teaches beginning college students today knows how much they have changed in recent years. Students are increasingly job-focused, technologically adept, concerned about the future, and unevenly prepared for college. Engaging and retaining today's students is a challenge at all levels but particularly in the first year. Since the early 1980s, college and university educators have recognized that the college success course or first-year seminar is a powerful tool in an overall plan to improve student success. But as students themselves change, so should these courses and course textbooks.

This ninth edition of *Your College Experience*, the first under the imprint of our new publisher, Bedford/St. Martins, responds to the dynamic nature of college success courses and to changing student needs. While it continues to address ongoing issues such as learning strategies, critical thinking, time management, relationships, and personal health, this text also adds a new focus on purpose, life planning, emotional intelligence, money management, and the growing role of technology.

What remains the same since the inception of the college success course over the past twenty-five years is our level of commitment and deep understanding of our students. Although this edition of *Your College Experience* has been significantly revised, it is still based on our collective knowledge and experience in teaching first-year students, as well as on feedback from generations of users. It is grounded in the growing body of research on student success and retention and includes many valuable contributions from leading experts in the field. Our contributors were chosen for their knowledge and currency in their fields as well as their own deep commitments to their students and to the discipline. Most of all, it is a text born from our devotion to students and to their success. Simply put, we do not like to see students fail. We are confident that if students both read and heed the information herein, they will be likely to become engaged in the college experience, to learn, and to persist to graduation.

We have written this text for students of any age in both two- and four-year residential and commuter institutions. Our writing style is intended to convey respect and admiration for students while recognizing their continued need for challenge and support. We have addressed every topic that our experience, our research, and our reviewers tell us is a concern for students at any type of school with any kind of educational background.

Whether you are considering this textbook for use in your first-year seminar or have already made a decision to adopt it, we thank you for your interest, and we trust that you will find it to be a valuable teaching aid. We also hope that this book will guide you and your campus in understanding the broad range of issues that can affect student success.

A SIMPLE AND LOGICAL ORGANIZATION

The first part of the book, "Preparing for Success," sets the stage by challenging students to explore their purpose for attending college and helping them learn how to apply that purpose to both short- and long-term goal setting. The chapters in this section also introduce readers to the fundamental elements of a college education. Part Two, "Preparing To Study," enumerates essential study skills and guides students in communicating and finding information. Part Three, "Preparing for Life," emphasizes practical considerations that all students must face, such as choosing a major, and money management, while also addressing the importance of learning about human and intellectual differences and the relationship between a healthy body and an eager mind.

A REVISION FOCUSED ON THE WHOLE STUDENT

Your College Experience has always helped students with their transition to college and throughout their time there, and as the spectrum of students and students' needs broadens, so does our coverage. This edition has been revised to address every aspect of the student's life with better coverage of academic skills and new coverage of topics critical to their personal and career success.

A new chapter devoted to emotional intelligence. Recognizing that the ability to identify behavior and understand and get along with people is central to success in school, work, and life, this new chapter discusses what emotional intelligence (EI) is, why everyone should understand it, and why it matters in college. This chapter discusses why EI skills—such as stress management, adaptability, and interpersonal skills—are crucial to student success and offers strategies for improving these and other EI competencies.

A new chapter on money management. This new chapter outlines important strategies that students can use both in college and in their lives after college, from how to create a budget and cut costs to how to obtain and keep financial aid. This chapter also includes the most up-to-date coverage of the Credit Card Act of 2009 and how it will affect college students.

The clearest coverage of critical thinking in any college success textbook. In an effort to make the complex but crucial topic of critical thinking easier to teach and learn, we have completely revised this chapter, shifting the emphasis to a more comprehensible, student-centered exploration of the value and practical application of critical thinking both inside and outside the classroom.

A revised and reorganized chapter on developing library, research, and information literacy skills. This chapter provides comprehensive and up-to-date advice on navigating the college library, evaluating sources, and gaining information literacy.

New end-of-chapter exercises help students assess what they've learned. Every chapter ends with a collection of exercises that provide multiple ways to help you and your students assess what they've learned. A one-minute paper prompt is a quick and easy assessment tool that will help alert you when students don't understand what was said or discussed in class. Short answer questions ask students to reflect on chapter material and its relevance to their academic and personal lives both now and in the future. Fully revised Building Your Portfolio exercises help students to assemble a collection of their own work.

More real models of how college works. Because many students learn best when they can see a model, we have included abundant examples—more than in any other college text—of the tasks required in college, such as annotating a textbook, multiple styles of note-taking, and other strategies for academic success.

A striking new design makes the book easier to use. As you page through the ninth edition of *Your College Experience*, you'll notice that reference material is easier to find, critical thinking exercises and activities are highlighted, and photographs and artifacts of student life have been included to grab students' attention.

INSTRUCTOR RESOURCES AND SUPPLEMENTS

- **Instructor's Annotated Edition.** A valuable tool for new and experienced instructors alike, the Instructor's Annotated Edition includes the full text of the student edition with abundant marginal annotations, chapter specific exercises, and helpful suggestions for teaching, fully updated and revised by the authors.

- **Instructor's Manual and Test Bank.** Written by Julie Alexander of the John N. Gardner Institute for Excellence in Undergraduate Education, the Instructor's Manual and Test Bank includes chapter objectives, teaching suggestions, additional exercises, test questions, a list of common concerns of first-year students, an introduction to the first-year experience course, a sample lesson plan for each chapter, and various case studies that are relevant to the topics covered. Available in print and online. ISBN-10: 0-312-59861-0; ISBN-13: 978-0-312-59861-7

- *VideoCentral* is a growing collection of online videos for the college success classroom. Visit to watch your colleagues talk about their own experiences teaching the course. Meet academic, real-world, and student writers, and listen to tips on writing for the classroom and life. Show our new "Student Life Videos" in your class to illustrate key concepts, skills, and situations. This resource is available for students and instructors. Learn more at bedfordstmartins.com/collegesuccess/catalog.

- **Custom with Care program.** Bedford/St. Martin's Custom Publishing offers the highest-quality books and media, created in consultation with publishing professionals who are committed to the discipline. Make *Your College Experience* more closely fit your course and goals by integrating your own materials, including only the parts of the text you intend to use in your course, or both. Contact your local Bedford/St. Martin's sales representative for more information.

- **TradeUP** Bring more value and choice to your students' first year experience by packaging *Your College Experience*, Ninth Edition, with one of a thousand titles from Macmillan publishers at a 50 percent discount from the regular price. See the inside back cover or contact your local Bedford/St. Martin's sales representative for more information.

STUDENT RESOURCES

- *Student Center for Your College Experience* bedfordstmartins.com/gardner. You and your students *need* value and *want* powerful online content that you can use anywhere, anytime. The *Student Center for Your College Experience* gives you both, with lots of free and open resources that you can use anywhere, anytime. These resources include a collection of *Student Life Videos* illustrating important concepts, skills, and situations that students will need to understand and master to become successful at college. Each video ends with questions to encourage further contemplation and discussion. Other features include topical quizzes that test students' knowledge of course concepts; downloadable podcasts that offer quick advice on note-taking, dealing with roommates, money management, succeeding on tests, and many more topics; a "Where to Go for Help" library of links directing students to further online resources for support; and much more. From the *Student Center*, you can also access instructor materials whenever you need them.

■ *CourseSmart e-Book for Your College Experience* We've partnered with CourseSmart to offer a downloadable version of *Your College Experience*, Ninth Edition, at about half the price of the print book. To learn more about this low-cost alternative, go to coursesmart.com. ISBN-10: 0-312-59860-2 / ISBN-13: 978-0-312-59860-0.

■ *The Bedford/St. Martin's Planner with Grammar Girl's Quick and Dirty Tips* includes everything that students need to plan and use their time effectively, with advice on preparing schedules and to-do lists, along with blank schedules and calendars (monthly and weekly) for planning. Integrated into the planner are tips from the popular Grammar Girl podcast (and from other podcast hosts); quick advice on fixing common grammar errors, note-taking, and succeeding on tests; an address book; and an annotated list of useful web sites. The planner fits easily into a backpack or purse, so students can take it anywhere. To order *The Bedford/St. Martin's Planner with Grammar Girl's Quick and Dirty Tips* packaged **free** with the text, use ISBN-10: 0-312-62854-4; ISBN-13: 978-0-312-62854-3. To order the planner stand-alone, use ISBN-10: 0-312-48023-7/ISBN-13: 978-0-312-48023-3.

■ *Bedford/St. Martin's Insider's Guides* These concise and student-friendly booklets on topics that are critical to college success are a perfect complement to your textbook and course. Bundle one with any Bedford/St. Martin's textbook at no additional cost. Topics include:

Insider's Guide to Credit Cards • *Insider's Guide to Test Anxiety* • *Insider's Guide to Time Management* • *Insider's Guide to Getting Involved on Campus* • *Insider's Guide to Community College*

For more information on ordering one of these guides **free** with the text, go to bedfordstmartins.com/gardner/catalog.

■ *Journal Writing: A Beginning* Designed to give students an opportunity to use writing as a way to explore their thoughts and feelings, this writing journal includes a generous supply of inspirational quotes placed throughout the pages, tips for journaling, and suggested journal topics. To order *Journal Writing: A Beginning* packaged **free** with the text, use ISBN-10: 0-312-62853-6; ISBN-13: 978-0-312-62853-6. To order the journal stand-alone, use ISBN 10: 0-312-59027-X / ISBN 13: 978-0-312-59027-7.

ACKNOWLEDGMENTS

Special thanks to the reviewers of this edition, whose wisdom and suggestions guided the creation of the ninth edition of the text:

Josie Adamo, Buffalo State College

Leigh A. Adams, Missouri State University–West Plains

Andrés Armijo, University of New Mexico

Camille J. Belolan, Bloomsburg University of Pennsylvania

Richard Conway, Nassau Community College

Matthew Gainous, Ogeechee Technical College

Wendy Grace, Holmes Community College

Janis M. Hausmann, Mount Marty College

Darby Johnsen, Oklahoma City Community College

Tamara Kuzmenkov, Tacoma Community College

Wendy McNeeley, Howard Payne University

Gail Malone Platt, South Plains College

Amy Reese, Baton Rouge Community College

Cristina C. Rodriguez, Los Angeles Pierce College

Rebecca Rogge, Louisiana State University

Janice Waltz, Harrisburg Area Community College

Jodi E. Webb, Bowling Green State University

We would also like to continue to thank our reviewers from the seventh and eighth editions, as they helped to shape the text you see today. **Eighth Edition:** Eunie Alsaker, Winona State University; Marianne Auten, Paradise Valley Community College; Joanne Baird Giordano, University of Wisconsin–Marathon County; Julia Brown, Northern Virginia Community College; Kara Craig, University of Southern Mississippi; Anne Dawson, Eastern Connecticut State University; Rosie DuBose, Century College; Melissa Gomez, Austin Peay State University; Laurene M. Grimes, Lorain County Community College; Kathleen Hangac, State University of New York at Oswego; Elizabeth H. Hicks, Central Connecticut State University; Claudette Jackson, Baylor University; Rebecca Jordan, University of Kentucky; Elizabeth Kennedy, Florida Atlantic University; Mary P. Lovelidge, Blinn College; Karen Mitchell, Northern Essex Community College; Kate Pandolpho, Ocean County College; Margaret Puckett, North Central State College; Christel Taylor, University of Wisconsin-Waukesha; Janice Waltz, Harrisburg Area Community College; Jodi E. Webb, Bowling Green State University; Nicole Weir, Montclair State University; Erika Wimby May, Dillard University; Michael B. Wood, Missouri State University; Janice E. Woods, Mohave Community College. **Seventh Edition:** Richard Conway, Nassau Community College; Joyce Deaton, Jackson State Community College; Gigi Derballa, Asheville Buncombe Technical Community College; Lisa Donato, Essex Community College; Diane Frazier, Colby Community College; Charles Frederick, Indiana University; Melanie Harring, University of Wisconsin, Oshkosh; Judy Jackman, Amarillo College; Rebecca Jordan, University of Kentucky; Harriet McQueen, Austin Peay State University; Jason Outlaw, Arizona State University; Bea Rogers, Monmouth University; Christel Taylor, University of Wisconsin–Waukesha; Susan M. Vladika, Marywood University; Linda S. York, Wallace Community College.

As we look to the future, we are excited about the numerous improvements to this text that our creative Bedford/St. Martin's team has made and will continue to make. Special thanks to Joan Feinberg, President of Bedford/St. Martin's; Denise Wydra, Editorial Director; Karen Henry, Editor in Chief; Carrie Brandon, Executive Editor; Julie Kelly, Development Editor; Casey Carroll, Marketing Manager; Nicholas Murphy, Editorial Assistant; Elise Kaiser, Assistant Director of Editing, Design, and Production; Kerri Cardone, Production Editor; and Ellen Kuhl Repetto, Editor.

Most of all, we thank you, the users of our book, for you are the true inspirations for our work.

CONTRIBUTORS

Although this text speaks with the voices of its three authors, it represents contributions from many other people. We gratefully acknowledge those contributions and thank these individuals, whose special expertise has made it possible to introduce new students to their college experience through the holistic approach we deeply believe in.

Catherine Andersen is Associate Provost for Enrollment at Gallaudet University. Before this appointment, she was interim Dean of Enrollment Management and General Studies as well Director of the First Year Experience at Gallaudet for ten years. She is a Teagle Assessment Scholar (as part of a national group that assists liberal arts colleges and universities in assessing student outcomes), is affiliated with the Policy Center on the First Year of College, and is a certified master trainer in emotional intelligence assessment. She received a B.S from Ohio University, an M.S. from Hofstra University, and her Ph.D. from Indiana University. She contributed her valuable expertise to the writing of the new Chapter 3, "Understanding Emotional Intelligence."

Throughout her career of more than thirty years, **Natala Kleather (Tally) Hart** has served students who have limited opportunities for higher education. Her work includes service in financial aid offices at the University of California-San Diego, Purdue University, Indiana University, and Ohio State University; public service as the head of the Indiana State Scholarship and Loan Commission; and service to institutions of higher education at the College Board. She has contributed widely to college student financial literacy initiatives to improve student retention and completion. She is the founding head of the Economic Access Initiative at Ohio State, developing and evaluating mechanisms to encourage college attendance among low-income fourth- through tenth-grade Ohio students and enrollment in graduate and professional programs for first-generation college students. She was a major contributor to the new Chapter 13, "Managing Your Money."

Kate Trombitas is the Assistant Director of the Ohio State University Student Wellness Center, where she serves as a financial specialist for undergraduate, graduate, and professional students. She holds a bachelor's degree in business administration from the Fisher College of Business and a master's degree in communications from Ohio State. She contributed her significant knowledge to the writing of the new Chapter 13, "Managing Your Money."

Reynol Junco is an Associate Professor and the Director of Disability Services in the Department of Academic Development and Counseling at Lock Haven University of Pennsylvania. He holds a doctoral degree in counselor education with a focus on college student development from Pennsylvania State University and a master's degree in clinical psychology, also from Penn State. He is a licensed professional counselor in the state of Pennsylvania, and he has taught first-year seminars for over eight years. His research focuses on using emerging technologies to help engage and support college students. He developed and wrote the "Wired Windows" features in this book and in the previous edition, and he wrote a section on social networking in Chapter 14, "Establishing and Maintaining Relationships in College."

Julie Alexander is the Associate Vice President for Assessment Administration at the John N. Gardner Institute for Excellence in Undergraduate Education. She actively engages with colleges and universities as they prepare for and conduct an intensive self-study of the first year of college. She holds an M.A. in college student development and a B.S. in psychology from Appalachian State University. While at Appalachian, she taught the three-credit hour first-year seminar and was involved in faculty development and support, peer leader recruitment and training, and planning and implementing Appalachian's residential summer bridge program. She developed and wrote the end of chapter review exercises and activities in this book.

Molly Reese is a senior in the Gallatin School of Individualized Study at New York University, studying French, Italian, and literature. She is particularly interested in world literature and literary translation and has studied abroad in both France and Italy. She liked France best and would like to live there someday. She currently works for a literary agency in New York and hopes to continue in the field of publishing. She conducted the student interviews for the "Confessions of a College Student" feature.

We would also like to acknowledge and thank the numerous colleagues who have contributed to this book in its previous editions:

Chapters 2, 6, 7, 8, 9: Jeanne L. Higbee, University of Minnesota, Twin Cities

Chapters 4, 14: Tom Carskadon, Mississippi State University

Chapter 7: Mary Ellen O'Leary, University of South Carolina at Columbia

Chapter 9: Christel Taylor, University of Wisconsin at Waukesha

Chapter 10: Constance Staley, University of Colorado at Colorado Springs

Chapter 10: R. Stephen Staley, Colorado Technical University

Chapter 11: Charles Curran, University of South Carolina at Columbia

Chapter 11: Rose Parkman Marshall, University of South Carolina at Columbia

Chapter 11: Margit Watts, University of Hawaii, Manoa

Chapter 12: Philip Gardner, Michigan State University

Chapter 15: Juan J. Flores, Folsom Lake College

Chapter 16: Michelle Murphy Burcin, University of South Carolina at Columbia

PART 1 → Preparing for SUCCESS

PART 2 Preparing to STUDY

PART 3 Preparing for LIFE

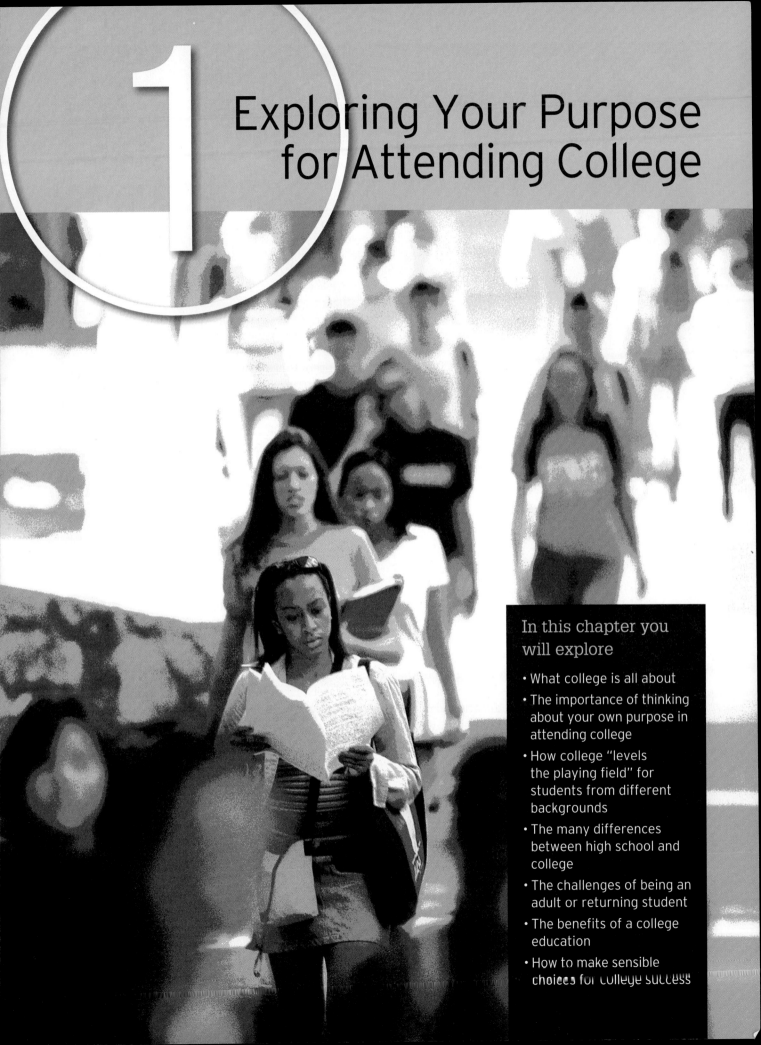

1 Exploring Your Purpose for Attending College

In this chapter you will explore

- What college is all about
- The importance of thinking about your own purpose in attending college
- How college "levels the playing field" for students from different backgrounds
- The many differences between high school and college
- The challenges of being an adult or returning student
- The benefits of a college education
- How to make sensible choices for college success

Confessions of a COLLEGE STUDENT...

> " I feel that college is basically my career until I get my career, and I've got to treat it like that. "

I wasn't a good student in high school. I went to college for a brief period, but I didn't know what I wanted to do. So I got a job and worked, for years and years. Now I'm a mom of two, and last year my husband passed. It was a whole life change. I decided I needed to get more training and a higher income so I could provide for my kids. I want to get my associate's degree in law enforcement and criminal justice and be an animal control officer.

I go to college part time right now because my son is in kindergarten. Next year I get to go full time. I feel that college is basically my career until I get my career, and I've got to treat it like that because if I'm not serious, I'm not going to get through it successfully. Coming back to college at this late stage, I have realized so many important things. You have to take on your own responsibility. You've got to figure out yourself what your goal is, and you've got to figure out how to reach it. As an adult, I understand why the instructors are doing what they do. I understand everything better. I've got life experience now. I can relate.

MINDY DEUEL, 40
Kalamazoo Valley Community College

IN 1900 fewer than 2 percent of Americans of traditional college age attended college. Today, new technologies and the information explosion are changing the workplace so drastically that in order to support themselves and their families adequately, most people will need some education beyond high school. College is so important that more than 67 percent of high school graduates (approximately 18 million students) attend. Because higher education can be essential to your future earning power and your overall well-being, we are committed to providing a set of strategies you can use to do your best. That's what this book is all about.

As you're settling into your new college routine, we want to welcome you to the world of higher education. The fact that you are reading this textbook probably means you are enrolled in a first-year seminar or "college success" course designed to introduce you to college and help you make the most of it. In this chapter, we'll discuss how you fit into the whole idea of college. We'll consider why the United States has more colleges and universities than any other country in the world. We'll also help you explore the purposes of college—many that your college might define for you. But even more important, we'll help you define your purposes for being here and offer many strategies to help you succeed.

The College Experience

So what is the college experience? Depending on who you are, your life circumstances, and why you decided to enroll, college can mean different things. College is often portrayed in books and films as a place where young people live away from home in ivy-covered residence halls. We frequently see college depicted as a place with a major focus on big-time sports, heavy drinking, and partying. And, yes, there is some of that at some colleges. But most students today don't move away from home, don't live on campus, and don't see much ivy. College is really far more than any single image you might carry around in your head.

There are many ways to define college. For starters, college is an established process designed to further formal education so that students who attend and graduate will be prepared for certain roles in society. These days, those roles are found especially in what has become known as "the information economy." This means most college graduates are going to be earning their living by creating, managing, and using information. Because the amount of available information expands all the time, your college classes can't possibly teach you all you need to know for years to come. The most important skill you will need to learn in college is how to keep learning throughout your life.

WHY COLLEGE IS IMPORTANT TO OUR SOCIETY

American society values higher education, which explains why the United States has so many colleges and universities—more than 4,400. College is the primary way in which people achieve upward social mobility, or the ability to attain a higher standard of living. In earlier centuries, a high standard of living was almost always a function of family background. Either you were born into power and money or you spent your life working for others who had power and money. But in most countries today, receiving a college degree helps to level the playing field for everyone. A college degree can minimize or eliminate differences due to background, race, ethnicity, family income level, national origin, immigration status, family lineage, and personal connections. Simply put, college participation is about ensuring that more people have the opportunity to be evaluated on the basis of merit rather than family status, money, or other forms of privilege. It makes achieving the American dream possible.

College is also important because it is society's primary means of preparing citizens for leadership roles. Without a college degree, it is difficult to be a leader in a community, company, profession, or the military.

Another purpose of a four-year college degree is to prepare students for continuing their education in a graduate or professional school. If you want to become a medical doctor, dentist, lawyer, or college professor, a four-year college degree is just the beginning.

> **YOUR TURN ▶**
>
> When you hear the phrase "American dream," what do you think of? How would you describe to someone else the meaning of these words?

WHY COLLEGE IS IMPORTANT FOR YOU

College is about thinking, and it will help you understand how to become a "critical thinker"—someone who doesn't believe everything he or she hears or reads but instead looks for evidence before forming an opinion. Developing critical-thinking skills will empower you to make sound decisions throughout your life.

Although college is often thought of as a time when traditional-age students become young adults, we realize that many of you are already adults. Whatever your age, college can be a time when you take some risks, learn new things, and meet new and different people—all in a relatively safe environment. It's OK to experiment in college, within limits, because that's what college is designed for.

College will provide you with many opportunities for developing a variety of social networks, both formal and informal. These will help you make friends and develop alliances with faculty members and fellow students who share your interests and goals. Social networking websites (such as Facebook and MySpace) provide a way to enrich your real-life social networks in college.

College definitely can and should be fun, and we hope it will be for you. You will meet new people, go to athletic events and parties, build camaraderie with new friends, and feel a sense of school spirit. Many college graduates relive memories of college days throughout their lives, fanatically root for their institution's athletic teams, return for homecoming and class reunions, and encourage their own children to attend their alma mater. In fact, you might be a legacy student—someone whose parents or grandparents attended the same institution.

In addition to being fun, college is a lot of work. Being a college student means spending hours studying each week, late nights, taking high-stakes exams, and possibly working harder than you ever have. For many students, college becomes much like a job, with defined duties, expectations, and obligations.

But most important, college will be a set of experiences that will help you to further define and achieve your own purpose. You might feel that you know exactly what you want to do with your life—where you want to go from here. Or, like many students, you might be struggling to find where you fit in life and work. It is possible that as you discover more about yourself and your abilities, your purpose for coming to college will change. In fact, the vast majority of college students change their academic major at least once during the college years, and some students find they need to transfer to another institution to meet their academic goals.

How would you describe your reasons for being in college and at this particular college? Perhaps you, like the vast majority of college students, see college as the pathway to a good job. Maybe you are in college to train or retrain for an occupation, or maybe you have recently experienced an upheaval in your life. Perhaps you are here to fulfill a lifelong dream of getting an education. Or maybe you are bored or in a rut and see college as a way out of it. Many students enter college without a purpose that has been clearly thought out. They have just been swept along by life's events, and now here they are.

Your college or university might require you to select a major during or before your first year, even before you have figured out your own purpose for college. Some institutions will allow you to be "undecided" or to select "no preference" for a year or two. Even if you are ready to select a major, it's a good idea to keep an open mind. There are so many avenues to pursue while you're in college—many that you might not have even considered. Or you might learn that the career you always dreamed of isn't what you thought it would be at all. You will learn more about choosing a major and a career later in this book, but you ought to use your first year to explore and think about your purpose for college and how that might connect with the rest of your life.

Wired WINDOW

USING THE INTERNET TO LEARN ABOUT YOUR COLLEGE OR UNIVERSITY

The Internet offers a number of ways to get connected online. As you might already know, social networking websites such as Facebook and MySpace are a great way to connect with your friends. Through Facebook you can find new schoolmates with similar interests, join clubs or interest groups, and find friends in your classes. Keep in mind that the information you post on Facebook is available to everyone in your network unless you adjust your privacy settings. This means that anyone with an e-mail address from your institution can see your entire profile unless you change your privacy settings. While most students use Facebook and MySpace appropriately, some students have faced conduct (and sometimes legal) sanctions for pictures and information they posted online. Therefore, it is important that you review your profile to make sure you are including only information you want the public to know about you. Ask yourself whether you want every Facebook user at your college or university to know personal information such as your residence hall room number or your cell phone number.

Another way in which you can learn about your specific college or university is by taking advantage of official and unofficial online campus resources. Your institution's website is one official resource that is useful for finding a range of information, from how to get help with your writing to when the term break begins. Unofficial resources include websites that rate professors and student-run wikis that have been created to help you find answers to common questions about your college or university.

Thinking Critically

A popular website for rating professors is www.RateMyProfessor.com. Keep in mind that ratings on such websites are not reviewed for accuracy, so use them only as a starting point to learn about a professor. Go to RateMyProfessor.com and search for one of your professors. What do the comments suggest about this professor's teaching style? How do the comments reflect on the students who wrote them? Use the information you gathered from reading the reviews to consider what you might do to be successful in a class taught by the professor you picked.

YOUR TURN ▶

How would you describe your reasons for coming to college at this time in your life? Do you think your reasons will change during your college career? Why or why not?

Outcomes of College

Although a college degree clearly will make you more professionally marketable, the college experience can enrich your life in many other ways. We hope you will take advantage of the many opportunities you'll have to learn the skills of leadership, experience diversity, explore other countries and cultures, clarify your beliefs and values, and make decisions about the rest of your life—not just what you want to do but also, more important, how you want to live.

When you made the decision to come to college, you probably didn't think about all of the positive ways in which college could affect the rest of your life. Your reasons for coming might have been more personal and more immediate. There are all sorts of reasons, circumstances, events, and pressures that bring students to college; and when you put different people with different motivations and purposes together, it creates an interesting environment for learning.

Many college graduates report that higher education changed them for the better. Read the information in the following box to learn how completing a college degree will make a positive difference for you.

OUTCOMES OF THE COLLEGE EXPERIENCE

- You will learn how to accumulate knowledge.
- You will be more likely to seek appropriate information before making a decision. Such information will also help you to realize how our lives are shaped by global and local, political, social, psychological, economic, environmental, and physical forces.
- You will grow intellectually through interactions with cultures, languages, ethnic groups, religions, nationalities, and socioeconomic groups other than your own.
- You will gain self-esteem and self-confidence, which will help you realize how you might make a difference in the world.
- You will tend to be more flexible in your views, more future-oriented, more willing to appreciate differences of opinion, and more interested in political and public affairs.
- If you have children, they will be more likely to have greater learning potential, which in turn will help them to achieve more in life.
- You will be an efficient consumer, save more money, make better investments, and be more likely to spend money on your home and on intellectual and cultural interests as well as on your children.
- You will be better able to deal with bureaucracies, the legal system, tax laws, and advertising claims.
- You will be more involved in education, hobbies, and civic and community affairs.
- You will be more concerned with wellness and preventive health care and through diet, exercise, stress management, a positive attitude, and other factors, will live longer and suffer fewer disabilities.

We know without a doubt that college will make your life different from the one you would have had if you had never been a college student. Consider the following list. You will note that the first item is that college graduates earn more money. (Look at Table 1.1 to see exactly how much more.) However, note that these differences go far beyond making more money. When compared to non-college graduates, those who graduate from college are more likely to:

- earn more money
- have a less erratic job history
- earn more promotions
- have fewer children
- be more involved in their children's school lives
- have more discretionary time and money
- become leaders in their communities and employment settings
- stay married longer to the same person
- be elected to public office
- participate in and enjoy the arts

When compared to nongraduates, college graduates are less likely to:

- be imprisoned
- become dependent on alcohol or drugs
- be duped, conned, or swindled
- be involuntarily unemployed
- use tobacco products

TABLE 1.1 ▶ Median* Earnings by Educational Attainment for Year-Round, Full-Time Workers Age 25+

Doctoral degree	$80,860
Master's degree	$63,856
Bachelor's degree	$50,856
Associate degree	$38,272
High school graduate	$30,732
Less than high school diploma	$22,152

*These are median earnings, meaning half the group earned less and half earned more. These figures are annual amounts based on weekly data through the second quarter of 2007.

Source: U.S. Department of Labor, Bureau of Labor Statistics, Current Population Survey, 2008. (http://www.bls.gov/emp/emptab7.htm)

Making the Transition

If you just graduated from high school, you will find some distinct differences between high school and college. For instance, you will probably be part of a more diverse student body, not just in terms of race but also in terms of age, religion, political opinions, and life experiences. If you attend a large college or university, you might feel like a number—not as special as you felt in high school. You will have more potential friends to choose from, but familiar assumptions about people based on where they live, where they go to church, or what high school they attend might not apply to the new people you're meeting.

You will be able to choose from many more types of courses, but managing your time is sure to be more complex because your classes will meet on various days and times, and you will have additional commitments, including work, family, activities, and sports. Your college classes might have many more students in them and meet for longer class periods. Tests are given less frequently in college—sometimes only twice a term—and you will most likely be required to do more writing in college. You will be encouraged to do original research and to investigate differing points of view on a topic. You will be expected to study outside of class, prepare assignments, do assigned reading, and be ready for in-class discussions. Your instructors might rely far less on textbooks and far more on lectures than your high school teachers did. Your instructors will rarely monitor your progress; you're on your own. But you will have more freedom to express views that are different from those of your instructors. They will usually have private offices and keep regular office hours in order to be available for you.

YOUR TURN ▶

In what ways are you already finding that college is different from high school? Did you anticipate these differences? Why or why not?

CHALLENGES AND OPPORTUNITIES FOR ADULT AND RETURNING STUDENTS

If you're a "returning" student—someone who might have experienced some college before—or if you are an adult living and working off campus, you might also find that college presents new challenges and opportunities. For instance, college might feel liberating, like a new beginning or a stimulating challenge or like a path to a career. However, working full-time and attending college at night, on weekends, or both can mean extra stress, especially with a family at home.

Adult students often experience a daunting lack of freedom because of many important conflicting responsibilities. Working, caring for a family, and meeting your other commitments will compete for the time and attention it takes to do your best or even to simply stay in college. You might wonder how you will ever get through college and still manage to care for your family. You might worry that they won't understand why you have to spend time in class and studying.

YOUR TURN ▶

As an adult or returning student, what challenges in college have you already faced? To whom can you turn for help? How might you avoid such challenges in the future?

In spite of your concerns, you should know that many college professors value working with adult students because, unlike eighteen-year-olds, your life experiences have shown you how important an education can be. Adult students tend to have intrinsic motivation that comes with maturity and experience, and that motivation will compensate for any initial difficulties you might have. You will bring a unique and rich perspective to what you're learning in your classes, a perspective that most eighteen-year-olds lack.

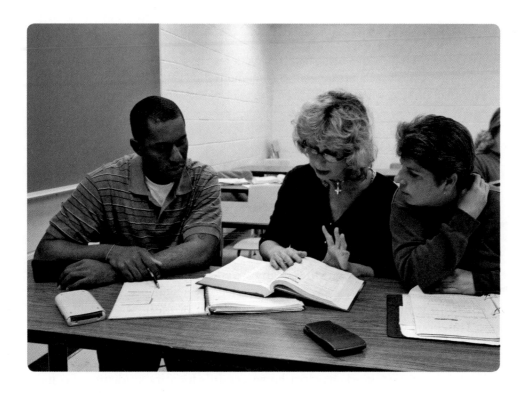

FIRST-YEAR MOTIVATION AND COMMITMENT

What attitudes and behaviors will help you to achieve your goals and be successful in college? If you are fresh out of high school, it will be important for you to learn to deal with newfound freedom. Your college professors are not going to tell you what, how, or when to study. If you live on campus, your parents won't be able to wake you in the morning, see that you eat properly and get enough sleep, monitor whether or how well you do your homework, or remind you to allow enough time to get to class. In almost every aspect of your life, you will have to assume primary responsibility for your own attitudes and behaviors.

If you are an adult student, you might find yourself with less freedom: You might have a difficult daily commute and have to arrange and pay for child care. You might have to juggle work and school responsibilities and still find time for family and other duties. As you walk around campus, you might feel uncertain about your ability to keep up with academic work. You also might find it difficult to relate to younger students, some of whom don't seem to take academic work seriously.

Whatever challenges you are facing, what will motivate you to be successful? And what about the enormous investment of time and money that getting a college degree requires? Are you convinced that the investment will pay off? Have you selected a major, or is this on your list of things to do after you arrive? Do you know where to go when you need help with a personal or financial problem? If you are a minority student on your campus, are you concerned about how you will be treated?

Thoughts like these are very common. Although your classmates might not say it out loud, many of them share your concerns, doubts, and fears. This course will be a safe place for you to talk about all of these issues with people who care about you and your success in college.

┌───┐
│ **YOUR TURN ▶**   │
│   │
│ On a scale of 1 to 5, with 5 being high, rate your own level of motivation for college. │
│ What do you think accounts for your current motivation level? If you don't think │
│ you are motivated, what strategies can you think of that would help motivate you? │
└───┘

What is Your Purpose in College?

Consider these differences in the way a student might feel about college:
I belong in college. . . . . versus . . . . .What on earth am I doing here? Where would you fall between these opposite attitudes? You might find that your exact position shifts depending on what's going on in your academic and personal life at any given time. But no matter how you feel on a particular day, as you begin college you will need to spend time sorting out your own sense of purpose and level of motivation. The clearer you are about why you're in college, the easier it will be to stay motivated, even when times are tough.

To build a clearer sense of purpose, look around you and get to know other students who work hard to be successful. Identify students who have the same major or the same career interests, and learn about the courses they have taken, work experiences they have had, and their plans for the future. Look for courses that are relevant to your interests—but don't stop there. Seek relevance in those required general education courses that might seem to be a waste of time or energy at first. Remember that general education courses are designed to give you the kinds of knowledge and skills you need for the rest of your life. Visit your career center, your library, and the Internet to investigate your interests and learn how to develop and apply them in college and beyond. A great website to help you research your career interests is the U.S. Department of Labor's Bureau of Labor Statistics (http://www.bls.gov), which includes information about average wages for each career by region, job growth statistics, and unemployment rates.

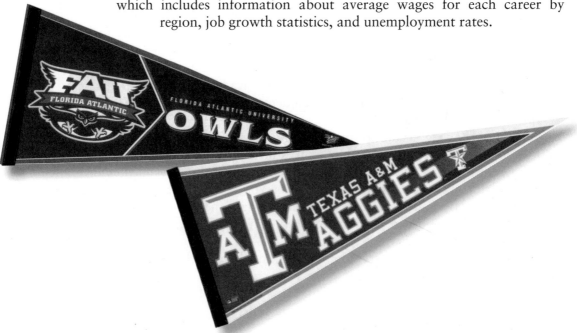

Talk to your residence hall advisors as well as your professors, academic advisors, and campus chaplains. College is designed to give you all the tools you need to find and achieve your purpose. It's all at your fingertips—but the rest is up to you.

A FORMULA FOR SUCCESS

- **Keep up with your weekly schedule and do your work on time.** Get a paper calendar or an electronic one, and use it consistently to keep track of assignments and appointments.
- **Be on time for class.** If you are frequently late, you give your instructors and fellow students the unspoken message that you don't think the class is important.
- **If you are a full-time student, limit the hours you work. If you must work, look for a job on campus.** Students who work a reasonable number of hours per week (about fifteen) and especially those who work on campus are more likely to do well in college.
- **Improve your study habits.** Find the most effective methods for reading textbooks, listening, taking notes, studying, and using information resources.
- **Use the academic skills center, library, and campus career center.** These essential services are there to help you be a better student and plan for your future.
- **Learn to think critically.** If you don't carefully examine and evaluate what you see, read, and hear, you're not really learning.
- **Strive to improve your writing and speaking.** The more you write and speak in public, the easier these skills will become now and in the future.
- **Speak up in class.** Research indicates that you will usually remember more about what goes on in class when you get involved.
- **Learn from criticism.** Criticism can be helpful to your learning. If you get a low grade, meet with your instructor to discuss how you can improve.
- **Study with a group.** Research shows that students who study in groups often earn the highest grades and have the fewest academic problems.
- **Become engaged in campus activities.** Visit the student activities office; join a club or organization that interests you; participate in community service.
- **Meet with your instructors out of class.** Instructors generally have office hours; successful students use them.
- **Find a competent and caring academic advisor or counselor.** If your personality and that of your advisor clash, ask the department office to find another advisor for you.
- **Take your health seriously.** How much you sleep, what you eat, whether you exercise, and how well you deal with stress will affect your college success.
- **Have realistic expectations.** If you are disappointed in your grades, remember that college is a new experience and your grades will probably improve if you continue to apply yourself.

Where to go FOR HELP...

ON CAMPUS ▶

To find the college support services you need, ask your academic advisor or counselor or consult your college catalog, phone book, and college website. Or call or visit student services (or student affairs) offices. Most of these services are free. In subsequent chapters, we will include a "Where to Go for Help" feature that is specific to the chapter topic.

Academic Advisement Center Help in choosing courses; information on degree requirements; help in finding a major.

Academic Skills Center Tutoring; help in study and memory skills; help in studying for exams.

Adult Reentry Center Programs for returning students; supportive contacts with other adult students; information about services such as child care.

Career Center Career library; interest assessments; counseling; help in finding a major; job and internship listings; co-op listings; interviews with prospective employers; help with résumés and interview skills.

Chaplains Worship services; fellowship; personal counseling.

Commuter Services List of off-campus housing, roommate lists, orientation to community, maps, public transportation guides, child-care listings.

Computer Center Minicourses, handouts on campus computer resources.

Counseling Center Confidential counseling for personal concerns, stress management programs.

Disabled Student Services Assistance in overcoming physical barriers or learning disabilities.

Financial Aid and Scholarship Office Information on financial aid programs, scholarships, and grants.

Health Center Help in personal nutrition, weight control, exercise, and sexuality; information on substance abuse programs and other health issues; often includes a pharmacy.

Housing Office Help in locating on- or off-campus housing.

Legal Services Legal aid for students; if your campus has a law school, possible assistance by senior law students.

Math Center Help with math skills.

Fitness Center Facilities and equipment for exercise and recreational sports.

Writing Center Help with writing assignments.

MY INSTITUTION'S RESOURCES ▶

_____

_____

_____

_____

_____

_____

_____

_____

_____

_____

_____

_____

_____

_____

_____

_____

_____

_____

_____

Chapter
REVIEW...

One-Minute PAPER...

Chapter 1 explores how deciding to go to college, experiencing college life, and finding your own path can be a unique journey. Sometimes things that seem simple have more depth if they are given some thought. Take a minute (or several) to think about and note what you found most useful or meaningful during this class. Did anything that was covered in this chapter leave you with more questions than answers?

Applying What You've LEARNED...

Now that you have read and discussed this chapter, consider how you can apply what you have learned to your academic and personal life. The following prompts will help you reflect on chapter material and its relevance to you both now and in the future.

1. Review the "Outcomes of College" section of this chapter. While landing a lucrative career is probably high on your list of goals after college, take a look at the other possible outcomes of obtaining a college degree. List five outcomes from this section that you can relate to the most. If you think of an outcome that is not noted in the chapter, add it to your top five. Why are these outcomes important to you?

2. College students often feel the stress of trying to balance their personal and academic lives. The ups and downs of life are inevitable, but we can control our choices and attitudes. As a first-year student, you will want to begin developing a personal strategy for bouncing back after a particularly difficult time. Your strategy should include at least three steps you can take to get back on track and move forward.

Building Your PORTFOLIO...

66 Life is what happens to you while you're busy making other plans. 99

–JOHN LENNON (1940-1980),
British singer and songwriter

WHAT'S IN IT FOR ME? SKILLS MATRIX

How might the courses in which you are enrolled right now affect your future? Although it might be hard to imagine that there is a direct connection to your career or lifestyle after college, the classes and experiences you are now engaged in can play an important role in your future.

Developing a Skills Matrix will help you reflect on your college experiences and track the skills that will eventually help you land a great summer job, the hard-to-get internship, a scholarship, and one day, a career.

1. Using Microsoft Excel, develop a skills matrix like the one on page 17 to identify courses and out-of-class experiences that enhance the following skills: communications, creativity, critical thinking, leadership, research, social responsibility, and teamwork.

2. Add any additional skills categories or courses you would like to track.

3. Indicate what you did in your courses or activities that helped you learn one of these skills. Be specific about the assignment, project, or activity that helped you learn.

4. Save your skills matrix on your computer, flash drive, or external hard drive.

5. Update your matrix often. Add new skills categories, courses, and activities. Change the title to indicate the appropriate time period (e.g., Skills Learned in my First Two Years of College.

6. Start an electronic collection of your college work. Save papers, projects, and other relevant material in one location on your computer or on an external storage device. Be sure to back up your work to avoid digital disasters!

Skills Learned During First Term in College	My Courses and Activities					
	English	Math	History	French	First-Year Seminar	Campus Activities
Communication	Improved my writing skills			E-mailed French students	Had to give three oral presentations	Participated in Toastmasters
Creativity	Writing original poetry					Designed float for homecoming
Critical Thinking			Class members debated Iraq war			
Leadership					Led a group project on college sports	Participated in Emerging Leaders
Research					Conducted research on memory	
Social Responsibility					Participated in Habitat for Humanity Project	Tutored 2nd grad-ers in reading
Teamwork		Had to study in a study group				Participated in intramural soccer

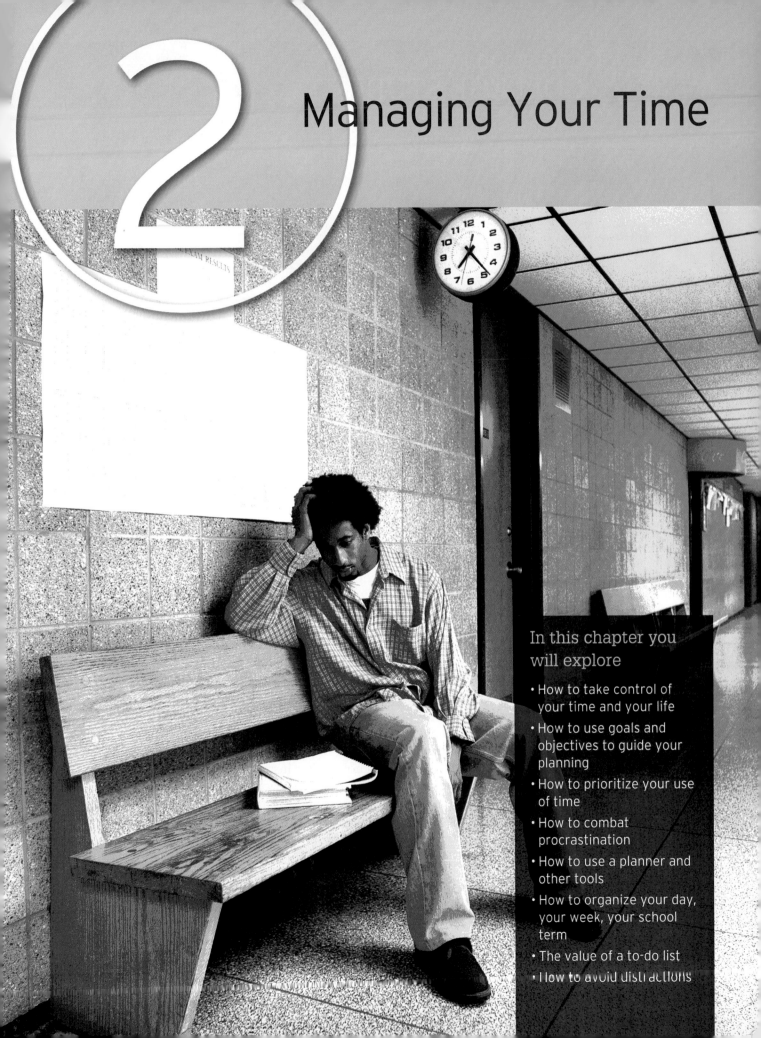

2 Managing Your Time

NICOLE BLAHUT, 18
Florida Atlantic University

❝ Without my planner, I'd be a mess. I keep everything in there. ❞

When I came to college, I thought that everyone would learn to be responsible about their free time and study time, but it seems as if a lot of people here don't know how to handle the freedom or responsibility of being on their own. They tend to want to hang out with their friends, to go out and party, and then schoolwork becomes a second priority, whereas it should always be first.

I'm a studious person. I have a nineteen-credit course load, and my classes are hard because I'm a biological sciences major. Procrastination is not good at all, especially with papers. Trying to write five or six pages the night before a paper is due doesn't exactly work out well; I've definitely learned my lesson on that. Now I usually start a week in advance and do a couple of pages at a time, so that by the night before, I only have a page or two left. Without my planner, I'd be a mess. I keep everything in there and make sure that I have everything planned out and that nothing's going to clash. If there happens to be a conflict, I always talk it out with whoever's involved, like the professor or someone, and work around it. I know it's my responsibility.

How do you approach time? You might find that you view this important resource differently than your classmates. Some of these differences might have to do with your personality and background. And often, these differences are so automatic and ingrained that you don't even think about them. For example, if you're a natural organizer, you probably enter all due dates for assignments on your calendar, cell phone, or PDA as soon as you receive each syllabus. If you take a more laid-back approach to life, you might prefer to be more flexible and go with the flow rather than following a daily or weekly schedule. You might be good at dealing with the unexpected, but you also might be a procrastinator.

Most fundamentally, how you manage time reflects what you value—what is most important to you and what consequences you are willing to accept when you make certain choices. For instance, when you value friendships above everything else, your academic work can take a back seat to social activities. What you value most and how that relates to the way you spend your time often change in college. How you manage this resource corresponds to how successful you will be in college and throughout life.

Time management involves:

- Knowing your goals
- Setting priorities to meet your goals
- Anticipating the unexpected
- Taking control of your time
- Making a commitment to punctuality
- Carrying out your plans

Taking Control of Your Time

The first step to effective time management is recognizing that you can be in control. How often do you find yourself saying, "I don't have time?" Once a week? Once a day? Several times a day? The next time you find yourself saying this, stop and ask yourself whether it is really true. Do you really not have time, or have you made a choice, consciously or unconsciously, not to make time for that particular task or activity?

When we say that we don't have time, we imply that we don't have a choice. But we do have a choice. We have control over how we use our time. We have control over many of the commitments we choose to make. And we also have control over many small decisions that affect our time-management success, such as what time we get up in the morning, how much sleep we get, what we eat, how much time we spend studying, and whether we get exercise. All of these small decisions have a big impact on our success in college and in life.

Being in control means that you make your own decisions. Two of the most often cited differences between high school and college are increased **autonomy**, or independence, and greater responsibility. If you are not a recent high school graduate, you have most likely already experienced a higher level of independence, but returning to school creates responsibilities above and beyond those you already have, whether those include employment, family, community service, or other activities.

Whether you are beginning college immediately after high school or are continuing your education after a break, make sure that the way you spend your time aligns with your most important values. For instance, if you value becoming an expert in a particular academic area, you'll want to learn everything you can in that field by taking related classes and participating in internships. If you value learning about many things and postponing a specific decision about your major, you might want to spend your time exploring many different areas of interest and taking as many different types of courses as possible. To take control of your life and your time and to guide your decisions, begin by setting some goals for the future.

OVERCOMING PROCRASTINATION

Procrastination is a serious problem that trips up many otherwise capable people. There are numerous reasons why students procrastinate. In the book, *Procrastination: Why You Do It, What to Do About It*, psychologists Jane Burka and Lenora Yuen summarize a number of research studies about procrastination.[1] According to these authors, even students who are highly motivated often fear failure, and some students even fear success (although

[1] Jane B. Burka and Lenora M. Yuen. *Procrastination: Why You Do It, What to Do About It* (Reading, MA: Addison-Wesley, 1983).

that might seem counterintuitive). Some students procrastinate because they are perfectionists; not doing a task might be easier than having to live up to your own very high expectations—or those of your parents, teachers, or peers. Others procrastinate because they find an assigned task boring or irrelevant or consider it "busy work," believing that they can learn the material just as effectively without doing the homework.

Simply not enjoying an assignment is not a good reason to put it off; it's an *excuse*, not a valid *reason*. Throughout life you'll be faced with tasks that you don't find interesting, and in many cases you won't have the option not to do them. For instance, when you work in an entry-level job, you might find that you are assigned tedious tasks that are generally reserved for new employees. On a more personal level, you might occasionally put off cleaning your house or your room until the day comes when you can't find an important file or document. At that point, cleaning your personal space becomes an essential task, not an optional one.

When you're in college, procrastinating can signal that it's time to reassess your goals and objectives; maybe you are not ready to make a commitment to academic priorities at this point in your life. Only you can decide, but a counselor or academic advisor can help you sort it out.

Here are some strategies for beating procrastination:

- Remind yourself of the possible consequences if you do not get down to work, then get started.
- Create a to-do list. Check off things as you get them done. Use the list to focus on the things that aren't getting done. Move them to the top of the next day's list, and make up your mind to do them. Working from a list will give you a feeling of accomplishment.
- Break big jobs into smaller steps. Tackle short, easy-to-accomplish tasks first.
- Promise yourself a reward for finishing the task, such as watching your favorite TV show or going out with friends. For more substantial tasks, give yourself bigger and better rewards.
- Find a place to study that's comfortable and doesn't allow for distractions and interruptions. Say "no" to friends and family members who want your attention; agree to spend time with them later.
- Don't talk on the phone, send e-mail or text messages, or surf the web during planned study sessions. If you study in your room, close your door.

If these ideas don't sufficiently motivate you to get to work, you might want to reexamine your purposes, values, and priorities. Keep coming back to some basic questions: Why am I in college here and now? Why am I in this course? What is really important to me? Are these values important enough to forgo some short-term fun or laziness in order to get down to work? Are my academic goals really my own, or were they imposed on me by family members, my employer, or societal expectations? If you are not willing to stop procrastinating and get to work on the tasks at hand, perhaps you should reconsider why you are in college and if this is the right time to pursue higher education.

Researchers at Carleton University in Canada have found that college students who procrastinate in their studies also avoid confronting other tasks and problems and are more likely to develop unhealthy habits, such as higher levels of alcohol consumption, smoking, insomnia, a poor diet, or lack of exercise.[2] If you cannot get procrastination under control, it is in your best interest to seek help at your campus counseling service before you begin to feel as though you are also losing control over other aspects of your life.

SETTING PRIORITIES

To help combat the urge to procrastinate, you should think about how to prioritize your tasks, goals, and values. Which goals and objectives are most important to you and most consistent with your values? Which are the most urgent? For example, studying in order to get a good grade on tomorrow's test might have to take priority over attending a job fair today. However, don't ignore long-term goals in order to meet short-term goals. With good time management you can study during the week prior to the test so that you can attend the job fair the day before. Skilled time managers often establish priorities by maintaining a to-do list (discussed in more detail later in this chapter), ranking the items on the list to determine schedules and deadlines for each task.

Another aspect of setting priorities while in college is finding an appropriate way to balance your academic schedule with the rest of your life. Social activities are an important part of the college experience. Time alone and time to think are also essential to your overall well-being.

For many students, the greatest challenge of prioritizing will be balancing school with work and family obligations that are equally important and are not optional. Good advance planning will help you meet these challenges. But you will also need to talk with your family members and your employer to make sure that they understand your academic responsibilities. Most professors will work with you when conflicts arise, but if you have problems that can't be

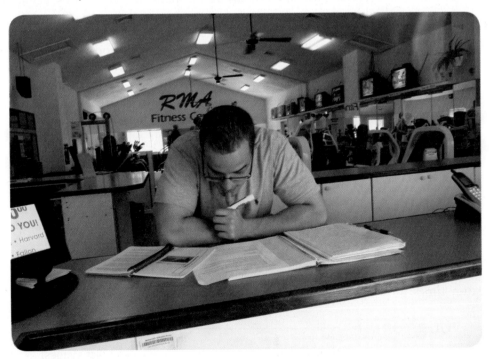

[2]Timothy A. Pychyl and Fuschia M. Sirois. *Procrastination: Costs to Health and Well-being*. Presentation at the APA Convention, August 22, 2002, Chicago.

resolved easily, be sure to seek support from the professionals in your college's counseling center. They will understand your challenges and help you manage and prioritize your many responsibilities.

> **YOUR TURN ▶**
>
> What are your most pressing obligations, other than your studies, that will have to fit into your time-management plan? Are any of them more important to you than doing well in college? Why or why not?

STAYING FOCUSED

Many of the decisions you make today are reversible. You can change your major, your career, and even your life goals. But it is important to take control of your life by establishing your own goals for the future, setting your priorities, and managing your time accordingly. Many first-year students, especially recent high school graduates, might temporarily forget their primary purposes for coming to college, lose sight of their goals, and spend their first term of college engaging in a wide array of new experiences. This is okay to do within limits, but some students spend the next four or five years trying to make up for poor decisions they made early in their college careers, such as skipping class and not taking their assignments seriously. Such decisions can lead to plummeting grade point averages (GPAs) and the threat of academic probation or, worse, academic dismissal. Staying focused means always keeping your eyes on your most important purposes for being in college. Ask yourself whether what you are doing at any moment contributes to, or detracts from, those purposes.

Many students of all ages question their decision to attend college and might sometimes feel overwhelmed by the additional responsibilities it brings. Prioritizing, rethinking some commitments, letting some things go, and weighing the advantages and disadvantages of attending school part-time versus full-time can help you work through this adjustment period. Again, keep your long-term goals in mind and find ways to manage your stress rather than reacting to it. While this book is full of suggestions for enhancing academic success, the bottom line is to stay focused and take control of your time and your life. Make a plan that begins with your priorities: attending classes, studying, working, and spending time with the people who are important to you. Then think about the necessities of life: sleeping, eating, exercising, and relaxing. Leave time for fun things such as talking with friends, checking out Facebook, watching TV, and going out. But finish what *needs* to be done before you move from work to pleasure. And don't forget about personal time. If you live in a residence hall or share an apartment with other students, talk with your roommates about how you can coordinate your class schedules so that each of you has some privacy. If you live with your family, particularly if you are a parent, work together to create special family times as well as quiet study times.

> **YOUR TURN ▶**
>
> List your current priorities in order of importance. What does your list suggest about why you consider some things more important? Less important? Have you put any items in the wrong place? What should you change, and why?

Getting Organized

In college, as in life, you will quickly learn that managing time is important to success. Almost all successful people use some sort of calendar or planner, either paper or electronic, to help them keep up with their appointments, assignments or tasks, and other important activities and commitments.

USE A PLANNER

Your college might design and sell a calendar in the campus bookstore designed specifically for your school, with important dates and deadlines already provided. Or you might prefer to use an online calendar or the calendar that comes on your computer, cell phone, or PDA. Regardless of the format you prefer (electronic or hard copy), it's a good idea to begin the term by completing a term assignment preview (Figure 2.1). This is a template you can use to map your schedule for an entire term.

To create a term assignment preview, begin by entering all of your commitments for each week: classes, assignment due dates, work hours, family commitments, and so on. Examine your toughest weeks during the term. If paper deadlines and test dates fall during the same week, find time to finish some assignments early to free up study and writing time. Note this in your cell phone, PDA, or calendar. If you use an electronic calendar, set a reminder for these important deadlines and dates. Break large assignments (term papers, for example) into smaller steps, such as choosing a topic, doing research, creating an outline, learning necessary computer skills, writing a first draft, and so on. Add deadlines in your term assignment preview for each of the smaller portions of the project. Breaking a large project into smaller steps is something you will probably have to do for yourself. Most professors won't provide this level of detailed assistance.

After you complete your term assignment preview, enter important dates and notes from the preview sheets into your calendar or planner and continue to enter all due dates as soon as you know them. Write down meeting times and locations, scheduled social events (including phone numbers in case you need to cancel), study time for each class you're taking, and so forth. It's best not to rely solely on an electronic calendar. Keep a backup copy on paper in case you lose your phone, you can't access the Internet, or your PDA or computer crashes. It's also a good idea to carry your calendar or planner with you in a place where you're not likely to lose it. Your first term of college is the time to get into the habit of using a planner to help you keep track of commitments and maintain control of your schedule. This practice will become invaluable to you in your career. Check your notes daily at the same time of day for the current week as well as the coming week. It takes just a moment to be certain that you aren't forgetting something important, and it helps to relieve stress.

	Monday	Tuesday	Wednesday	Thursday	Friday
Week 1			First day of Classes!	Read Ch. 1-2 English	Discuss Ch. 1-2 History in Class Work 2-5
Week 2	English Quiz Ch. 1-2 Work 4-7	Psych Quiz Ch. 1	English Essay #1 Due Work 4-7	History Quiz Ch. 1-2	English Quiz Ch. 1-2 Work 2-5
Week 3	English Quiz Ch. 3-4 Work 4-7	Psych Quiz Ch. 2 Read Bio Ch. 1-2	English Essay Due Work 4-7	Be Ready for Bio Lab Experiment	Discuss English pp. 151-214 Work 2-5
Week 4	Work 4-7	Read English pp. 214-275	English Essay Due Work 4-7 Discuss pp. 214-275	Read English pp. 276-311	Discuss English 276-311 Work 2-5

	Monday	Tuesday	Wednesday	Thursday	Friday
Week 5	Work 4-7	Psych Quiz Ch. 3-4	English Essay Due Work 4-7	Bio Lab Experiment	Prepare Psych Experiment Work 2-5
Week 6	Work 4-7	Present Psych Experiment	English Essay Due Work 4-7	Bio Lab Experiment	Work 2-5
Week 7	Work 4-7	Study for English Mid-Term	English Mid-Term!! Work 4-7	Bio Lab Experiment	Study Psych Mid-Term Work 2-5
Week 8	Study for Psych Mid-Term Work 4-7	Psych Mid-Term!!	Study for History Mid-Term Work 4-7	Bio Lab Experiment Study for History Mid-Term	History Mid-Term!! Work 2-5

▲ **FIGURE 2.1**

Term Assignment Preview. Using the course syllabi provided
by your instructors, create your own term calendar. You can find blank templates on
the book's website at bedfordstmartins.com/gardner. Remember, for longer assignments, such as term papers,
divide the task into smaller parts and establish your own deadline for each part of the assignment, such as
deadlines for choosing a topic, completing your library research, developing an outline of the paper, writing a first
draft, and so on.

┌─ **YOUR TURN** ▶ ───┐

What kind of planner do you currently use, if any? Does your method of planning
work for you? Why or why not?

└──┘

CHART A WEEKLY TIMETABLE

Now that you have created a term preview, the weekly timetable model in
Figure 2.2 can help you tentatively plan how to spend your hours in a typical week. Here are some tips for creating a weekly schedule:

- As you create your schedule, try to reserve at least two hours of study
  time for each hour spent in class. This universally accepted "two-for-
  one" rule reflects faculty members' expectations for how much work you
  should be doing to earn a good grade in their classes. This means that
  if you take a typical full-time class load of fifteen credits, for example,
  you should plan to study an additional 30 hours per week. Think of this
  forty-five-hour-per-week commitment as comparable to a full-time job.
  If you are also working, reconsider how many hours per week it will be
  reasonable for you to be employed above and beyond this commitment,
  or consider reducing your credit load.

- Depending on your **biorhythms** (predictable daily patterns of physical,
  emotional, and mental activity), obligations, and potential distractions,
  decide whether you study more effectively in the day or in the evening,
  or a combination of both. Determine whether you are capable of getting
  up very early in the morning to study or how late you can stay up at
  night and still wake up for morning classes.

- Not all assignments are equal. Estimate how much time you will need for
  each one, and begin your work early. A good time manager frequently
  finishes assignments before actual due dates to allow for emergencies.

Keep track of how much time it takes you to complete different kinds of
tasks. For example, depending on your skills and interests, it might take longer to read a chapter in a biology text than to read one in a literature text.
Keeping track of your time will help you estimate how much time to allocate
for similar tasks in the future. How long does it really take you to solve a set
of twenty math problems or to write up a chemistry lab? Use your weekly
timetable to track how you actually spend your time for an entire week.

┌─ **YOUR TURN** ▶ ───┐

What are the best and worst times for you to study? Why? Have you found a
particular time when it's easier for you to concentrate or be creative?

└──┘

	Sunday	Monday	Tuesday	Wednesday	Thursday	Friday	Saturday
6:00							
7:00							
8:00			BREAKFAST	⟶			
9:00	SLEEP IN!	Review English	PSYCH 101	Review English	PSYCH 101	Review English	
10:00		English 101	Review PSYCH	English 101	Review PSYCH	English 101	ENJOY!
11:00		LUNCH		LUNCH			
12:00	PICNIC	HISTORY 101	LUNCH	HISTORY 101	LUNCH	HISTORY 101	
1:00	W/JANE,						
2:00	ALEX ,	BIO 101		BIO 101	BIO 101 LAB	WORK	BE LAZY!
3:00	MICHELLE, etc.						
4:00		WORK		WORK			
5:00							GO
6:00	STUDY ENGLISH	DINNER	DINNER	DINNER	DINNER	DINNER	OUT
7:00	HISTORY		STUDY ENGLISH		STUDY ENGLISH		WITH
8:00			HISTORY		HISTORY		FRIENDS
9:00		STUDY PSYCH	BIO	STUDY PSYCH			
10:00							
11:00							

▲ **FIGURE 2.2**

Weekly Timetable. Using your term calendar, create your own weekly timetable. You can find blank templates on the book's website at bedfordstmartins.com/gardner. As you complete your timetable, keep in mind the suggestions in this chapter. Do you want your classes back to back or with breaks in between? How early in the morning are you willing to start classes? Do you prefer—or do work or family commitments require you—to take evening classes? Are there times of day when you are more alert? Less alert? How many days per week do you want to attend classes? At some institutions you can go to school full-time by attending classes exclusively on Saturday. Plan how you will spend your time for the coming week. Track all of your activities for a full week by entering into your schedule everything you do and how much time each task requires. Use this record to help you estimate the time you will need for similar activities in the future.

MAINTAIN A TO-DO LIST

Once you have plotted your future commitments with a term planner and decided how your time will be spent each week, you can stay on top of your obligations with a to-do list, which is especially handy for last-minute reminders. It can help you keep track of errands you need to run, appointments you need to make, e-mail messages you need to send, and so on—anything you're prone to forget. You can keep this list on your cell phone or in your notebook, or you can post it on your bulletin board. Some people start a new list every day or once a week. Others keep a running list, and throw a page away only when everything on the list is done. Whichever method you prefer, use your to-do list to keep track of all the tasks you need to remember, not just academics. You might want to develop a system for prioritizing the items on your list: highlight; different colors of ink; one, two, or three stars; or lettered tasks with A, B, C (see Figure 2.3). As you complete each task, cross it off your list. You might be surprised by how much you have accomplished—and how good you feel about it.

TO DO
TODAY: MONDAY

School:
  Review notes for tomorrow's classes
  ***2:15 Meet Professor Gardner
    to discuss paper
  ***Final draft of lab report
  Read History and Philosophy for Tues cl
  **Make final copies of minutes for
    chapter meeting at 7:00
  **7:30 Meet in Lounge –
    math study group

Other
  Order B'day gift for Dad from LL Bean
  Pay Visa bill
  E-mail Mom for $
  Catch rerun of Lost at 9:00

TO DO
THIS WEEK

School:
  ***Prepare note cards for persuasion
    speech next week
  ***Write first draft of book review –
    due next Wed
  ***Share draft with Sue before Friday
  **Organize study group for
    math exam next Monday
  **Go to Spanish lab every day
  *Make appt to see Prof Jewler

Other
  Draw posters for SGA election
  Get up and run MWF
  Make eye appt
  Take dry cleaning in by Wed
  Arrange ride home by Thursday
  Order concert tickets for Saturday

◄ **FIGURE 2.3**
Daily and Weekly To-do Lists

Making Sure Your Schedule Works for You

As a first-year student, you might not have had much flexibility in determining your course schedule; by the time you were allowed to register for classes, some sections of the courses you needed might already have been closed. You also might not have known whether you would prefer taking classes back to back or giving yourself a break between classes.

How might you wisely use time between classes? This might have been your first opportunity to take classes that do not meet five days a week. Do you prefer spreading your classes over five or six days of the week, or would you like to go to class just two or three days a week or even once a week for a longer class period? Your attention span and other commitments should influence your decision. In the future, you might have more control over how

Wired WINDOW

GETTING THINGS DONE

A popular process to help you with time management and procrastination is the Getting Things Done (GTD) system created by David Allen. GTD is very popular with people who are heavy users of computers and technology, since it offers simple, straightforward, and easy-to-accomplish ways to help get your life in order. Although engaging in the GTD process does not require a computer or other technology tool, many websites and applications are dedicated to supporting the GTD process.

The basic premise behind GTD is that we are bombarded by things we have to do. These things are always tugging at us, even when we aren't consciously thinking about them. The constant tug, whether conscious or unconscious, causes us undue stress and negatively affects our thinking process. While the complete GTD system addresses both physical and mental items, let's focus on the application of GTD to your to-do list. (To learn more about the GTD system, visit http://www.43folders.com/2004/09/08/getting-started-with-getting-things-done.)

Here is the process:

1. Identify all of the things that demand your attention (these include courses, projects, work, family, etc.).
2. Allow yourself the freedom to forget about the things that aren't important.
3. *Create* a reliable and portable to-do list (you can use whatever works best for you. Some examples include a small notepad that you carry with you, an application on your computer or cell phone, or a three-ring binder). It is helpful to organize this list by contexts (such as home, school, computer, phone calls, errands, etc.)
4. *Write down everything* on your to-do list in the form of a *next task* (for instance, when you need to write a term paper for your philosophy class, you might want to list the next task as "Choose a topic for Philosophy term paper").
5. Do the things on your list when you are in the right context (for example, send an e-mail to your professor when you are at your computer).
6. Start at the beginning and go through the process again.

Think Critically

Try out the GTD system of keeping a to-do list. If you would like a technology-based tool that will help you implement the system, try Chandler (http://chandlerproject.org), a free application that is available for all computer operating systems. After a few days of using the GTD system, ask yourself: Is this method of keeping a to-do list right for me? Why or why not? Are there ways in which you can improve this system to fit with your personality style?

you schedule your classes. Before you register, think about how to make your class schedule work for you, in other words, how you can create a schedule that allows you to use your time more efficiently. Also consider your own biorhythms and recognize the part of the day or evening in which you are most alert and engaged.

ORGANIZE YOUR DAYS

Being a good student does not necessarily mean studying day and night and doing little else. Keep the following points in mind as you organize your day:

- **Set realistic goals for your study time.** Assess how long it takes to read a chapter in different types of textbooks and how long it takes you to review your notes from different instructors, and schedule your time accordingly. Give yourself adequate time to review and then test your knowledge when preparing for exams.

- **Use waiting time to review** (on the bus, before class, before appointments). Prevent forgetting what you have learned by allowing time to review as soon as is reasonable after class. (Reviewing immediately after class might be possible but not reasonable if you are too burned out to concentrate!)

- **Know your best times of day to study.** Schedule other activities, such as laundry, e-mail, or spending time with friends, for times when it will be difficult to concentrate.

- **Restrict repetitive, distracting, and time-consuming tasks** such as checking your e-mail, Facebook, or cell phone to a certain time, not every hour.

- **Avoid multitasking.** Even though you might actually be quite good at it, or at least think that you are, the reality is (and research shows) that you will be able to study most effectively and retain the most information if you concentrate on one task at a time.

- **Be flexible.** You cannot anticipate every disruption to your plans. Build extra time into your schedule so that unexpected interruptions do not prevent you from meeting your goals.

CREATE A WORKABLE CLASS SCHEDULE

If you live on campus, you might want to create a schedule that situates you near a dining hall at mealtimes or allows you to spend breaks between classes at the library. Or you might need breaks in your schedule for relaxation, catching up with friends, or spending time in a student lounge, college union, or campus center. You might want to avoid returning to your residence hall room to take a nap between classes if the result is likely to be feeling lethargic or oversleeping and missing later classes. Also, if you attend a large university, be sure that you allow adequate time to get from one class to another.

If you're a commuter student or if you must carry a heavy workload to afford going to school, you might prefer to schedule your classes in blocks without breaks. However, while taking back-to-back classes allows you to cut travel time by attending school one or two days a week and might provide for more flexible scheduling of a job or family commitments, it can also have significant drawbacks.

Month(s)   October

Monday the _____ 5 _____

Time		Time	
7 AM		2	Review for stats Quiz–Wed!
8		3	Do English reading assignment
9		4	↓
10	Stats	5	
11	English 101	6	Gym
NOON		7	
1 PM	Lunch w/Jenn	8	

Tuesday the _____ 6 _____

Time		Time	
7 AM		2	
8		3	History (3:30)
9	Gym	4	
10		5	Review for stats Quiz
11	Volunteer @ MSPCA	6	Work 6–11
NOON		7	
1 PM	Biology (1:30)	8	↓

Wednesday the _____ 7 _____

Time		Time	
7 AM		2	Do English Reading Assignment
8	Review for stats Quiz	3	
9		4	
10	Stats (Quiz Today!)	5	Meet w/Bio Study Group
11	English 101	6	
NOON		7	
1 PM		8	Volleyball

When all your classes are scheduled in a block of time, you run several risks. If you become ill on a class day, you could fall behind in all of your classes. You might also become fatigued from sitting in class after class. When one class immediately follows another, it will be difficult for you to have a last-minute study period immediately before a test because you will be attending another class and are likely to have no more than a fifteen-minute break. Finally, remember that for back-to-back classes, several exams might be held on the same day. Scheduling classes in blocks might work better if you have the option of attending lectures at alternative times in case you are absent, if you alternate classes with free periods, and if you seek out instructors who are flexible with due dates for assignments.

> **YOUR TURN ▶**
>
> Knowing what you know now about your schedule, what will you do differently next term? Will you try to schedule classes close together or spread them apart? Why?

DON'T OVEREXTEND YOURSELF

Being overextended is a primary source of stress for college students. Determine what a realistic workload is for you, but note that this can vary significantly from one person to another. Although being involved in campus life is very important, don't allow your academic work to take a backseat to extracurricular activities or other time commitments. Do not take on more than you can handle. Learn to say "no." Do not feel obligated to provide a reason; you have the right to decline requests that will prevent you from getting your own work done.

Even with the best intentions, some students who use a time-management plan overextend themselves. If there is not enough time to carry your course load and meet your commitments, drop a course before the drop deadline so that you won't have a low grade on your permanent record. If you receive financial aid, keep in mind that you must be registered for a minimum number of credit hours to be considered a full-time student and thereby maintain your current level of financial aid.

If dropping a course is not feasible or if other activities are lower on your list of priorities, which is likely for most college students, assess your other time commitments and let go of one or more. Doing so can be very difficult, especially if you think that you are letting other people down. However, it is far preferable to excuse yourself from an activity in a way that is respectful to others than to fail to come through at the last minute because you have committed to more than you can possibly achieve.

REDUCE DISTRACTIONS

Where should you study? Some students find that its best not to study in places associated with leisure, such as the kitchen table, the living room, or in front of the TV, because these places lend themselves to interruptions and other distractions. Similarly, it might be unwise to study on your bed because you might drift off to sleep when you need to study or learn to associate your bed with studying and not be able to go to sleep when you need to. Instead, find quiet places, both on campus and at home, where you can concentrate and develop a study mind-set each time you sit down to do your work.

Try to stick to a routine as you study. The more firmly you have established a specific time and a quiet place to study, the more effective you will be in keeping up with your schedule. If you have larger blocks of time available on the weekend, for example, take advantage of that time to review or catch up on major projects, such as term papers, that can't be completed effectively in fifty-minute blocks. Break down large tasks and take one thing at a time; you will make more progress toward your ultimate academic goals.

Here are some more tips to help you deal with distractions:

- Turn off the computer, TV, CD player, DVD, iPod, or radio unless the background noise or music really helps you concentrate on your studies or drowns out more distracting noises (people laughing or talking in other rooms or hallways, for instance). Consider silencing your cell phone so that you aren't distracted by incoming calls or text messages.

- Stay away from the computer if you're going to be tempted to check e-mail or Facebook.

- Try not to let personal concerns interfere with studying. If necessary, call a friend or write in a journal before you start to study, and then put your worries away.

- Develop an agreement with your roommate(s) or family about quiet hours. If that's not possible, find a quiet place where you can go to concentrate.

Respecting Others' Time

How does time management relate to respect? Think of the last time you made an appointment with someone who either forgot the appointment entirely or was very late. Were you upset or disappointed by the person for wasting your time? Most of us have experienced the frustration of having someone else disrespect our time. In college, if you repeatedly arrive late for class or leave before class periods have officially ended, you are breaking the basic rules of politeness, and you are intentionally or unintentionally showing a lack of respect for your instructors and your classmates.

At times, instructors might perceive certain behaviors to be inappropriate or disrespectful. In college, punctuality is a virtue. This might be a difficult adjustment for some students, but you need to be aware of faculty members' expectations at your college or university.

Be in class on time. Arrive early enough to shed your coat, shuffle through your backpack, and have your assignments, notebooks, and writing utensils ready to go. Likewise, be on time for scheduled appointments. Avoid behaviors that show a lack of respect for both the instructor and other students, such as leaving class to feed a parking meter or answer your cell phone, returning five or ten minutes later, thus disrupting class twice. Similarly, text messaging, sending instant messages, doing homework for another class, falling asleep, or talking (even whispering) disrupts the class. Make adequate transportation plans in advance, get enough sleep at night, wake up early enough to be on time for class, and complete assignments prior to class.

Time management is a lifelong skill. Securing a good job after college will likely mean managing your own time and possibly that of other people you supervise. If you decide to go to graduate or professional school, time management will continue to be essential to your success. But not only is time management important for you, it is also a way in which you show respect for others: your friends, family, and your college instructors.

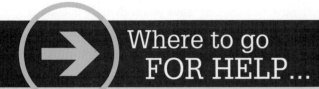

Where to go FOR HELP...

ON CAMPUS ▶

Academic Skills Center Along with assistance in studying for exams, reading textbooks, and taking notes, your campus academic skills center has specialists in time management who can offer advice for your specific problems.

Counseling Center If your problems with time management involve emotional issues you are unable to resolve, consider visiting your school's counseling office.

Your Academic Advisor/Counselor If you have a good relationship with this person, he or she might be able to offer advice or to refer you to another person on campus, including those in the offices mentioned above.

A Fellow Student A friend who is a good student and willing to help you with time management can be one of your most valuable resources.

MY INSTITUTION'S RESOURCES ▶

_____

_____

_____

_____

_____

_____

One-Minute PAPER...

Chapter 2 gives you a lot of tips for managing your time. It can be frustrating to realize that you have to spend time organizing yourself in order to manage your time effectively. Did any of the time management tips in this chapter really appeal to you? If so, which ones and why? Did anything in this chapter leave you with more questions than answers? If so, what are your questions?

Applying What You've LEARNED...

Now that you have read and discussed this chapter, consider how you can apply what you have learned to your academic and personal life. The following prompts will help you to reflect on chapter material and its relevance to you both now and in the future.

1. Review the "overcoming procrastination" section of this chapter. Think of one upcoming assignment in any of your current classes and describe how you can avoid waiting until the last minute to get it done. Break down the assignment, and list each step that you will take to complete the assignment. Give yourself a due date for each step and one for completing the assignment.

2. After reading about effective time management strategies, consider the way in which you manage your own time. If you were grading your current set of time management skills, what grade (A, B, C, or lower) would you give yourself? Why? What is your biggest challenge to becoming a more effective time manager?

Building Your PORTFOLIO...

66 If time be of all things the most precious, wasting time must be the greatest prodigality. 99

–BENJAMIN FRANKLIN (1706–1790),
American statesman, scientist, philosopher, printer, writer, and inventor

TIME IS OF THE ESSENCE

This chapter includes many great tips for effectively managing your time. Those skills are necessary for reducing the stress of everyday life, but have you thought about managing your time over the long term? What are your long-term goals? Preparing yourself for a particular career is probably high on your list, and it's not too early to begin thinking about what kind of preparation is necessary for the career (or careers) you are considering.

First, to help you determine the careers you're most interesting in pursuing, schedule an appointment with the career center on your campus and ask for information on career assessments to help you identify your preferences and interests. This portfolio assignment will help you realize that it is important to plan ahead and consider what implications your long-term goals have for managing your time right now.

1. In a Word document or Excel spreadsheet create a table like the example below.

2. Choose a career or careers in which you're most interested. In this example, a student needs to plan ahead for activities that will help to prepare for a future as a certified public accountant. It is okay if you have not decided on just one major or career; this is a process that you can repeat as your interests change. An "action step" is something that you need to do in within a certain time frame.

3. Talk with someone in the career center, a professor, an upperclass student in your desired major, or a professional in your chosen career to get an idea of what you need to be considering, even now.

4. Fill in the action steps, to-dos, time line, and notes sections of your own chart, and update the chart as you learn more about the career you are exploring.

Example Career: Certified Public Accountant (CPA)			
Action Step	**To-do**	**Time line**	**Notes**
Make sure I'm taking the courses necessary to pursue this career.	Set up an appointment to talk with my academic advisor.	I should do this as soon as possible.	What prerequisites do I need for these courses?
Consider job shadowing.	Check with the career center to learn whether they can help me job shadow with a college alum in this career.	I should do this as soon as possible.	This action step will help me to determine whether this is really a career that I wish to pursue.
Check out campus clubs, organizations, and volunteer work.	Join a club or organization and consider becoming an officer, such as treasurer.	I should do this as soon as possible.	This will give me practical experience that relates to my field.
Determine whether I need a master's degree, certificate, or license.	Explore these options and the benefits of each.	I should begin thinking about this in my junior and senior year.	I need to know how long a degree will take and consider how to finance it.
Consider internships.	Find out whether this is a requirement.	I should begin thinking about this in my junior and senior year.	Where would I do an internship?

5. Save your work in your portfolio on your personal computer or flash drive.

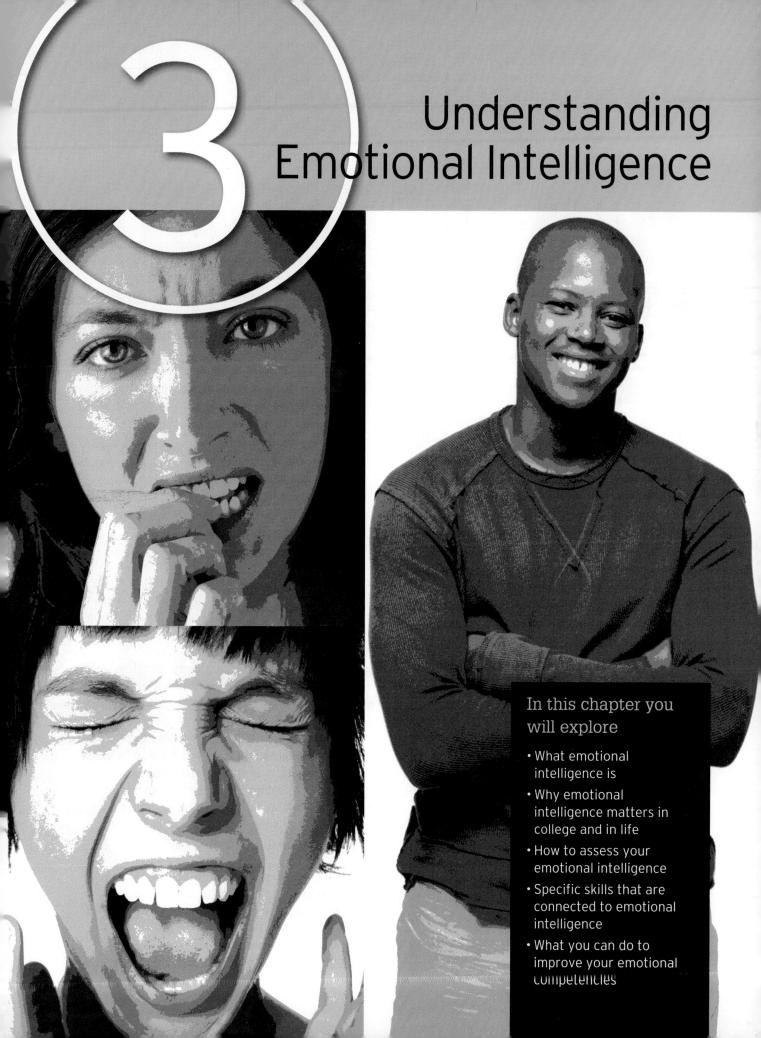

3

Understanding
Emotional Intelligence

In this chapter you will explore

- What emotional intelligence is
- Why emotional intelligence matters in college and in life
- How to assess your emotional intelligence
- Specific skills that are connected to emotional intelligence
- What you can do to improve your emotional competencies

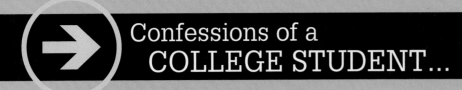

Confessions of a
COLLEGE STUDENT...

GENEVIEVE TIMMONS, 19
New York University

> **❝ I learned that I was more assertive than I thought—that I can face a problem, find a solution, and not stress out. ❞**

Spending a semester in Paris taught me so many things about myself I never would have discovered otherwise. I was thrown into a complete whirlwind for the first couple of weeks, maybe even the first two months. It was a huge adjustment. I had to be completely independent, living in a foreign country and picking up a second language. You have to be more aggressive in France than in the U.S. You kind of have to push your way through; you have to grow a backbone.

While I was there, I was notified that I was no longer eligible for university housing in New York. It turned out that the school lost my deposit, and so I was kind of homeless. Being across the ocean, it was difficult to deal with the situation, but I wrote appeal after appeal, and I called housing numerous times. Finally everything worked out and I got a place to live, but it was pretty stressful. I'm proud of how I handled that situation. I learned that I was more assertive than I knew—that I could face a problem, find a solution, and not stress out about it. It's going to get done; it will pass.

It has been said that many successful businesspeople and politicians were C students who spent more time in college socializing than studying. That's not necessarily true, but the popular belief embodies a key aspect of education that is often overlooked. The ability to understand and get along with people is vital for success in school, work, and life. Another element of success is the ability to manage time well and get things done. Why do some individuals handle stressful situations with ease while others fall apart? Although we tend to think of these abilities as inborn personality traits that can't be changed, the fact is that social skills and stress-management skills can be learned and improved.

Particularly in the first year of college, many students who are intellectually capable of succeeding have difficulty establishing positive relationships with others, dealing with pressure, or making wise decisions. Other students exude optimism and happiness and seem to adapt to their new environment without any trouble. The difference lies not in academic talent but in emotional intelligence (EI), or the ability to recognize and manage moods, feelings, and attitudes. A growing body of evidence shows a clear connection between students' EI and whether or not they stay in college.

As you read this chapter, you will develop an understanding of emotional intelligence, and you will learn how to use it to become a more successful student and person. You will begin to look at yourself and others through an EI lens, observe the behaviors that help people do well, get to know yourself better, and take the time to examine why you are feeling the way that you do before you act. Then, as you read each subsequent chapter in this book, try to apply what you have learned about EI and think about how it might relate to the behaviors of successful college students. You can't always control the challenges and frustrations of life, but with practice you *can* control how you respond to them.

What Is Emotional Intelligence?

Emotional intelligence is the ability to identify, use, understand, and manage emotions. Emotions are a big part of who you are; you should not ignore them. The better the emotional read you have on a situation, the more appropriately you can respond to it. Being aware of your own and others' feelings helps you to gather accurate information about the world around you and allows you to respond in appropriate ways.

YOUR TURN ▶

Do you know anybody (including yourself) who is "book smart" but not very good with people? Do you know anyone who has serious problems managing time? What kinds of challenges do these people face? How would improving emotional awareness help?

There are many competing theories about EI, some of them very complex. While experts vary in their definitions and models, all agree that emotions are real, can be changed for the better, and have a profound impact on whether or not a person is successful.

In the simplest terms, emotional intelligence consists of two general abilities:

- **Understanding emotions** involves the capacity to monitor and label feelings accurately (nervous, happy, angry, relieved, and so forth) and to determine why you feel the way you do. It also involves predicting how others might feel in a given situation. Emotions contain information, and the ability to understand and think about that information plays an important role in behavior.

- **Managing emotions** builds on the belief that feelings can be modified, even improved. At times, you need to stay open to your feelings, learn from them, and use them to take appropriate action. Other times, it is better to disengage from an emotion and return to it later. Anger, for example, can blind you and lead you to act in negative or antisocial ways; used positively, however, the same emotion can help you overcome adversity, bias, and injustice.

Identifying and using emotions can help you know which moods are best for different situations and learn how to put yourself in the "right" mood. Developing an awareness of emotions allows you to use your feelings to enhance your thinking. If you are feeling sad, for instance, you might view the world in a certain way, while if you feel happy, you are likely to interpret the same events differently. Once you start paying attention to emotions, you can learn not only how to cope with life's pressures and demands, but also how to harness your knowledge of the way you feel for more effective problem solving, reasoning, decision making, and creative endeavors.[1]

Assessing Your Emotional Intelligence

A number of sophisticated tools can be used to assess emotional intelligence. Some first-year seminars and many campus counseling centers offer the opportunity to complete a professionally administered questionnaire, such as the Emotional Quotient Inventory (EQ-i), which provides a detailed assessment of your emotional skills and a graphic representation of where you stand in comparison with other students. But even without a formal test, you can take a number of steps to get in touch with your own EI. You'll have to dig deep inside yourself and be willing to be honest about how you really think and how you really behave. This can take time, and that's fine. Think of your EI as a work in progress.

EMOTIONAL INTELLIGENCE QUESTIONNAIRE

Your daily life gives you many opportunities to take a hard look at how you handle emotions. Here are some questions that can help you begin thinking about your own EI.

1. What do you do when you are under stress?
   - ☐ a. I tend to deal with it calmly and rationally.
   - ☐ b. I get upset, but it usually blows over quickly.
   - ☐ c. I get upset but keep it to myself.

2. My friends would say that:
   - ☐ a. I will play, but only after I get my work done.
   - ☐ b. I am ready for fun anytime.
   - ☐ c. I hardly ever go out.

3. When something changes at the last minute:
   - ☐ a. I easily adapt.
   - ☐ b. I get frustrated.
   - ☐ c. It doesn't matter, since I don't really expect things to happen as I plan.

4. My friends would say that:
   - ☐ a. I am sensitive to their concerns.
   - ☐ b. I spend too much time worrying about other people's needs.
   - ☐ c. I don't like to deal with other people's petty problems.

5. When I have a problem to solve, such as too many things due at the end of the week:
   - ☐ a. I write down a list of the tasks I must complete, come up with a plan indicating specifically what I can accomplish and what I cannot, and follow my plan.
   - ☐ b. I am very optimistic about getting things done and just dig right in and get to work.
   - ☐ c. I get a little frazzled. Usually I get a number of things done and then push aside the things that I can't do.

Review your responses. A responses indicate that you probably have a good basis for strong emotional intelligence. **B** responses indicate you may have some strengths and some challenges in your EI. **C** responses indicate that your success in life and school could be negatively affected by your EI.

[1]Adapted with permission from EI Skills Group, "Ability Model of Emotional Intelligence," http://www.emotionaliq.com/. © 2005–2009.

Identifying Competencies

Emotional intelligence includes many capabilities and skills that influence a person's ability to cope with life's pressures and demands. Reuven Bar-On, a professor at the University of Texas, Austin, and world-renowned EI expert, developed a model that demonstrates how these categories of emotional intelligence directly affect general mood and lead to effective performance (see Figure. 3.1).

◀ FIGURE 3.1

Bar-On Model of
Emotional Intelligence

Let's take a closer look at the specific skills and competencies that Bar-On has identified as the pieces that make up a person's emotional intelligence.[2] It's something like a jigsaw puzzle, and when you have put all of the pieces together, you will begin to see yourself and others more clearly.

INTRAPERSONAL SKILLS

The first category, intrapersonal, relates to how well you know and like yourself, as well as how effectively you can do the things you need to do to stay happy. This category is made up of five specific competencies:

- **Emotional self-awareness.** Knowing how and why you feel the way you do.

---

[2]Adapted from R. Bar-On. "The Bar-On Model of Emotional-Social Intelligence (ESI)," *Psicothema*, 2006, 18 (suppl. 13-25): 21. http://www.eiconsortium.org/pdf/baron_model_of_emotional_social_intelligence.pdf

- **Assertiveness.** Standing up for yourself when you need to without being too aggressive.
- **Independence.** Making important decisions on your own without having to get everyone's opinion.
- **Self-regard.** Liking yourself in spite of your flaws (and we all have them).
- **Self-actualization.** Being satisfied and comfortable with what you have achieved in school, work, and your personal life.

Understanding yourself and why you think and act as you do is the glue that holds all of the EI competencies together. Knowledge of self is strongly connected to respect for others and their way of life. If you don't understand yourself and why you do the things you do, it can be difficult for you to understand others. What's more, if you don't like yourself, you can hardly expect others to like you.

INTERPERSONAL SKILLS

Recent studies have shown that people with extensive support networks are generally happier and tend to enjoy longer, healthier lives. Forging relationships and getting along with other people depend on the competencies that form the basis for the interpersonal category:

- **Empathy.** Making an effort to understand another person's situation or point of view.
- **Social responsibility.** Establishing a personal link with a group or community and cooperating with other members in working toward shared goals.
- **Interpersonal relationships.** Seeking out healthy and mutually beneficial relationships—such as friendships, professional networks, family connections, mentoring, and romantic partnerships—and making a persistent effort to maintain them.

ADAPTABILITY

Things change. Adaptability, the ability to adjust your thinking and behavior when faced with new or unexpected situations, helps you cope and ensures that you'll do well in life, no matter what the challenges. This category includes three key competencies:

- **Reality testing.** Ensuring that your feelings are appropriate by checking them against external, objective criteria.
- **Flexibility.** Adapting and adjusting your emotions, viewpoints, and actions as situations change.
- **Problem solving.** Approaching challenges step by step and not giving up in the face of obstacles.

STRESS MANAGEMENT

In college, at work, and at home, now and in the future, you'll be faced with what can seem like never-ending pressures and demands. Managing the inevitable resulting stress depends on two skills:

- **Stress tolerance.** Recognizing the causes of stress and responding in appropriate ways. Staying strong under pressure
- **Impulse control.** Thinking carefully about potential consequences before you act and delaying gratification for the sake of achieving long-term goals

GENERAL MOOD AND EFFECTIVE PERFORMANCE

It might sound sappy, but having a positive attitude really does improve your chances of doing well. Bar-On emphasizes the importance of two emotions in particular:

- **Optimism.** Looking for the "bright side" of any problem or difficulty and being confident that things will work out for the best.
- **Happiness.** Being satisfied with yourself, with others, and with your situation in general.

It makes sense: If you feel good about yourself and manage your emotions, you can expect to get along with others and enjoy a happy, successful life.

YOUR TURN ▶

On the basis of what you have learned so far about EI and the competencies that are involved, choose three competencies and describe how being strong in those dimensions will help a student succeed in college.

Wired WINDOW

HOW YOU EXPRESS EI ONLINE

We express our EI in many different ways, sometimes without ever being conscious that we are doing it. One space in which students express themselves in subtle and not-so-subtle ways is on social networking sites such as Facebook and MySpace. You may have intentionally posted information in your profile to help others learn about the kind of person you are, your hobbies, your sense of humor, and your personality style. The words that you use and the way in which you try to come across can also tell others about you. Take the groups to which you belong on Facebook, for example. What does being a member of these groups tell others about you? You can learn a lot about people by what they have chosen to share (and what they do not share) on their profile pages. Have you ever read a friend's status update and realized that he or she was having a rough time without your

friend's having to say so explicitly? That is an example of one of the subtle ways in which we communicate information about our EI online.

Think Critically

Now that you have examined your groups on Facebook, think critically about your entire profile with a focus on EI. What does your profile (and your online activity such as wall posts) tell you (and others) about how you get along with other people? What other EI dimensions does your profile communicate? Are you assertive? Can you put off having fun until after you've gotten work done? Are you generally happy? Do you handle stress well? Have you found differences in the way in which you communicate your EI online and your actual EI? If so, how can you fix these discrepancies?

How Emotions Affect Success

Emotions are strongly tied to physical and psychological well-being. For example, some studies have suggested that cancer patients who have strong EI live longer. People who are aware of the needs of others tend to be happier than people who are not. A large study done at the University of Pennsylvania found that the best athletes do well in part because they're extremely optimistic. In light of tremendous obstacles and with the odds stacked against them, emotionally intelligent people nonetheless go on to succeed.

YOUR TURN ▶

Describe yourself as a successful person ten years after college. What kinds of skills will you have? Don't just focus on your degree or a job description; include the EI competencies that help explain why you have become successful.

A number of studies link strong emotional intelligence skills to college success in particular. Here are a few highlights:

- **Emotionally intelligent students get higher grades.** Researchers looked at students' grade point averages at the end of the first year of college. Students who had tested high for intrapersonal skills, stress tolerance, and adaptability when they entered in the fall did better academically than those who had lower overall EI test scores.

- **Students who can't manage their emotions struggle academically.** Some students have experienced full-blown panic attacks before tests. Others who are depressed can't concentrate on coursework. And far too many turn to risky behaviors (drug and alcohol abuse, eating disorders, and worse) in an effort to cope. Dr. Richard Kadison, Chief of Mental Health Service at Harvard University, notes that "the emotional well-being of students goes hand-in-hand with their academic development. If they're not doing well emotionally, they are not going to reach their academic potential."[3] Even students who manage to succeed academically in spite of emotional difficulties can be at risk if unhealthy behavior patterns follow them after college.

- **Students who can delay gratification tend to do better overall.** Impulse control leads to achievement. In the famous "Marshmallow Study" performed at Stanford University, researchers examined the long-term behaviors of individuals who, as four-year olds, did or did not practice delayed gratification. The children were given one marshmallow and told that if they didn't eat it right away, they could have another. Fourteen years later, the children who ate their marshmallow immediately were more likely to experience significant stress, irritability, and inability to focus on goals. The children who waited scored an average of 210 points higher on the SAT; had better confidence, concentration, and reliability;

[3]Richard Kadison and Theresa Foy DiGeronimo, *College of the Overwhelmed: The Campus Mental Health Crisis and What to Do About It* (San Francisco: Jossey-Bass, 2004), p. 156.

held better-paying jobs; and reported being more satisfied with life. The following box details the differences between the two groups of students after fourteen years.

THE STANFORD MARSHMALLOW STUDY

Impulse Controlled	Impulsive
■ Assertive	■ Indecisive
■ Cope with frustration	■ Overreact to frustration
■ Work better under pressure	■ Overwhelmed by stress
■ Self-reliant, confident	■ Lower self-image
■ Trustworthy	■ Stubborn
■ Dependable	■ Impulsive
■ Delay gratification	■ Don't delay gratification
■ Academically competent	■ Poorer students
■ Respond to reason	■ Prone to jealousy and envy
■ Concentrate	■ Provoke arguments
■ Eager to learn	■ Sharp temper
■ Follow through on plans	■ Give up in face of failure
■ SAT: 610 verbal, 652 math	■ SAT: 524 verbal, 528 math

Source: Y. Shoda, W. Mischel, and P. K. Peake, "Predicting Adolescent Cognitive and Self-Regulatory Competencies from Preschool Delay of Gratification," *Developmental Psychology*, 1990, 26(6), 978-986.

- **EI skills can be enhanced in a first-year seminar.** In two separate studies, one conducted in Australia and another conducted in the United States, researchers found that college students enrolled in a first-year seminar who demonstrated good EI skills were more likely to do better in college than students who did not exhibit those behaviors. A follow-up study indicated that the students who had good EI skills also raised their scores on a measure of emotional intelligence.

Without strong EI in college, it is possible to do well enough to get by, but you might miss out on the full range and depth of competencies and skills that can help you to succeed in your chosen field and have a fulfilling and meaningful life.

How to Improve Your Emotional Intelligence

Developing your EI is an important step toward getting the full benefit of a college education. Think about it. Do you often give up because something is just too hard or you can't figure it out? Do you take responsibility for what you do, or do you blame others if you fail? Can you really be successful in life if you don't handle change well or if you are not open to diverse groups and their opinions? How can you communicate effectively if you are not assertive or if you are overly aggressive? If you're inflexible, how can you solve problems, get along with coworkers and family members, or learn from other people's points of view?

The good news is you can improve your EI. It might not be easy—old habits are hard to change—but it can definitely be done. Here are some suggestions:

1. **Identify your strengths and weaknesses.** Take a hard look at yourself, and consider how you respond to situations. Most people have trouble assessing their own behaviors realistically, so ask someone you trust and respect for insight. And if you have an opportunity to take a formal emotional intelligence test or to meet with a behavioral counselor, by all means, do.

2. **Set realistic goals.** As you identify areas of emotional intelligence that you would like to improve, be as specific as possible. Instead of deciding to be more assertive, for example, focus on a particular issue that is giving you trouble, such as nagging resentment toward a friend who always orders the most expensive thing on the menu and then expects to split the whole check evenly.

3. **Formulate a plan.** With a particular goal in mind, identify a series of steps you could take to achieve the goal, and define the results that would indicate success. As you contemplate your plan, consider all of the emotional competencies discussed on pages 43–45 of this chapter: You might find that to be more assertive with your friend about the restaurant situation, for instance, you need to figure out why you're frustrated (emotional self-awareness), identify possible causes for your friend's behavior (empathy), and consider what you might be doing to encourage it (reality testing).

4. **Check your progress on a regular basis.** Continually reassess whether or not you have met your goals, and adjust your strategy as needed.

Suppose you know that you don't handle stress well. When things get tough—too many things are due at once, your roommate leaves clothes and leftover food all over the place, and your significant other seems a bit distant—you begin to fall apart. Here is a model you might use for improving the way you handle stress.

> **EI competency:** Stress tolerance
>
> **Specific goal:** To get control of the things that are causing stress this week
>
> **Plan:** Identify each stressor, and select a strategy for addressing it.

- List everything that needs to be done this week. Allot time for each item on the list, and stick to a schedule. Reassess the schedule many times during the week.

- Ask yourself whether your roommate is bothering you only because you are stressed. Do you do some of the same things your roommate does? Ask yourself what the next step should be: Talking to your roommate? Looking for another place to study?

- Ask yourself whether your significant other is acting differently for any reason. Is he or she under stress? Are you overreacting because you feel insecure in the relationship? After answering these questions, decide what the next step will be: Talking to your significant other and sharing your feelings with him or her? Reassessing the situation in another week when things calm down?

- Identify what reduces stress for you and still allows you to stay on target to get things done. Is it exercise? Working in small chunks with rewards when you finish something? Playing a musical instrument?

Success Indicator: You are feeling less stressed, and you have accomplished many of the things on your list. You are working out three times a week. Your significant other seems just fine, and your place is still a mess but it's not bothering you. You leave your room and decide to study in the library.

YOUR TURN ▶

Using the preceding example as a model, select an EI competency that you would like to improve, choose a specific goal, and formulate a plan for accomplishing it. What kinds of results do you hope to achieve? How will improving your EI in this area help you become a happier, more confident person?

It's important not to try to improve everything at once. Instead, identify specific EI competencies that you can define, describe, and identify, and then set measurable goals for change. Don't expect success overnight. Remember that it took you a while to develop your specific approach to life, and it will take commitment and practice to change it.

Where to go
FOR HELP...

If you think that you might need some help developing some of these EI skills, especially if you feel that you are not happy or optimistic or you're not handling stress well, do something about it. Although you can look online and get some tips about being an optimistic person, for example, there is nothing like getting some help from a professional. Consider visiting your academic advisor or a wellness or counseling center on campus. Look for any related workshops that are offered on campus or nearby. Remember that the good news about EI is that with persistence it can be improved.

MY INSTITUTION'S RESOURCES ▶

_____

_____

_____

_____

_____

_____

_____

Chapter REVIEW...

One-Minute PAPER...

"Emotional intelligence" might be a term that you were not familiar with before reading this chapter. What did you find to be the most interesting information in this chapter? Make a note of any information that was hard to understand or apply to your own life. What kinds of questions do you still have for your instructor?

Applying What You've LEARNED...

Now that you have read and discussed this chapter, consider how you can apply what you have learned to your academic and personal life. The following prompts will help you reflect on the chapter material and its relevance to you both now and in the future.

1. Managing stress is an important skill in college. Take a look through your course syllabi, and make a list of assignments, exams, and the due dates. Do any of your assignments or exams seem to cluster around the same time in the term? Can you anticipate times when you might be especially likely to get stressed? What can you do in advance to avoid becoming overwhelmed and overstressed?

2. College life offers many opportunities to meet new people and to develop a new support network. But finding friends and mentors you can trust is not always easy. What steps have you taken so far to meet new people and build a network of support in college?

Building Your PORTFOLIO...

66 Knowing others is wisdom, knowing thyself is enlightenment. 99

–LAO TZU (~6TH CENTURY B.C.E.),
Philosopher in ancient China

KNOW THYSELF

Understanding your own behavior can sometimes be more difficult than understanding someone else's. Review the questionnaire on page 42 of this chapter. Were you honest in your assessment of yourself?

1. In a Word document, list the questions from page 42 that you answered with a B or a C. For example, did you rate yourself with a B or a C on a question such as "I am okay when things change at the last minute"?

2. Next, note the EI competencies that relate to each question. For the example above, the key competency is adaptability, as evidenced in reality testing, flexibility, and problem solving.

3. For each question that you have listed, describe your strategy for improving your response to certain situations. For example, when things change suddenly, you might say, "I am going to take a few minutes to think about what I need to do next. I will remind myself that I am still in control of my actions."

4. Save your responses in your portfolio on your personal computer or flash drive. Revisit your responses to the questions listed above as you experience similar situations.

Pay special attention to how your emotional intelligence affects your daily life. As you become more aware of your emotions and actions, you will begin to see how you can improve in the areas that are most difficult for you.

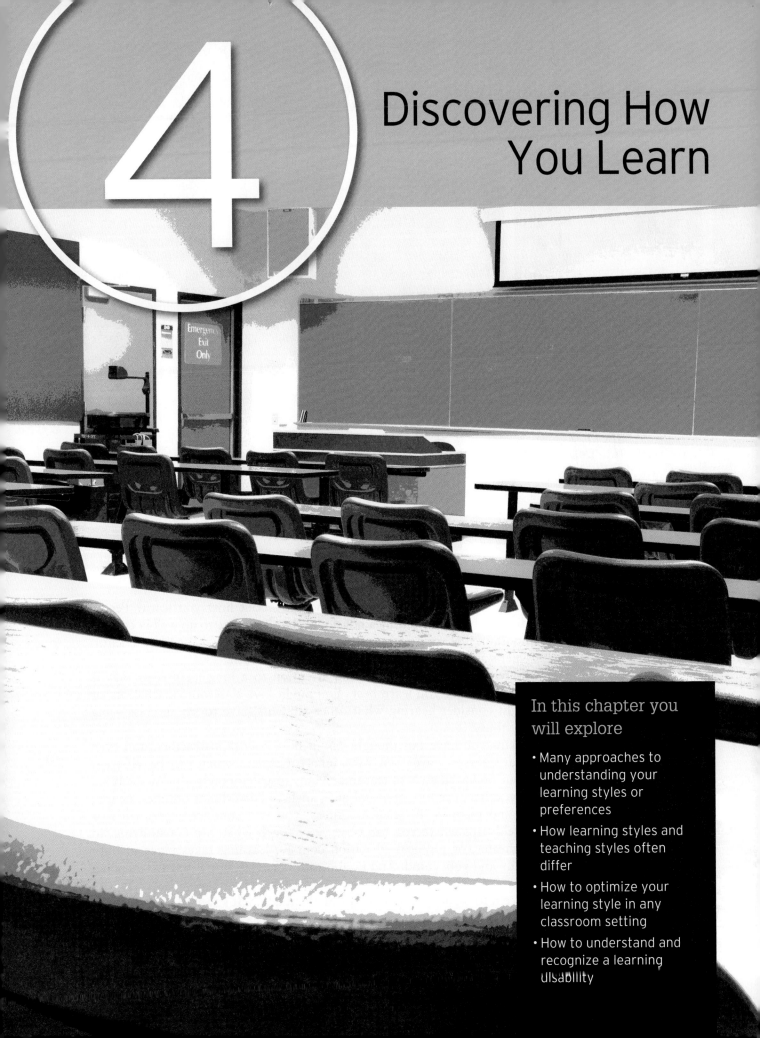

4

Discovering How You Learn

In this chapter you will explore

- Many approaches to understanding your learning styles or preferences
- How learning styles and teaching styles often differ
- How to optimize your learning style in any classroom setting
- How to understand and recognize a learning disability

Confessions of a
COLLEGE STUDENT...

BILLIE DIVER, 20
University of North Dakota

> 66 Once I discovered how I learn best and what I wanted to do, I became a lot more interested in my classes, and I started trying a lot harder. 99

I'm a visual, hands-on person. If an instructor is just lecturing or talking continuously, I can't picture anything; it just goes in one ear and out the other, and I don't learn anything at all. Especially with classes like chemistry and anatomy, it's hard if they're talking forever. I need PowerPoints or something like that. And I need to be involved. When I was taking all my general classes, I realized that in the ones I didn't care about I didn't really try, and so I didn't do well in them. Once I found what I wanted to do—I'm pre-nursing now—I became a lot more interested in my classes, and I started trying a lot harder.

Working on my own is a little bit hard for me. I can usually teach myself pretty well, but if I'm really stuck on something, I feel like there isn't anything I can do. Some of my instructors are really good about helping out. They have office hours, and they're available by e-mail or telephone. Other instructors are not so helpful, and that's really frustrating. So I use Facebook. If I have a question about a class, I always see if anyone in my class is online, and just ask them. It's a lot easier for me that way.

Have you

ever thought about how you learn? People learn differently. This is hardly a novel idea, but if you are to do well in college, it is important that you become aware of your preferred way, or style, of learning. Experts agree that there is no one best way to learn.

Maybe you have trouble paying attention to a long lecture, or maybe listening is the way you learn best. You might love classroom discussion, or you might consider hearing what other students have to say in class a big waste of time.

Perhaps you have not thought about how college instructors, and even particular courses, have their own inherent styles, which can be different from your preferred style of learning. Many instructors rely almost solely on lecturing; others use lots of visual aids, such as PowerPoint outlines, charts, graphs, and pictures. In science courses, you will conduct experiments or go on field trips where you can observe or touch what you are studying. In dance, theater, or physical education courses, learning takes place in both your body and your mind. And in almost all courses, you'll learn by reading both textbooks and other materials. Some instructors are friendly and warm; others seem to want little interaction with students. It's safe to say that in at least some of your college courses, you won't find a close match between the way you learn most effectively and the way you're being taught. This chapter will help you first to understand how you learn best and then to think of ways in which you can create a link between your style of learning and the expectations of each course and instructor.

There are many ways of thinking about and describing **learning styles.** Some of these will make a lot of sense to you; others might initially seem confusing or counterintuitive. Some learning style theories are very simple, and some are complex. You will notice some overlap between the different theories, but using several of them might help you do a more precise job of discovering your learning style. If you are interested in reading more about learning styles, the library and campus learning center will have many resources.

In addition to its focus on learning styles, this chapter will also explore **learning disabilities,** which are very common among college students. You might know someone who has been diagnosed with a learning disability, such as dyslexia or attention deficit disorder. It is also possible that you have a special learning need and are not aware of it. This chapter seeks to increase your self-awareness and your knowledge about such challenges to learning. In reading this chapter, you will learn more about common types of learning disabilities, how to recognize them, and what to do if you or someone you know has a learning disability.

YOUR TURN ▶

Which of your current classes would you describe as your favorite? Do you think that your choice has anything to do with the instructor's teaching style? Why or why not?

The VARK Learning Styles Inventory

The VARK Inventory focuses on how learners prefer to use their senses (hearing, seeing, writing, reading, or experiencing) to learn. The acronym VARK stands for "Visual," "Aural," "Read/Write," and "Kinesthetic." Visual learners prefer to learn information through charts, graphs, symbols, and other visual means. Aural learners prefer to hear information. Read/Write learners prefer to learn information that is displayed as words. Kinesthetic learners prefer to learn through experience and practice, whether simulated or real. To determine your learning style according to the VARK Inventory, respond to the following questionnaire.

THE VARK QUESTIONNAIRE, VERSION 7.0

This questionnaire is designed to tell you something about your preferences for the way you work with information. Choose answers that explain your preference. Check the box next to those items. Please select as many boxes as apply to you. If none of the response options apply to you, leave the item blank.

1. You are helping someone who wants to go to your airport, town center, or railway station. You would:
   - ☐ a. go with her.
   - ☐ b. tell her the directions.
   - ☐ c. write down the directions (without a map).
   - ☐ d. draw, or give her a map.

2. You are not sure whether a word should be spelled "dependent" or "dependant." You would:
   - ☐ a. see the words in your mind and choose by the way they look.
   - ☐ b. think about how each word sounds and choose one.
   - ☐ c. find it in a dictionary.
   - ☐ d. write both words on paper and choose one.

3. You are planning a holiday for a group. You want some feedback from them about the plan. You would:
   - ☐ a. describe some of the highlights.
   - ☐ b. use a map or website to show them the places.
   - ☐ c. give them a copy of the printed itinerary.
   - ☐ d. phone, text, or email them.

4. You are going to cook something as a special treat for your family. You would:
   - ☐ a. cook something you know without the need for instructions.
   - ☐ b. ask friends for suggestions.
   - ☐ c. look through the cookbook for ideas from the pictures.
   - ☐ d. use a cookbook where you know there is a good recipe.

5. A group of tourists want to learn about the parks or wildlife reserves in your area. You would:
   - ☐ a. talk about, or arrange a talk for them, about parks or wildlife reserves.
   - ☐ b. show them Internet pictures, photographs or picture books.
   - ☐ c. take them to a park or wildlife reserve and walk with them.
   - ☐ d. give them a book or pamphlets about the parks or wildlife reserves.

6. You are about to purchase a digital camera or mobile phone. Other than price, what would most influence your decision?
   - ☐ a. Trying or testing it.
   - ☐ b. Reading the details about its features.
   - ☐ c. It is a modern design and looks good.
   - ☐ d. The salesperson telling me about its features.

7. Remember a time when you learned how to do something new. Try to avoid choosing a physical skill (e.g., riding a bike). You learned best by:
   - ☐ a. watching a demonstration.
   - ☐ b. listening to somebody explaining it and asking questions.
   - ☐ c. diagrams and charts—visual clues.
   - ☐ d. written instructions—e.g., a manual or textbook.

8. You have a problem with your knee. You would prefer that the doctor:
   - ☐ a. gave you a web address or something to read about it.
   - ☐ b. used a plastic model of a knee to show what was wrong.
   - ☐ c. described what was wrong.
   - ☐ d. showed you a diagram of what was wrong.

9. You want to learn a new program, skill, or game on a computer. You would:
   - ☐ a. read the written instructions that came with the program.
   - ☐ b. talk with people who know about the program.
   - ☐ c. use the controls or keyboard.
   - ☐ d. follow the diagrams in the book that came with it.

10. You like websites that have:
    - ☐ a. things you can click on, shift, or try.
    - ☐ b. interesting design and visual features.
    - ☐ c. interesting written descriptions, lists, and explanations.
    - ☐ d. audio channels where you can hear music, radio programs, or interviews.

11. Other than price, what would most influence your decision to buy a new nonfiction book?
    - ☐ a. The way it looks is appealing.
    - ☐ b. Quickly reading parts of it.
    - ☐ c. A friend talks about it and recommends it.
    - ☐ d. It has real-life stories, experiences, and examples.

12. You are using a book, CD, or website to learn how to take photos with your new digital camera. You would like to have:
    - ☐ a. a chance to ask questions and talk about the camera and its features.
    - ☐ b. clear written instructions with lists and bullet points about what to do.
    - ☐ c. diagrams showing the camera and what each part does.
    - ☐ d. many examples of good and poor photos and how to improve them.

13. You prefer a teacher or a presenter who uses:
    - ☐ a. demonstrations, models, or practical sessions.
    - ☐ b. question and answer, talk, group discussion, or guest speakers.
    - ☐ c. handouts, books, or readings.
    - ☐ d. diagrams, charts, or graphs.

14. You have finished a competition or test and would like some feedback. You would like to have feedback:
    - ☐ a. using examples from what you have done.
    - ☐ b. using a written description of your results.
    - ☐ c. from somebody who talks it through with you.
    - ☐ d. using graphs showing what you had achieved.

15. You are going to choose food at a restaurant or café. You would:
    - ☐ a. choose something that you have had there before.
    - ☐ b. listen to the waiter or ask friends to recommend choices.
    - ☐ c. choose from the descriptions in the menu.
    - ☐ d. look at what others are eating or look at pictures of each dish.

16. You have to make an important speech at a conference or special occasion. You would:
    - ☐ a. make diagrams or get graphs to help explain things.
    - ☐ b. write a few key words and practice saying your speech over and over.
    - ☐ c. write out your speech and learn from reading it over several times.
    - ☐ d. gather many examples and stories to make the talk real and practical.

Source: www.vark-learn.com/english/index.asp

SCORING THE VARK

Use the following scoring chart to find the VARK category to which each of your answers belongs. Circle the letters that correspond to your answers. For example, if you answered b and c for question 3, circle V and R in the 3 row.

Question	A Category	B Category	C Category	D Category
3	K	(V)	(R)	A

Count the number of each of the VARK letters you have circled to get your score for each VARK category.

SCORING CHART

Question	A Category	B Category	C Category	D Category
1	K	A	R	V
2	V	A	R	K
3	K	V	R	A
4	K	A	V	R
5	A	V	K	R
6	K	R	V	A
7	K	A	V	R
8	R	K	A	V
9	R	A	K	V
10	K	V	R	A
11	V	R	A	K
12	A	R	V	K
13	K	A	R	V
14	K	R	A	V
15	K	A	R	V
16	V	A	R	K

Total number of **V**s circled = _____

Total number of **A**s circled = _____

Total number of **R**s circled = _____

Total number of **K**s circled = _____

Because you could choose more than one answer for each question, the scoring is not just a simple matter of counting. It is like four stepping stones across some water. Enter your scores **from highest to lowest** on the stones in the figure, with their V, A, R, and K labels.

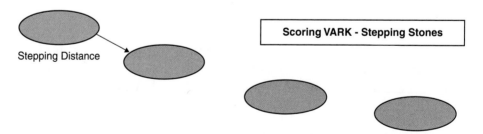

Stepping Distance

Scoring VARK - Stepping Stones

Your stepping distance comes from this table:

The total of my four VARK scores is	My stepping distance is
16-21	1
22-27	2
28-32	3
More than 32	4

Follow these steps to establish your preferences.

1. Your first preference is always your highest score. Check that first stone as one of your preferences.

2. Now subtract your second highest score from your first. If that figure is larger than your stepping distance, you have a single preference. Otherwise, check this stone as another preference and continue with step 3.

3. Subtract your third score from your second one. If that figure is larger than your stepping distance, you have a bimodal preference. If not, check your third stone as a preference and continue with step 4.

4. Last, subtract your fourth score from your third one. If that figure is larger than your stepping distance, you have a trimodal preference. Otherwise, check your fourth stone as a preference, and you have all four modes as your preferences!

Note: If you are bimodal or trimodal or you have checked all four modes as your preferences, you can be described as *multimodal* in your VARK preferences.

YOUR TURN ▶

Did your VARK score surprise you at all? Did you know what type of learner you were before taking the test? If so, when did you discover this? How do you use your modality to your benefit?

USING VARK RESULTS TO STUDY MORE EFFECTIVELY

How can knowing your VARK score help you do better in your college classes? The following table offers suggestions for using learning styles to develop your own study strategies.

Study Strategies by Learning Style

Visual	Aural	Read/Write	Kinesthetic
Underline or highlight your notes.	Talk with others to verify the accuracy of your lecture notes.	Write and rewrite your notes.	Use all your senses in learning: sight, touch, taste, smell, and hearing.
Use symbols, charts, or graphs to display your notes.	Put your notes on tape and listen or tape class lectures.	Read your notes silently.	Supplement your notes with real-world examples.
Use different arrangements of words on the page.	Read your notes out loud; ask yourself questions and speak your answers.	Organize diagrams or flow charts into statements.	Move and gesture while you are reading or speaking your notes.
Redraw your pages from memory.		Write imaginary exam questions and respond in writing.	

Kolb Inventory of Learning Styles

A learning model that is more complex than the VARK Inventory is the widely used and referenced Kolb Inventory of Learning Styles. While the VARK Inventory investigates how learners prefer to use their senses in learning, the Kolb Inventory focuses on abilities we need to develop in order to learn. This inventory, developed in the 1980s by David Kolb, is based on a four-stage cycle of learning (see Figure 4.1).

According to Kolb, effective learners need four kinds of abilities:

- *Concrete experience* abilities, which allow them to be receptive to others and open to other people's feelings and specific experiences. An example of this type of ability is learning from and empathizing with others.
- *Reflective observation* abilities, which help learners to reflect on their experiences from many perspectives. An example of this type of ability is remaining impartial while considering a situation from a number of different points of view.
- *Abstract conceptualization* abilities, which help learners to integrate observations into logically sound theories. An example of this type of ability is analyzing ideas intellectually and systematically.
- *Active experimentation* abilities, which enable learners to make decisions, solve problems, and test what they have learned in new situations. An example of this type of ability is being ready to move quickly from thinking to action.

Kolb's Inventory of Learning Styles measures differences along two basic dimensions that represent opposite styles of learning. The first dimension is *abstract-concrete*; the second is *active-reflective*. See Figure 4.1 to visualize how these polar-opposite characteristics link together to create four discrete groups of learners: *divergers, assimilators, convergers,* and *accommodators*.

Doing well in college will require you to adopt some behaviors that are characteristic of each of these four learning styles. Some of them might be uncomfortable for you, but that discomfort will indicate that you're growing, stretching, and not relying on the learning style that might be easiest or most natural (Kolb, 1981).

If you are a diverger, you are adept at reflecting on situations from many viewpoints. You excel at brainstorming, and you're imaginative, people ori-

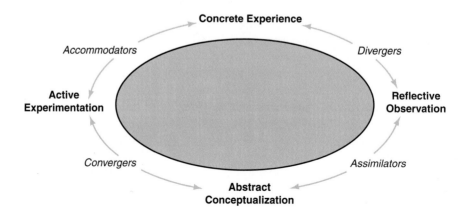

FIGURE 4.1 ▶
Kolb's Four-Stage Cycle of Learning

ented, and sometimes emotional. On the downside, you sometimes have difficulty making decisions. Divergers tend to major in the humanities or social sciences.

If you are an assimilator, you like to think about abstract concepts. You are comfortable in classes where the instructor lectures about theoretical ideas without relating the lectures to real-world situations. Assimilators often major in math, physics, or chemistry.

If you are a converger, you like the world of ideas and theories, but you also are good at thinking about how to apply those theories to real-world, practical situations. You differ from divergers in your preference for tasks and problems rather than social and interpersonal issues. Convergers tend to choose health-related and engineering majors.

If you are an accommodator, you prefer hands-on learning. You are skilled at making things happen, and you rely on your intuition. You like people, but you can be pushy and impatient at times, and you might use trial and error, rather than logic, to solve problems. Accommodators often major in business, especially in marketing or sales.[1]

[1]Adapted from David A. Kolb, "Learning Styles and Disciplinary Differences," in *The Modern American College*, ed. Arthur W. Chickering (San Francisco: Jossey Bass, 1981), pp. 232–35.

Wired WINDOW

USING TECHNOLOGY TO AID LEARNING

If you scored as having an aural, visual, or read/write preference on the VARK Inventory, you can use technology to enhance how you learn course material. Students with an aural preference can use a digital recorder or microcassette recorder to record lectures and then listen to them again later. If you have an iPod, you can purchase a microphone attachment that allows you to use the iPod as a digital audio recorder, and you can organize your recorded lectures using iTunes. Many other MP3 players also have recording capabilities. Before you record any lecture, make sure that you have your professors' permission to do so. In addition to recording lectures, you can find supplemental course material through podcasts and via iTunes. A number of institutions provide podcasts for many of their courses for free on iTunes. You can browse through course offerings in the iTunesU section, or you can search for a term in the iTunes store and limit it to iTunesU results. Try searching the web to find podcasts and audio files to help you enhance your knowledge of a certain topic. (Hint: Try searching for a specific subject and the word *podcast*. For instance, you might search "Introduction to Philosophy podcast.")

Students with a visual preference can use websites such as YouTube to help supplement their learning. Institutions such as Stanford University have their own profiles on YouTube, and they post videos that feature faculty members explaining concepts in their field of study. In the same way you search for audio files on the web and iTunesU, you can search YouTube to find videos to enhance your knowledge of concepts covered in class. (For your psychology class, for example, you might watch a video based on Stanley Milgram's obedience experiments.)

Thinking Critically

Search for an audio or video file to supplement a concept or lecture from one of your courses. Once you have found the file, evaluate it on the basis of the criteria for evaluating Internet sources found in Chapter 11. Can you identify the creator of the work? Is the person reliable? Does the podcast or video cite the sources that are used? Is the information in this podcast or video more or less reliable than the information contained in your textbook? In what way?

In all your classes, but especially in liberal arts and social science courses, you will need to develop the strengths of divergers: imagination, brainstorming, and listening with an open mind. The abilities that are characteristic of assimilators, developing theories and concepts, are valuable for all students, especially those in the sciences. If you major in the health sciences or in engineering, you will routinely practice the skills of convergers: experimenting with new ideas and choosing the best solution. Finally, whatever your major and ultimate career, you'll need to get things done, take some risks, and become a leader—skills that are characteristic of accommodators.

> **YOUR TURN ▶**
>
> On the basis of the descriptions we have provided here, where do you see yourself in the Kolb Inventory? Are you more like a diverger, assimilator, converger, or accommodator? How can you use this knowledge in your courses?

The Myers-Briggs Type Indicator

One of the best-known and most widely used personality inventories that can also be used to describe learning styles is the Myers-Briggs Type Indicator, or MBTI.[2] While the VARK measures your preferences for using your senses to learn and the Kolb Inventory focuses on learning abilities, the MBTI investigates basic personality characteristics and how those relate to human interaction and learning. The MBTI was created by Isabel Briggs Myers and her mother, Katharine Cook Briggs. The inventory identifies and measures psychological type as developed in the personality theory of Carl Gustav Jung, the great twentieth-century psychoanalyst. The MBTI is given to several million people around the world each year. Employers often use this test to give employees insight into how they perceive the world, go about making decisions, and get along with other people. Many first-year seminar or college success courses also

[2]Isabel Briggs Myers, *Introduction to Type*, 6th ed. (Palo Alto, CA: CPP, 1998).

include a focus on the MBTI because it provides a good way to begin a dialogue about human interaction and how personality type affects learning.

All the psychological types described by the MBTI are normal and healthy; there is no good or bad or right or wrong—people are simply different. When you complete the Myers-Briggs survey instrument, your score represents your "psychological type"—the combination of your preferences on four different scales. These scales measure how you take in information and how you then make decisions or come to conclusions about that information. Each preference has a one-letter abbreviation. The four letters together make up your type. Although this book doesn't include the actual survey, you will find a description of the basic MBTI types below. Which one sounds most like you?

EXTRAVERSION (E) VERSUS INTROVERSION (I): THE INNER OR OUTER WORLD

The E-I preference indicates whether you direct your energy and attention primarily toward the outer world of people, events, and things or the inner world of thoughts, feelings, and reflections.

Extraverts tend to be outgoing, gregarious, and talkative. They often think "with the volume on," saying out loud what is going through their minds. They are energized by people and activity, and they seek this in both work and play. They are people of action; they like to spend more time doing things than thinking about them. At their best, they are good communicators who are quick to act and lead. However, they might seem to talk too much and too loudly, drowning others out or acting before they think. (Note that when the term is being used in the context of psychological type and the MBTI, "extravert" is spelled with an "a" and not an "o," even though "extrovert" is the more common spelling.)

Introverts prefer to reflect carefully and think things through before taking action. They think a lot, but if you want to know what's on their minds, you might have to ask them. They are refreshed by quiet and privacy. At their best, introverts are good, careful listeners whose thoughts are deep and whose actions are well considered. On the other hand, they might seem too shy and not aware enough of the people and situations around them, or they can think about things so long that they neglect to actually start doing anything.

YOUR TURN ▶

After reading this description, do you consider yourself an extravert or an introvert? Why? Do you ever wish you were like the other? If so, when and why?

SENSING (S) VERSUS INTUITION (N): FACTS OR IDEAS

The S-N preference indicates how you perceive the world and take in information: directly, through your five senses, or indirectly, by using your intuition.

Sensing types are interested above all in the facts, what is known and what they can be sure of. Typically sensing types are practical, factual, realistic, and down-to-earth. They can be very accurate, steady, precise, patient, and effective with routine and details. They are often relatively traditional and conventional. They dislike unnecessary complication, and they prefer to practice skills they already know. At their best, sensing types can be counted on to do things right, taking care of every last detail. However, they can plod along while missing the point of why they are doing what they do, not seeing the forest (the whole picture) for the trees (the details).

Intuitive types are fascinated by possibilities—not so much the facts themselves, but what those facts mean, what concepts might describe those facts, how those might relate to other concepts, and what the implications of the facts would be. Intuitive types are less tied to the here and now and tend to look farther into the future and the past. They need inspiration and meaning for what they do, and they tend to work in bursts of energy and enthusiasm. Often, they are original, creative, and nontraditional. They can have trouble with routine and details, however, and they would rather learn a new skill than keep practicing one they have already mastered. They can exaggerate facts sometimes without realizing it. At their best, intuitive types are bright, innovative people who thrive in academic settings and the world of invention and ideas, although they can also be impractical dreamers whose visions fall short because of inattention to detail.

THINKING (T) VERSUS FEELING (F): LOGIC OR VALUES

The T-F preference indicates how you prefer to make your decisions: through logical, rational analysis or through your subjective values, likes, and dislikes. *Thinking* types are usually logical, rational, analytical, and critical. They pride themselves on reasoning their way to the best possible decisions. They tend to decide things relatively impersonally and objectively, and they are less swayed by feelings and emotions—both their own and other people's. In fact, other people's feelings sometimes puzzle or surprise them. They can deal with interpersonal disharmony and can be firm and assertive when they need to be. In all of their dealings, they need and value fairness. At their best, thinking types are firm, fair, logical, and just. On the other hand, they can seem cold, insensitive to other people's feelings, and overly blunt and hurtful in their criticisms.

Feeling types are typically warm, empathic, sympathetic, and interested in the happiness of others as well as themselves. They need and value harmony, and they can become distressed and distracted by argument and conflict. They sometimes have trouble being assertive when it would be appropriate to do so. Above all, they need and value kindness. At their best, feeling types are warm and affirming, and they facilitate cooperation and goodwill among those around them while pursuing the best human values. However, feeling types can be illogical, emotionally demanding, reluctant to tackle unpleasant tasks, and unaffected by objective reason and evidence.

JUDGING (J) VERSUS PERCEIVING (P): ORGANIZATION OR ADAPTABILITY

The J-P preference indicates how you characteristically approach the outside world: by making decisions and judgments or by observing and perceiving instead.

Judging types approach the world in a planned, orderly, organized way; they try to order and control their part of it as much as possible. They make their decisions relatively quickly and easily because they like to make and follow plans. They are usually punctual and tidy, and they appreciate those traits in others. At their best, judging types are natural organizers who get things done and get them done on time. However, judging types might jump to conclusions prematurely, be too judgmental of people, make decisions too hastily without enough information, and have trouble changing their plans even when those plans are not working.

Perceiving types don't try to control their world as much as adapt to it. Theirs is a flexible, wait-and-see approach. They deal comfortably and well with changes, unexpected developments, and emergencies, adjusting their plans and behaviors as needed. They tend to delay decisions so that they can keep their options open and gather more information. They might procrastinate to a serious degree, however, and they can try to juggle too many things at once without finishing any of them. At their best, perceiving types are spontaneous, flexible individuals who roll with the punches and find ways to take the proverbial lemons in life and turn them into lemonade. On the other hand, perceiving types can be messy, disorganized procrastinators.

HOW TO USE YOUR STRONGEST- AND WEAKEST-PREFERENCES

Because there are two possible choices for each of four different preferences, there are sixteen possible psychological types. No matter what your Myers-Briggs type, all components of personality have value in the learning process. The key to success in college, therefore, is to use all of the attitudes and functions (E, I, S, N, T, F, J, and P) in their most positive sense. As you go about your studies, here is a system we recommend:

1. *Sensing*: Get the facts. Use sensing to find and learn the facts. How do we know facts when we see them? What is the evidence for what is being said?

2. *Intuition*: Get the ideas. Now use intuition to consider what those facts mean. Why are those facts being presented? What concepts and ideas are being supported by those facts? What are the implications? What is the big picture?

3. *Thinking*: Critically analyze. Use thinking to analyze the pros and cons of what is being presented. Are there gaps in the evidence? What more do we need to know? Do the facts really support the conclusions? Are there alternative explanations? How well does what is presented hang together logically? How could our knowledge of it be improved?

4. *Feeling*: Make informed value judgments. Why is this material important? What does it contribute to people's good? Why might it be important to you personally? What is your personal opinion about it?

5. *Introversion*: Think it through. Before you take any action, carefully review everything you have encountered so far.

6. *Judging*: Organize and plan. Don't just dive in! Now is the time to organize and plan your studying so you will learn and remember everything you need to. Don't just plan in your head either; write your plan down, in detail.

7. *Extraversion*: Take action. Now that you have a plan, act on it. Do whatever it takes. Create note cards, study outlines, study groups, and so on. If you are working on a paper, now is the time to start writing.

8. *Perceiving*: Change your plan as needed. Be flexible enough to change something that isn't working. Expect the unexpected, and deal with the unforeseen. Don't give up the whole effort the minute your original plan stops working. Figure out what's wrong, and come up with another, better plan and start following that.

Multiple Intelligences

Another way of measuring how we learn is the theory of *multiple intelligences*, developed in 1983 by Dr. Howard Gardner, a professor of education at Harvard University. Gardner's theory is based on the premise that the traditional notion of human intelligence is very limited. He proposes eight different intelligences to describe how humans learn.

As you might imagine, Gardner's work is controversial because it questions our long-standing definitions of intelligence. Gardner argues that students should be encouraged to develop the abilities they have and that evaluation should measure all forms of intelligence, not just linguistic and logical-mathematical intelligence.

As you think of yourself and your friends, what kinds of intelligences do you have? Do college courses measure all the ways in which you are intelligent? Here is a short inventory that will help you recognize your multiple intelligences.

MULTIPLE INTELLIGENCES INVENTORY

According to Gardner, all human beings have at least eight different types of intelligence. Depending on your background and age, some intelligences are likely to be more developed than others. This activity will help you find out what your intelligences are. Knowing this, you can work to strengthen the other intelligences that you do not use as often. Put a check mark next to the items that apply to you.

Verbal/Linguistic Intelligence

_____ I enjoy telling stories and jokes.

_____ I enjoy word games (for example, Scrabble and puzzles).

_____ I am a good speller (most of the time).

_____ I like talking and writing about my ideas.

_____ If something breaks and won't work, I read the instruction book before I try to fix it.

Logical/Mathematical Intelligence

_____ I really enjoy my math class.

_____ I like to find out how things work.

_____ I enjoy computer and math games.

_____ I love playing chess, checkers, or Monopoly.

_____ If something breaks and won't work, I look at the pieces and try to figure out how it works.

Visual/Spatial Intelligence

_____ I prefer a map to written directions.

_____ I enjoy hobbies such as photography.

_____ I like to doodle on paper whenever I can.

_____ In a magazine, I prefer looking at the pictures rather than reading the text.

_____ If something breaks and won't work, I tend to study the diagram of how it works.

Bodily/Kinesthetic Intelligence

_____ My favorite class is gym because I like sports.

_____ When looking at things, I like touching them.

_____ I use a lot of body movements when talking.

_____ I tend to tap my fingers or play with my pencil during class.

_____ If something breaks and won't work, I tend to play with the pieces to try to fit them together.

Musical/Rhythmic Intelligence

_____ I enjoy listening to CDs and the radio.

_____ I like to sing.

_____ I like to have music playing when doing homework or studying.

_____ I can remember the melodies of many songs.

_____ If something breaks and won't work, I tend to tap my fingers to a beat while I figure it out.

Interpersonal Intelligence

_____ I get along well with others.

_____ I have several very close friends.

_____ I like working with others in groups.

_____ Friends ask my advice because I seem to be a natural leader.

_____ If something breaks and won't work, I try to find someone who can help me.

Intrapersonal Intelligence

_____ I like to work alone without anyone bothering me.

_____ I don't like crowds.

_____ I know my own strengths and weaknesses.

_____ I find that I am strong-willed, independent, and don't follow the crowd.

_____ If something breaks and won't work, I wonder whether it's worth fixing.

Naturalist Intelligence

_____ I am keenly aware of my surroundings and of what goes on around me.

_____ I like to collect things like rocks, sports cards, and stamps.

_____ I like to get away from the city and enjoy nature.

_____ I enjoy learning the names of living things in the environment, such as flowers and trees.

_____ If something breaks down, I look around me and try to see what I can find to fix the problem.

A verbal/linguistic learner likes to read, write, and tell stories and is good at memorizing information. A logical/mathematical learner likes to work with numbers and is good at problem-solving and logical processes. A visual/spatial learner likes to draw and play with machines and is good at puzzles and reading maps and charts. A bodily/kinesthetic learner likes to move around and is good at sports, dance, and acting. A musical/rhythmic learner likes to sing and play an instrument and is good at remembering melodies and noticing pitches and rhythms. An interpersonal learner likes to have many friends and is good at understanding people, leading others, and mediating conflicts. Intrapersonal learners like to work alone, understand themselves well, and are original thinkers. A naturalistic learner likes to be outside and is good at preservation, conservation, and organizing a living area. You can use your intelligences to help you make decisions about a major, choose activities, and investigate career options. Which intelligences best describe you?

TOTAL SCORE

_____ Verbal/Linguistic
_____ Musical/Rhythmic
_____ Logical/Mathematical
_____ Interpersonal
_____ Visual/Spatial
_____ Intrapersonal
_____ Bodily/Kinesthetic
_____ Naturalist

Add the number of check marks you made in each section. Your score for each intelligence will be a number between 1 and 5. Your high scores of 3 or more will help you to get a sense of your own multiple intelligences.

Source: www.ldrc.ca/projects/miinventory/mitest.html.

YOUR TURN ▶

Do you agree with Howard Gardner that there are eight styles of learning? Why or why not?

When Learning Styles and Teaching Styles Conflict

Educators who study learning styles maintain that instructors tend to teach in ways that conform to their own particular styles of learning. So an introverted instructor who prefers abstract concepts and reflection (an assimilator, according to Kolb) and learns best in a read/write mode or aural mode will probably structure the course in a lecture format with little opportunity for either interaction or visual and kinesthetic learning. Conversely, an instructor who needs a more interactive, hands-on environment will likely involve students in discussion and learning through experience.

Do you enjoy listening to lectures, or do you find yourself gazing out the window or dozing? When your instructor assigns a group discussion, what is your immediate reaction? Do you dislike talking with other students, or is that the way you learn best? How do you react to lab sessions when you have to conduct an actual experiment? Is this an activity you look forward to or one that you dread? Each of these learning situations appeals to some students more than others, but each is inevitably going to be part of your college experience. Your college or university has intentionally designed courses for you to have the opportunity to listen to professors who are experts in their field, interact with other students in structured groups, and learn through doing. Because these are all important components of your college education, it's important for you to make the most of each situation.

When you recognize a mismatch between how you best learn and how you are being taught, it is important that you take control of your learning process. Don't depend on the instructor or the classroom environment to give you everything you need to maximize your learning. Employ your own preferences, talents, and abilities to develop many different ways to study and retain information. Look back through this chapter to remind yourself of the ways in which you can use your own learning styles to be more successful in any class you take.

Learning With a Disability

While everyone has a learning style, a portion of the population has what is characterized as a learning disability. Learning disabilities are usually recognized and diagnosed in grade school, but some students can successfully compensate for a learning problem, perhaps without realizing that's what it is, and reach college without having been properly diagnosed or assisted.

Learning disabilities affect people's ability to interpret what they see and hear or to link information across different parts of the brain. These limitations can show up as specific difficulties with spoken and written language, coordination, self-control, or attention. Such difficulties can impede learning to read, write, or do math. The term "learning disability" covers a broad range of possible causes, symptoms, treatments, and outcomes. Because of this, it is difficult to diagnose a learning disability or pinpoint the causes. The types of learning disabilities that most commonly affect college students are attention disorders and disorders that affect the development of academic skills including reading, writing, and mathematics.

ATTENTION DISORDERS

Attention disorders are common in children, adolescents, and adults. Some students who have attention disorders appear to daydream excessively, and once you get their attention, they can be easily distracted. Individuals with attention deficit disorder (ADD) or attention deficit hyperactivity disorder (ADHD) often have trouble organizing tasks or completing their work. They don't seem to listen to or follow directions, and their work might be messy or appear careless. Although they are not strictly classified as learning disabilities, ADD and ADHD can seriously interfere with academic performance, leading some educators to classify them along with other learning disabilities.

If you have trouble paying attention or getting organized, you won't really know whether you have ADD or ADHD until you are evaluated. Check out resources on campus or in the community. After you have been evaluated, follow the advice you get, which might or might not mean taking medication. If you do receive a prescription for medication, be sure to take it according to the physician's directions. In the meantime, if you're having trouble getting and staying organized, whether or not you have an attention disorder, you can improve your focus through your own behavioral choices. The National Institutes of Mental Health offer the following suggestions (found on their website) for adults with attention disorders:

> Adults with ADD or ADHD can learn how to organize their lives by using "props," such as a large calendar posted where it will be seen in the morning, date books, lists, and reminder notes. They can have a special place for keys, bills, and the paperwork of everyday life. Tasks can be organized into sections so that completion of each part can give a sense of accomplishment. Above all, adults who have ADD or ADHD should learn as much as they can about their disorder (http://www.nimh.nih.gov/health/publications/attention-deficit-hyperactivity-disorder/can-adults-have-adhd.shtml).

COGNITIVE LEARNING DISABILITIES

Other learning disabilities are related to cognitive skills. Dyslexia, for example, is a common developmental reading disorder. A person can have problems with any of the tasks involved in reading. However, scientists have found that a significant number of people with dyslexia share an inability to distinguish or separate the sounds in spoken words. For instance, dyslexic individuals sometimes have difficulty assigning the appropriate sounds to letters, either individually or when letters combine to form words. However, there is more to reading than recognizing words. If the brain is unable to form images or relate new ideas to those stored in memory, the reader can't understand or remember the new concepts. So other types of reading disabilities can appear when the focus of reading shifts from word identification to comprehension.

Writing, too, involves several brain areas and functions. The brain networks for vocabulary, grammar, hand movement, and memory must all be in good working order. So a developmental writing disorder might result from problems in any of these areas. Someone who can't distinguish the sequence of sounds in a word will often have problems with spelling. People with writing disabilities, particularly expressive language disorders (the inability to express oneself using accurate language or sentence structure), are often unable to compose complete, grammatical sentences.

A student with a developmental arithmetic disorder will have difficulty recognizing numbers and symbols, memorizing facts such as the multiplication table, aligning numbers, and understanding abstract concepts such as place value and fractions.

Anyone who is diagnosed with a learning disability is in good company. The pop star Jewel; Michael Phelps, the Olympic goal medal swimmer; and actors Keira Knightley, Orlando Bloom, Patrick Dempsey, and Vince Vaughn are just a few of the famous and successful people who have diagnosed learning disabilities. A final important message: A learning disability is a learning difference but is in no way related to intelligence. Having a learning disability is not a sign that you are stupid. In fact, some of the most intelligent individuals in human history have had a learning disability.

The following questions may help you determine whether you or someone you know should seek further screening for a possible learning disability:

- Do you perform poorly on tests even when you feel you have studied and are capable of performing better?
- Do you have trouble spelling words?
- Do you work harder than your classmates at basic reading and writing?
- Do your instructors tell you that your performance in class is inconsistent, such as answering questions correctly in class but incorrectly on a written test?
- Do you have a really short attention span, or do your family members or instructors say that you do things without thinking?

Although responding "yes" to any of these questions does not mean that you have a disability, the resources of your campus learning center or the office for student disability services can help you address any potential problems and devise ways to learn more effectively.

Where to go
FOR HELP...

ON CAMPUS ▶

To learn more about learning styles and learning disabilities, talk to your first-year seminar instructor about campus resources. Most campuses have a learning center or a center for students with disabilities. You might also find that instructors in the areas of education or psychology have a strong interest in the processes of learning. Finally, don't forget your library or the Internet. A great deal of published information is available to describe how we learn.

BOOKS ▶

Learning Outside the Lines   Edward M. Hallowell (Foreword), Jonathan Mooney, and David Cole, *Two Ivy League Students with Learning Disabilities and ADHD Give You the Tools for Academic Success and Educational Revolution* (New York: Fireside, 2000).

Kathleen G. Nadeau, *Survival Guide for College Students with ADD or LD* (Washington, DC: Magination Press, 1994).

ADD and the College Student   Patricia O. Quinn, MD (ed.), *A Guide for High School and College Students with Attention Deficit Disorder* (Washington, DC: Magination Press, 2001).

ONLINE ▶

LD Pride   www.ldpride.net/learningstyles.MI.htm. This site was developed in 1998 by Liz Bogod, an adult with learning disabilities. It provides general information about learning styles and learning disabilities and offers an interactive diagnostic tool to determine your learning style.

Support 4 Learning   www.support4learning.org.uk/ education/learning_styles.cfm. This site is supported by HERO (Higher Education and Research Opportunities), which is the official online gateway to U.K. universities, colleges, and research organizations. The site provides

learning style inventories and helpful hints about how to use your learning style to do well in college courses.

National Center for Learning Disabilities   www.ncld .org. This is the official website of the National Center for Learning Disabilities. The site provides a variety of resources on diagnosing and understanding learning disabilities.

Facebook   www. facebook.com. There are groups on Facebook that were created by students who have learning disabilities or ADHD. These groups are a great way to connect with other students with learning disabilities at your college or university or at other institutions. If you have been diagnosed with a disability, the members of these groups can offer support and help you seek out appropriate resources in order to be successful in college.

MY INSTITUTION'S RESOURCES ▶

_____

_____

_____

_____

_____

_____

_____

_____

_____

_____

_____

_____

_____

_____

_____

One-Minute PAPER...

Recognizing that people have different ways of learning can be a relief. After reading this chapter, do you have a better understanding of your own learning style? What did you find to be the most interesting point in this chapter? What would you like to learn more about?

Applying What You've LEARNED...

1. It is almost certain that you will find yourself in a class where your learning style conflicts with your instructor's preferred style of teaching. After reading this chapter, describe what you can do to take control and make the most of your strongest learning preferences.

2. It is important to understand various learning styles in the context of education, but it is also important to understand how learning preferences affect career choices. Considering your own learning styles, what might be the best careers for you? Why?

Building Your PORTFOLIO...

66 It is what we think we know already that often prevents us from learning. 99

–CLAUDE BERNARD (1813-1878), French physiologist

ARE WE ON THE SAME PAGE?

After reading about the Myers-Briggs Type Indicator in this chapter, can you guess what type you are?

1. Create a Word document, and note each type that you think best fits your personality.

Example

Extravert **or I**ntrovert
I think I am an _____

Sensing **or** Intuitio**N**
I think I am _____

Thinking **or F**eeling
I think I am _____

Judging **or P**erceiving
I think I am _____

---

2. Note what you think your four MBTI letters would be (for example, ESTP).

3. Using your favorite Internet search engine, search for "suggested careers for MBTI types." You will find several websites that suggest specific careers based on specific personality types.

4. Visit one site, and list at least two careers that are recommended for the MBTI type that you identify. Have you thought about these careers before? Do you think they would be a good fit for you? Why or why not?

   (Example: Careers recommended for ESTP: Sales representatives, marketers, police, detectives, paramedics, medical technicians, computer technicians, computer technical support, entrepreneurs. Suggestions found at http://www .geocities.com/lifexplore/mbcareer.htm.)

5. Save your findings in your portfolio on your personal computer or flash drive. Revisit this document as you continue to explore different majors and careers.

PART 1   Preparing for SUCCESS

PART 2 → Preparing to STUDY

PART 3   Preparing for LIFE

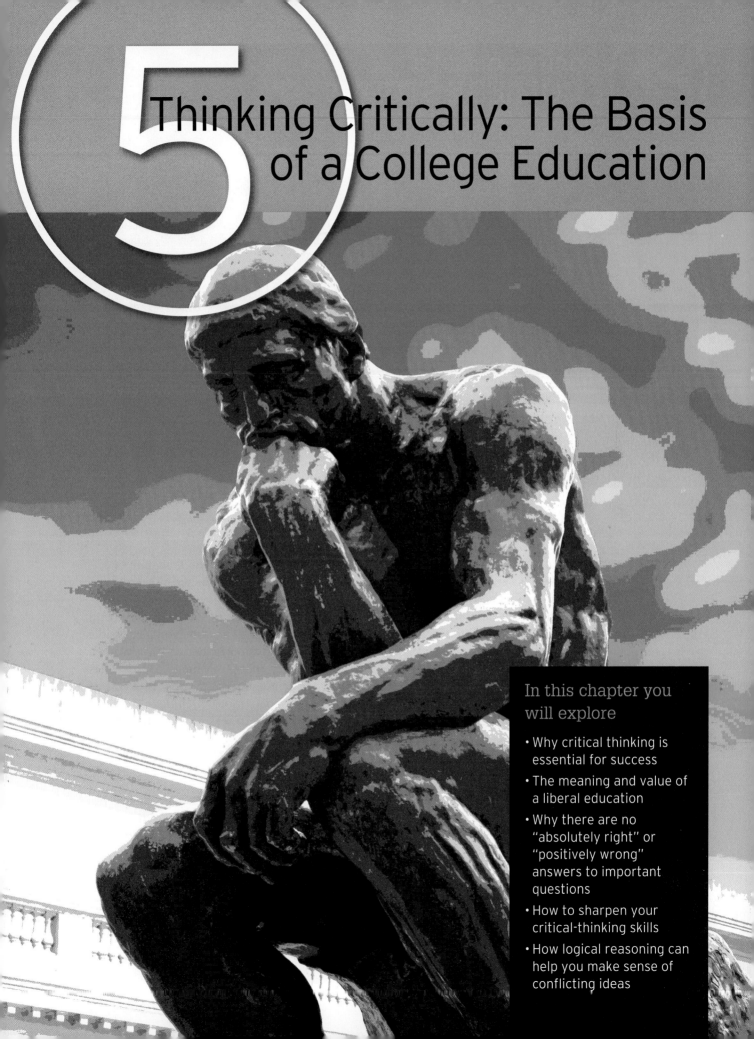

5 Thinking Critically: The Basis of a College Education

In this chapter you
will explore

• Why critical thinking is
essential for success

• The meaning and value of
a liberal education

• Why there are no
"absolutely right" or
"positively wrong"
answers to important
questions

• How to sharpen your
critical-thinking skills

• How logical reasoning can
help you make sense of
conflicting ideas

Confessions of a
COLLEGE STUDENT...

AMANDA ZELL, 19
University of Sioux Falls

❝ Before I accept something as true, it must come from more than one valid source. ❞

I learn from observation and from hearing other people's opinions. I'm never really one to state my opinion unless I'm called on. But my freshman English instructor liked to get the class members talking, and he encouraged us to voice our opinions. He had a list of controversial topics, and every class period he'd start us off with a prompt. We would always end up arguing because it would be a very complicated issue. The class never really got out of control, but his prompts sparked conversation and let us express our views.

A couple of times in that class I did speak out on issues I thought were important. But for the most part, I already knew where I stood, so I tried to be very open to what other people thought. Sometimes I have been wrong. It's interesting to see the background behind what other people think about an issue. I might view things differently, and maybe I don't agree. Before I accept something as true, it must come from more than one valid source. Even in class if I hear something interesting, I don't always believe it.

Arguably the most important skill you'll acquire in college is the ability and confidence to think for yourself. Courses in every discipline will encourage you to ask questions, to sort through competing information and ideas, to form well-reasoned opinions, and to defend them. A liberal college education teaches you to investigate all sides of an issue and all possible solutions to a problem before you reach a conclusion or decide on a plan of action. Indeed, the word *liberal* (from the Latin *libero*, meaning "to free") has no political connotation in this context but represents the purpose of a college education: to liberate your mind from biases, superstitions, prejudices, and lack of knowledge so that you'll be in a better position to seek answers to difficult questions.

> **YOUR TURN ▶**
>
> In your own words, define "liberal education." Why would a "free" mind be an asset for you now and in the future?

If you have just completed high school, you might be experiencing an awakening as you adjust to college. If you're an older returning student, discovering that your instructors trust you to find valid answers could be both surprising and stressful. If a high school teacher asked, "What are the three branches of the U.S. government?" there was only one acceptable answer: "legislative, executive, and judicial." A college instructor, on the other hand, might ask, "Under what circumstances might conflicts arise among the three branches of government, and what does this reveal about the democratic process?" There is no simple—or single—answer, and that's the point of higher education. Questions that suggest complex answers engage you in the process of critical thinking.

Most important questions don't have simple answers, and satisfying answers can be elusive. To reach them, you will have to discover numerous ways to view important issues. You will need to become comfortable with uncertainty. And you must be willing to challenge assumptions and conclusions, even those presented by so-called experts. It is natural to find critical thinking difficult, to feel frustrated by answers that are seldom entirely wrong or right. Yet the complicated questions are usually the ones that are most worthy of study, and working out the answers can be both intellectually exciting and personally rewarding. In this chapter, we will explain how developing and applying your critical-thinking skills can make the search for truth a worthwhile and stimulating adventure.

What Is Critical Thinking and Why Is it Important?

Let's start with what critical thinking is *not*. By "critical," we do not mean "negative" or "harsh." Rather, the term refers to thoughtful consideration of the information, ideas, and arguments that you encounter. Critical thinking is the ability to think for yourself and to reliably and responsibly make the decisions that affect your life.

As Richard Paul and Linda Elder of the National Council for Excellence in Critical Thinking explain it, "critical thinking is that mode of thinking about any subject, content, or problem in which the thinker improves the quality of his or her thinking by skillfully . . . imposing intellectual standards upon [his or her thoughts]."[1] They believe that much of our thinking, left to itself, is biased, distorted, partial, uninformed, or downright prejudiced. Yet the quality of our life and the quality of what we produce, make, or build depend precisely on the quality of our thought.

Paul and Elder also caution that shoddy thinking is costly. How so? You probably know people who simply follow authority. They do not question, are not curious, and do not challenge people or groups who claim special knowledge or insight. These people do not usually think for themselves but rely on others to think for them. They might indulge in wishful, hopeful, and emotional thinking, assuming that what they believe is true simply because they wish it, hope it, or feel it to be true. As you might have noticed, such people tend not to have much control over their circumstances or to possess any real power in business or society.

Critical thinkers, in contrast, investigate problems, ask questions, pose new answers that challenge the status quo, discover new information, question authorities and traditional beliefs, challenge received dogmas and doctrines,

[1]Richard Paul and Linda Elder, *The Miniature Guide to Critical Thinking Concepts and Tools* (Dillon Beach, CA: Foundation for Critical Thinking Press, 2008).

make independent judgments, and develop creative solutions. When employers say they want workers who can find reliable information, analyze it, organize it, draw conclusions from it, and present it convincingly to others, they are seeking individuals who are critical thinkers.

YOUR TURN ▶

On the basis of the explanation above, how would you rate yourself as a critical thinker?

Whatever else you do in college, make it a point to develop and sharpen your critical-thinking skills. You won't become an accomplished critical thinker overnight. But with practice, you can learn how to tell whether information is truthful and accurate. You can make better decisions, come up with fresh solutions to difficult problems, and communicate your ideas strategically and persuasively.[2]

Becoming a Critical Thinker

In essence, critical thinking is a search for truth. In college and in life, you'll be confronted by a mass of information and ideas. Much of what you read and hear will seem suspect, and a lot of it will be contradictory. (If you have ever talked back to a television commercial or doubted a politician's campaign promises, you know this already.) How do you decide what to believe?

Paul and Elder remind us that there may be more than one right answer to any given question. The task is to determine which of the "truths" you read or hear are the most plausible and then draw on them to develop ideas of your own. Difficult problems practically demand that you weigh options and think through consequences before you can reach an informed decision. Critical thinking also involves improving the way you think about a subject, statement, or idea. To do that, you'll need to ask questions, consider several different points of view, and draw your own conclusions.

YOUR TURN ▶

Think of a problem you had to solve in the past. How did you do it? How can you draw on that experience to improve your ability to solve academic problems?

ASK QUESTIONS

The first step of thinking critically is to engage your curiosity. Instead of accepting statements and assertions at face value, question them. When you come across an idea or a "fact" that strikes you as interesting, confusing, or suspicious, ask yourself first what it means. Do you fully understand what is being said, or do you need to pause and think to make sense of the idea? Do you agree with the statement? Why or why not? Can the material be interpreted in more than one way?

[2]Liz Brown, *Critical Thinking* (New York: Weigl Publishers, 2008), p. 4.

Don't stop there. Ask whether you can trust the person or institution making a particular claim, and ask whether they have provided enough evidence to back up an assertion (more on this later). Ask who might be likely to agree or disagree and why. Ask how a new concept relates to what you already know, where you might find more information about the subject, and what you could do with what you learn. Finally, ask yourself about the implications and consequences of accepting

something as truth. Will you have to change your perspective or give up a long-held belief? Will it require you to do something differently? Will it be necessary to investigate the issue further? Do you anticipate having to try to bring other people around to a new way of thinking?

YOUR TURN ▶

Imagine that your state has just approved a license plate design incorporating a cross and the slogan "I Believe." Almost immediately, a number of organizations begin protesting that this is a violation of the First Amendment of the U.S. Constitution. What kinds of questions will you ask to get at the truth?

CONSIDER MULTIPLE POINTS OF VIEW

Once you start asking questions, you'll typically discover a slew of different possible answers competing for your attention. Don't be too quick to latch onto one and move on. To be a critical thinker, you need to be fair and open-minded, even if you don't agree with certain ideas at first. Give them all a fair hearing, because your goal is to find the truth or the best action, not to confirm what you already believe.

Often, you will recognize the existence of competing points of view on your own, perhaps because they're held by people you know personally. You might discover them in what you read, watch, or listen to for pleasure. Reading assignments might deliberately expose you to conflicting arguments and theories about a subject, or you might encounter differences of opinion as you do research for a project.

In class discussions, also, your instructors might often insist that more than one valid point of view exists: "So, for some types of students, you agree that bilingual education might be best? What types of students might not benefit?" Your instructors will expect you to explain in concrete terms any point you reject: "You think this essay is flawed. Well, what are your reasons?" They might challenge the authority of experts: "Dr. Fleming's theory sounds impressive. But here are some facts he doesn't account for . . .." Your instructors will also sometimes reinforce your personal views and experiences: "So something like this happened to you once, and you felt exactly the same way. Can you tell us why?"

The more ideas you entertain, the more sophisticated your own thinking will become. Ultimately, you will discover not only that is it okay to change your mind, but that a willingness to do so is the mark of a reasonable, educated person.

DRAW CONCLUSIONS

Once you have considered different points of view, it's up to you to reach your own conclusions, to craft a new idea based on what you've learned, or to make a decision about what you'll do with the information you have.

This process isn't necessarily a matter of figuring out the best idea. Depending on the goals of the activity, it might be simply the one that you think is the most fun or the most practical, or it might be a new idea of your own creation. For a business decision, it might involve additional cost-benefit analysis to decide which computer equipment to purchase for your office. In a chemistry lab, it might be a matter of interpreting the results of an experiment. In a creative writing workshop, students might collaborate to select the most workable plot for a classmate's short story. Or a social worker might conduct multiple interviews before recommending a counseling plan for a struggling family.

Drawing conclusions involves looking at the outcome of your inquiry in a more demanding, critical way. If you are looking for solutions to a problem, which ones really seem most promising after you have conducted an exhaustive search for materials? Do some answers conflict with others? Which ones can be achieved? If you have found new evidence, what does that new evidence show? Do your original beliefs hold up? Do they need to be modified? Which notions should be abandoned? Most important, consider what you would need to do or say to persuade someone else that your ideas are valid. Thoughtful conclusions aren't very useful if you can't share them with others.

How Collaboration Fosters Critical Thinking

A 1995 study by Professor Anuradha A. Gokhale at Western Illinois University, published in the *Journal of Technology Education*, found that students who participated in collaborative learning performed significantly better on a test requiring critical thinking than did students who studied individually. The study also found that the two groups did equally well on a test that required only memorization.[3]

[3]Anuradha Gokhale, "Collaborative Learning Enhances Critical Thinking," *Journal of Technology Education*, 1995, 7.1.

Having more than one student involved in the learning process generates a greater number of ideas. People think more clearly when they are talking as well as listening (a very good reason to participate actively in your classes). Creative brainstorming and group discussion encourage original thought. These habits also teach participants to consider alternative points of view carefully and to express and defend their own ideas clearly. As a group negotiates ideas and learns to agree on the most reliable thoughts, it moves closer to a surer solution.

YOUR TURN ▶

If you never have worked with a study group, now is the time to try it and discover how much more learning can take place in a shorter period of time. How do you think you could benefit from joining a study group? What reasons might you give for not joining one?

Collaboration occurs not only face to face, but also over the Internet. Christopher P. Sessums, creator of an award-winning blog, writes:

> Weblogs offer several key features that I believe can support a constructive, collaborative, reflective environment. For one, it's convenient. The medium supports self-expression and "voice." Collaboration and connectivity can be conducted efficiently, especially in terms of participants' time or place. Publishing your thoughts online forces you to concretize your thoughts.

"Collaborative weblogs," Sessums concludes, "promote the idea of learners as creators of knowledge, not merely consumers of information."[4] So do online discussion groups, wikis (which allow users to add, update, and otherwise improve material that others have posted), and, of course, face-to-face collaboration.

Whether in person or through electronic communication, teamwork improves your ability to think critically. As you leave college and enter the world of work, you will find that collaboration is essential in almost any career you pursue, not only with people in your work setting, but also with others around the globe.

[4]Christopher Sessums, Eduspaces weblog, November 9, 2005. Available at: http://eduspaces.net/csessums/weblog/archive/2005/11.

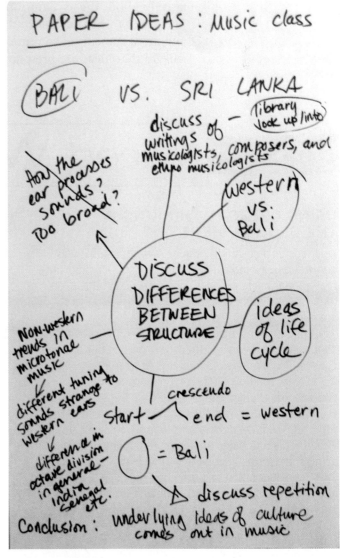

▶ FIGURE 5.1   Brainstorming on Paper

Thinking Critically About Arguments

What does the word *argument* mean to you? If you're like most people, the first image it conjures up might be an ugly fight you had with a friend, a yelling match you witnessed on the street, or a heated disagreement between family members. True, such unpleasant confrontations are arguments. But the word also refers to a calm, reasoned effort to persuade someone of the value of an idea.

When you think of it this way, you'll quickly recognize that arguments are central to academic study, work, and life in general. Scholarly articles, business memos, and requests for spending money all have something in common: The effective ones make a general claim, provide reasons to support it, and back up those reasons with evidence. That's what argument is.

As we have already seen, it's important to consider multiple points of view, or arguments, in tackling new ideas and complex questions. But arguments are not all equally valid. Good critical thinking involves thinking creatively about the assumptions that might have been left out and scrutinizing the quality of the evidence that is used to support a claim. Whether examining an argument or communicating one, a good critical thinker is careful to ensure that ideas are presented in an understandable, logical way.

Wired WINDOW

USING CRITICAL THINKING IN THE BLOGOSPHERE

Web logs or blogs allow anyone, even those with limited web publishing experience, to post online journals that appear professional. Blogs emerged in 2003, and their popularity has exploded since then. Bloggers are currently posting over 900,000 new entries every day.[5] Because there are so many blogs, they cover just about any topic you can think of—from politics to purchasing, from movies to money, sex to Silicon Valley. If you want to know bloggers' opinions about anything, you can find them in the blogosphere. Because there are so many blogs, opinions about an issue can range widely among bloggers—some supporting a certain viewpoint, some being against it, and many others being somewhere in between. Keep in mind that that vast majority of bloggers are not experts in their field and that most blogs are not reviewed for accuracy. This allows for a richer examination of all possible viewpoints, but you must hone your critical-thinking skills to evaluate blogs effectively.

Thinking Critically

Blogs present a wonderful opportunity for you to improve your critical-thinking skills. Many bloggers are perfectly comfortable sharing their thinking process with their audience. Can you find a blogger who discusses a common topic yet provides a viewpoint that is not represented in the mainstream? Search for a blog with commentary on a current event that you find interesting. (Hint: Search for the topic keywords plus the word *blog*.) Find two blogs with different viewpoints on the same topic. Then answer the following questions: What is each blogger's viewpoint? Do the people who leave comments generally agree or disagree with the blogger's point of view? Why does the blogger hold that point of view? Is there any evidence on the blog that supports the blogger's view? Do you have an opinion on the topic? Which blogger do you most agree with? Why?

[5]Technorati, 2008. Available at: http://technorati.com/blogging/state-of-the-blogosphere.

CHALLENGE ASSUMPTIONS

All too often, our beliefs are based on gut feelings or on blind acceptance of something we've heard or read. To some extent, that's unavoidable. If we made a habit of questioning absolutely everything, we would have trouble making it through the day. Yet some assumptions should be examined more thoughtfully, especially if they will influence an important decision or serve as the foundation for an argument.

For an example, imagine that the mayor of the city where your school is located has announced that he wants to make a bid to host the Olympic Games. Many people on campus are excited at the prospect, but your friend Richard is less than thrilled.

"The Olympic Games just about ruined my hometown," Richard tells you. "Road signs all over Atlanta had to be changed so that visitors could find the game sites easily. Because the city couldn't supply enough workers to complete the task on time, the organizers brought thousands of immigrants to town to help with the task, and some of them were illegal aliens.

The Games are intended to foster national and international pride, but these immigrants could care less about that. They were there to earn money for their families. The Hispanic population nearly doubled once the Games were over. And if people understood how much political corruption went on behind the scenes, they would understand why the Olympic Games are not healthy for a host city."

> **YOUR TURN ▶**
>
> So far, what unstated assumptions do you see in Richard's argument? Explain why you question some of his claims.

Another friend, Sally, overhears your conversation, and she's not buying Richard's conclusions. "How do you know all of that is accurate?" she asks. "I just know it," says Richard.

Eager to get at the truth of the matter, Sally decides to look into other points of view. She does a quick web search and finds an article about the Atlanta Olympics in the *American Historical Review*, the journal of record for the history profession in the United States. Its author notes that "the Games provided an enormous engine for growth" and comments that the city's "surging population is the most obvious marker of Atlanta's post-Olympic transformation." The article continues: "By the 1996 Games the metro population had reached three million, and today [is] 4,458,253. Winning the Olympic bid marked a turning point that put Atlanta on the world's radar screen."[6]

> **YOUR TURN ▶**
>
> What's the difference between Richard's approach to the truth and Sally's? Which is more sensible? Why?

[6]Mary G. Rolinson, visiting lecturer in the Georgia State University History Department, "Atlanta Before and After the Olympics." Copyright © American Historical Association. Available at: http://www.historians.org/perspectives/issues/2006/0611/0611ann6.cfm.

Although Sally has found good information from a reputable source, you should be uncomfortable with the totally upbeat tone of the article. If you and Sally dig a little further, you might land on the website of the Utah Office of Tourism, which includes a report that was prepared when that state was investigating the potential impacts of hosting the 2002 Winter Games in Salt Lake City. According to the report, "Among the key legacies of the Atlanta Olympics was the regeneration of certain downtown districts that had fallen into urban decay." The authors also note that "the Olympic-spurred development in [Atlanta] has provided a much-needed stimulus for revitalization."[7]

Finding a second positive analysis would give you a compelling reason to believe that the Olympic Games are good for a city, but Richard might easily discover a report from the European Tour Operators Association, which concludes that visitors are likely to stay away from host countries during and following the Games, causing a significant long-term decline in revenue for hotels and other businesses that depend on tourism.[8]

Unfortunately, simply learning more about the benefits and costs of hosting the Olympics doesn't yield any concrete answers. Even so, you, Richard, and Sally have uncovered assumptions and have developed a better understanding of the issue. That's an important first step.

YOUR TURN ▶

In your opinion, is hosting the Olympics good or bad for a city? Why? How can you reconcile Richard's views on the subject with Sally's findings? If you think the truth lies in between, how would you go about discovering it?

EXAMINE THE EVIDENCE

The evidence that is offered as support for an argument can vary in quality. While Richard started with no proof other than his convictions ("I just know it"), Sally looked to expert opinion and research studies for answers to her question. Even so, one of her sources sounded overly positive, prompting a need to confirm the author's claims with additional evidence from other sources.

Like Sally, critical thinkers are careful to check that the evidence supporting an argument—whether someone else's or their own—is of the highest possible quality. To do that, simply ask a few questions about the arguments as you consider them:

- What general idea am I being asked to accept?
- Are good and sufficient reasons given to support the overall claim?
- Are those reasons backed up with evidence in the form of facts, statistics, and quotations?
- Does the evidence support the conclusions?
- Is the argument based on logical reasoning, or does it appeal mainly to the emotions?

---

[7]Utah Office of Tourism, *Observations from Past Olympic Host Communities: Executive Summary*. Available at: http://travel.utah.gov/research_and_planning/2002_olympics.

[8]"Olympics Have Negative Effect on Tourism," July 10, 2008. Available at: http://www.travelbite.co.uk.

- Do I recognize any questionable assumptions?
- Can I think of any counterarguments? What facts can I muster as proof?
- What do I know about the person or organization making the argument?

┌───┐
│ **YOUR TURN ▶**   │
│   │
│ What, if anything, is wrong with making decisions purely on the basis of your │
│ emotions?   │
└───┘

If, after you have evaluated the evidence used in support of a claim, you're still not certain of its quality, it's best to keep looking. Drawing on questionable evidence for an argument has a tendency to backfire. In most cases, a little persistence will help you find something better. (You can find tips on how to find and evaluate sources in Chapter 11, "Developing Library, Research, and Information Literacy Skills.")

BEWARE OF LOGICAL FALLACIES

A critical thinker has an attitude—an attitude of wanting to avoid nonsense, to find the truth and to discover the best action. It's an attitude that rejects intuiting what is right in favor of requiring reasons. Instead of being defensive or emotional, critical thinkers aim to be logical.

Although logical reasoning is essential to solving any problem, whether simple or complex, you need to go one step further to make sure that an argument hasn't been compromised by faulty reasoning. Here are some of the most common missteps people make in their use of logic:

- **Attacking the person.** It's perfectly acceptable to argue against other people's positions or to attack their arguments. It is not okay, however, to go after their personalities. Any argument that resorts to personal attack ("Why should we believe a cheater?") is unworthy of consideration.

- **Begging.** "Please, officer, don't give me a ticket because if you do, I'll lose my license, and I have five little children to feed and won't be able to feed them if I can't drive my truck." None of the driver's statements offer any evidence, in any legal sense, as to why she shouldn't be given a ticket. Pleading *might* work, if the officer is feeling generous, but an appeal to facts and reason would be more effective: "I fed the meter, but it didn't register the coins. Since the machine is broken, I'm sure you'll agree that I don't deserve a ticket."

- **Appealing to false authority.** Citing authorities, such as experts in a field or the opinions of qualified researchers, can offer valuable support for an argument. But a claim based on the authority of someone whose expertise is questionable relies on the appearance of authority rather than real evidence. We see this all the time in advertising: Sports stars who are not doctors, dieticians, or nutritionists urge us to eat a certain brand of food, or famous actors and singers who are not dermatologists extol the medical benefits of a pricey remedy for acne.

- **Jumping on a bandwagon.** Sometimes we are more likely to believe something if a lot of other people believe it. Even the most widely accepted truths, however, can turn out to be wrong. There was a time when nearly everyone believed that the world was flat—until someone came up with evidence to the contrary.

- **Assuming that something is true because it hasn't been proven false.** Go to a bookstore, and you'll find dozens of books detailing close encounters with flying saucers and extraterrestrial beings. These books describe the person who had the close encounter as beyond reproach in integrity and sanity. Because critics could not disprove the claims of the witnesses, the events are said to have really occurred. Even in science, few things are ever proved completely false, but evidence can be discredited.

- **Falling victim to false cause.** Frequently, we make the assumption that just because one event followed another, the first event must have caused the second. This reasoning is the basis for many superstitions. The ancient Chinese once believed that they could make the sun reappear after an eclipse by striking a large gong, because they knew that the sun reappeared after a large gong had been struck on one such occasion. Most effects, however, are usually the result of a complex web of causes. Don't be satisfied with easy before-and-after claims; they are rarely correct.

- **Making hasty generalizations.** If someone selected one green marble from a barrel containing a hundred marbles, you wouldn't assume that the next marble would be green. After all, there are still ninety-nine marbles in the barrel, and you know nothing about the colors of those marbles. However, given fifty draws from the barrel, each of which produced a green marble after the barrel had been shaken thoroughly, you would be more willing to conclude that the next marble drawn would be green, too. Reaching a conclusion based on the opinion of one source is like figuring that all the marbles in the barrel are green after pulling out only one.

YOUR TURN ▶

Have you ever used any of these fallacies to justify a decision? Why was it wrong to do so? Can you think of other errors of logic that might push you farther from the truth?

Fallacies like these can slip into even the most careful reasoning. One false claim can derail an entire argument, so be on the lookout for weak logic in what you read and write. Never forget that accurate reasoning is a key factor for success in college and in life.

Critical Thinking in College and Everyday Life

As you practice the skills of critical thinking in college, they start to become a natural part of your life. Eventually, you will be able to think your way through many everyday situations, such as these:

- You try to reach a classmate on the phone to ask a question about tomorrow's quiz. When you can't reach her, you become so anxious that you can't study or sleep.
- On the day an important paper is due, a heavy snowstorm rolls in. You brave the cold to get to class. When you arrive, no one—including the teacher—is there. You take a seat and wait.

Now let's transform you into a critical thinker and examine the possible outcomes:

- When you can't reach a classmate on the phone to ask a question about tomorrow's quiz, you review the material once more, then call one or more other classmates. Then you consider their views and those of your textbook and class. Instead of deciding on one point of view for each important topic, you decide to keep in mind all of those that make sense, leaving your final decision until you have the quiz in your hand.
- Before heading out to class in a big snowstorm, you check the college website and discover that classes have been canceled. You stay at home.

YOUR TURN ▶

Suppose you're shopping for a surround-sound system. One good friend urges you to buy the top of the line. Another well-meaning friend steers you to a different brand, claiming it's just as good as the more expensive brand leader. Now all you know is that two of your good friends have offered information that might or might not be true. How do you think critically about which system to choose?

If you hang onto the guidelines in this chapter, we can't promise your classes will be easier, but they will certainly be more interesting. You will now know how to use critical thinking to figure things out instead of depending purely on how you feel or what you've heard. As you listen to a lecture, try to predict where it is heading and why. When other students raise issues, ask yourself whether they have enough information to justify what they have said. And when you raise your hand, remember that asking a sensible question can be more important than trying to find the elusive—and often nonexistent— "right answer."

Imagine a world in which physicians tried a new procedure on a patient before it had been tested, your history course was taught by someone who never studied history, and you put your total faith in a hair restorer just because the advertising said it would grow hair in two weeks.

As a critical thinker, you would know better.

Where to go
FOR HELP...

ON CAMPUS ▶

Logic Courses Check out your philosophy department's introductory course in logic. This might be the single best course designed to teach you critical-thinking skills. Nearly every college offers such a course.

Argument Courses and Critical Thinking Courses These are usually offered in the English department. They will help you develop the ability to formulate logical arguments and avoid such pitfalls as logical fallacies.

Debating Skills Some of the very best critical thinkers developed debating skills during college. Go to either your student activities office or your department of speech/drama, and find out whether your campus has a debate club or team. Debating can be fun, and chances are you will meet some interesting student thinkers that way.

LITERATURE ▶

12 Angry Men **by Reginald Rose** (New York: Penguin Classics, 2006) This is a reprint of the original teleplay, which was written in 1954 and made into a film in 1958. It is also available on DVD. The stirring courtroom drama pits twelve jurors against one another as they argue the outcome of a murder trial in which the defendant is a teenage boy. Where critical thinking is needed to arrive at the truth, all but one juror employ every noncritical argument in the book to arrive at a guilty verdict until the analysis of the one holdout produces remarkable changes in their attitudes.

ONLINE ▶

Check the following website for a critical review of *The Encyclopedia of Stupidity:* http://arts.independent.co.uk/books/reviews/article112328.ece.

A Guide to Critical Thinking About What You See on the Web: http://www.ithaca.edu/library/training/think.html.

MY INSTITUTION'S RESOURCES ▶

_____

_____

_____

_____

_____

_____

_____

_____

_____

_____

_____

_____

_____

_____

_____

_____

One-Minute PAPER...

One major shift from being a high school student to being a college student involves the level of critical thinking your college instructors expect of you. After reading this chapter, how would you describe critical thinking to a high school student?

Applying What You've LEARNED...

Now that you have read and discussed this chapter, consider how you can apply what you have learned to your academic and personal life. The following prompts will help you reflect on chapter material and its relevance to you both now and in the future.

1. After reading this chapter, think of professions (for example, physicians, engineers, marketing professionals) for whom problem solving and thinking "outside of the box" is necessary. Choose one career, and describe why you think critical thinking is a necessary and valuable skill.

2. In your opinion, is it harder to think critically than to base your arguments on how you feel about a topic? Why or why not? What are the advantages of finding answers based on your feelings? Based on critical thinking? How might you use both approaches in seeking answers?

Building Your PORTFOLIO...

66 We all take different paths in life, but no matter where we go, we take a little of each other everywhere. 99

–TIM McGRAW (b. 1967),
American country music singer

MY INFLUENCES

Our past experiences have shaped the way in which we think and perceive the world around us. Sometimes it is easy to interpret things without stopping to think about why we feel the way we do. How have other people shaped the way you see the world today?

1. In your personal portfolio, create a Word document and

- Describe at least three people (such as family, friends, celebrities, national leaders) who you feel have most influenced the way you think.

- Describe how these individuals' values, actions, expectations, and words have shaped the way you think about yourself and the world.

2. Describe a situation that you have dealt with since coming to college that has challenged you to think about an issue in a new and different way.

3. Save your work on your personal computer or flash drive.

6
Being Engaged in Learning: Listening, Taking Notes, and Participating in Class

In this chapter you will explore

- How to use your senses in learning and remembering
- How to prepare before class
- Why you should participate in class by speaking up
- How to listen critically
- How to assess and improve your note-taking skills
- Why it is important to review your notes and textbook materials soon after class
- How being engaged in the classroom improves your learning

Confessions of a
COLLEGE STUDENT . . .

VINCENT ADAME, 19
California State University,
San Bernardino

> ❝ You're on your own in college, so you have to try to do the best you can. ❞

I'm not a big fan of school. I find it sometimes hard to pay attention to lectures. If it's not really a lecture or if we're doing other things, it's pretty easy for me to listen. But as far as sitting there for an hour and fifty minutes straight hearing a professor just go on and on about the subject, it's hard to focus. And if they turn the lights off for PowerPoint or something, I tend to fall asleep and that's that.

Some instructors talk more quickly than others. Sometimes I'll take my laptop to class, but I write faster than I type, so I usually write my notes by hand. It helps me pay attention too, if I'm taking notes. Then later I can look over what I wrote in class and try to remember what the instructor was saying. Books and study guides are available, but good notes are the best aid. You're on your own in college, so you have to try to do the best you can. Go to class, put your study hours in, and you should be successful.

In virtually every college class you take, you'll need to master certain skills to earn high grades, such as listening, taking notes, and being engaged in learning. Engagement in learning means that you take an active role in your classes by listening critically, asking questions, contributing to discussions, and providing answers. These active learning behaviors will enhance your ability to understand abstract ideas, find new possibilities, organize those ideas, and recall the material once the class is over.

Your academic success relies on practicing the habits of active engagement both in and out of class. In the classroom, engagement starts with the basics: listening, taking notes, and participating in class discussions. Many of the questions on college exams will be drawn from class lectures and discussions. Therefore you need to attend each class and be actively involved. In addition to taking notes, you might consider recording the lecture and discussion if you have the instructor's permission. If there are points you don't understand, take the time to meet with the instructor after class or during office hours. Another strategy to increase your engagement and your learning is to meet with a study group to compare your understanding of course material with that of your classmates.

94

This chapter reviews several note-taking methods. Choose the one that works best for you. Because writing down everything the instructor says is probably not possible and you might not be sure what is most important, ask questions in class. This will ensure that you clearly understand your notes. Reviewing your notes with a tutor, someone from your campus learning center, or a friend from class can also help you clarify your understanding of the most important points.

Most of all, be sure to speak up. When you have a question to ask or a comment to share, don't let embarrassment or shyness stop you. You will be more likely to remember what happens in class if you are an active participant.

YOUR TURN ▶

What kind of notes did you take in high school? Do you think you learned how to take good notes? Is the same method working for you now? Why or why not?

Using Your Senses in the Learning Process

You can enhance your memory by using as many of your senses as possible while learning. How do you believe you learn most effectively?

1. **Aural:** Are you an auditory learner? Do you learn by listening to other people talk, or does your mind begin to wander when you listen passively for more than a few minutes?

2. **Visual:** Do you like reading? Do you learn best when you can see the words on the printed page? During a test, can you actually visualize where the information appears in your text? Can you remember data best when it's presented in the form of a picture, graph, chart, map, or video?

3. **Interactive:** Do you enjoy discussing course work with friends, classmates, or the teacher? Does talking about information from the lecture or the text help you remember it?

4. **Tactile:** Do you learn through your sense of touch? Does typing your notes help you remember them?

5. **Kinesthetic:** Can you learn better when your body is in motion? When you are participating in sports, dancing, or working out, do you know immediately if a movement feels right? Do you learn more effectively by doing something than by listening or reading about it?

6. **Olfactory:** Does your sense of taste or smell contribute to your learning process? Do you cook using a recipe or by tasting and adding ingredients? Are you sensitive to odors?

Two or three of these modes probably describe your preferred ways of learning better than the others. At the college level, faculty members tend to share information primarily via lecture and the textbook. However, many students like to learn through visual and interactive means. This creates a mismatch between learning and teaching styles. Is this a problem? Not necessarily. It is a problem only if you do not learn how to adapt lecture material and the text to your preferred modes of learning.

Preparing for Class

Have you ever noticed how easy it is to learn the words of a song? We remember songs more easily than other kinds of information because songs follow a tune and have a beat and because they often have a personal meaning for us: We often relate songs to something in our everyday lives. We remember prose less easily unless we make an effort to relate it to what we already know. In your first-year classes, you'll be listening to and reading material that might seem hard to understand. Beginning on the first day of class, you will be more likely to remember what you hear and read if you try to link it to something you have already learned or experienced.

Because some lectures are hard to follow and understand, you need to be prepared before class begins. You would not want to be unprepared to give a speech, interview for a job, plead a case in court, or compete in a sport. For each of these situations, you would prepare in some way. For the same reasons, you should begin listening, learning, and remembering before the lecture.

Even if lectures don't allow for active participation, you can do a number of things to become more engaged and to make your listening and note-taking more efficient. You will then learn and remember more, understand what the instructor considers important, and ultimately earn better grades.

Participating in Class

Learning is not a spectator sport. To really learn, you must listen critically, talk about what you are learning, write about it, relate it to past experiences, and make what you learn part of yourself. Participation is the heart of **active learning**. When we say something in class, we are more likely to remember it than we will when someone else says something. So when a teacher tosses a question your way or you have a question to ask, you're actually making it easier to remember the day's lesson.

LISTENING CRITICALLY AND WITH AN OPEN MIND

Listening in class is not like listening to a TV show, listening to a friend, or even listening to a speaker at a meeting. Knowing how to listen in class can help you get more out of what you hear, understand better what you have heard, and save time.

Here are some suggestions:

1. **Be ready for the message.** Prepare yourself to hear, to listen, and to receive the message. If you have done the assigned reading, you will already know details from the text, so you can focus your notes on key concepts during the lecture. You will also be able to notice information that the text does not cover, and you will be prepared to pay closer attention when the instructor is presenting unfamiliar material.

BEFORE CLASS TIPS

1. **Do the assigned reading.** Otherwise, you might find the lecturer's comments disjointed, and you might not understand some terms that your instructor will use. Some instructors refer to assigned readings for each class session; others might distribute a **syllabus** (course outline) and assume you are keeping up with the assigned readings. Completing assigned reading on time will help you listen better and pick out the most important information when taking notes in class. As you read, take good notes. In books that you own, **annotate** (add critical or explanatory margin notes), highlight, or underline the text. In books that you do not own, such as library books, make a photocopy of the pages and then annotate or highlight.

2. **Pay careful attention to your course syllabus.** Syllabi are formal statements of course expectations, requirements, and procedures. Instructors assume that students will understand and follow course requirements with few or no reminders once they have received a syllabus.

3. **Make use of additional materials provided by the instructors.** Many instructors post lecture outlines or notes on a website before class. Download and print these materials for easy reference during class. They often provide hints about the topics that the instructor considers most important; they also can create an organizational structure for taking notes.

4. **Warm up for class** by reviewing chapter introductions and summaries, referring to related sections in your text, and scanning your notes from the previous class period. This prepares you to pay attention, understand, and remember.

5. **Get organized.** Decide what type of notebook will work best for you. Many study skills experts suggest using three-ring binders because you can punch holes in syllabi and other course handouts and keep them with class notes. You might want to buy notebook paper with a larger left-hand margin (sometimes called "legal-ruled"), which will help you to easily annotate your lecture notes. If you take notes on your laptop, keep your files organized in separate folders for each of your classes, and make sure that the file name of each document reflects the date and topic of the class.

Philosophy 101: Introduction to Philosophy
Descartes: Meditations on First Philosophy
Meditation 1

Lecture Notes

Historical Introduction

- b. 1596, LaHaye (now 'Descartes'), France; d. 1650, Stockholm, Sweden.
- Trained in classical literature, history, rhetoric, higher mathematics, and philosophy.
- Unimpressed with traditional, scholastic philosophy; all of it open to doubt; shaky foundations.
- Sought to develop a new model for science and philosophy based on the certainty of mathematical reasoning.

Introduction to the *Meditations*

- Not a philosophical treatise, but an exercise in thinking.
- Written as a thought process, "stream of consciousness".
- Written in first person, allows reader to imagine him/herself as engaging in this thought process.
- Goal: discover a foundation for knowledge.

Meditation 1

- Foundation of knowledge must be certain.
- Why? Anything built upon certainty will also be certain. Anything built upon uncertain foundations will also be uncertain.

Relation between knowledge and belief

- To know something X, one must belief X.
- Belief is a necessary condition for knowledge.

What kinds of beliefs do we have?

- Observational beliefs (grass is green, I have hands, etc.)
- Predictive beliefs (the sun will rise tomorrow)
- General inductive beliefs (all swans are white)
- General definitional beliefs (all bachelors are unmarried)
- Mathematical beliefs (2 + 3 = 5)

Descartes only focuses on two of these categories: observational beliefs and mathematical beliefs.

- Can we be certain with respect to either of these categories of belief?
- Observational
  - Sources of doubt: senses sometimes deceive; we could be dreaming.
- Mathematical
  - Sources of doubt: omnipotent God, omnipotent evil genius.

Can we be certain about any belief?

- Descartes finds such a belief in Meditation 2.

End of Meditation 1

- While doubt forces us to discard practically all of our beliefs, we naturally fall back into agreement with them.

2. **Listen to the main concepts and central ideas, not just to fragmented facts and figures.** Although facts are important, they will be easier to remember and will make more sense when you can place them in a context of concepts, themes, and ideas.

3. **Listen for new ideas.** Even if you are an expert on a topic, you can still learn something new. Do not assume that college instructors will present the same information you learned in a similar course in high school. Even if you're listening to the lecture again (perhaps because you recorded your lectures), you will pick out and learn new information. As a critical thinker, make a note of questions that arise in your mind as you listen, but save the judgments for later.

4. **Repeat mentally.** Words can go in one ear and out the other unless you make an effort to retain them. Think about what you hear, and restate it silently in your own words. If you cannot translate the information into your own words, ask the instructor for further clarification.

5. **Decide whether what you have heard is not important, somewhat important, or very important.** If it's really not important, let it go. If it's very important, make it a major point in your notes by highlighting or underscoring it, or use it as a major topic in your outline if that's the method you use for taking notes. If it's somewhat important, try to relate it to a very important topic by writing it down as a subset of that topic.

6. **Keep an open mind.** Every class holds the promise of letting you discover new ideas and uncover different perspectives. Some teachers might intentionally present information that challenges your value system. One of the purposes of college is to teach you to think in new and different ways and to learn to provide support for your own beliefs. Instructors want you to think for yourself; they don't necessarily expect you to agree with everything they or your classmates say. However, if you want people to respect your values and ideas, you must show respect for theirs as well, by listening to what they have to say with an open mind.

7. **Ask questions.** Early in the term, determine whether the instructor is open to responding to questions during lecture. Some teachers prefer to save questions for the end or want students to ask questions during separate discussion sections or office hours. To some extent, this might depend on the nature and size of the class, such as a large lecture versus a small seminar. If your teacher answers questions as they arise, do not hesitate to ask if you did not hear or understand what was said. It is best to clarify things immediately, if possible, and other students are likely to have the same questions. If you can't hear another student's question or response, ask that it be repeated.

8. **Sort, organize, and categorize.** When you listen, try to match what you are hearing with what you already know. Take an active role in deciding how best to recall what you are learning.

SPEAKING UP

Naturally, you will be more likely to participate in a class in which the teacher emphasizes interactive discussion, calls on students by name, shows signs of approval and interest, and avoids criticizing students for an incorrect answer. Often, answers you and others offer that are not quite correct can lead to new perspectives on a topic.

In large classes instructors often use the lecture method, and large classes can be intimidating. If you speak up in a class of 100 and think you have made a fool of yourself, you also believe that 99 other people will know it. That's somewhat unrealistic, since you have probably asked a question that others were too timid to ask, and they'll silently thank you for doing so. If you're lucky, you might even find that the instructor takes time out to ask or answer questions. To take full advantage of these opportunities, try using the following techniques:

1. **Take a seat as close to the front as possible.** If students are seated by name and your name begins with Z, visit your professor during office hours and request to be moved up front.

2. **Keep your eyes trained on the teacher.** Sitting up front will make this easier to do.

3. **Focus on the lecture.** Do not let yourself be distracted. It might be wise not to sit near friends who can distract you.

4. **Raise your hand when you don't understand something.** The instructor might answer you immediately, ask you to wait until later in the class, or throw your question to the rest of the class. In each case, you benefit in several ways. The instructor will get to know you, other students will get to know you, and you will learn from both the instructor and your classmates. But don't overdo it. The instructor and your peers will tire of too many questions that disrupt the flow of the class.

5. **Speak up in class.** Ask a question or volunteer to answer a question or make a comment. This becomes easier every time you do it.

6. **Never feel that you're asking a stupid question.** If you don't understand something, you have a right to ask for an explanation.

7. **When the instructor calls on you to answer a question, don't bluff.** If you know the answer, give it. If you're not certain, begin with, "I think . . . , but I'm not sure I have it all correct." If you don't know, just say so.

YOUR TURN ▶

Is it hard or easy for you to raise your hand and ask questions in most of your classes? Why? How can you become more involved?

---

8. **If you have recently read a book or article that is relevant to the class topic, bring it in.** Use it either to ask questions about the topic or to provide information that was not covered in class.

Taking Effective Notes

What are "effective notes"? They are notes that cover all the important points of the lecture or reading material without being too detailed or too limited. Most important, effective notes prepare you to do well on quizzes or exams. Becoming an effective note-taker takes time and practice, but this skill will help you improve your learning and your grades in the first year and beyond.

NOTE-TAKING FORMATS

You can make class time more productive by using your listening skills to take effective lecture notes, but first you have to decide on a system. Any system can work as long as you use it consistently.

Cornell Format. Using the Cornell format, one of the best-known methods for organizing notes, you create a "recall" column on each page of your notebook by drawing a vertical line about two to three inches from the left border (see Figure 6.1). As you take notes during lecture—whether writing down ideas, making lists, or using an outline or paragraph format—write only in the wider column on the right; leave the recall column on the left blank. (If you have large handwriting and this method seems unwieldy, consider using the back of the previous notebook page for your recall column.) The recall column is the place where you write down the main ideas and important details for tests and examinations as you sift through your notes as soon after class as is feasible, preferably within an hour or two. Many students have

FIGURE 6.1 ▶

Note-taking in the Cornell Format

> Psychology 101, 1/31/09
> Theories of Personality
>
> **Personality trait: define**
> Personality trait = "durable disposition to behave in a particular way in a variety of situations"
>
> **Big 5: Name + describe them**
> Big 5 – McCrae + Costa – (1)extroversion, (or positive emotionality)=outgoing, sociable, friendly, upbeat, assertive.; (2) neuroticism=anxious, hostile, self-conscious, insecure, vulnerable; (3)openness to experience=curiosity, flexibility, imaginative.; (4) agreeableness=sympathetic, trusting, cooperative, modest; (5)conscientiousness=diligent, disciplined, well organized, punctual, dependable
>
> **Psychodynamic Theories: Who?**
> Psychodynamic Theories–focus on unconscious forces
> Freud–psychoanalysis–3 components of personality–(1)id=primitive, instinctive, operates according to pleasure principle (immediate gratification);
>
> **3 components of personality: name and describe**
> (2)ego=decision-making component, operates according to reality principle (delay gratification until appropriate); (3)superego=moral component, social standards, right + wrong
>
> **3 levels of awareness: name and describe**
> 3 levels of awareness–(1) conscious=what one is aware of at a particular moment; (2)preconscious=material just below surface, easily retrieved; (3)unconscious=thoughts, memories, + desires well below surface, but have great influence on behavior

found the recall column to be a critical part of effective note-taking, one that becomes an important study device for tests and exams.

Outline Format. Some students find that an outline is the best way for them to organize their notes. You probably already know what a formal outline looks like, with key ideas represented by Roman numerals and other ideas relating to each key idea represented in order by uppercase letters, numbers, and lowercase letters. If you use this approach, try to determine the instructor's outline and recreate it in your notes. Add details, definitions, examples, applications, and explanations (see Figures 6.2 and 6.5).

Paragraph Format. You might decide to write summary paragraphs when you are taking notes on what you are reading. This method might not work as well for class notes because it's difficult to summarize a topic until your instructor has covered it completely. By the end of the lecture, you might have forgotten critical information (see Figures 6.3 and 6.5).

Psychology 101, 1/31/09: Theories of Personality

I. Personality trait = "durable disposition to behave in a particular way in a variety of situations"
II. Big 5-McCrae + Costa
   A. Extroversion, (or positive emotionality)=outgoing, sociable, friendly, upbeat, assertive
   B. Neuroticism=anxious, hostile, self-conscious, insecure, vulnerable
   C. Openness to experience=curiosity, flexibility, imaginative
   D. Agreeableness=sympathetic, trusting, cooperative, modest
   E. Conscientiousness=diligent, disciplined, well organized, punctual, dependable
III. Psychodynamic Theories-focus on unconscious forces-- Freud-psychoanalysis
   A. 3 components of personality
     1. Id=primitive, instinctive, operates according to pleasure principle (immediate gratification)
     2. Ego=decision-making component, operates according to reality principle (delay gratification until appropriate)
     3. Superego=moral component, social standards, right + wrong
   B. 3 levels of awareness
     1. Conscious=what one is aware of at a particular moment
     2. Preconscious=material just below surface, easily retrieved
     3. Unconscious=thoughts, memories, + desires well below surface, but have great influence on behavior

◄ **FIGURE 6.2**

Note-taking in the Outline Format

Psychology 101, 1/31/09: Theories of Personality

A personality trait is a "durable disposition to behave in a particular way in a variety of situations"

Big 5: According to McCrae + Costa most personality traits derive from just 5 higher-order traits: extroversion (or positive emotionality), which is outgoing, sociable, friendly, upbeat, assertive,; neuroticism, which means anxious, hostile, self-conscious, insecure, vulnerable; openness to experience characterized by curiosity, flexibility, imaginative,; agreeableness, which is sympathetic, trusting, cooperative, modest; and conscientiousness, means diligent, disciplined, well organized, punctual, dependable

Psychodynamic Theories: Focus on unconscious forces

Freud, father of psychoanalysis, believed in 3 components of personality: id, the primitive, instinctive, operates according to pleasure principle (immediate gratification); ego, the decision-making component, operates according to reality principle (delay gratification until appropriate); and superego, the moral component, social standards, right + wrong

Freud also thought there are 3 levels of awareness: conscious, what one is aware of at a particular moment; preconscious, the material just below surface, easily retrieved; and unconscious, the thoughts, memories, + desires well below surface, but have great influence on behavior

FIGURE 6.3 ▶

Note-taking in the Paragraph Format

List Format. This format can be effective in taking notes on lists of terms and definitions, facts, or sequences, such as the body's pulmonary system. It is easy to use lists in combination with the Cornell format, with key terms on the left and their definitions and explanations on the right (see Figure 6.4).

Once you have decided on a format for taking notes, you might also want to develop your own system of abbreviations. For example, you might write "inst" instead of "institution" or "eval" instead of "evaluation." Just make sure you will be able to understand your abbreviations when it's time to review.

YOUR TURN ▶

Which of these four note-taking methods (Cornell, outline, paragraph, list) is most like the one you use? How well does your current system work for you? Explain your answer. What changes will you make in how you take notes now that you have read this portion of the chapter?

Psychology 101, 1/31/09: Theories of Personality

- A personality trait is a "durable disposition to behave in a particular way in a variety of situations"
- Big 5: According to McCrae + Costa most personality traits derive from just 5 higher-order traits
    - extroversion, (or positive emotionality)=outgoing, sociable, friendly, upbeat, assertive
    - neuroticism=anxious, hostile, self-conscious, insecure, vulnerable
    - openness to experience=curiosity, flexibility, imaginative
    - agreeableness=sympathetic, trusting, cooperative, modest
    - conscientiousness=diligent, disciplined, well organized, punctual, dependable
- Psychodynamic Theories: Focus on unconscious forces
- Freud, father of psychoanalysis, believed in 3 components of personality
    - id=primitive, instinctive, operates according to pleasure principle (immediate gratification)
    - ego=decision-making component, operates according to reality principle (delay gratification until appropriate)
    - superego=moral component, social standards, right + wrong
- Freud also thought there are 3 levels of awareness
    - conscious=what one is aware of at a particular moment
    - preconscious=material just below surface, easily retrieved
    - unconscious=thoughts, memories, + desires well below surface, but have great influence on behavior

◄ **FIGURE 6.4**

Note-taking in the List Format

NOTE-TAKING TECHNIQUES

Whatever note-taking system you choose, follow these important steps:

1. **Identify the main ideas.** Well-organized lectures always contain key points. The first principle of effective note-taking is to identify and write down the most important ideas around which the lecture is built. Although supporting details are important as well, focus your note-taking on the main ideas. Such ideas can be buried in details, statistics, anecdotes, or problems, but you will need to identify and record them for further study.

   Some instructors announce the purpose of a lecture or offer an outline, thus providing you with the skeleton of main ideas, followed by the details. Other instructors develop PowerPoint presentations. If they make these materials available on a class website before the lecture, you can print them and take notes on the teacher's outline or next to the PowerPoint slides.

Personality trait	I. Personality trait = "durable disposition to behave in a particular way in a variety of situations"
	II. Big 5-McCrae + Costa
Big 5: Who? Name + describe them	A. Extroversion, (or positive emotionality)=outgoing, sociable, friendly, upbeat, assertive
	B. Neuroticism=anxious, hostile, self-conscious, insecure, vulnerable
	C. Openness to experience=curiosity, flexibility, imaginative
	D. Agreeableness=sympathetic, trusting, cooperative, modest
	E. Conscientiousness=diligent, disciplined, well organized, punctual, dependable
	III. Psychodynamic Theories-focus on unconscious forces-- Freud-psychoanalysis
Psychodynamic Theories: Who? 3 components. Name, define, relate each to a principle	A. 3 components of personality
	1. Id=primitive, instinctive, operates according to pleasure principle (immediate gratification)
	2. Ego=decision-making component, operates according to reality principle (delay gratification until appropriate)
	3. Superego=moral component, social standards, right + wrong
	B. 3 levels of awareness
	1. conscious=what one is aware of at a particular moment
3 levels of awareness: name and describe	2. preconscious=material just below surface, easily retrieved
	3. unconscious=thoughts, memories, + desires well below surface, but have great influence on behavior

FIGURE 6.5 ▶

Cornell Format combined with Outline Format

Some lecturers change their tone of voice or repeat themselves for each key idea. Some ask questions or promote discussion. If a lecturer says something more than once, chances are it is important. Ask yourself, "What does my instructor want me to know at the end of today's class?"

2. **Don't try to write down everything.** Some first-year students try to do just that. They stop being thinkers and become stenographers. As you take notes, leave spaces so that you can fill in additional details that you might have missed during class but remember later. Take the time to review and complete your notes as soon after class as possible.

3. **Don't be thrown by a disorganized lecturer.** When a lecture is disorganized, it's your job to try to organize what is said into general and specific frameworks. When the order is not apparent, you will need to indicate in your notes where the gaps lie. After the lecture, consult the reading material or classmates to fill in these gaps, or ask your instructor. Most instructors

have regular office hours for student appointments, yet it is amazing how few students use these opportunities for one-on-one instruction. Asking questions can help your instructor find out which parts of the lecture need more attention and clarification.

4. **Keep your notes and supplementary materials for each course in a separate three-ring binder.** Label the binder with the course number and name. If the binders are too bulky to carry in your backpack, create a separate folder for each class, stocked with loose-leaf notebook paper. Before class, label and date the paper you will be using for taking notes. Then, as soon after class as possible, move your notes from the folder to the binder.

5. **Download any notes, outlines, or diagrams, charts, graphs, and other visuals** from the instructor's website before class and bring them with you. You might be able to save yourself considerable time during the lecture if you do not have to try to copy complicated graphs and diagrams while the instructor is talking. Instead, you can focus on the ideas being presented while adding your own labels and notes to the visual images.

6. **Organize your notes chronologically in your binder.** Then create separate tabbed sections for homework, lab assignments, returned tests, and other materials.

7. **If handouts are distributed in class, label them and place them in your binder** near the notes for that day. Buy a portable three-ring hole-punch that can be kept in your binder. Do not let handouts accumulate in your folders; add any handouts to your binders as you review your notes each day.

Taking Notes in Nonlecture Courses. Always be ready to adapt your note-taking methods to match the situation. Group discussion is becoming a popular way to teach in college because it engages students in active participation. On your campus you might also have **Supplemental Instruction** (SI) classes that provide further opportunity to discuss the information presented in lectures. How do you keep a record of what's happening in such classes? Assume you are taking notes in a problem-solving group assignment. You would begin your notes by asking yourself, "What is the problem?" and writing down the answer. As the discussion progresses, you would list the solutions that are offered. These would be your main ideas. The important details might include the positive and negative aspects of each view or solution. The important thing to remember when taking notes in nonlecture courses is that you need to record the information presented by your classmates as well as by the instructor and to consider all reasonable ideas, even though they might differ from your own.

When a course has separate lecture and discussion sessions, you will need to understand how the discussion sessions relate to and augment the lectures. If different material is covered in lecture or discussion, you might need to ask for guidance in organizing your notes. When similar topics are covered, you can combine your notes so that you have comprehensive, unified coverage of each topic.

How to organize the notes you take in a class discussion depends on the purpose or form of the discussion. It usually makes good sense to begin with the list of issues or topics that the discussion leader announces. Another approach is to list the questions that participants raise for discussion. If the discussion explores reasons for and against a particular argument, divide your notes into columns or sections for pros and cons. When conflicting views are presented in discussion, record different perspectives and the rationales behind them. Your teacher might ask you to defend your own opinions in light of those of other students.

Taking Notes in Science and Mathematics Courses. Many mathematics and science courses build on each other from term to term and from year to year. When you take notes in these courses, you will likely need to refer to them in the future. For example, when taking organic chemistry, you might need to refer to notes taken in earlier chemistry courses. This can be particularly important when time has passed since your last related course, such as after a summer break. Taking notes in math and science courses can be different from taking notes in other types of classes. Here are some tips to keep in mind specifically when taking notes in quantitative and scientific classes.

TIPS FOR NOTE-TAKING IN QUANTITATIVE AND SCIENCE CLASSES

- Write down any equations, formulas, diagrams, charts, graphs, and definitions that the instructor puts on the board or screen.
- Quote the instructor's words as precisely as possible. Technical terms often have exact meanings and cannot be paraphrased.
- Use standard symbols, abbreviations, and scientific notation.
- Write down all worked problems and examples, step by step. They often provide the template for exam questions. Actively engage in solving the problem yourself as it is being solved at the front of the class. Be sure that you can follow the logic and understand the sequence of steps. If you have questions you cannot ask during lecture, write them down in your notes so that you can ask them in discussion, in the lab, or during the instructor's office hours.
- Consider taking your notes in pencil or erasable pen. You will probably need to use an eraser or make changes in your notes when copying long equations while also trying to pay attention to the instructor or when you copy problems that other students are solving at the board. You want to keep your notes as neat as possible. Later, you can use colored ink to add other details.
- Listen carefully to other students' questions and the instructor's answers. Take notes on the discussion and during question-and-answer periods.
- Use asterisks, exclamation points, question marks, or symbols of your own to highlight important points in your notes or questions that you need to come back to when you review.
- Refer back to the textbook after class; the text might contain more accurate diagrams and other visual representations than you can draw while taking notes in class. If they are not provided in handouts or on the instructor's website, you might even want to scan or photocopy diagrams from the text and include them with your notes in your binder.
- Keep your binders for math and science courses until you graduate (or even longer if there is any chance that you will attend graduate school at some point in the future). They will serve as beneficial review materials for later classes in math and science and for preparing for standardized tests such as the Graduate Record Exam (GRE) or Medical College Admission Test (MCAT). In some cases, these notes can also prove helpful in the workplace.

Using Technology to Take Notes. While some students use laptops for note-taking, others prefer taking notes by hand so they can easily circle important items or copy complex equations or diagrams while these are being presented. If you handwrite your notes, entering them on a computer after class for review purposes might be helpful, especially if you are a kinesthetic learner. After class you can also cut and paste diagrams and other visual representations into your notes and print a copy that might be easier to read than notes you wrote by hand.

Some students, especially aural learners, find it is advantageous to record lectures. But if you record, resist the temptation to become passive in class instead of actively listening. Students with specific types of disabilities might be urged to record lectures or use the services of note-takers who type on a laptop while the student views the notes on a separate screen.

Wired WINDOW

TECHNOLOGY TO HELP YOU TAKE NOTES

You will discover many options for using technology to enhance your note-taking skills and your engagement with learning. Some students prefer to bring their laptops to class and either type their notes or use the tablet feature to handwrite their notes into digital files. We think it's important to strike a balance between taking notes on your computer and paying attention to class discussion. Most students can't type as quickly as they can write and will need to be very selective about the information they choose to enter on a computer, so you might face a greater challenge extracting the most important points of the lecture or discussion while it is happening. Evernote (evernote.com), a free service, allows you to take pictures of documents, including PowerPoint presentations, whiteboard notes, and overheads, using your cell phone and have these converted to digital documents automatically. If you choose to use such a service, make sure you have obtained permission from your professors to reproduce their notes. Evernote has a useful web interface and offers a free desktop application that

allows you to search for text within your notes. Using the web interface or the application, you can organize your notes in "notebooks" (it is helpful to keep a notebook for each of your courses). With Evernote, you don't have to worry about making sure that you copy every detail from your professor's notes, and you can stay focused on the topic being discussed.

Think Critically

What note-taking method do you prefer (notebook, laptop, Evernote, recorder)? Why is this method effective for you? What are some adjustments that you can make to your preferred method to enhance your note-taking success? One example, if you use your laptop to take notes, might be finding a better way to organize your files on your computer so they are easier to find. What are some other examples? If you have never used a service such as Evernote before, think about whether this kind of service would be helpful to you. In what ways would it help? In what ways might it detract from your learning?

Reviewing Your Notes

Most forgetting takes place within the first twenty-four hours of encountering the information, a phenomenon known as "the forgetting curve." So if you do not review your notes almost immediately after class, it can be difficult to retrieve the material later. In two weeks, you will have forgotten up to 70 percent of it! Forgetting can be a serious problem when you are expected to learn and remember many different facts, figures, concepts, and relationships for a number of classes. Once you understand how to improve your ability to remember, you will retain information more easily and completely. Retaining information will help your overall understanding as well as your ability to recall important details during exams.

Don't let the forgetting curve take its toll on you. As soon after class as possible, review your notes and fill in the details you still remember but missed writing down. One way to remember is to recite important data to yourself every few minutes. If you are an aural learner, you might want to repeat your notes out loud. Another idea is to tie one idea to another idea, concept, or name so that thinking of one will prompt recall of the other. Or you might want to create your own poem, song, or slogan using the information.

For interactive learners, the best way to learn something might be to teach it to someone else. You will understand something better and remember it longer if you try to explain it. This helps you discover your own reactions and uncover gaps in your comprehension of the material. (Asking and answering questions in class can also provide you with the feedback you need to make certain your understanding is accurate.) Now you're ready to embed the major points from your notes in your memory. Use the following three important steps for remembering the key points from the lecture.

These three ways to engage with the material will pay off later, when you begin to study for your exams.

KEYS TO REMEMBERING

1. **Write down the main ideas.** For five or ten minutes, quickly review your notes and select key words or phrases that will act as labels or tags for main ideas and key information in your notes.

2. **Recite your ideas out loud.** Recite a brief version of what you understand from the class. If you don't have a few minutes after class when you can concentrate on reviewing your notes, find some other time during that same day to review what you have written. You might also want to ask your instructor to glance at your notes to determine whether you have identified the major ideas.

3. **Review your notes from the previous class just before the next class session.** As you sit in class the next time it meets, waiting for the lecture to begin, use the time to quickly review your notes from the previous class session. This will put you in tune with the lecture that is about to begin and prompt you to ask questions about material from the previous lecture that might not have been clear to you.

What if you have three classes in a row and no time for studying between them? Recall and recite as soon after class as possible. Review the most recent class first. Never delay recall and recitation longer than one day; if you do, it will take you longer to review, select main ideas, and recite. With practice, you can complete the review of your main ideas from your notes quickly, perhaps between classes, during lunch, or while riding the bus.

COMPARING NOTES

You might be able to improve your notes by comparing notes with another student or in a study group, Supplemental Instruction session, or a learning community, if one is available to you. Knowing that your notes will be seen by someone else will prompt you to make your notes well organized, clear, and accurate. Compare your notes: Are they as clear and concise as those of other students'? Do you agree on the most important points? Share with each other how you take and organize your notes. You might get new ideas for using abbreviations. Take turns testing each other on what you have learned. This will help you predict exam questions and determine whether you can answer them. Comparing notes is not the same as copying somebody else's notes. You simply cannot learn as well from someone else's notes, no matter how good they are, if you have not attended class.

If your campus has a note-taking service, check with your instructor about making use of this for-pay service, but keep in mind that such notes are intended to supplement the ones you take, not to substitute for them. Some students choose to copy their own notes as a means of review or because they think their notes are messy and that they will not be able to understand them later. Unless you are a tactile learner, copying or typing your notes might not help you learn the material. A more profitable approach might be to summarize your notes in your own words.

Finally, have a backup plan in case you need to be absent because of illness or a family emergency. Exchange phone numbers and e-mail addresses with other students so that you can contact one of them to learn what you missed and get a copy of their notes. Also contact your instructor to explain your absence and set up an appointment during office hours to make sure you understand the work you missed.

CLASS NOTES AND HOMEWORK

Good class notes can help you complete homework assignments. Follow these steps:

1. **Take ten minutes to review your notes.** Skim the notes, and put a question mark next to anything you do not understand at first reading. Draw stars next to topics that warrant special emphasis. Try to place the material in context: What has been going on in the course for the past few weeks? How does today's class fit in?

2. **Do a warm-up for your homework.** Before doing the assignment, look through your notes again. Use a separate sheet of paper to rework examples, problems, or exercises. If there is related assigned material in the textbook, review it. Go back to the examples. Cover the solution, and attempt to answer each question or complete each problem. Look at the author's work only after you have made a serious effort to remember it. Keep in mind that it can help to go back through your course notes, reorganize them, highlight the essential items, and thus create new notes that let you connect with the material one more time and could be better than the originals.

3. **Do any assigned problems, and answer any assigned questions.** When you start doing your homework, read each question or problem and ask: What am I supposed to find or find out? What is essential and what is extraneous? Read each problem several times, and state it in your own words. Work the problem without referring to your notes or the text, as though you were taking a test. In this way, you will test your knowledge and know when you are prepared for exams.

4. **Persevere.** Don't give up too soon. When you encounter a problem or question that you cannot readily handle, move on only after a reasonable effort. After you have completed the entire assignment, come back to any items that stumped you. Try once more, and then take a break. You might need to mull over a particularly difficult problem for several days. Let your unconscious mind have a chance. Inspiration might come when you are waiting at a stoplight or just before you fall asleep.

5. **Complete your work.** When you finish an assignment, talk to yourself about what you learned from it. Think about how the problems and questions were different from one another, which strategies were successful, and what form the answers took. Be sure to review any material you have not mastered. Seek assistance from the instructor, a classmate, a study group, the campus learning center, or a tutor to learn how to answer questions that stumped you.

YOUR TURN ▶

What is your reaction to these suggestions about taking notes and studying for class? Which ideas will you implement in your note-taking strategies? Why? Do you think they have the potential to help you earn better grades? If so, in what way?

Becoming Engaged in Learning

No matter how good your listening and note-taking techniques are, you will not get the most out of college unless you become an engaged learner. Engaged students devote the time and the energy necessary to develop a real love of learning, both in and out of class.

Although you might acquire knowledge by listening to a lecture, you might not be motivated to think about what that knowledge means to you.

When you are actively engaged in learning, you will learn not only the material in your notes and textbooks, but also how to:

- Work with others
- Improve your critical thinking, listening, writing, and speaking skills
- Function independently and teach yourself
- Manage your time
- Gain sensitivity to cultural differences

Engagement in learning requires that you be a full and active participant in the learning process. Your instructors will set the stage and provide valuable information, but it's up to you to do the rest. Your college experience will be most rewarding if you take advantage of the resources your college offers, including the library, cultural events, the faculty, and other students. This approach to learning has the potential to make you well rounded in all aspects of life. The hexagon in Figure 6.6 depicts seven aspects of development, with intellectual development at its center. Optimal development depends on each area supporting every other area.

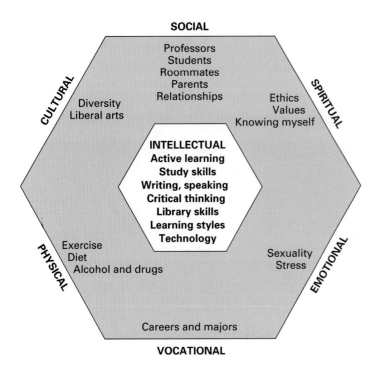

▲ **FIGURE 6.6**

Aspects of Student Development

OTHER TIPS FOR ENGAGEMENT

- Before choosing a class, ask friends which instructors encourage active learning.
- Go beyond the required reading. Investigate other information sources in the library or on the Internet.
- If you disagree with what your instructor says, politely offer your opinion. Most instructors will listen. They might still disagree with you, but they might also think more of you for showing you can think independently.
- Interact with professors, staff members, and other students. One easy way is through e-mail. Some professors offer first-year students the opportunity to collaborate in research projects and service activities. You will also find many opportunities to become involved in campus organizations. Getting involved in out-of-class opportunities will help you develop relationships with others on campus.
- Use Facebook to connect with other students and with campus activities and groups. Join in discussions that are happening in those groups.

Where to go FOR HELP . . .

ON CAMPUS ▶

Learning Assistance Center   Almost every campus has one of these, and this chapter's topic is one of their specialties. More and more, the best students—and good students who want to be better students—use learning centers as much as students who are having academic difficulties. Services at learning centers are offered by both full-time professionals and highly skilled student tutors.

Fellow College Students   Often, the best help we can get comes from those who are closest to us: fellow students. Keep an eye out in your classes, residence hall, co-curricular groups, and other places for the most serious, purposeful, and directed students. Those are the ones to seek out. Find a tutor. Join a study group. Students who do these things are most likely to stay in college and be successful. It does not diminish you in any way to seek assistance from your peers.

ONLINE ▶

Toastmasters International offers public speaking tips at http://www.toastmasters.org.

See guidelines for speaking in class at http://www.school-for-champions.com/grades/speaking.htm.

MY INSTITUTION'S RESOURCES ▶

_____

_____

_____

_____

_____

_____

_____

_____

_____

_____

_____

_____

_____

_____

_____

_____

6 Chapter REVIEW...

One-Minute PAPER...

This chapter explores multiple strategies for being an effective listener and being engaged in class. What new strategies did you learn that you had never thought about or used before? What questions about effective note-taking do you still have?

Applying What You've LEARNED...

Now that you have read and discussed this chapter, consider how you can apply what you have learned to your academic and personal life. The following prompts will help you to reflect on chapter material and its relevance to you both now and in the future.

1. Review the "Using Your Senses in the Learning Process" section of this chapter. Which modes of learning seem to work best for you? If you are not an aural learner, how can you use your preferred ways of learning to master the information that is presented in lecture-style courses? Brainstorm ways to convert lecture material into a format that is a better match for how you best use your five senses in the learning process.

2. Making an intentional effort to learn is not easy. As you try the suggestions in this chapter, consider ways in which you can encourage yourself to keep up the hard work. For example, if you have a big project, try breaking it up into several smaller pieces. As you complete each piece, reward yourself by hanging out with friends or taking time to do something you enjoy.

Building Your PORTFOLIO...

    66 It is important that students bring a certain ragamuffin, barefoot irreverence to their studies; they are not here to worship what is known, but to question it. **99**

– JACOB BRONOWSKI (1908-1974),
Polish–English mathematician

MAKING MEANING

Chapter 6 includes several examples of note-taking strategies, but did you catch the emphasis on what you should do with your notes after class? Sometimes it is helpful to associate a concept with an interest you have. And preparing to teach someone else how to do something or explaining a complex idea to others can help you to understand the information more fully.

    Test this idea for yourself.

1. Choose a set of current class notes (it doesn't matter which class they are from), and specifically look for connections between the subject matter and your personal interests and goals (future career, social issue, sports, hobbies, etc.).

2. Next, develop a five-minute presentation using PowerPoint that both outlines your class notes and shows the connection to your interests. Develop the presentation as though you were going to teach a group of students about the concept. Use a combination of graphics, photos, music, and video clips to help your imaginary audience to connect with the material in a new and interesting way.

3. Save the PowerPoint in your portfolio on your personal computer or flash drive. Use your PowerPoint presentation as one way to study for your next exam in that course.

You probably won't be creating PowerPoint presentations for all of your class notes, but making a habit of connecting class content to your life is an easy way to help yourself remember information. When it is time to prepare for a test, try pulling your notes into a presentation that you would feel comfortable presenting to your classmates.

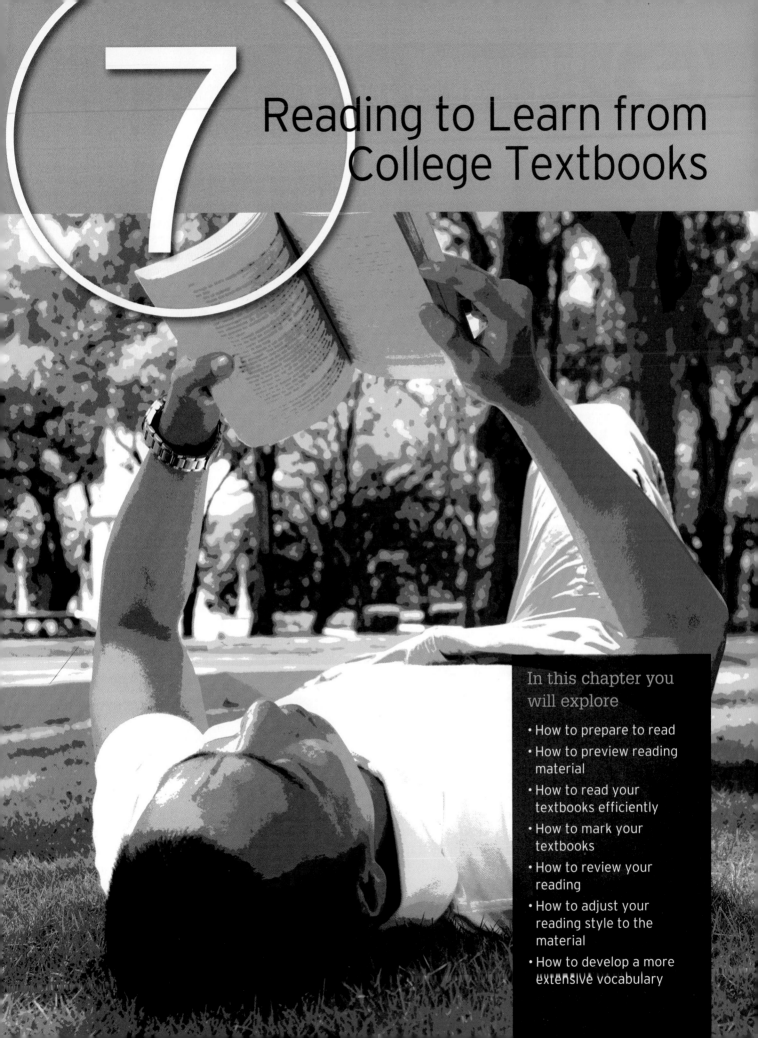

7

Reading to Learn from College Textbooks

In this chapter you will explore

- How to prepare to read
- How to preview reading material
- How to read your textbooks efficiently
- How to mark your textbooks
- How to review your reading
- How to adjust your reading style to the material
- How to develop a more extensive vocabulary

BREE SCHIPPER, 29
Kalamazoo Valley Community
College

> ❝ I'll read if I have to, when I have to, and how many times I have to, but I don't like it. ❞

I hate reading with a passion. I don't read novels or sit down and read a book for pleasure. I never have. If a book's not important to me or interesting to me, I'll read a page and not know what I just read because it's not something I enjoy. I'll continue to read if I have to, when I have to, and how many times I have to in order to understand something, but I don't really like it. I'm more right-brained, a hands-on learner. That's the way I've always been. It's something I just have to live with.

With some things, I need to go beyond reading because I might not absorb it all or I'll have to read it a couple times in order to remember what I read. Engineering and technology textbooks are different. They're more informational and have a lot of things that I want to learn about. I really enjoy looking at my computer-aided drafting books because they've got the parts in there and the dimensions and metric sizes and all that technical stuff. And I actually did read my college success strategies textbook because I was learning about myself and other kinds of people. I keep referring back to that—I have highlights in it, notes in the margins, underlines, circles, everything. Who couldn't learn more about how to study better?

Why is reading college textbooks more challenging than reading high school texts or reading for pleasure? College texts are loaded with concepts, terms, and complex information that you are expected to learn on your own in a short period of time. To accomplish all this, you will find it helpful to learn and use the active reading strategies in this chapter. They are intended to help you get the most out of your college reading.

A Plan for Active Reading

The following plan for active reading is designed to help you read college textbooks. When you read actively, you use strategies that help you stay focused. Active reading is different from readings novels or magazines for pleasure. Pleasure reading doesn't require you to annotate, highlight, or take notes. But as you read college textbooks, you'll use all these strategies and more. This plan will increase your focus and concentration, promote greater understanding of what you read, and prepare you to study for tests and exams. The four steps in active reading are

1. Previewing
2. Marking
3. Reading with Concentration
4. Reviewing

YOUR TURN ▶

Which of these four steps do you always, sometimes, or never do? Do any of them seem unnecessary? If so, why? After you read this chapter, go back and see whether you have changed your mind.

PREVIEWING

The purpose of previewing is to get the big picture, that is, to understand how what you are about to read connects with what you already know and to the material the instructor covers in class. Begin by reading the title of the chapter. Ask yourself: What do I already know about this subject? Next, quickly read through the introductory paragraphs. Then read the summary at the beginning or end of the chapter if there is one. Finally, take a few minutes to skim the chapter, looking at the headings and subheadings. Note any study exercises at the end of the chapter.

As part of your preview, note how many pages the chapter contains. It's a good idea to decide in advance how many pages you can reasonably expect to cover in your first study period. This can help build your concentration as you work toward your goal of reading a specific number of pages. Before long, you'll know how many pages are practical for you.

Keep in mind that different types of textbooks can require more or less time to read. For example, depending on your interests and previous knowledge, you might be able to read a psychology text more quickly than a logic text that presents a whole new symbol system.

Mapping. Mapping the chapter as you preview it provides a visual guide for how different chapter ideas fit together. Because many students identify themselves as visual learners, visual mapping is an excellent learning tool for test preparation, as well as reading (see chapter 4, Discovering How You Learn). To map a chapter, use either a wheel structure or a branching structure as you preview the chapter (see Figure 7.1). In the wheel structure, place the central idea of the chapter in the circle. The central idea should be in the introduction to the chapter and might be apparent in the chapter title. Place secondary ideas on the spokes emanating from the circle, and place offshoots of those ideas on the lines attached to the spokes. In the branching map, the main idea goes at the top, followed by supporting ideas on the second tier and so forth. Fill in the title first. Then, as you skim the chapter, use the headings and subheadings to fill in the key ideas.

Alternatives to Mapping. Perhaps you prefer a more linear visual image. If so, consider making an outline of the headings and subheadings in the chapter. You can fill in the outline after you read. Alternatively, make a list. A list can be particularly effective when you are dealing with a text that introduces many new terms and their definitions. Set up the list with the terms in the left column, and fill in definitions, descriptions, and examples on the right after you read. Divide the terms on your list into groups of

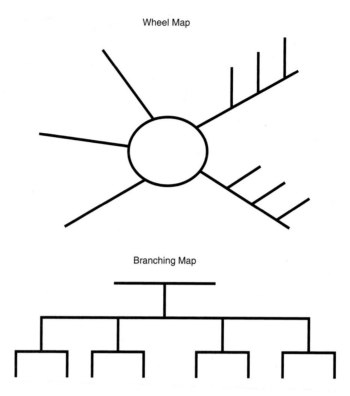

FIGURE 7.1 ▶

Wheel and Branching Maps

five, seven, or nine, and leave white space between the clusters so that you can visualize each group in your mind. This practice is known as **chunking**. Research indicates that we learn material best when it is in chunks of five, seven, or nine.

If you are an interactive learner, make lists or create a flash card for each heading and subheading. Then fill in the back of each card after reading each section in the text. Use the lists or flash cards to review with a partner, or recite the material to yourself.

Previewing, combined with mapping, outlining, or flash cards, might require more time up front, but it will save you time later because you will have created an excellent review tool for quizzes and tests. You will be using your visual learning skills as you create advanced organizers to help you associate details of the chapter with the larger ideas. Such associations will come in handy later. As you preview the text material, look for connections between the text and the related lecture material. Call to mind the related terms and concepts that you recorded in the lecture. Use these strategies to warm up. Ask yourself: Why am I reading this? What do I want to know?

MARKING YOUR TEXTBOOK

After completing your preview, you are ready to read the text actively. With your skeleton map or outline, you should be able to read more quickly and with greater comprehension. To avoid marking too much or marking the wrong information, first read without using your pencil or highlighter.

Think a moment about your goals for making marks in your own texts. Some students report that **marking** is an active reading strategy that helps them to focus and concentrate on the material as they read. In addition, most students expect to use their text notations when they study for tests. To meet these goals, some students like to underline, some prefer to highlight, and others use margin notes or annotations. Figure 7.2 provides an example of each method. No matter what method you prefer, remember these two important guidelines:

1. **Read before you mark.** Finish reading a section before you decide which are the most important ideas and concepts. Mark only those particular ideas, using your preferred methods (highlighting, underlining, circling key terms, annotating).
2. **Think before you mark.** When you read a text for the first time, everything can seem important. Only after you have completed a section and have reflected on it will you be ready to identify the key ideas. Ask yourself: What are the most important ideas? What will I see on the test? This can help you avoid marking too much material.

Two other considerations might affect your decisions about textbook marking. First, if you just make notes or underline directly on the pages of your textbook, you are committing yourself to at least one more viewing of all the pages that you have already read—all or most pages of your anatomy or art history textbook, for instance. A more productive use of your time might be taking notes, creating flash cards, making lists, or outlining textbook chapters. These methods are also more practical if you intend to review with a friend or study group.

Second, sometimes highlighting or underlining can provide you with a false sense of security. You might have determined what is most important, but you have not necessarily tested yourself on your understanding of the material. When you force yourself to put something in your own words while taking notes, you are not only predicting exam questions but also assessing whether you can answer them. Although these active reading strategies take more time initially, they can save you time in the long run because they not only promote concentration as you read but also make it easy to review. If you can use these strategies effectively, you probably won't have to pull an all-nighter before an exam.

READING WITH CONCENTRATION

Students commonly have trouble concentrating or understanding the content when they read textbooks. Many factors can affect your ability to concentrate and understand texts: the time of day, your energy level, your interest in the material, and your study location.

Consider these suggestions, and decide which would help you improve your reading ability:

- Find a study location that is removed from traffic and distracting noises such as the campus library. Turn off your cell phone's ringer, and store the phone in your purse or book bag (someplace where you can't easily feel it vibrating). If you are reading an electronic document on your computer, download the information that you need and disconnect from the network to keep you from easily going online and chatting, e-mailing, or using Facebook or MySpace.

CULTURE AND HUMAN BEHAVIOR 12.1

The Stress of Adapting to a New Culture

differences affecting cultural stress

Refugees and immigrants are often unprepared for the dramatically different values, language, food, customs, and climate that await them in their new land. Coping with a new culture can be extremely stress-producing (Johnson & others, 1995). The process of changing one's values and customs as a result of contact with another culture is referred to as *acculturation.* Thus, the term **acculturative stress** describes the stress that results from the pressure of adapting to a new culture (Berry, 1994, 2003).

acceptance of new culture reduces stress also speaking new language, education, & social support

Many factors can influence the degree of acculturative stress that a person experiences. For example, when the new society is one that accepts ethnic and cultural diversity, acculturative stress is reduced (Shuval, 1993). The ease of transition is also enhanced when the person has some familiarity with the new language and customs, advanced education, and social support from friends, family members, and cultural associations (Finch & Vega, 2003).

how attitudes affect stress

Cross-cultural psychologist John Berry has found that a person's *attitudes* are important in determining how much acculturative stress is experienced. When people encounter a new cultural environment, they are faced with two fundamental questions: (1) Should I seek positive relations with the dominant society? (2) Is my original cultural identity of value to me, and should I try to maintain it?

4 patterns of acculturation

The answers to these questions result in one of four possible patterns of acculturation: integration, assimilation, separation, or marginalization (see the diagram). Each pattern represents a different way of cop-

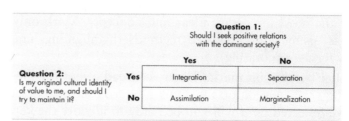

	Question 1: Should I seek positive relations with the dominant society?	
	Yes	**No**
Question 2: Is my original cultural identity of value to me, and should I try to maintain it? **Yes**	Integration	Separation
No	Assimilation	Marginalization

Patterns of Adapting to a New Culture According to cross-cultural psychologist John Berry (1994, 2003), there are four basic patterns of adapting to a new culture. Which pattern is followed depends on how the person responds to the two key questions shown.

ing with the stress of adapting to a new culture (Berry, 1994, 2003).

1* *Integrated* individuals continue to value their original cultural customs but also seek to become part of the dominant society. Ideally, the integrated individual feels *comfortable* in both her culture of origin and the culture of the dominant society, moving easily from one to the other (LaFromboise, Coleman, & Gerton, 1993). The successfully integrated individual's level of acculturative stress will be low (Ward & Rana-Deuba, 1999).

2* *Assimilated* individuals give up their old cultural identity and try to become part of the new society. They may adopt the new clothing, religion, and social values of the new environemnt and *abandon* their old customs and language.

Assimilation usually involves a moderate level of stress, partly because it involves psychological loss—one's previous cultural identity. People who follow this pattern also

possible rejection by both cultures

face the possibility of being rejected either by members of the majority culture or by members of their original culture (LaFromboise & others, 1993). The process of learning new behaviors and suppressing old behaviors can also be moderately stressful.

*separation may be self-imposed or discriminating

3* Individuals who follow the pattern of *separation* maintain their cultural identity and avoid contact with the new culture. They may refuse to learn the new language, live in a neighborhood that is primarily populated by others of the same ethnic background, and socialize only with members of their own ethnic group.

higher stress with separation

In some instances, such withdrawal from the larger society is self-imposed. However, separation can also be the result of discrimination by the dominant society, as when people of a particular ethnic group are discouraged from fully participating in the dominant society. Not surprisingly, the level of acculturative stress associated with separation is likely to be very high.

4* Finally, the *marginalized* person lacks cultural and psychological contact with *both* his traditional cultural group and the culture of his new society. By taking the path of marginalization, he has lost the important features of his traditional culture but has not replaced them with a new cultural identity.

*marginalized = higher level of stress

Marginalized individuals are likely to experience the greatest degree of acculturative stress, feeling as if they don't really belong anywhere. Essentially, they are stuck in an unresolved conflict between the traditional culture and the new social environment. They are also likely to experience feelings of alienation and a loss of identity (Berry & Kim, 1988).

Acculturative Stress As this Sikh family crossing a busy street in Chicago has discovered, adapting to a new culture can be a stressful process. What factors can make the transition less stressful? How can the acculturation process be eased?

▲ FIGURE 7.2

Using a combination of highlighting, lines, and marginal notes, the reader has boiled down the content of this page for easy review. Without reading the text, note the highlighted words and phrases and the marginal notes, and see how much information you can gather from them. Then read the text itself. Does the markup serve as a study aid? Does it cover the essential points? Would you have marked this page any differently? Why or why not?

- Read in blocks of time, with short breaks in between. Some students can read for fifty minutes; others find that a fifty-minute reading period is too long. By reading for small blocks of time throughout the day instead of cramming in all your reading at the end of the day, you should be able to process material more easily.

- Set goals for your study period, such as "I will read twenty pages of my psychology text in the next fifty minutes." Reward yourself with a ten-minute break after each fifty-minute study period.

- If you have trouble concentrating or staying awake, take a quick walk around the library or down the hall. Stretch or take some deep breaths, and think positively about your study goals. Then resume studying.

- Jot study questions in the margins, take notes, or recite key ideas. Reread confusing parts of the text, and make a note to ask your instructor for clarification.

- Focus on the important portions of the text. Pay attention to the first and last sentences of paragraphs and to words in italics or bold print.

- Use the glossary in the text or a dictionary to define unfamiliar terms.

YOUR TURN ▶

Do you have trouble concentrating while you read your textbooks? What strategies do you use to make sure that your mind doesn't wander?

REVIEWING

The final step in active textbook reading is reviewing. Many students expect to read through their text material once and be able to remember the ideas four, six, or even twelve weeks later at test time. More realistically, you will need to include regular reviews in your study process. Here is where your notes, study questions, annotations, flash cards, visual maps, or outlines will be most useful. Your study goal should be to review the material from each chapter every week.

Consider ways to use your many senses to review. Recite aloud. Tick off each item in a list on each of your fingertips. Post diagrams, maps, or outlines around your living space so that you will see them often and will likely be able to visualize them while taking the test.

Strategies for Reading Textbooks

As you begin reading, be sure to learn more about the textbook and its author by reading the front matter in the book, such as the preface, foreword, introduction, and author's biographical sketch. The preface is usually written by the author (or authors) and will tell you why they wrote the book and what material it covers. Textbooks often have a preface written to the instructor and a separate preface for the students. The foreword is often an endorsement of the book written by someone other than the author, which can add to your understanding of the book and its purpose. Some books have an additional introduction that reviews the book's overall organization and its contents chapter by chapter. Front matter might also include biographical information about the authors that will give you important details about their background.

> **YOUR TURN ▶**
>
> Look at the front material in this book. What does it tell you about the authors and their purpose in writing this book? How do the authors' biographies influence the way you think about what's written in this book?

Some textbooks include questions at the end of each chapter that you can use as a study guide or as a quick check on your understanding of the chapter's main points. Take time to read and respond to these questions, whether or not your instructor requires you to do so.

Textbooks must try to cover a lot of material in a fairly limited space. Although many textbooks seem detailed, they won't necessarily provide all the things you want to know about a topic—the things that can make your reading more interesting. If you find yourself fascinated by a particular topic, go to the **primary sources**—the original research or document. You'll find those referenced in many textbooks, either at the end of the chapters or in the back of the book. You can read more information about primary and supplementary sources on page 126.

You might also go to other related sources that are credible—whatever makes the text more interesting and informative for you. Remember that most texts are not designed to treat topics in depth. Your textbook reading will be much more interesting if you dig a bit further in related sources. Because some textbooks are sold with test banks that are available to instructors, your instructors might draw their examinations directly from the text, or they might use the textbook only to supplement the lectures. Ask your instructors,

Wired WINDOW

AMAZON KINDLE AND THE FUTURE OF ELECTRONIC READING

Amazon.com has developed the Kindle, hoping to popularize electronic reading among mainstream audiences. The Kindle is a book-sized gadget that has a screen, expandable memory, and wireless capability. Electronic readers are not new; however, Amazon.com has made some improvements to make the device more useful and marketable. Kindle allows you to download content and even to sample chapters before you agree to purchase the entire book. A growing number of textbooks are available through Kindle, and colleges and universities are starting to experiment with adopting Kindle in their libraries and for use in the curriculum. You might already have read some of your course material digitally. If you have taken an online course, a course that has an online component, or a course shell such as Blackboard or WebCT, then odds are good that you've read a document online posted by your professor. Some of the active reading strategies you might use for a print book (such as annotating) might not be easy or possible when you are reading something in a digital format.

Think Critically

Pretend that you have been assigned all of your books in a digital format this semester. How would you go about using some of the strategies you've read about in this chapter? How would you take notes on the reading? If you took notes on paper, would you keep them on paper or convert them to a digital format by typing them into a word processing document? How would you highlight the material that you read? How would it feel to be using this kind of technology for reading? Would it be an improvement over traditional books and readings? Why or why not? How do you retain the material that you currently read online (such as news, blog postings, or your friends' status updates)?

if they have not made it clear, what the tests will cover and the types of questions that will be used. In addition, you might try to find a student who has taken a course with your instructor so that you can get a better idea of how that instructor designs tests. Some instructors expect that you will learn the kinds of detail that you can get only through the textbook. Other instructors are much more concerned that you be able to understand broad concepts that come from lectures in addition to texts and other readings.

Finally, not all textbooks are equal. Some are simply better designed and written than others. If your textbook is exceptionally hard to understand or seems disorganized, let your instructor know your opinion. On the basis of what you say, your instructor might focus on explaining the text and how it is organized or might decide to use a different text for future classes.

YOUR TURN ▶

What is your favorite text in one of your current courses? Why? Which is your least favorite text? Why?

MATH TEXTS

While the previous suggestions about textbook reading apply across the board, mathematics textbooks present some special challenges because they tend to have lots of symbols and very few words. Each statement and every line in the solution of a problem need to be considered and digested slowly. Typically, the author presents the material through definitions, theorems, and sample problems. As you read, pay special attention to definitions. Learning all the terms that relate to a new topic is the first step toward understanding.

Math texts usually include derivations of formulas and proofs of theorems. You must understand and be able to apply the formulas and theorems, but unless your course has a particularly theoretical emphasis, you are less likely to be responsible for all the proofs. So if you get lost in the proof of a theorem, go on to the next item in the section. When you come to a sample problem, it's time to get busy. Pick up pencil and paper, and work through the problem in the book. Then cover the solution and think through the problem on your own. Of course, the exercises that follow each text section form the heart of any math book. A large portion of the time you devote to the course will be spent completing assigned textbook exercises. It is absolutely vital that you do this homework in a timely manner, whether or not your instructor collects it. Success in mathematics requires regular practice, and students who keep up with math homework, either alone or in groups, perform better than students who don't.

$$\frac{2X}{Y} + \frac{Z}{3X} - \frac{5Y}{3} = 3$$

After you complete the assignment, skim through the other exercises in the problem set. Reading the unassigned problems will deepen your understanding of the topic and its scope. Finally, talk the material through to yourself, and be sure your focus is on understanding the problem and its solution, not on memorization. Memorizing something might help you remember how to work through one problem, but it does not help you understand the steps involved so that you can employ them for other problems.

SCIENCE TEXTS

Your approach to your science textbook will depend somewhat on whether you are studying a math-based science, such as physics, or a text-based science, such as biology. In either case, you need to become acquainted with the overall format of the book. Review the table of contents and the glossary, and check the material in the appendices. There, you will find lists of physical constants, unit conversions, and various charts and tables. Many physics and chemistry books also include a minireview of the math you will need in science courses.

Notice the organization of each chapter, and pay special attention to graphs, charts, and boxes. The amount of technical detail might seem overwhelming, but—believe it or not—the authors have sincerely tried to present the material in an easy-to-follow format. Each chapter might begin with chapter objectives and conclude with a short summary, sections that can be useful to study both before and after reading the chapter. You will usually find answers to selected problems in the back of the book. Use the answer key or the student solutions manual to promote your mastery of each chapter.

As you begin an assigned section in a science text, skim the material quickly to gain a general idea of the topic. Begin to absorb the new vocabulary and technical symbols. Then skim the end-of-chapter problems so you'll know what to look for in your detailed reading of the chapter. State a specific goal: "I'm going to learn about recent developments in plate tectonics," or "I'm going to distinguish between mitosis and meiosis," or "Tonight I'm going to focus on the topics in this chapter that were stressed in class."

Should you underline and highlight, or should you outline the material in your science textbooks? You might decide to underline or highlight for a subject such as anatomy, which involves a lot of memorization. But use restraint with a highlighter; it should pull your eye only to important terms and facts. If highlighting is actually a form of procrastination for you (you are reading through the material but planning to learn it at a later date) or if you are highlighting nearly everything you read, your highlighting might be doing you more harm than good. You won't be able to identify important concepts quickly if they're lost in a sea of color. Ask yourself whether the frequency of your highlighting is helping you be more active in your learning process. If not, you might want to highlight less or try a different technique such as margin notes or annotations.

In most sciences, it is best to outline the text chapters. You can usually identify main topics, subtopics, and specific terms under each subtopic in your text by the size of the print. For instance, in each chapter of this textbook, the main topics (or level-1 headings) are in capital blue letters with a rule below. Following each major topic heading, you will find subtopics, or level-2 headings, printed in smaller blue letters. The level-3 headings, which tell more about the subtopics, are in bold, blue capital letters, but are much smaller than the level-1 headings.

To save time when you are outlining, you won't write full sentences, but you will include clear explanations of new technical terms and symbols. Pay

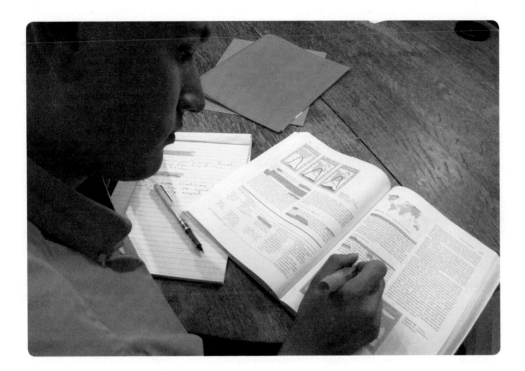

special attention to topics that the instructor covered in class. If you aren't sure whether your outlines contain too much or too little detail, compare them with the outlines members of your study group have made. You could also consult with your instructor during office hours. In preparing for a test, it's a good idea to make condensed versions of your chapter outlines so that you can see how everything fits together.

SOCIAL SCIENCE AND HUMANITIES TEXTS

Many of the suggestions that apply to science textbooks also apply to reading in the social sciences (sociology, psychology, anthropology, economics, political science, and history). Social science texts are filled with special terms or jargon that is unique to the particular field of study. These texts also describe research and theory building and contain references to many primary sources. Your social science texts might also describe differences in opinions or perspectives. Social scientists do not all agree on any one issue, and you might be introduced to a number of ongoing debates about particular issues. In fact, your reading can become more interesting if you seek out different opinions about a common issue. You might have to go beyond your particular textbook, but your library will be a good source of various viewpoints about ongoing controversies.

Textbooks in the **humanities** (philosophy, religion, literature, music, and art) provide facts, examples, opinions, and original material, such as stories or essays. You will often be asked to react to your reading by identifying central themes or characters.

Some instructors believe that the way in which colleges and universities structure courses and majors artificially divides human knowledge and experience. For instance, they argue that subjects such as history, political science, and philosophy are closely linked and that studying each subject separately results in only partial understanding. By stressing the links between courses, these instructors encourage students to think in an **interdisciplinary** manner.

You might be asked to consider how the book or story you're reading or the music you're studying reflects the political atmosphere or the culture of the period. Your art history instructor might direct you to think about how a particular painting gives you a window on the painter's psychological makeup or religious beliefs.

YOUR TURN ▶

Are you ever tempted not to buy a textbook for one of your courses? Why? What can you do as an alternative? How important do you think textbooks are in your courses? In what other ways can you access the information you want and need to learn?

SUPPLEMENTARY MATERIAL

Whether or not your instructor requires you to read material in addition to the textbook, your understanding will be enriched if you go to some of the primary and supplementary sources that are referenced in each chapter of your text. These sources can take the form of journal articles, research papers, dissertations (the major research papers that students write to earn a doctoral degree), or original essays, and they can be found in your library and on the Internet. Reading source material will give you a depth of detail that few textbooks accomplish.

Many sources were originally written for other instructors or researchers. Therefore they often use language and refer to concepts that are familiar to other scholars but not necessarily to first-year college students. If you are reading a journal article that describes a theory or research study, one technique for easier understanding is to read from the end to the beginning. Read the article's conclusion and discussion sections. Then go back to see how the author performed the experiment or formulated the ideas. If you aren't concerned about the specific method used to collect the data, you can skip over the "methodology" section. In almost all scholarly journals, articles are introduced by an abstract, a paragraph-length summary of the methods and major findings. Reading the **abstract** is a quick way to get the gist of a research article before you dive in. As you're reading research articles, always ask yourself: So what? Was the research important to what we know about the topic, or, in your opinion, was it unnecessary?

Monitoring Your Reading

An important step in textbook reading is to monitor your comprehension. As you read, ask yourself: Do I understand this? If not, stop and reread the material. Look up words that are not clear. Try to clarify the main points and how they relate to one another.

Another way to check comprehension is to try to recite the material aloud, either to yourself or your study partner. Using a study group to monitor your comprehension gives you immediate feedback and is highly motivating. After you have read and marked or taken notes on key ideas from the first section of the chapter, proceed to each subsequent section until you have finished the chapter.

YOUR TURN ▶

How do you monitor your own reading comprehension? On the basis of the material in this chapter, what are some strategies you could use to ensure you understand what you are reading?

After you have completed each section and before you move on to the next section, ask again: What are the key ideas? What will I see on the test? At the end of each section, try to guess what information the author will present in the next section.

Improving Your Reading

With effort, you can improve your reading dramatically, but remember to be flexible. How you read should depend on the material. Assess the relative importance and difficulty of the assigned readings, and adjust your reading style and the time you allot accordingly. Connect one important idea to another by asking yourself: Why am I reading this? Where does this fit in? When the textbook material is virtually identical to the lecture material, you can save time by concentrating mainly on one or the other. It takes a planned approach to read textbook materials and other assigned readings with good understanding and recall.

DEVELOPING YOUR VOCABULARY

Textbooks are full of new terminology. In fact, one could argue that learning chemistry is largely a matter of learning the language of chemists and that mastering philosophy, history, or sociology requires a mastery of the terminology of each particular **discipline**.

If words are such a basic and essential component of our knowledge, what is the best way to learn them? Follow the basic vocabulary-building strategies outlined in the following box.

VOCABULARY-BUILDING STRATEGIES

- During your overview of the chapter, notice and jot down unfamiliar terms. Consider making a flash card for each term or making a list of terms.

- When you encounter challenging words, consider the context. See whether you can predict the meaning of an unfamiliar term by using the surrounding words.

- If context by itself is not enough, try analyzing the term to discover the root, or base part, or other meaningful parts of the word. For example, *emissary* has the root "to emit" or "to send forth," so we can guess that an emissary is someone who is sent forth with a message. Similarly, note prefixes and suffixes. For example, *anti* means "against," and *pro* means "for." Use the glossary of the text, a dictionary, or the online **Merriam-Webster Dictionary** (http://www.merriam-webster.com) to locate the definition. Note any multiple definitions, and search for the meaning that fits this usage.

- Take every opportunity to use these new terms in your writing and speaking. If you use a new term a few times, you'll soon know it. In addition, studying new terms on flash cards or study sheets can be handy at exam time.

IF ENGLISH IS NOT YOUR FIRST LANGUAGE

The English language is one of the most difficult languages to learn. Words are often spelled differently from the way they sound, and the language is full of idioms—phrases that are peculiar and cannot be understood from the individual meanings of the words. If you are learning English and are having trouble reading your texts, don't give up. Reading slowly and reading more than once can help you improve your comprehension. Make sure that you have two good dictionaries—one in English and one that links English with your primary language—and look up every word that you don't know. Be sure to practice thinking, writing, and speaking in English, and take advantage of your college's helping services. Your campus might have ESL (English as a Second Language) tutoring and workshops. Ask your advisor or your first-year seminar instructor to help you locate those services.

Listening, note-taking, and reading are the essentials for success in each of your classes. You can perform these tasks without a plan, or you can practice some of the ideas presented in this chapter. If your notes are already working, great. If not, now you know what to do.

Where to go FOR HELP . . .

ON CAMPUS ▶

Learning Assistance Center Most campuses have learning centers that specialize in reading assistance. Both the best students and struggling students use learning centers, where full-time professionals and skilled student tutors offer services.

Fellow students Your best help can come from a fellow student. Look for the best students—those who appear to be the most serious and conscientious. Hire a tutor if you can, or join a study group. You are much more likely to be successful.

ONLINE ▶

Middle Tennessee State University: http://www.mtsu.edu/~studskl/Txtbook.html. The "Study Skills Help" web page has a link to "Reading Your Textbooks."

Niagara University's Office for Academic Support: http://www.niagara.edu/oas/learning_center/study_reading_ strategies/21_Tips_For_Better_Textbook_Reading.htm. Read these "21 Tips for Better Textbook Reading."

MY INSTITUTION'S RESOURCES ▶

_____
_____
_____
_____
_____
_____
_____
_____
_____
_____
_____
_____
_____
_____

One-Minute PAPER . . .

This chapter is full of suggestions for effectively reading your college textbooks. What suggestions did you find the most doable? What do you think is your biggest challenge in using these suggestions to improve your reading habits?

Applying What You've LEARNED . . .

Now that you have read and discussed this chapter, consider how you can apply what you have learned to your academic life and your personal life. The following prompts will help you reflect on the chapter material and its relevance to you both now and in the future.

1. Choose a reading assignment for one of your upcoming classes. After previewing the material, begin reading until you reach a major heading or until you have read at least a page or two. Now stop and write down what you remember from the material. Go back and review what you read. Were you able to remember all of the main ideas?

2. It is easy to say that there is not enough time in the day to get everything done, especially a long reading assignment. However, your future depends on how well you do in college. Challenge yourself not to use that excuse. How can you modify your daily activities to make time for reading?

Building Your PORTFOLIO . . .

66 The more that you read, the more things you will know. The more that you learn, the more places you'll go. 99

–THEODOR SEUSS GEISEL
a.k.a. DR. SEUSS (1904-1991),
American writer and cartoonist

THE BIG PICTURE

This chapter introduces a reading strategy called **mapping** as a visual tool for getting the "big picture" of what you are preparing to read. Mapping a textbook chapter can help you quickly recognize how different concepts and terms fit together and make connections to what you already know about the subject. A number of ways of mapping, including wheel maps and branching maps, are described in this chapter. You might also use other types of maps, such as *matrixes* to compare and contrast ideas or show cause and effect, a *spider web* to connect themes, or *sketches* to illustrate images, relationships, or descriptions.

1. Look through your course syllabi, and identify a reading assignment that you need to complete in the next week.

2. Begin by previewing the first chapter of the reading assignment.

3. Practice mapping the chapter by creating your own map using the drawing toolbar in Microsoft Word.

4. Save your map in your portfolio on your personal computer or flash drive.

Example

1. Place the central idea of the chapter in the center of the wheel.

2. Place supporting ideas on the spokes of the wheel.

3. Place important details on the lines attached to the spokes.

Tip: A good place to start is with chapter headings and subheadings. Then move on to terms in bold and graphics such as charts, tables, and diagrams. Textbooks often have study questions at the end of the chapter, which can give you clues about what the author considers the most important concepts.

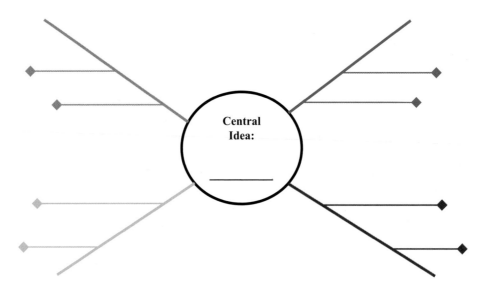

Reading a textbook efficiently and effectively requires that you develop reading strategies that will help you to make the most of your study time. Mapping can help you to organize and retain what you have read, making it a good reading and study tool. Writing, reciting, and organizing the main points, supporting ideas, and key details of the chapter will help you to recall the information on test day.

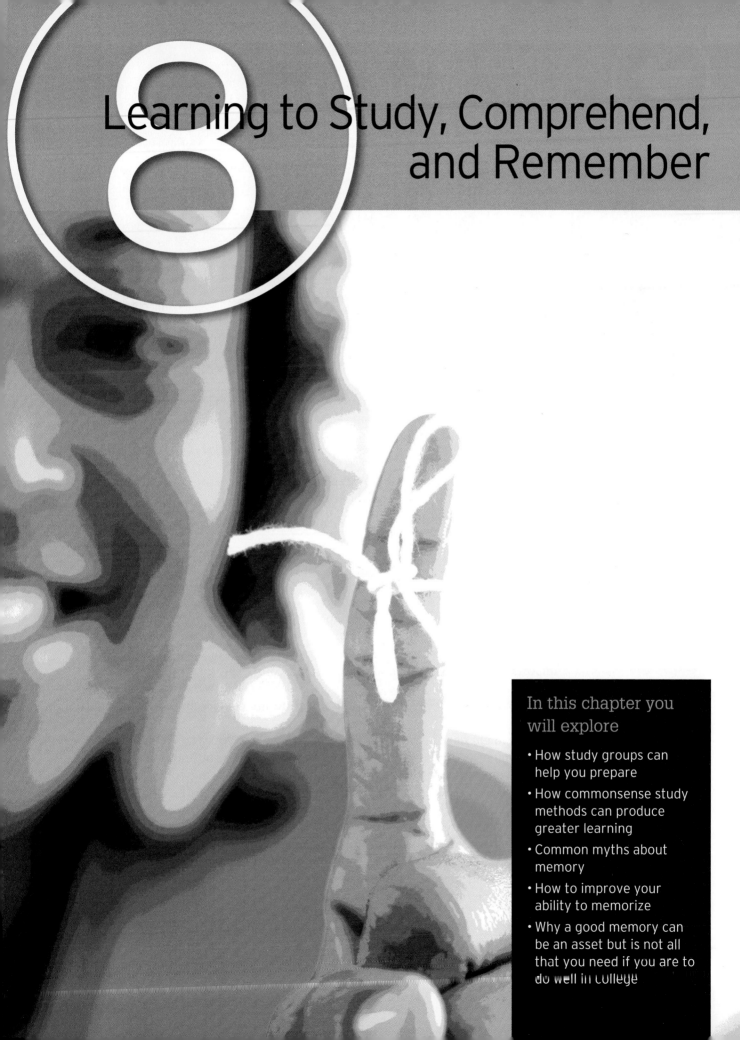

8 Learning to Study, Comprehend, and Remember

In this chapter you will explore

- How study groups can help you prepare
- How commonsense study methods can produce greater learning
- Common myths about memory
- How to improve your ability to memorize
- Why a good memory can be an asset but is not all that you need if you are to do well in college

Confessions of a
COLLEGE STUDENT . . .

MADISON DURRETT, 19
Wofford College

66 **You can study with your friends in groups, and you pick up study habits that you haven't thought of.** 99

Freshman year was a crash course in study skills for me. I've been involved in theater, oh my gosh, since I was little, and I thought I knew how to study; then I got to college and I had to reevaluate that. I'm a sophomore now, and I think I have gotten the hang of it.

I usually am better studying by myself, in my room, trying to focus. But residence life can be very distracting, with people coming in and out of rooms all the time and everyone wanting to go out a lot. The good part about residence life is that you can study with your friends in groups, and you pick up study habits from them that you haven't thought of. I study pretty well with friends. Some of them spend hours upon hours every day in the library, but I wouldn't call it my favorite study environment. Honestly, it's a really cold building temperature-wise and not very comfortable. It's hard to relax there, too, so it doesn't always work for me. I would say my favorite place to study would be in a coffee shop or at a bookstore. Usually I just bring all my notes and spend Saturday or Sunday afternoon reviewing or writing. It's a really relaxed environment, and I feel like I get more work done there than I do anywhere else.

Studying, comprehending, and remembering are essential

to getting the most out of your college experience. Although many students think that the only reason for studying is to do well on exams, a far more important reason is to learn and understand course information. If you study to increase your understanding, you are more likely to remember and apply what you learn not only to tests, but also to future courses and to life beyond college.

You might have learned to study effectively while you were in high school, or you might be finding that you need to learn more about how to study. In college you will need to spend time out of class reviewing course material, doing assigned reading, and keeping up with your homework. Occasionally, you will also want to go the extra mile by doing additional (unassigned) reading and investigating particular topics that interest you.

This chapter offers you a number of strategies for making the best use of your study time. It also addresses the important topic of memory. There's no getting around it: If you can't remember what you have read or heard, you won't do well on course exams.

TIPS FOR EFFECTIVE STUDYING

Whether you are completing class assignments or preparing for a test, these strategies will help you study more effectively:

1. **Make studying a part of your daily routine**. Don't allow days to go by when you don't crack a book or keep up with course assignments.

2. **Manage your study time wisely**. Create a schedule that will allow you to prepare for exams and complete course assignments on time. Be aware of "crunch times" when you might have several exams or papers due at once. And create some flexibility in your schedule to allow for unexpected distractions.

3. **Collaborate with others**. One of the most effective ways to study is in a group with other students. In your first year of college, gather a group of students who study together. Study groups can meet throughout the term, or they can review for midterms or final exams.

4. **Make your learning style work for you as you study**. Look back at your VARK score from Chapter 4. If you are a visual learner, create diagrams, lists, flash cards, or other visual aids that will enhance memory. If you are an aural learner, be sure to attend discussions and tutorials. Use a digital recorder or tape recorder in class, and replay the lecture when it's study time. Aural learners often find that talking out loud is more effective than reciting in their heads. This might mean that you'll occasionally need to study alone so you won't bother others when you're talking to yourself. If you are a read/ write learner, take notes on your notes as you reread them. Turn diagrams and charts into words. If you are a kinesthetic learner, move around the room while you study. Gesture with your arms and hands. Try to convert your notes into real-life examples.

5. **Be alert for external distractions**. Choose a place to study where you can concentrate. That might be in your residence hall or room at home, or you might have to go somewhere else. The campus library is often the best place to go for uninterrupted study.

6. **Get enough sleep**. Don't cut back on your sleep to cram in additional study hours. Remember that most tests will require you to be able to think clearly about the concepts that you have studied. Especially during final exam weeks, it is important to be well rested so that you can stay alert for extended periods of time.

7. **Follow a regular exercise program**. Walking, jogging, swimming, or other aerobic activities might help you think more clearly and can provide positive and needed study breaks. Exercise releases endorphins in the brain, so it can help improve your mood. Furthermore, research has shown that exercise can potentially increase your brain power by generating new neurons in the hippocampus, an area of the brain that controls learning and memory.[1]

8. **Get a tutor**. Tutoring is not just for students who are failing. Often, the best students seek tutorial assistance to ensure that they understand course material. Most tutors are students, and most campus tutoring services offer their services for free. Ask your academic advisor, counselor, or campus learning center about the availability of tutoring or other kinds of academic support.

[1]http://serendip.brynmawr.edu/bb/neuro/neuro05/web2/mmcgovern.html.

Studying to Understand and Remember

Studying will help you accomplish two goals: understanding and remembering. While memory is a necessary tool for learning, what's most important is that you study to develop a deep understanding of course information. When you truly comprehend what you are learning, you will be able to place names, dates, and specific facts in context. You will also be able to exercise your critical thinking abilities.

The human mind has discovered ingenious ways to understand and remember information. Here are some methods that might be useful to you as you're trying to nail down the causes of World War I, remember the steps in a chemistry problem, or absorb a mathematical formula:

1. **Pay attention to what you're hearing or reading**. This suggestion is perhaps the most basic and the most important. If you're sitting in class thinking about everything except what the professor is saying or if you're reading and you find that your mind is wandering, you're wasting your time. Force yourself to focus.

> **YOUR TURN ▶**
>
> When you're in class, how would you rate your level of concentration on what the instructor is saying? Is it good, fair, or poor? In which classes do you concentrate best? In which is your concentration worst? Why do you think it's easier to concentrate in some classes than in others?

2. **"Overlearn" the material**. After you know and think you understand the material you're studying, go over it again to make sure that you'll retain it for a long time. Test yourself, or ask someone else to test you. Recite aloud, in your own words, what you're trying to remember.

3. **Check the Internet**. If you're having trouble remembering what you have learned, Google a key word, and try to find interesting details that will engage you in learning more, not less, about the subject. Many first-year courses cover such a large amount of material that you'll miss the more interesting details unless you seek them out for yourself. As your interest increases, so will your memory for the topic.

4. **Be sure you have the big picture.** Whenever you begin a course, make sure that you're clear on what the course will cover. You can talk with someone who has already taken the course, or you can take a brief look at all the reading assignments. Having the big picture will help you understand and remember the details of what you're learning.

5. **Look for connections between your life and what's going on in your courses.** College courses might seem irrelevant to you, but if you look more carefully, you'll find many connections between course material and your daily life. Seeing those connections will make your courses more interesting and will help you remember what you're learning. For example, if you're taking a music theory course and studying chord patterns, listen for those patterns in contemporary music.

6. **Get organized.** If your desk or your computer is organized, you'll spend less time trying to remember a file name or where you put a particular document. And as you rewrite your notes, putting them in a logical order (either chronological or thematic) that makes sense to you will help you learn and remember them.

YOUR TURN ▶

Look around your room and at your computer desktop. Is your living environment neat and organized? How about your "electronic environment"? Does a lack of organization ever cause you to waste time? What strategies could you use to become better organized?

---

7. **Reduce stressors in your life.** Although there's no way to determine the extent to which worry or stress causes you to be unable to focus or to forget, most people will agree that stress can be a distraction. Healthy, stress-reducing behaviors, such as meditation, exercise, and sleep, are especially important for college students. Many campuses have counseling or health centers that can provide resources to help you deal with whatever might be causing stress in your daily life.

How Memory Works

Kenneth Higbee describes two different processes involved in memory. The first is **short-term memory**, defined as how many items you are able to perceive at one time. Higbee found that information stored in short-term memory is forgotten in less than thirty seconds (and sometimes much faster) unless you take action to either keep that information in short-term memory or move it to long-term memory.

Although short-term memory is significantly limited, it has a number of uses. It serves as an immediate but temporary holding tank for information, some of which might not be needed for long. It helps you maintain a reasonable attention span so that you can keep track of topics mentioned in conversation, and it enables you to stay on task with the goals you are pursuing at any moment. But even these simple functions of short-term memory fail on occasion. If the telephone rings, if someone asks you a question, or if you're interrupted in any way, you might find that your attention suffers and that you essentially have to start over in reconstructing short-term memory.

The second memory process is **long-term memory**, and this is the type of memory that you will need to improve so that you will remember what you're learning in college. Long-term memory can be described in three ways. *Procedural memory* is knowing how to do something, such as solving a mathematical problem or playing a musical instrument. *Semantic memory* involves facts and meanings without regard to where and when you learned those things. *Episodic memory* deals with particular events, their time, and place.[2]

You are using your procedural memory when you get on a bicycle you haven't ridden in years, when you can recall the first piece you learned to play on the piano, when you effortlessly type a letter or class report, and when you drive a car. Your semantic memory is used continuously to recall word meanings or important dates, such as your mother's birthday. Episodic memory allows you to remember events in your life—a vacation, your first day in school, the moment you opened your college acceptance letter. Some people can recall not only the event but also the very date and time the event happened. For others, although the event stands out, the dates and times are harder to remember immediately.

TABLE 8.1 ▶ Long-Term and Short-Term Memory

Short-Term Memory	Long-Term Memory
Stores information for about thirty seconds	Procedural: remembering how to do something
Can contain from five to nine chunks of information at one time	Semantic: remembering facts and meanings
Information either forgotten or moved to long-term memory	Episodic: remembering the time and place of events

[2]W. F. Brewer and J. R. Pani, "The Structure of Human Memory," in G. H. Bower (Ed.), *The Psychology of Learning and Motivation: Advances in Research and Theory*, vol. 17 (New York: Academic Press, 1983), pp 1–38.

CONNECTING MEMORY TO DEEP LEARNING

It can be easy to blame a poor memory on the way we live; multitasking has become the norm for college students and instructors. Admittedly, it's hard to focus on anything for very long if your life is full of daily distractions and competing responsibilities or if you're not getting the sleep you need. Have you ever had the experience of walking into a room with a particular task in mind and immediately forgetting what that task was? You were probably interrupted either by your own thoughts or by someone or something else. Or have you ever felt the panic that comes from blanking on a test, even though you studied hard and thought you knew the material? You might have pulled an all-nighter, and studying and exhaustion raised your stress level, causing your mind to go blank. Such experiences happen to everyone at one time or another. But obviously, to do well in college—and in life—it's important that you improve your ability to remember what you read, hear, and experience. As one writer put it, "there is no learning without memory."[3] On the other hand, not all memory involves real learning.

Is a good memory all you need to do well in college? Most memory strategies tend to focus on helping you remember names, dates, numbers, vocabulary, graphic materials, formulas—the bits and pieces of knowledge. However, if you know the date the Civil War began and the fort where the first shots were fired but you don't really know why the Civil War was fought, you're missing the point of a college education. College is about **deep learning**, understanding the "why" and "how" behind the details. So don't forget that while recall of specific facts is certainly necessary, it isn't sufficient. To do well in college courses, you will need to understand major themes and ideas, and you will also need to hone your ability to think critically about what you're learning. Critical thinking is discussed in depth in Chapter 5 of this book.

MYTHS ABOUT MEMORY

Although scientific knowledge about how our brains function is increasing all the time, Kenneth Higbee suggests that you might have heard some myths about memory (and maybe you even believe them). Here are five of these memory myths, and what experts say about them:

1. **Myth:** Some people are stuck with bad memories.

   Reality: Although there are probably some differences among people in innate memory (the memory ability a person is born with), what really gives you the edge are memory skills that you can learn and use. Virtually anyone can improve the ability to remember and recall.

2. **Myth:** Some people have photographic memories.

   Reality: Although a few individuals have truly exceptional memories, most research has found that these abilities result more often from learned strategies, interest, and practice than from some innate ability. Even though you might not have what psychologists would classify as an exceptional memory, applying the memory strategies presented later in this chapter can help you improve it.

[3]Harry Lorayne, *Super Memory, Super Student: How to Raise Your Grades in 30 Days* (Boston: Little, Brown and Company, 1990).

3. **Myth:** Memory benefits from long hours of practice.

   Reality: Practicing memorizing can help improve memory. If you have ever been a server in a restaurant, you might have been required to memorize the menu. You might even have surprised yourself at your ability to memorize not only the main entrees, but also sauces and side dishes. Experts acknowledge that practice often improves memory, but they argue that the way you practice, such as using special creative strategies, is more important than how long you practice.

4. **Myth:** Remembering too much can clutter your mind.

   Reality: For all practical purposes, the storage capacity of your memory is unlimited. In fact, the more you learn about a particular topic, the easier it is to learn even more. How you organize the information is more important than the quantity.

5. **Myth:** People only use 10 percent of their brain power.

   Reality: No scientific research is available to accurately measure how much of our brain we actually use. However, most psychologists and learning specialists believe that we all have far more mental ability than we actually tap.

Wired WINDOW

REMEMBER (ALMOST) EVERYTHING

Do you ever wish that you could store memories the way your computer does? Well, you can . . . sort of. Using online and handheld tools can help lift some of the burdens of keeping long to-do lists and important dates in mind. You might already have your own PDA. Most computers, cell phones, and iPods have calendar and/or to-do list software built in. Search your computer, cell phone, or MP3 player menus to see whether you have a calendar function. (Hint: The calendar is found under "Extras" in the main menu on the classic iPod and by selecting the Calendar icon on the iPod Touch and iPhone.) It is important to sync your MP3 player or cell phone with an online calendar or one on your computer in case your device ever crashes or gets lost. Syncing the calendar with an external source is easier to manage with an iPod Touch or iPhone than with a classic iPod; you can get detailed instructions by Googling "ipod calendar sync" or by searching the Apple support website (http://support.apple.com/manuals/#ipod) for your model.

Thinking Critically

Try using an electronic calendar for a few weeks. Input all of your assignment due dates and activities that you don't want to forget. Use reminders to alert you of upcoming dates. At the end of your trial period, ask yourself whether it helped to use these features. How would you get information about using other types of devices to keep your calendar and/or to-do lists? You'll find plenty of free calendar services online. For instance, Google offers Google Calendar, which integrates with Gmail; other sites such as Yahoo!, Facebook, and MySpace also provide calendars. Try using an online calendar for a few weeks. Some institutions offer access to an online calendar that is saved on a campus server (such as the calendar included in Microsoft Outlook). Campus-based calendars have the added feature of allowing you to schedule appointments and events directly with other students, faculty members, and staff. Of course, there can be a danger in becoming too dependent on technology and losing trust in your own memory. Technological devices are valuable as aids for memory and time management, but be careful not to rely on them exclusively. Any electronic device can crash or be lost or stolen, so be sure to keep backups of important information. How helpful are electronic calendars to you? In what ways can they help you remember? Do you think it's risky to become too reliant on them? Why or why not?

Improving Your Memory

Throughout history, human memory has been a topic of great interest and fascination for scientists and the general public. Although severe problems with memory are extremely rare, you're in good company if you find that your memory occasionally lets you down, especially if you're nervous or stressed or when grades depend on immediate recall of what you have read, heard, or written.

So how can you improve your ability to store information in your brain for future use? Psychologists and learning specialists have conducted research on memory and have developed a number of strategies that you can use as part of a study-skills regimen. Some of these strategies might be new to you, but others will be simple commonsense ways to maximize your learning—ideas that you've heard before, though perhaps not in the context of improving your memory.

The benefits of having a good memory are obvious. In college, your memory will help you retain information and ace tests. After college, the ability to recall names, procedures, presentations, and appointments will save you energy and time and will prevent a lot of embarrassment.

There are many ways to go about remembering. Have you ever had to memorize a speech or lines from a play? How you approach committing the lines to memory might depend on your learning style. If you're an aural learner, you might choose to record your lines as well as lines of other characters and listen to them on tape. If you're a visual learner, you might remember best by visualizing where your lines appear on the page in the script. If you learn best by reading, you might simply read the script over and over. If you're a kinesthetic learner, you might need to walk or move across an imaginary stage as you read the script.

YOUR TURN ▶

How can you apply your learning style to remembering material for an exam? List some strategies that you already use or might want to try in the future.

Although knowing specific words will help, remembering concepts and ideas can be much more important. To embed such ideas in your mind, ask yourself these questions as you review your notes and books:

1. What is the essence of the idea?
2. Why does the idea make sense? What is the logic behind it?
3. How does this idea connect to other ideas in the material?
4. What are some possible arguments against the idea?

MNEMONICS

Mnemonics (pronounced "ne MON iks") are various methods or tricks to aid the memory. Mnemonics tend to fall into four basic categories:

1. **Acronyms.** New words created from the first letters of several words can be helpful in remembering. The Great Lakes can be more easily recalled by remembering the word "HOMES" for Huron, Ontario, Michigan, Erie, and Superior.

2. **Acrostics.** An acrostic is a verse in which certain letters of each word or line form a message. Many piano students were taught the notes on the treble clef lines (E, G, B, D, F) by remembering the acrostic "Every Good Boy Deserves Fudge."

3. **Rhymes or songs.** Do you remember learning "Thirty days hath September, April, June, and November. All the rest have 31, excepting February alone. It has 28 days time, but in leap years it has 29"? If so, you were using a mnemonic rhyming technique to remember the days in each month.

4. **Visualization.** You use visualization to associate words, concepts, or stories with visual images. The more ridiculous the image, the more likely you are to remember it. So use your imagination to create mental images when you're studying important words or concepts. For example, as you're driving to campus, choose some landmarks along the way to help you remember material for your history test. The next day, as you pass those landmarks, relate them to something from your class notes or readings. A white picket fence might remind you of the British army's eighteenth-century approach to warfare, with its official uniforms and straight lines of infantry, while a stand of trees of various shapes and sizes might remind you of the Continental army's less organized approach.

Mnemonics work because they make information meaningful through the use of rhymes, patterns, and associations. They impose meaning where meaning might be hard to recognize. Mnemonics provide a way of organizing material, a sort of mental filing system. Mnemonics probably aren't needed if what you are studying is very logical and organized, but they can be quite useful for other types of material.

Although mnemonics are a time-tested way of remembering, the method has some limitations. The first is time. Thinking up rhymes, associations, or visual images can take longer than simply learning the words themselves through repetition. Also, it is often difficult to convert abstract concepts into concrete words or images, and you run the risk of being able to remember an image without recalling the underlying concept. Finally, memory specialists debate whether learning through mnemonics actually helps with long-term knowledge retention and whether this technique helps or interferes with deeper understanding.

USING REVIEW SHEETS, MIND MAPS, AND OTHER TOOLS

To prepare for an exam that will cover large amounts of material, you need to condense the volume of notes and text pages into manageable study units. Review your materials with these questions in mind: Is this one of the key ideas in the chapter or unit? Will I see this on the test? As suggested in Chapter 7, you might prefer to highlight, underline, or annotate the most important ideas or create outlines, lists, or visual maps.

Use your notes to develop review sheets. Make lists of key terms and ideas (from the recall column if you've used the Cornell method) that you need to remember. Also, don't underestimate the value of using your lecture notes to test yourself or others on information presented in class.

A **mind map** is essentially a review sheet with a visual element. Its word and visual patterns provide you with highly charged clues to jog your memory. Because they are visual, mind maps help many students recall information more easily.

Figure 8.1 shows what a mind map might look like for a chapter on listening and learning in the classroom. Try to reconstruct the ideas in the chapter by following the connections in the map. Then make a visual mind map for this chapter, and see how much more you can remember after studying it a number of times.

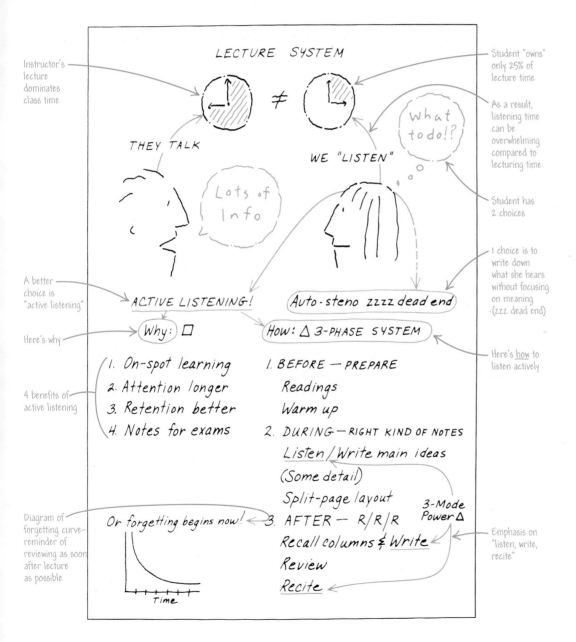

◀ **FIGURE 8.1**

Sample Mind Map on Listening and Learning in the Classroom

In addition to review sheets and mind maps, you might want to create flash cards. One of the advantages of flash cards is that you can keep them in a pocket of your backpack or jacket and pull them out to study anywhere, even when you might not think that you have enough time to take out your notebook to study. Also, you always know where you left off. Flash cards can help you make good use of time that might otherwise be wasted, such as time spent on the bus or waiting for a friend.

Bicameral: Having two Legislative Chambers

SUMMARIES

Writing summaries of class topics can be helpful in preparing for essay and short-answer exams. By condensing the main ideas into a concise written summary, you store information in your long-term memory so you can retrieve it to answer an essay question. Here's how:

1. Predict a test question from your lecture notes or other resources.
2. Read the chapter, supplemental articles, notes, or other resources. Underline or mark main ideas as you go, make notations, or outline on a separate sheet of paper.
3. Analyze and abstract. What is the purpose of the material? Does it compare two ideas, define a concept, or prove a theory? What are the main ideas? How would you explain the material to someone else?
4. Make connections between main points and key supporting details. Reread to identify each main point and the supporting evidence. Create an outline to assist you in this process.
5. Select, condense, and order. Review underlined material, and begin putting the ideas into your own words. Number what you underlined or highlighted in a logical order.
6. Write your ideas precisely in a draft. In the first sentence, state the purpose of your summary. Follow this statement with each main point and its supporting ideas. See how much of the draft you can develop from memory without relying on your notes.
7. Review your draft. Read it over, adding missing transitions or insufficient information. Check the logic of your summary. Annotate with the material you used for later reference.
8. Test your memory. Put your draft away, and try to recite the contents of the summary to yourself out loud, or explain it to a study partner who can provide feedback on the information you have omitted.
9. Schedule time to review summaries, and double-check your memory shortly before the test. You might want to do this with a partner, but some students prefer to review alone. Some faculty members also might be willing to assist you in this process and provide feedback on your summaries.

Where to go
FOR HELP . . .

ON CAMPUS ▶

Your campus probably has a study skills center or learning center that can help you develop effective memory strategies. Other students and faculty members can also give you tips on how they remember course material. And your college library will have many books on the topic of memory. Some were written by researchers for the research community, but others were written for people like you who are trying to improve their memory.

BOOKS ▶

Buzan, Tony. *Use Your Perfect Memory*, 3rd rev. ed. New York: Penguin Books, 1991.

Higbee, Kenneth L., Ph.D. *Your Memory: How It Works and How to Improve It*, 2nd rev. ed. New York: Marlowe & Co., 2001.

Lorayne, Harry. *Super Memory, Super Student: How to Raise Your Grades in 30 Days*. Boston: Little, Brown and Company, 1990.

ONLINE ▶

Review of the Research on Memory and College Student Learning: http://www.ferris.edu/htmls/academics/center/Teaching_and_Learning_Tips/Memory/indexMemory.htm. This website is designed for instructors, though it also includes lots of interesting information for students.

Memorization Techniques: http://www.accd.edu/ sac/history/keller/ACCDitg/SSMT.htm. This excellent website is maintained by the Alamo Community College District.

MY INSTITUTION'S RESOURCES ▶

_____

_____

_____

_____

_____

_____

_____

_____

_____

_____

_____

_____

_____

_____

One-Minute PAPER...

Doing well on exams is important, but being able to study, comprehend, and remember what you learn has bigger implications for your life. After reading this chapter, do you find yourself thinking about these concepts in a different way? If so, how? What kinds of questions would you ask your instructor about this chapter?

Applying What You've LEARNED...

Now that you have read and discussed this chapter, consider how you can apply what you have learned to your academic and personal life. The following prompts will help you reflect on the chapter material and its relevance to you both now and in the future.

1. Give mnemonics a try. Choose a set of class notes that you need to study for an upcoming quiz or exam. As you study, pick one concept, and create your own acronym, acrostic, rhyme or song, or visualization to help you remember.

2. The way in which students study in high school is often very different from the way they need to study in college. It can be difficult to adapt to new ways of doing things. Describe the way in which you studied in high school. Describe how you can improve on those habits to do well in college.

Building Your PORTFOLIO...

66 The sense of smell can be extraordinarily evocative, bringing back pictures as sharp as photographs of scenes that had left the conscious mind. 99

–THALASSA CRUSO (1909-1997)
English horticulturalist and writer

TAKES ME BACK

Is there a song that reminds you, every time you hear it, of a certain time in your life or even the exact moment when something happened? Or maybe you have a photo that you take out every so often for a trip down memory lane? Our senses often trigger memories.

1. Recall a photo, song, or object that prompts you to recall a life event or time period. Create a new document in your word processing software, and describe just what it is about the photo, song, or object that reminds you of something else.

2. Describe your memory in as much detail as possible.

3. Describe how this memory makes you feel.

4. Describe how you might use photos or drawings, songs, or mnemonics to remember ideas or concepts in one of the classes you are currently taking.

5. Save these musings in your portfolio on your personal computer or flash drive. If possible, save the photos or music files that you described along with your document.

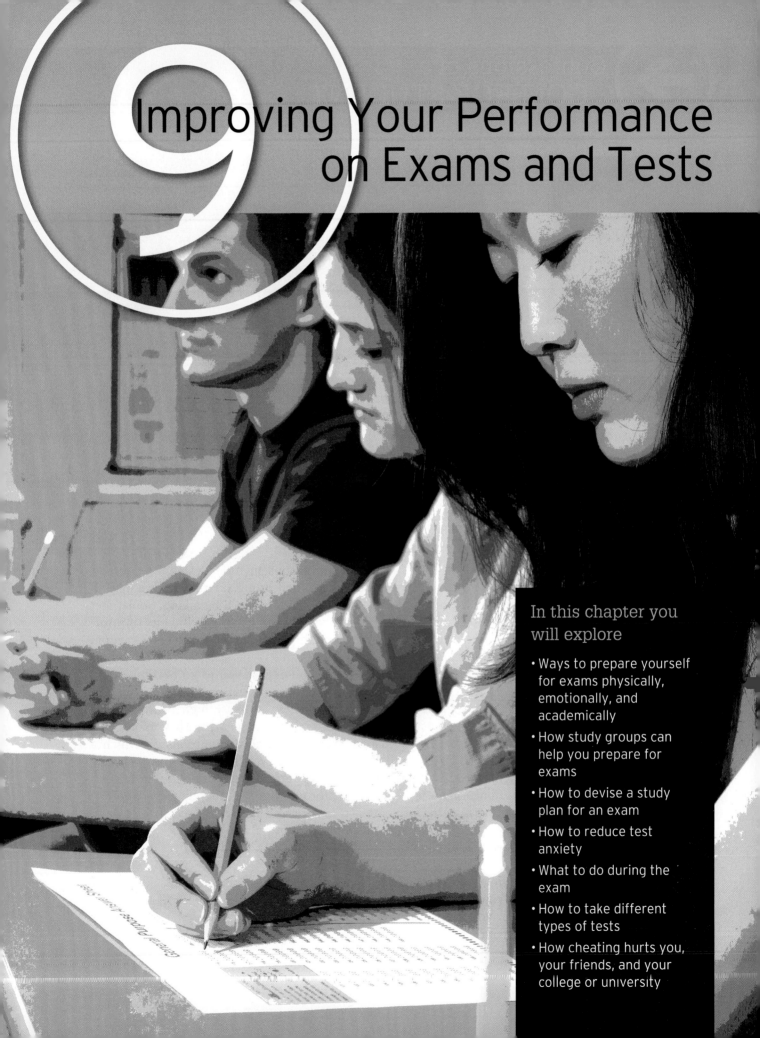

9 Improving Your Performance on Exams and Tests

In this chapter you will explore

- Ways to prepare yourself for exams physically, emotionally, and academically
- How study groups can help you prepare for exams
- How to devise a study plan for an exam
- How to reduce test anxiety
- What to do during the exam
- How to take different types of tests
- How cheating hurts you, your friends, and your college or university

DAN BAKER, 19
The University of New Haven

66 I study hard, but sometimes it just doesn't get through and I kind of choke. 99

I'm not really a good test taker. I mean, I study hard and everything, but sometimes it just doesn't get through, especially if I feel a lot of pressure. I can get nervous about the test and kind of choke. I've always been like that. I went to a private high school, and they gave us a lot of homework, a couple of hours every night for each class, so I didn't really prepare much for tests. Whenever I had one, I would just freak out about the problems that I didn't know and then forget everything that I did know.

It's a little weird: College feels like less work because the classes are split up differently, two a day rather than six. So I just to try to study as much as possible. If I have everything fresh in my head, it just kind of comes to me during a test, and I don't panic or worry. Another thing that helps, especially for math tests, is that first I write down any equations that are in my head on the back of the test paper, so I can always look at them if I forget an equation while trying to work on another problem. I think my study skills are pretty good, but I need to work harder.

You can prepare for exams in many ways, and certain methods are more effective than others, depending on the subject matter, your preferred learning style, and the type of test you'll be taking. Sometimes you'll need to be able to recall names, dates, and other specific bits of information, especially if you are taking a multiple-choice or short-answer exam. Many instructors, especially in humanities and social science courses such as literature, history, and political science, will expect you to go beyond names and dates and have a good conceptual understanding of the subject matter. They often prefer essay exams that require you to use higher-level critical thinking skills, such as *analysis, synthesis*, and *evaluation*. They expect you to be able to provide the reasons, arguments, and assumptions on which a given position is based, and the evidence that you believe confirms or discounts it. They want you to be able to support your opinions so they can see how you think. They are not looking for answers that merely prove you can memorize the material presented in lecture and the text. Even in math and science courses, your instructors want you not only to remember the correct theory, formula, or equation but also to understand and apply what you have learned.

Knowing your preferred learning style will also help you decide the best ways for you to study, no matter what kind of text or exam you are facing. Remember your VARK score, and review the material in Chapter 4 that helps you link your learning style to strategies for exam preparation.

◀ **FIGURE 9.1**

Exam Schedule from
Sample Course Syllabus

**History 111, US History to 1865
Fall 2009**

Examinations
Note: In this course, most of your exams will be on Fridays,
except for the Wednesday before Thanksgiving and the final.
This is to give you a full week to study for the exam and
permit me to grade them over the weekend and return the
exams to you on Monday. I believe in using a variety of
types of measurements. In addition to those scheduled
below, I reserve the right to give you unannounced quizzes
on daily reading assignments. Also, current events are fair
game on any exam! Midterm and final exams will be
cumulative (on all material since beginning of the course).
Other exams cover all classroom material and all readings
covered since the prior exam. The schedule is as follows:

Friday, 9/4: Objective type

Friday, 9/18: Essay type

Friday, 10/16: Midterm: essay and objective

Friday, 10/30: Objective

Friday, 11/13: Open-book type

Wednesday, 11/25: Essay

Tuesday, 12/15: Final exam; essay and objective

Getting Prepared for Tests and Exams

Believe it or not, you actually begin preparing for a test on the first day of
the term. All of your lecture notes, assigned readings, and homework are
part of that preparation. As the test day nears, you should know how much
additional time you will need for review, what material the test will cover,
and what format the test will take. It is very important to double-check the
exam dates on your syllabi, as in Figure 9.1, and to incorporate these dates
into your overall plans for time management, for example, in your daily and
weekly to-do lists.

Here are some specific suggestions to help you prepare well for any exam:

1. **Ask your instructor.** Find out the purpose, types of questions, conditions (how much time you will have to complete the exam), and content to be covered on the exam. Talk with your instructor to clarify any misunderstandings you might have about your reading or lecture notes. Some instructors might let you see copies of old exams so you can see the types of questions they use. Never miss the last class before an exam, because your instructor might summarize valuable information.

2. **Manage your preparation time wisely.** Create a schedule that will give you time to review effectively for the exam without waiting until the night before. Make sure your schedule has some flexibility to allow for unexpected distractions. If you are able to spread your study sessions over several days, your mind will continue to process the information between study sessions, which will help you during the test. Also, let your friends and family know when you have important exams coming up and how that will affect your time with them.

3. **Focus your study.** Figure out what you can effectively review that is likely to be on the exam. Collaborate with other students to share information, and try to attend all test or exam review sessions offered by your instructor.

PREPARE PHYSICALLY

Maintain your regular sleep routine. To do well on exams, you will need to be alert so that you can think clearly. And you are more likely to be alert when you are well rested. Last-minute, late-night cramming that robs you of sufficient sleep isn't an effective study strategy.

Follow your regular exercise program. Another way to prepare physically for exams is by walking, jogging, or engaging in other kinds of physical activity. Exercise is a positive way to relieve stress and to give yourself a needed break from long hours of studying.

Eat right. Eat a light breakfast before a morning exam, and avoid greasy or acidic foods that might upset your stomach. Limit the amount of caffeinated beverages you drink on exam day, because caffeine can make you jittery. Choose fruits, vegetables, and other foods that are high in energy-rich complex carbohydrates. Avoid eating sweets before an exam. The immediate energy boost they create can be quickly followed by a loss of energy and alertness. Ask the instructor whether you may bring a bottle of water with you to the exam.

PREPARE EMOTIONALLY

Know your material. If you have given yourself adequate time to review, you will enter the classroom confident that you are in control. Study by testing yourself or quizzing others in a study group or learning community so that you will be sure you really know the material.

Practice relaxing. Some students experience upset stomachs, sweaty palms, racing hearts, or other unpleasant physical symptoms of test anxiety. Consult your counseling center about relaxation techniques. Some campus learning centers also provide workshops on reducing test anxiety. If this is a problem you experience, read the section on test anxiety later in this chapter.

Use positive self-talk. Instead of telling yourself, "I never do well on math tests" or "I'll never be able to learn all the information for my history essay exam," make positive statements, such as "I have attended all the lectures, done my homework, and passed the quizzes. Now I'm ready to pass the test!"

YOUR TURN ▶

Are there times when you engage in negative predictions about your academic performance? What do you think causes you to be so hard on yourself? Do you think that changing your predictions could change your performance? Why or why not? How can you reverse your thinking and compliment yourself on your work?

PREPARE FOR TEST TAKING

Find out about the test. Ask your instructor what format the test will have, such as essay, multiple-choice, true/false, fill-in-the-blank, short-answer, or something else. Ask how long the test will last and how it will be graded. Ask whether all questions will have the same point value.

Design an exam plan. Use the information about the test as you design a plan for preparing. Build that preparation into a schedule of review dates. Develop a to-do list of the major steps you need to take to be ready. Be sure you have read and learned all the material by one week before the exam. That way, you will be able to use the final week to review and prepare for the exam. The week before the exam, set aside a schedule of one-hour blocks of time for review, and make notes on specifically what you plan to accomplish during each hour.

Join a study group. You have seen the suggestion to join or form a study group in other chapters because this is one of the most effective strategies for doing well in college, especially in preparing for exams. You can benefit from different views of your instructors' goals, objectives, and emphasis; have your study partners quiz you on facts and concepts; and gain the support and friendship of others to help sustain your motivation.

Some instructors will provide time in class for the formation of study groups. Otherwise, ask your teacher, advisor, or campus tutoring or learning center to help you identify interested students and decide on guidelines for the group. Study groups can meet throughout the term, or they can just review for midterms or final exams. Group members should complete their assignments before the group meets and prepare study questions or points of discussion ahead of time. If your study group decides to meet just before exams, allow enough time to share notes and ideas.

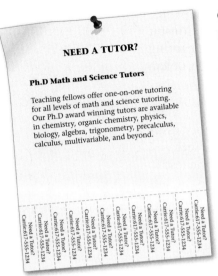

NEED A TUTOR?

Ph.D Math and Science Tutors

Teaching fellows offer one-on-one tutoring for all levels of math and science tutoring. Our Ph.D award winning tutors are available in chemistry, organic chemistry, physics, biology, algebra, trigonometry, precalculus, calculus, multivariable, and beyond.

Need a Tutor? Carrie:617-555-1234

Get a tutor. Most campus tutoring services offer their services for free. Ask your academic advisor or counselor or campus learning center about arranging for tutoring. Many learning centers employ student tutors who have done well in the same courses you are taking. These students might have some good advice on how to prepare for tests given by particular instructors. Learning centers often have computer tutorials that can help you refresh basic skills.

PREPARE FOR MATH AND SCIENCE EXAMS

Math and science exams often require additional preparation techniques. Here are some suggestions for doing well on these exams:

1. Do your homework regularly, even if it is not graded, and do all the assigned problems. As you do your homework, write out your work as carefully and clearly as you will be expected to do on your tests. This practice will allow you to use your homework as a review for the test.

2. Attend each class, and always be on time. Many instructors use the time at the beginning of class to review homework.

3. Create a review guide throughout the term. As you begin your homework each day, write out a random problem from each homework section in a notebook that you have set up for reviewing material for that course. As you review later, you will be able to come back to these problems to make sure you have a representative problem from each section you've studied.

4. Throughout the term, keep a list of definitions or important formulas. (These are great to put on flash cards.) Review one or two of these as part of every study session. Another technique is to post the formulas and definitions in prominent areas in your living space (e.g., on the bathroom wall, around your computer work area, or on the door of the microwave). Seeing this information frequently will help embed it in your mind.

Taking Tests and Exams

Throughout your college career you will take tests in many different formats, in many subject areas, and with many different types of questions. The following box offers test-taking tips that apply to any test situation.

TIPS FOR SUCCESSFUL TEST TAKING

1. **Write your name on the test** (unless you are directed not to) and on the answer sheet.

2. **Analyze, ask, and stay calm**. Before you start the test, take a long, deep breath and slowly exhale. Carefully read all the directions before beginning the test so that you understand what to do. Ask the instructor or exam

monitor for clarification if you don't understand something. Be confident. Don't panic. Answer one question at a time.

3. **Make the best use of your time**. Quickly survey the entire test and decide how much time you will spend on each section. Be aware of the point values of different sections of the test. If some questions are worth more points than others, they deserve more of your time.

4. **Jot down idea-starters before the test**. Before you even look at the test questions, turn the test paper over and take a moment to write down the formulas, definitions, and major ideas that you have been studying. (Check with your instructor ahead of time to be sure that this is okay.) This will help you go into the test with a feeling of confidence and knowledge, and it will provide quick access to the information while you are taking the test.

5. **Answer the easy questions first**. Expect that you'll be puzzled by some questions. Make a note to come back to them later. If different sections consist of different types of questions (such as multiple-choice, short-answer, and essay questions), complete the types of question you are most comfortable with first. Be sure to leave enough time for any essays.

6. **If you feel yourself starting to panic or go blank, stop whatever you are doing**. Take a long, deep breath and slowly exhale. Remind yourself you will be okay and that you do know the material and can do well on this test. Then take another deep breath. If necessary, go to another section of the test and come back later to the item that triggered your anxiety.

7. **If you finish early, don't leave**. Stay and check your work for errors. Reread the directions one last time. If you are using a Scantron answer sheet, make sure that all bubbles are filled in accurately and completely.

ESSAY QUESTIONS

Many college instructors have a strong preference for essay exams for a simple reason: Essay exams promote higher-order critical thinking, whereas other types of exams tend to be exercises in memorization. Generally, advanced courses are more likely to include essay exams. To be successful on essay exams, follow these guidelines:

1. **Budget your exam time**. Quickly survey the entire exam, and note the questions that are the easiest for you, along with their point values. Take a moment to weigh their values, estimate the approximate time you should allot to each question, and write the time beside each item number. Be sure you know whether you must answer all the questions or choose among questions. Remember, writing profusely on easy questions that have low value can be a costly error because it takes up precious time you might need for more important questions. Wear a watch so you can monitor your time, and include time at the end for a quick review.

2. **Develop a very brief outline of your answer before you begin to write**. Start working on the questions that are easiest for you, and jot down a few ideas before you begin to write. First, make sure that your outline responds to all parts of the question. Then use your first paragraph

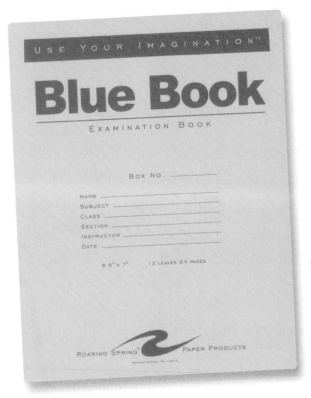

to introduce the main points and subsequent paragraphs to describe each point in more depth. If you begin to lose your concentration, you will be glad to have the outline to help you regain your focus. If you find that you are running out of time and cannot complete an essay, provide an outline of key ideas at the very least. Instructors usually assign points on the basis of your coverage of the main topics from the material. Thus you will usually earn more points by responding briefly to all parts of the question than by addressing just one aspect of the question in detail. An outline will often earn you partial credit even if you leave the essay unfinished.

3. **Write concise, organized answers.** Many well-prepared students write good answers to questions that were not asked because they did not read a question carefully or didn't respond to all parts of the question. Other students hastily write down everything they know on a topic. Instructors will give lower grades for answers that are vague and tend to ramble or for articulate answers that don't address the actual question.

4. **Know the key task words in essay questions.** Being familiar with the **key task word** in an essay question will help you answer it more specifically. The key task words in Table 9.1 appear frequently on essay tests. Take time to learn them so that you can answer essay questions as accurately and precisely as possible.

MULTIPLE-CHOICE QUESTIONS

Preparing for multiple-choice tests requires you to actively review all of the material that has been covered in the course. Reciting from flash cards, summary sheets, mind maps, or the recall column in your lecture notes is a good way to review these large amounts of material.

Take advantage of the many cues that multiple-choice questions contain. Careful reading of each item might uncover the correct answer. Always question choices that use absolute words such as *always*, *never*, and *only*. These choices are often (but not always) incorrect. Also, read carefully for terms such as *not*, *except*, and *but*, which are introduced before the choices. Often, the answer that is the most inclusive is correct. Generally, options that do not agree grammatically with the first part of the item are incorrect. For instance, what answers could you rule out in the example in Figure 9.2?

Some students are easily confused by multiple-choice answers that sound alike. The best way to respond to a multiple-choice question is to read the first part of the item and then predict your own answer before reading the options. Choose the letter that corresponds to the option that best matches your prediction.

TABLE 9.1 ▶ Key Task Words

Analyze	Divide something into its parts in order to understand it better; show how the parts work together to produce the overall pattern.
Compare	Look at the characteristics or qualities of several things, and identify their similarities or differences. Don't just describe the traits; define how the things are alike and how they are different.
Contrast	Identify the differences between things.
Criticize/ Critique	Analyze and judge something. Criticism can be positive, negative, or both. A criticism should generally contain your own judgments (supported by evidence) and those of authorities who can support your point.
Define	Give the meaning of a word or expression. Giving an example sometimes helps to clarify a definition, but an example by itself is not a definition.
Describe	Give a general verbal sketch of something in narrative or other form.
Discuss	Examine or analyze something in a broad and detailed way. Discussion often includes identifying the important questions related to an issue and attempting to answer these questions. A good discussion explores all relevant evidence and information.
Evaluate	Discuss the strengths and weaknesses of something. Evaluation is similar to criticism, but the word *evaluate* stresses the idea of how well something meets a certain standard or fulfills some specific purpose.
Explain	Clarify something. Explanations generally focus on why or how something has come about.
Interpret	Explain the meaning of something. In science you might explain what an experiment shows and what conclusions can be drawn from it. In a literature course you might explain—or interpret—what a poem means beyond the literal meaning of the words.
Justify	Argue in support of some decision or conclusion by showing sufficient evidence or reasons in its favor. Try to support your argument with both logical and concrete examples.
Narrate	Relate a series of events in the order in which they occurred. Generally, you will also be asked to explain something about the events you are narrating.
Outline	Present a series of main points in an appropriate order. Some instructors want an outline with Roman numerals for main points followed by letters for supporting details. If you are in doubt, ask the instructor whether he or she wants a formal outline.
Prove	Give a convincing logical argument and evidence in support of some statement.
Review	Summarize and comment on the main parts of a problem or a series of statements. A review question usually also asks you to evaluate or criticize.
Summarize	Give information in brief form, omitting examples and details. A summary is short but covers all important points.
Trace	Narrate a course of events. Whenever possible, you should show connections from one event to the next.

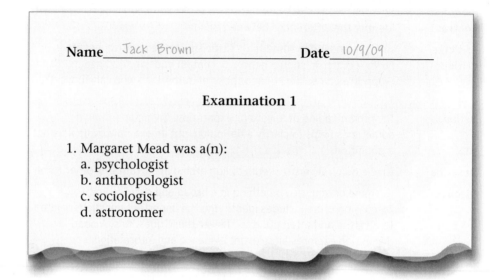

FIGURE 9.2 ▶

Multiple-choice question

If you are totally confused by a question, place a checkmark in the margin, leave it, and come back later, but always double-check that you are filling in the answer for the right question. Sometimes another question will provide a clue for a question you are unsure about. If you have absolutely no idea, look for an answer that at least contains some shred of information. If there is no penalty for guessing, fill in an answer for every question, even if it is just a guess. If there is a penalty for guessing, don't just choose an answer at random; leaving the answer blank might be a wiser choice.

FILL-IN-THE-BLANK QUESTIONS

In many ways preparing for fill-in-the-blank questions is similar to getting ready for multiple-choice items, but fill-in-the-blank questions can be harder because you do not have a choice of possible answers right in front of you. Not all fill-in-the-blank questions are constructed the same. Some teachers will provide a series of blanks to give you a clue about the number of words in the answer, but if just one long blank is provided, you can't assume that the answer is just one word. If possible, ask the teacher whether the answer is supposed to be a single word per blank or can be a longer phrase.

TRUE/FALSE QUESTIONS

Remember that for a statement to be true, every detail of the sentence must be true. Questions containing words such as *always*, *never*, and *only* tend to be false, whereas less definite terms such as *often* and *frequently* suggest the statement might be true. Read through the entire exam to see whether information in one question will help you answer another. Do not begin to second-guess what you know or doubt your answers just because a sequence of questions appears to be all true or all false.

MATCHING QUESTIONS

The matching question is the hardest type of question to answer by guessing. In one column you will find the terms, and in the other you will find their descriptions. Before answering any question, review all of the terms and descriptions. Then match the terms you are sure of. As you do so, cross out both the term and its description, and use the process of elimination to assist you in answering the remaining items. To prepare for matching questions, try using flash cards and lists that you create from the recall column in your notes.

Types of Tests

While you are in college, you will encounter many types of tests. Some tend to be used in particular disciplines; others can be used in any class you might take.

PROBLEM-SOLVING TESTS

In the physical and biological sciences, mathematics, engineering, statistics, and symbolic logic, some tests will require you to solve problems showing all steps. Even if you know a shortcut, it is important to document how you got from step A to step B. On other tests, all that will matter will be whether you have the correct solution to the problem, but doing all the steps will still help ensure that you get the right answer. For these tests, you must also be very careful that you have made no errors in your scientific notation. A misplaced sign, parenthesis, bracket, or exponent can make all the difference.

If you are allowed to use a calculator during the exam, it is important to check that your input is accurate. The calculator does what you tell it to, and if you miss a zero or a negative sign, the calculator will not give you the correct answer to the problem.

Be sure that you read all directions carefully. Are you required to reduce the answer to simplest terms? Are you supposed to graph the solution? Be careful when canceling terms, cross-multiplying, distributing terms, and combining fractions. Whenever possible, after you complete the problem, work it in reverse to check your solution, or plug your solution back into the equation and make sure it adds up. Also check to be sure that your solution makes sense. You can't have negative bushels of apples, for example, or a fraction of a person, or a correlation less than negative 1 or greater than 1. Write out each step clearly, with everything lined up as the instructor has indicated in class (lining up the equal signs with each other, for example).

MACHINE-SCORED TESTS

It is important that you carefully follow the directions for machine-scored tests. In addition to your name, be sure to provide all the necessary information on the answer sheet, such as the instructor's name, the number for the class section, or your student ID number. Each time you fill in an answer, make sure that the number on the answer sheet corresponds to the number of the item on the test. If you have questions that you want to come back to (if you are allowed to do so), mark them on the test rather than on the answer sheet.

Although scoring machines have become more sophisticated over time, stray marks on your answer sheet can still be misread and throw off the scoring. When a machine-scored test is returned to you, check your answer sheet against the scoring key, if one is provided, to make sure that you receive credit for all the questions you answered correctly.

COMPUTERIZED TESTS

Your comfort with taking computerized tests might depend on how computer literate you are in general for objective tests as well as your keyboarding skills for essay exams. If your instructor provides the opportunity for practice tests, be sure to take advantage of this chance to get a better sense of how the tests will be structured. There can be significant variations depending on the kind of test, the academic subject, and whether the test was constructed by the teacher or by a textbook company or by another source.

For multiple-choice and other objective forms of computerized tests, you might be allowed to scroll down and back through the entire test, but this is not always the case. Sometimes you are allowed to see only one question at a time, and after you complete that question, you might not be allowed to go back to it. In this situation you cannot skip questions that are hard and come back to them later, so be sure that you try to answer every question.

For computerized tests in math and other subjects that require you to solve each problem, record an answer and then move to the next problem. Be sure to check each answer before you submit it. Also, know in advance what materials you are allowed to have on hand, including a calculator and scratch paper for working the problems.

LABORATORY TESTS

In many science courses and in some other academic disciplines, you will be required to take lab tests during which you rotate from one lab station to the next and solve problems, identify parts of models or specimens, explain chemical reactions, and complete other tasks similar to those that you have been performing in lab. At some colleges and universities, lab tests are now administered at computer terminals via simulations. To prepare for lab tests, always attend lab, take good notes, including diagrams and other visual representations as necessary, and be sure to study your lab notebook carefully before the test. If possible, create your own diagrams or models, and then see whether you can label them without looking at your book.

You might also have lab tests in foreign language courses. These tests can include both oral and written components. Work with a partner or study group to prepare for oral exams. Ask each other questions that require using key vocabulary words. Try taping your answers to work on your pronunciation. You might also have computerized lab tests that require you to identify syllables or words and indicate the order and direction of the strokes required to create them, particularly in a foreign language that uses a different symbol system, such as Chinese. The best way to prepare for these tests is to learn the meanings and parts of the symbols and regularly practice writing them.

OPEN-BOOK AND OPEN-NOTE TESTS

If you never had open-book or open-note tests in high school, you might be tempted to study less thoroughly, thinking that you will have access to all the information you need during the test. This is a common misjudgment on the part of first-year students. Open-book and open-note tests are usually harder than other exams, not easier.

Most students don't really have time to spend looking things up during an open-book exam. The best way to prepare is to begin the same way you would study for a test in which you cannot refer to your notes or text. But as you do so, develop a list of topics and the page numbers where they are covered in your text. You might want to use the same strategy in organizing your lecture notes. Number the pages in your notebook. Later, type a three-column grid (or use an Excel spreadsheet) with your list of topics in alphabetical order in the first column and corresponding pages from your textbook and notebook in the second and third columns so that you can refer to them quickly if necessary. Or you might want to stick colored tabs onto your textbook or notebook pages for different topics. But whatever you do, study as completely as you would for any other test, and do not be fooled into thinking that you don't need to know the material thoroughly.

Wired WINDOW

TAKING ONLINE EXAMS

Even if you are typically enrolled in traditional face-to-face courses, you will undoubtedly take an increasing number of your exams online through course management systems (such as WebCT and Blackboard).

Some of the tips for successful test taking also apply to online exams. Ensure that you will be in a quiet area that is free of distractions while you take the exam. Learn about constraints (e.g., time limit, due date) before the exam by asking your instructor or logging in early to see if the constraints are posted online. If you haven't already done so, take a practice test so that you are familiar with the testing interface. If there is no time limit, take a break after you complete the exam and then go back and recheck your answers. If there is a time limit and the course management system does not show a timer, use a stopwatch or countdown timer to track your progress. (A good rule of thumb is to have the countdown timer sound once with enough time left for you to review the entire exam and then again with five minutes left.) Since you won't have a paper exam, you'll be unable to make notes on the exam itself. Be prepared to have a notepad with you to jot down notes.

You also won't be able to move easily back and forth between the pages of the exam to review your answers or skip questions for later. Therefore when reviewing your answers or going back to previous questions, make sure that you have saved every page of the exam. If you save your exam and have not yet submitted it for grading, you can use your browser's back button to review questions and answers on previous pages.

Thinking Critically

Consider the major differences between taking a paper-and-pencil exam in the classroom and taking it online. What are some ways in which you can apply test-taking strategies to an online environment? What challenges might you encounter when taking exams online? For instance, other open applications and websites might distract you. To reduce distractions, close applications and websites that you don't need before starting the exam. How can you deliberately set up your desktop workspace and the surrounding area so that you'll do your best on online exams?

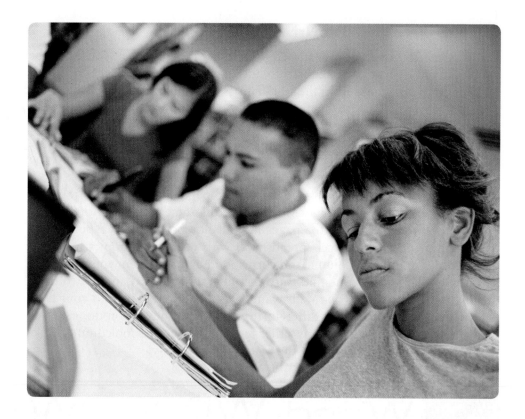

During the test, monitor your time carefully. Don't waste time unnecessarily looking up information in your text or notes to double-check yourself if you are reasonably confident of your answers. Instead, wait until you have finished the test, and then, if you have extra time, go back and look up answers and make any necessary changes. But if you have really studied, you probably will not find this necessary.

Sometimes the only reason a teacher allows open books or open notes is for students to properly reference their sources when responding to essay or short-answer tests. Make sure to clarify whether you are expected to document your answers and provide a reference or works cited list.

TAKE-HOME TESTS

Like open-book and open-note tests, take-home tests are usually more difficult than in-class tests. Many take-home tests are essay tests, though some teachers will give take-home objective tests. Be sure to allow plenty of time to complete a take-home test. Read the directions and questions as soon as you receive the test to help you gauge how much time you will need. If the test is all essays, consider how much time you might allocate to writing several papers of the same length. Remember that your teacher will expect your essay answers to look more like assigned out-of-class papers than like the essays you would write during an in-class test.

Unfortunately, issues of academic honesty can arise for take-home tests. If you are accustomed to working with a study group or in a learning community for the course, check with the teacher in advance to determine the extent to which collaboration is allowed on the test. One thing that can be very confusing for students is to be encouraged to work together throughout the academic term and then to be told that there should be no communication outside of class about a take-home test.

Overcoming Test Anxiety

Test anxiety takes many different forms. Part of combating test anxiety is understanding its sources and identifying its symptoms. Whatever the source, be assured that test anxiety is common.

Test anxiety has many sources. It can be the result of the pressure that students put on themselves to succeed. Without any pressure, students would not be motivated to study; some stress connected with taking exams is natural and can enhance performance. However, when students put too much pressure on themselves or set unrealistic goals, the result is stress that is no longer motivating, only debilitating.

The expectations of parents, a spouse, friends, and other people who are close to you can also induce test anxiety. Sometimes, for example, students who are the first in their families to attend college bear the weight of generations before them who have not had this opportunity. The pressure can be overwhelming!

Finally, some test anxiety is caused by lack of preparation—by not keeping up with assigned reading, homework, and other academic commitments leading up to the test. Procrastination can begin a downward spiral because after you do poorly on the first test in a course, there is even more pressure to do well on subsequent tests to pull up your course grade. This situation becomes even more dire if the units of the course build on one another, as in math and foreign languages, or if the final exam is cumulative. While you are having to master the new material after the test, you are still trying to catch up on the old material as well.

Some test anxiety comes from a negative prior experience. Transcending the memory of negative past experiences can be a challenge. But remember that the past is not the present. Perhaps there are good reasons why you performed poorly in the past. You might not have prepared for the test, you might not have read the questions carefully, or you might not have studied with other students or sought prior assistance from your professor or a tutor. If you carefully follow the strategies in this chapter, you are very likely to do well on all your tests. Remember that a little anxiety is okay. But if you find that anxiety is getting in the way of your performance on tests and exams, be sure to seek help from your campus counseling center.

YOUR TURN ▶

Do you experience any type of test anxiety? If so, what causes you to be anxious? If not, what strategies do you use to stay calm?

TYPES OF TEST ANXIETY

Students who experience test anxiety under some circumstances don't necessarily feel it in all testing situations. For example, you might do fine on classroom tests but feel anxious during standardized examinations such as the SAT and ACT. One reason standardized tests are so anxiety provoking is the notion that they determine your future. Believing that the stakes are so high can create unbearable pressure. One way of dealing with this type of test anxiety is to ask yourself: What is the worst that can happen? Remember that no matter what the result, it is not the end of the world. How you do on standardized tests might limit some of your options, but going into these tests with a negative attitude will certainly not improve your chances. Attending preparation workshops and taking practice exams not only can better prepare you for standardized tests, but also can assist you in overcoming your anxiety. And remember that many standardized tests can be taken again at a later time, giving you the opportunity to prepare better and pull up your score.

Some students are anxious only about some types of classroom tests. Practice always helps in overcoming test anxiety; if you fear essay exams, try predicting exam questions and writing sample essays as a means of reducing your anxiety.

Some students have difficulty taking tests at a computer terminal. Some of this anxiety might be related to lack of computer experience. On the other hand, not all computerized tests are user-friendly. You might be allowed to see only one item at a time. Often, you do not have the option of going back and checking over all your answers before submitting them. In preparation for computerized tests, ask the instructor questions about how the test will be structured. Also, make sure you take any opportunities to take practice tests at a learning center or lab.

Test anxiety can often be subject-specific. For example, some students have math test anxiety. It is important to distinguish between anxiety that arises from the subject matter itself and more generalized test anxiety. Perhaps subject-specific test anxiety relates to old beliefs about yourself, such as "I'm no good at math" or "I can't write well." Now is the time to try some positive self-talk and realize that by preparing well, you can be successful even in your hardest courses. If the problem persists, talk to someone in your campus counseling center to develop strategies to overcome irrational fears that can prevent you from doing your best.

SYMPTOMS OF TEST ANXIETY

Test anxiety can manifest itself in many ways. Some students feel it on the very first day of class. Other students begin showing symptoms of test anxiety when it's time to start studying for a test. Others do not get nervous until the night before the test or the morning of an exam day. And some students experience symptoms only while they are actually taking a test.

Symptoms of test anxiety can include butterflies in the stomach, queasiness or nausea, severe headaches, a faster heartbeat, hyperventilating, shaking, sweating, or muscle cramps. During the exam itself, students who are overcome with test anxiety can experience the sensation of "going blank," that is, being unable to remember what they actually know. At this point, students can undermine both their emotional and academic preparation for the test and convince themselves that they cannot succeed.

Test anxiety can impede the success of any college student, no matter how intelligent, motivated, and prepared. That is why it is critical to seek help from your college or university's counseling service or another professional if you think that you have significant test anxiety. If you are not sure where to go for help, ask your advisor, but seek help promptly! If your symptoms are so severe that you become physically ill (with migraine headaches, hyperventilating, or vomiting), you should also consult your physician or campus health service.

STRATEGIES FOR COMBATING TEST ANXIETY

In addition to studying, eating right, and getting plenty of sleep, there are a number of simple strategies you can use to overcome the physical and emotional impact of test anxiety. First, any time that you begin to feel nervous or upset, take a long, deep breath and slowly exhale to restore your breathing to a normal level. This is the quickest and easiest relaxation device, and no one even needs to know that you are doing it.

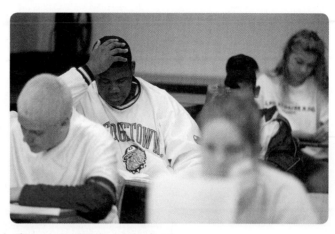

Before you go into the test room, especially before a multiple-hour final exam or before sitting through several exams on the same day, it can help to stretch your muscles just as you would when preparing to exercise. Stretch your calf and hamstring muscles, and roll your ankles. Stretch your arms, and roll your shoulders. Tilt your head to the right, front, and left to stretch your neck muscles.

When you sit down to take the test, pay attention to the way you are sitting. Sit with your shoulders back and relaxed, rather than shrugged forward, and put your feet flat on the floor. Smooth out your facial muscles rather than wrinkling your forehead or frowning. Resist the temptation to clutch your pencil or pen tightly in your fist; take a break and stretch your fingers now and then.

Anxiety-reducing techniques that might be available through your campus counseling center include systematic desensitization, progressive muscle relaxation, and visualization. One of the most popular techniques is creating your own peaceful scene and mentally taking yourself there when you need to relax. Try to use all five senses to recreate your peaceful scene in your mind: What would you see, hear, feel, taste, or smell?

These strategies can assist you in relaxing physically, but meanwhile, you must also pay attention to the mental messages that you are sending yourself. Focus on the positive! If you are telling yourself that you are not smart enough, that you did not study the right material, or that you are going to fail, you need to turn those messages around with a technique called **cognitive restructuring**. We all talk to ourselves, so make sure that your messages are encouraging rather than stress provoking. When you are studying, practice sending yourself positive messages: I really know this stuff. I am going to ace this test!

Similarly, do not allow others, including classmates, your spouse, parents, or friends, to undermine your confidence. If you belong to a study group, discuss the need to stay positive. Sometimes, getting to the test room early will expose you to other students who are asking questions or making comments that are only going to make you nervous. Get to the building early, but wait until just a few minutes before the exam begins to approach the classroom itself. If at any point during a test you begin to feel like you cannot think clearly, or you have trouble remembering or you come to a question you cannot answer, stop for a brief moment, and take another long, deep breath and slowly exhale. Then remind yourself of the positive self-messages you have been practicing.

GETTING THE TEST BACK

Students react differently when they receive their test grades and papers. For some students the thought of seeing the actual graded test produces high levels of anxiety. But unless you look at the instructor's comments and your answers (the correct and incorrect ones), you will have no way to evaluate your own knowledge and test-taking strengths. You might also find that the instructor made an error in the grade that might have cost you a point or two. Be sure to let the instructor know if you find an error.

It is important that you review your graded test. You might find that your mistakes were caused by failing to follow directions, being careless with words or numbers, or overanalyzing a multiple-choice question. If you have any questions about your grade, be sure to talk to the instructor. You might be able to negotiate a few points in your favor, but in any case, you will let your instructor know that you are concerned and want to learn how to do better on graded tests and examinations.

> **YOUR TURN ▶**
>
> What actions do you take when you look at graded tests? Take a look at an exam you got back in one of your classes. What can you learn from it? Would you challenge an instructor if you thought he or she had made a mistake in your grade? Why or why not?

Academic Honesty and Misconduct

Imagine what our world would be like if researchers reported fraudulent results that were then used to develop new machines or medical treatments or to build bridges, airplanes, or subway systems. Integrity is a cornerstone of higher education, and activities that compromise that integrity damage everyone: your country, your community, your college or university, your classmates, and yourself.

CHEATING

Institutions vary widely in how they define broad terms such as "lying" or "cheating." One university defines cheating as "intentionally using or attempting to use unauthorized materials, information, notes, study aids, or other devices . . . [including] unauthorized communication of information during an academic exercise." This would apply to looking over a classmate's shoulder for an answer, using a calculator when it is not authorized, obtaining or discussing an exam (or individual questions from an exam) without permission, copying someone else's lab notes, purchasing term papers over the Internet, watching the video instead of reading the book, and duplicating computer files.

PLAGIARISM

Plagiarism, or taking another person's ideas or work and presenting them as your own, is especially intolerable in academic culture. Just as taking someone else's property constitutes physical theft, taking credit for someone else's ideas constitutes intellectual theft.

On most tests, you don't have to credit specific sources. (But some instructors do require this. When in doubt, ask!) In written reports and papers, however, you must give credit any time you use (a) another person's actual words, (b) another person's ideas or theories—even if you don't quote them directly, or (c) any other information that is not considered common knowledge.

Many schools prohibit certain activities in addition to lying, cheating, unauthorized assistance, and plagiarism. Some examples of prohibited behaviors are intentionally inventing information or results, earning credit more than once for the same piece of academic work without permission, giving your work or exam answers to another student to copy during the actual exam or before that exam is given to another section, and bribing in exchange for any kind of academic advantage. Most schools also outlaw helping or attempting to help another student commit a dishonest act.

CONSEQUENCES OF CHEATING AND PLAGIARISM

Although you might see some students who seem to be getting away with cheating or plagiarizing, the consequences of such behaviors can be severe and life-changing. Recent cases of cheating on examinations and plagiarizing major papers have caused some college students to be suspended or expelled and even to have their college degrees revoked. Writers and journalists whose plagiarism has been discovered, such as Jayson Blair, formerly of the *New York Times*, and Stephen Glass, formerly of the *New Republic*, have lost their jobs and their journalistic careers. Even college presidents have occasionally been found guilty of "borrowing" the words of others and using them as their own in speeches and written documents. Such discoveries result not only in embarrassment and shame, but also in lawsuits and criminal actions.

Because plagiarism can be a problem on college campuses, faculty members are now using electronic systems such as www.turnitin.com to identify passages in student papers that have been plagiarized. Many instructors routinely check their students' papers to make sure that the writing is original. So even though the temptation to cheat or plagiarize might be strong, the chance of possibly getting a better grade isn't worth misrepresenting yourself or your knowledge and suffering the potential consequences.

REDUCING THE LIKELIHOOD OF ACADEMIC DISHONESTY

To avoid becoming intentionally or unintentionally involved in academic misconduct, consider the reasons why it could happen:

- **Ignorance.** In a survey at the University of South Carolina, 20 percent of students incorrectly thought that buying a term paper wasn't cheating. Forty percent thought using a test file (a collection of actual tests from previous terms) was fair behavior. Sixty percent thought it was acceptable to get answers from someone who had taken the exam earlier in the same or in a prior term. What do you think?
- **Cultural and campus differences.** In other countries and on some U.S. campuses, students are encouraged to review past exams as practice exercises. Some student government associations maintain test files for use by students. Some campuses permit sharing answers and information for homework and other assignments with friends. Make sure you know the policy on your specific campus.

- **Different policies among instructors.** Because there is no universal code that dictates such behaviors, ask your instructors for clarification. When a student is caught violating the academic code of a particular school or instructor, pleading ignorance of the rules is a weak defense.

- **A belief that grades are all that matter.** This might reflect our society's competitive atmosphere. It also might be the result of pressure from parents, peers, or teachers. In truth, grades are nothing if one has cheated to earn them. Even if your grades help you get a job, it is what you have actually learned that will help you keep the job and be promoted. If you haven't learned what you need to know, you won't be ready to work in your chosen field.

- **Lack of preparation or inability to manage time and activities.** If you are tempted to cheat because you are unprepared, ask an instructor to extend a deadline so that a project can be done well.

The following box outlines some steps you can take to reduce the likelihood of problems:

GUIDELINES FOR ACADEMIC HONESTY

1. **Know the rules.** Learn the academic code for your college by going to its website. Also learn about any department guidelines on cheating or plagiarism. Study course syllabi. If a teacher does not clarify standards and expectations, ask exactly what they are.

2. **Set clear boundaries.** Refuse when others ask you to help them cheat. This might be hard to do, but you must say no. In test settings, keep your answers covered and your eyes down, and put all extraneous materials away, including cell phones. Now that cell phones enable text messaging, instructors are rightfully suspicious when they see students looking at their cell phones during an exam.

3. **Improve time management.** Be well prepared for all quizzes, exams, projects, and papers. This might mean unlearning habits such as procrastination (see Chapter 2, "Managing Your Time").

4. **Seek help.** Find out where you can obtain assistance with study skills, time management, and test taking. If your methods are in good shape but the content of the course is too difficult, consult your instructor, join a study group, or visit your campus learning center or tutorial service.

5. **Withdraw from the course.** Your institution has a policy about dropping courses and a deadline to drop without penalty. You might decide to drop only the course that's giving you trouble. Some students choose to withdraw from all classes and take time off before returning to school if they find themselves in over their heads or if a long illness, a family crisis, or some other unexpected occurrence has caused them to fall behind. Before withdrawing, you should ask about campus policies as well as ramifications in terms of federal financial aid and other scholarship programs. See your advisor or counselor.

6. **Reexamine goals.** Stick to your own realistic goals instead of giving in to pressure from family members or friends to achieve impossibly high standards. You might also feel pressure to enter a particular career or profession that is of little or no interest to you. If that happens, sit down with counseling or career services professionals or your academic advisor and explore alternatives.

Where to go
FOR HELP . . .

ON CAMPUS ▶

Learning Assistance Support Center Almost every campus has one of these, and studying for tests is one of its specialties. The best students, good students who want to be the best students, and students with academic difficulties use learning centers and tutoring services. These services are offered by both full-time professionals and highly skilled student tutors and usually are free.

Counseling Services College and university counseling centers offer a wide array of services, often including workshops and individual or group counseling for test anxiety. Sometimes these services are also offered by the campus health center.

Fellow College Students Often the best help we can get is the closest to us. Keep an eye out in your classes, residence hall, and extracurricular activities for the best students, those who appear to be the most serious, purposeful, and directed. Find a tutor. Join a study group. Students who do these things are much more likely to be successful.

ONLINE ▶

The Academic Center for Excellence, University of Illinois at Chicago: http://www.uic.edu/depts/counselctr/ace/examprep.htm.

This website provides a list of tips to help you prepare for exams.

Learning Centre of the University of New South Wales in Sydney, Australia: http://www.lc.unsw.edu.au/onlib/exam.html.

Includes the popular SQ3R method.

MY INSTITUTION'S RESOURCES ▶

_____

_____

_____

_____

_____

_____

_____

_____

_____

_____

_____

_____

_____

One-Minute PAPER . . .

As you were reading the tips for improving your performance on exams and tests, were you surprised to see different tips for different subjects, such as math and science, and for different kinds of tests, such as multiple-choice and essay? What did you find to be the most useful information in this chapter? What material was unclear to you?

Applying What You've LEARNED . . .

Now that you have read and discussed this chapter, consider how you can apply what you have learned to your academic and personal life. The following prompts will help you reflect on the chapter material and its relevance to you both now and in the future.

1. Identify your next upcoming test or exam. What class is it for? When is it scheduled (morning, afternoon, or evening)? What type of test will it be (problem solving, computerized, etc.)? List the specific strategies described in this chapter that will help you prepare for and take this test.

2. Is there one particular course that you find more difficult than others? You probably deal with some form of anxiety when it comes to taking a test in that class. To help you deal with that anxiety, adopt a positive self-message or "mantra"—something to help you stay focused. Think of a phrase or sentence to say to yourself when you begin to doubt your ability to succeed. It could be one of your favorite quotes, lyrics from a song, or even something as simple as "I know I can do this!"

Building Your PORTFOLIO . . .

66 I desire so to conduct the affairs of this administration that if at the end, when I come to lay down the reins of power, I have lost every other friend on earth, I shall at least have one friend left, and that friend shall be down inside me. 99

–ABRAHAM LINCOLN (1809-1865),
Sixteenth President of the United States

A HIGH PRICE TO PAY

Academic integrity is a supreme value on college and university campuses. Faculty members, staff, and students are held to a strict code of academic integrity, and the consequences of breaking that code can be severe and life-changing. Create a Word document to record your responses to the following activity.

1. Imagine that your college or university has hired you to conduct a month-long academic integrity awareness campaign so that students will learn about and take seriously your campus's guidelines for academic integrity. To prepare for your "new job":

    a. Visit your institution's website and use the search feature to find the academic integrity code or policy. Take the time to read through the code, violations, and sanctions.

    b. Visit the judicial affairs office on your campus to learn more about the way your institution deals with violations of academic integrity policies.

    c. Research online resources from other campuses, such as information from the Center for Academic Integrity, hosted by Clemson University (http://www.academicintegrity.org/). This link describes the university's Fundamental Values Project.

    d. Check out several other college and university academic integrity policies and/or honor codes. How do they compare to your institution's code or policy?

2. Outline your month-long awareness campaign. Here are a few ideas to get you started:

    • Plan a new theme every week. Don't forget Internet-related violations.

    • Develop eye-catching posters to display around campus. (Check out the posters designed by students at Elizabethtown College in Pennsylvania, found at http://www.rubberpaw.com/integrity/)

    • Consider guest speakers, debates, skits, or other presentations.

    • Come up with catchy slogans or phrases.

    • Send students a postcard highlighting your institution's policies or honor code.

    • Consider the most effective ways to communicate your message to different groups on campus.

Academic Integrity Awareness Campaign	Events Plan
Week 1	
Week 2	
Week 3	
Week 4	

3. Consider what you have learned through your research. You might want to share your campaign ideas with other students in your class and even select the best ideas for presentation to your campus student affairs office or judicial board.

4. Save your work in your portfolio on your personal computer or flash drive.

10 Writing and Speaking Effectively

In this chapter you will explore

- How writing is a process that leads to a product
- Ways to review and revise your writing
- The importance of recognizing the difference between formal and informal writing
- Six steps to success in preparing a speech
- How best to use your voice and body language
- How to sound organized when speaking on the spot

NICK MURPHY, 23
Bridgewater State College

66 For a long time, I thought that having to revise something was proof that I had failed. But that's crazy. 99

I really like English. It may a sound a little nerdy, but I would honestly get excited about going to a poetry class. I was even asked to be a writer for a school paper. Yet writing freezes me up sometimes. I think it's because I'm a bit of a perfectionist. I want to get the words down right the first time, and for a long time, I thought that having to revise something was proof that I had failed. But that's crazy.

I'm a musician, so I know how important practice is. I spent hours in my dorm room just playing guitar, and I became a better guitar player for it. Finally I realized that the same principle applies to writing: The more you do it, the better you get. And it pays to take risks. When I'm working on a song, I'll toy around with different parts—the chords, the tempo, the phrasing, whatever—until I like the way it sounds. Why shouldn't I do the same thing with a paper? Giving myself permission to experiment and to make mistakes has made writing so much easier. I can try out different ideas and see where they go, and if I don't like the results, it's no big deal. I just try something different. With each attempt, I'm improving what I write.

Writing

and speaking are the two basic forms of communication. The ability to write well and speak well makes a tremendous difference in how the rest of the world perceives you and how well you will be able to communicate throughout your life. But you will find that you often need to communicate differently depending on who is reading or listening to your words. Each time you speak or write, you are addressing an audience. The audience might be one person—a friend, family member, professor, or a potential employer—or your audience might be a group, such as your classmates in college. Some audiences might be unknown to you. For instance, if you're writing a book or an article for publication, a blog entry, or something on your Facebook or MySpace page, you never know who might read your words. To communicate effectively, it's important to think about your audience, what they will understand and expect, and how they will react to what you are saying or writing. It's generally okay to use informal language with your friends, family, and other college students, for example, but your instructors and potential employers will expect more formal writing and speaking.

Experts suggest that there's no single, universally accepted standard for how to speak or write American English. Even so, school systems, professional communicators, and businesses all have standards, and, not surprisingly, the rules do not vary dramatically from place to place. If they did, we would have a hard time understanding one another. Our purpose in this chapter is not to teach you grammar and punctuation (we'll save that for your English classes), but to get you to think of writing and speaking as processes (how you get there) as well as products (the final paper or script) and to help you overcome those writer's and speaker's blocks we all encounter from time to time.

You might wonder: Why can't more people express themselves effectively? The answers vary, but all come back to the same theme: Most people do not think of writing and speaking as processes to be mastered step by step. Instead, they view writing and speaking as products; you knock them out and you're done. Nothing could be further from the truth.

Whatever career you choose, you will be expected to think, create, communicate, manage, and lead. A 2002 survey by the Plain English Network found that 96 percent of the nation's 1,000 largest employers say that employees must have good communication skills to get ahead. This means you will have to be able to write and speak well. You will have to write reports about your work and the performance of others, e-mails to describe problems and propose solutions, and position papers to explain and justify to your superiors why the organization must make certain changes.

As you lead and manage others, you also will need strong speaking skills in order to explain, report, motivate, direct, encourage, and inspire. You might have to give presentations in meetings to your superiors and their subordinates and then follow up with a written report or e-mail. So as you prepare yourself for a career, you need to start thinking of yourself as a person who is both a good thinker and an outstanding communicator.

WRITING

William Zinsser, author of several books on writing, claims, "The act of writing gives the teacher a window into the mind of the student."[1] In other words, your writing provides tangible evidence of how well you think and how well you understand concepts related to the courses you are taking. Your writing might also reveal a good sense of humor, a compassion for the less fortunate, a respect for family, and many other things. Zinsser reminds us that writing is not merely something that writers do; it is a basic skill for getting through life. He claims that far too many Americans cannot perform useful work because they never learned to express themselves.

Using Freewriting to Discover What You Want to Say

Writing expert Peter Elbow asserts that it's impossible to write effectively if you simultaneously try to organize, check grammar and spelling, and offer intelligent thoughts to your readers.[2] He argues that it can't all be done at once, mainly because you use the right—or creative—side of your brain to create thoughts, whereas you use the left—or logical—side for grammar, spelling, organization, and so forth.

[1] William Zinsser, *On Writing Well* (New York: Harper Resource 25th Anniversary Edition, 2001).
[2] Peter Elbow, *Writing without Teachers* (New York: Oxford University Press, 1973).

Elbow argues that we can free up our writing and bring more energy and voice into it by writing more like the way we speak and trying to avoid the heavy overlay of editing in our initial efforts to write. This preliminary step in the writing process is called "freewriting." By freewriting, Elbow simply means writing that is temporarily unencumbered by mechanical processes, such as punctuation, grammar, spelling, and context. Freewriting is also a way to break the habit of trying to write and edit at the same time.

The freewriting process can be difficult at first because it goes against the grain of how we are accustomed to writing. We normally edit as we write, pausing to collect our thoughts, to recollect the correct spelling of a word, to cross out a sentence that does not belong, to reject a paragraph that doesn't fit with the argument that we are making, or to mentally outline a structure of the argument that we are trying to make. Once you get the hang of it, though, it can become second nature.

YOUR TURN ▶

Have you tried freewriting before? To see what freewriting feels like, write, "My writing speaks for me." Write for at least ten minutes, nonstop, about that statement. Don't think about organization, grammar, punctuation, or spelling, and don't stop writing until the time is up. Discuss with your classmates your reactions to writing this way and what each of you wrote.

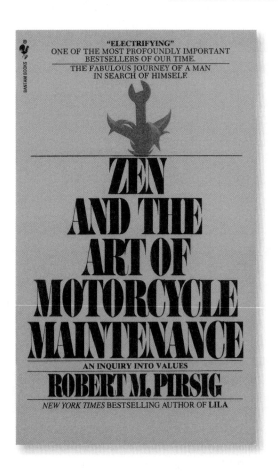

"ELECTRIFYING"
ONE OF THE MOST PROFOUNDLY IMPORTANT
BESTSELLERS OF OUR TIME.
THE FABULOUS JOURNEY OF A MAN
IN SEARCH OF HIMSELF.

ZEN AND THE ART OF MOTORCYCLE MAINTENANCE

AN INQUIRY INTO VALUES

ROBERT M. PIRSIG

NEW YORK TIMES BESTSELLING AUTHOR OF *LILA*

NARROWING YOUR TOPIC

In *Zen and the Art of Motorcycle Maintenance*,[3] Robert Pirsig tells a story about a first-year English class he had taught. Each week he assigned students a 500-word essay to write. One week, a student failed to submit her paper about the town where the college was located, explaining that she had "thought and thought, but couldn't think of anything to write about." Pirsig gave her an additional weekend to complete the assignment. As he said this, an idea flashed through his mind. "I want you to write a 500-word paper just about Main Street, not the whole town," he said. She gasped and stared at him angrily. How was she to narrow her thinking to just one street when she couldn't think of a thing to write about the entire town? On Monday she arrived in tears. "I'll never learn to write," she said. Pirsig's answer: "Write a paper about one building on Main Street. The opera house. And start with the first brick on the lower left side. I want it next class."

The student's eyes opened wide. She walked into the next class with a 5,000-word paper on the opera house. In writing this paper, she had been freewriting but hadn't realized it. "I don't know what happened," she exclaimed. "I sat across the street and wrote about the first brick, then the second, and all of a sudden I couldn't stop." What

[3]Robert Pirsig, *Zen and the Art of Motorcycle Maintenance* (New York: Bantam Books, 1984).

had Pirsig done for this person? He had helped her find a focus and a place to begin. Getting started is what blocks most students from approaching writing properly. Faced with an ultimatum, the student probably began to see the beauty of the opera house for the first time and had gone on to describe it, to find out more about it in the library, to ask others about it, and to comment on its setting among the other buildings on the block.

Very few writers—even professionally published ones—say what they want to say on their first try. And the sad fact is that really good writers are in the minority. But through practice, an understanding of the writing process, and dedication, more people can improve their writing skills. And good writers can make good money.

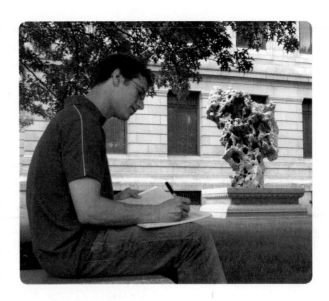

EXPLORATORY WRITING

Another way to think about writing is to distinguish between exploratory writing and explanatory writing. Those terms practically define themselves, but here are some clearer definitions: **Exploratory writing**, like freewriting, helps you discover what you want to say; **explanatory writing** then allows you to transmit those ideas to others. Explanatory writing is "published," meaning you have chosen to allow others to read it (your teacher, your friends, other students, or the public at large), but it is important that most or all of your exploratory writing be private, to be read only by you as a series of steps toward your published work. Keeping your early drafts under wraps frees you to say what you mean and mean what you say. Later, you will come back and make adjustments, and each revision will strengthen your message.

Some writers say they gather their best thoughts through exploratory writing: by researching their topic, writing down ideas from their research, and adding their questions and reactions to what they have gathered. As they write, their minds begin to make connections between ideas. At this stage, they don't attempt to organize, to find exactly the right words, or to think about structure. But when they move from exploratory writing to explanatory writing, their preparation will help them form crystal clear sentences, spell correctly, and have their thoughts organized so that their material flows naturally from one point to the next.

The Writing Process

One of the more popular ways of thinking about the writing process includes the following steps:

1. **Prewriting or rehearsing (freewriting).** This step includes preparing to write by filling your mind with information from other sources. It is generally considered the first stage of exploratory writing.
2. **Writing or drafting.** This step is when exploratory writing becomes a rough explanatory draft.

3. **Rewriting or revision.** This step is when you polish your work until it clearly explains what you want to communicate and is ready for your audience.

Many students turn in poorly written papers because they skip the first and last steps and make do with the middle one. Perhaps they don't have time because they have overloaded their schedule or they put off things until the night before the paper is due. Whatever the reason, the result is often a poorly written assignment, since the best writing is usually done over an extended period of time, not as a last-minute task. Most professional writers and speakers would never start preparing an assignment only a day or hours before it has to be delivered. For one thing, the mere anxiety such a situation creates would be more than enough to shut down any manner of intelligent thinking. Worrying about your grammar and spelling as you write what might be your only draft can lead to a low grade or a rejection from a career inquiry.

YOUR TURN ▶

Describe your writing process. What steps do you go through when you write a major paper?

PREWRITING: THE IDEA STAGE

Many writing experts, such as Donald Murray,[4] believe that of all the steps, **prewriting** (or freewriting) should take the longest. During freewriting you might question things that seem illogical. You might recall what you've heard other people say. This should lead you to write more, to ask yourself whether your views are more reliable than those of others, whether the topic might be too broad or too narrow, and so forth.

What constitutes an appropriate topic or thesis? When is it neither too broad nor too narrow? Test your topic by writing, "The purpose of this paper is to convince my readers that . . ." (but don't use that stilted line in your eventual paper). Pay attention to the assignment. Know the limits of your knowledge, the limitations on your time, and your ability to do the necessary research.

WRITING: THE BEGINNING OF ORGANIZATION

Once you have completed your research and feel you have exhausted the information sources and ideas, it's time to move to the writing, or drafting, stage. It might be a good idea to begin with a **thesis statement** and an outline so that you can put things where they logically belong. A thesis statement is a short statement that clearly defines the purpose of the paper (see Figure 10.1).

Once you have a workable outline and thesis, you can begin paying attention to the flow of ideas from one sentence to the next and from one paragraph to the next, including subheadings where needed. If you have chosen the thesis carefully, it will help you check to see that each sentence relates to your main idea. When you have completed this stage, you will have the first draft of your paper in hand.

[4]Donald Murray, *Learning by Teaching: Selected Articles on Writing and Teaching* (Portsmouth, NH: Boynton/Cook, 1982).

Thesis: Napoleon's dual personality can be explained by examining incidents throughout his life.
1. Explain why I am using the term "dual personality" to describe Napoleon
2. Briefly comment on his early life and his relationship with his mother.
3. Describe Napoleon's rise to fame from soldier to emperor. Stress the contradictions in his personality and attitudes.
4. Describe the contradictions in his relationship with Josephine.
5. Summarize my thoughts about Napoleon's personality.
6. Possibly conclude by referring to opening question: "Did Napoleon actually have a dual personality?"

◄ **FIGURE 10.1**
Thesis Statement

REWRITING: THE POLISHING STAGE

Are you finished? Not by a long shot. Next comes the stage at which you take a good piece of writing and do your best to make it great. The essence of good writing is rewriting. You read. You correct. You add smoother transitions. You slash through wordy sentences and paragraphs, removing anything that is repetitious or adds nothing of value to your paper. You substitute stronger words for weaker ones. You double-check spelling and grammar. It also

Wired WINDOW

WIKIPEDIA: A GOOD SOURCE?

Wikipedia is an online encyclopedia that contains content generated by its users. You might have used Wikipedia to do research for term papers in high school. Unlike the content in traditional encyclopedias, what is found on Wikipedia is never systematically reviewed by topic experts. So who can add or edit content on Wikipedia? The answer is anyone. Sometimes, this creates chaos on Wikipedia pages when users spend a lot of time quarreling over facts. In theory, these discussions can lead to better content on the more popular Wikipedia pages; however, on less popular pages, information can be grossly inaccurate. Knowing this, you should not be surprised that many of your professors will not allow the use of Wikipedia as a source for your research papers.

The discussion of whether or how Wikipedia can be used as a legitimate source continues in the academic world. Many faculty members at one extreme of the debate argue that Wikipedia is nothing more than an opinion-based website, while those on the other end argue that the "crowdsourcing" that occurs because of Wikipedia is the ultimate form of peer review. The main point of the argument is that Wikipedia arrives at knowl-

edge by bypassing the established process of scientific inquiry, which includes conducting research that meets certain criteria and publishing research in periodicals reviewed by experts in the field. So before you begin your research papers, check with your professors to see whether they will allow you to use Wikipedia as a reference. If they do, use it sparingly, focusing on its ability to provide a quick source of potential information that you can verify (or discount) using other sources that are more acceptable to your instructors.

Thinking Critically

What's your opinion of Wikipedia? Do you think that faculty members should consider Wikipedia the "ultimate form of peer review," or should they treat it as useless? Search for a popular Wikipedia entry that you can corroborate with an external source (such as a textbook or a research article). Are there differences of opinion between the external source and the Wikipedia article? If so, how would you judge what information is correct? How would you suggest improving Wikipedia to make it more acceptable to the academic world?

might help to share your paper with one or more of your classmates to get their feedback. This is typically called "peer review." Once you have talked with your reviewers about their suggested changes, you can either accept or reject them. At this point, you are ready to finalize your writing and "publish" (turn in) your paper.

ALLOCATING TIME

When writer Donald Murray was asked how long a writer should spend on each of the three stages, he suggested the following:

Prewriting: 85 percent (including research and rumination)

Writing: 1 percent (the first draft)

Rewriting: 14 percent (revising until it's suitable for "publication")

When readers offer meaningful feedback, you might want to begin the process again, returning to prewriting, then writing, then rewriting (Figure 10.2).

If Murray's figures surprise you, here's a true story about a writer who was assigned to create a brochure. He had other jobs to do and kept avoiding that one. But the other work he was doing had a direct bearing on the brochure he was asked to write. So as he was putting this assignment off, he was also "researching" material for it.

After nearly three months, he finally decided it was time to move forward on the brochure. He sat at his computer and dashed the words off in just under thirty minutes. The more he wrote, the faster the ideas popped into his head. He actually was afraid to stop until he had finished. He read his words, made revisions, sent the result around the office for peer review, incorporated some suggestions, and the brochure was published.

He had spent a long time prewriting (working with related information without trying to write the brochure). He went through the writing stage quickly because his mind was primed for the task. As a result, he had time to polish his work before the first draft.

You can use a similar process. Begin writing the day you get the assignment, even if it's only for ten or fifteen minutes. That way, you won't be confronting a blank screen or piece of paper later. Write something on the

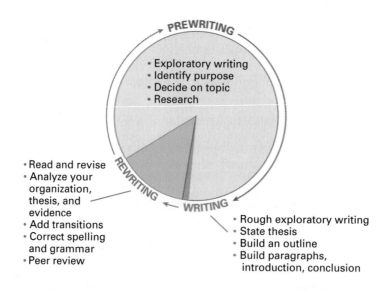

FIGURE 10.2 ▶

The Writing Process

assignment every day; the more you write, the better you'll write. Dig for ideas. *Reject nothing* at first, and then revise later. Read good writing; it will help you find your own writing style. Above all, know that becoming a better thinker and writer takes hard work, but practice can make near perfect.

Choosing the Best Way to Communicate with Your Audience

Before you came to college, you probably spent much more time writing informally than writing formally. Think about all the time you've spent writing e-mails, Facebook and blog comments, text messages, and instant messages (IMs). Now think about all the time you've spent writing papers for school or work. Typically, writing for wired communications is informal. This can be a detriment to your writing skills. The grammar and structure of e-mail and other types of electronic communication resemble a conversation instead of a formal piece of writing. Additionally, communications via IM and text messaging often use spelling and grammar conventions all their own. As a shortcut, people often condense text messages and IMs by using abbreviations such as "brb," "lol," "y?," and "ttyl." They are abbreviated for good reason—imagine how long it would take to thumb this sentence into a text message. The downside of text message and IM shortcuts is that they have gradually crept into our writing habits and caused many of us to become careless in our formal writing. It is important to be aware of when it's okay to be sloppy and when you have to be meticulous.

Electronic communication does not convey emotions as well as face-to-face or even telephone conversations do. Electronic communication lacks vocal inflection, visible gestures, and a shared environment. Your correspondent might have difficulty telling whether you are serious or kidding, happy or sad, frustrated or euphoric. Sarcasm is particularly dangerous to use in electronic messages. Therefore your electronic compositions will be different from both your paper compositions and your speech.

Being aware of the differences between formal writing and informal writing will help you build appropriate writing skills for college work. How would you write an e-mail to friends telling them about the volunteer work you did this past weekend? How would you write that same e-mail to a potential employer who might hire you for your first job after college? Another way to improve your writing is to consider the reader's point of view. For the next week, before sending any MySpace or Facebook messages, e-mails, or text messages, reread them and consider how the people who will receive them will perceive your tone. What kind of mood will they think you are in? Will they feel that you are happy to have them as a friend? In how many different ways might your message be interpreted?

YOUR TURN ▶

Have you ever sent or received an e-mail or text message that could be interpreted in more than one way? What did you learn from that experience?

Writing for class projects might be a challenge at first. Visit your institution's writing center when you are starting to work on your paper. Professional staff and trained peer consultants who work in writing centers are available to help students express their ideas clearly through writing. Ask your instructor for examples of papers that have received good grades. You might also ask your instructor to help you review your writing after you have worked with the writing center. Most important, you can practice by using a correct writing style when IMing and text messaging. You'll find that your friends won't fault you for it. (Have you ever seen an IM asking you to "pls stop using proper grammar"?) Since you spend more time with online forms of communication, it's a great way to get real-world practice in the art of academic writing.

SPEAKING

The advice about writing also applies to speaking in public. The major difference, of course, is that you not only have to write the speech, you also have to present it to an audience. Because many people believe that fear of public speaking ranks up there with the fear of death, you might be thinking: What if I plan, organize, prepare, and rehearse, but calamity strikes anyway? What if my mind goes completely blank, I drop my note cards, or I say something totally embarrassing? Remember that people in your audience have been in your position and will understand your anxiety. Just accentuate the positive, rely on your wit, and keep speaking. Your recovery is what they are most likely to recognize; your success is what they are most likely to remember. The guidelines in this chapter can help you improve your speaking skills tremendously, including losing your fear of speaking publicly.

Preparing a Speech

Successful speaking involves six fundamental steps:

Step 1. Clarify your objective.
Step 2. Analyze your audience.
Step 3. Collect and organize your information.
Step 4. Choose your visual aids.
Step 5. Prepare your notes.
Step 6. Practice your delivery.

STEP 1. CLARIFY YOUR OBJECTIVE

Begin by identifying what you want to accomplish. Do you want to persuade your listeners that your campus needs additional student parking? Inform your listeners about the student government's accomplishments? What do you want your listeners to know, believe, or do when you are finished?

STEP 2. ANALYZE YOUR AUDIENCE

You need to understand the people you'll be talking to. Ask yourself:

- **What do they already know about my topic?** If you're going to give a presentation on the health risks of fast food, you'll want to find out how much your listeners already know about fast food so you don't risk boring them or wasting their time.
- **What do they want or need to know?** If your presentation will be about fast food and health, how much interest do your classmates have in nutrition? Would they be more interested in some other aspect of college life?
- **Who are my listeners?** What do the members of your audience have in common with you? How are they different from you?
- **What are their attitudes toward me, my ideas, and my topic?** How are they likely to feel about the ideas you are planning to present? For instance, what are your classmates' attitudes about fast food?

STEP 3. COLLECT AND ORGANIZE YOUR INFORMATION

Now comes the most critical part of the process: building your presentation by selecting and arranging blocks of information. One useful analogy is to think of yourself as guiding your listeners through the maze of ideas they already have to the new knowledge, attitudes, and beliefs you would like them to have. You can apply the suggestions from earlier in this chapter about creating an outline for writing to composing an outline for a speech.

STEP 4. CHOOSE YOUR VISUAL AIDS

Research has shown that when visual aids are added to presentations, listeners can absorb 35 percent more information, and over time they can recall 55 percent more. You might choose to prepare a chart, show a video clip, write on the board, or distribute handouts. You might also use your computer to prepare overhead transparencies or dynamic PowerPoint presentations. As you select and use your visual aids, consider these rules of thumb:

- Make visuals easy to follow. Use readable lettering, and don't overload your audience by trying to cover too much on one slide.
- Explain each visual clearly.
- Allow your listeners enough time to process visuals.
- Proofread carefully. Misspelled words hurt your credibility as a speaker.
- Maintain eye contact with your listeners while you discuss the visuals. Don't turn around and address the screen.

A fancy PowerPoint slideshow can't make up for inadequate preparation or poor delivery skills, but using clear, attractive visual aids can help you organize your material and help your listeners understand what they're hearing. The quality of your visual aids and your skill in using them can contribute to making your presentation effective (see Figure 10.3).

Step 4. Choose Your Visual Aids

When visual aids are added to presentations, listeners can absorb 35 percent more information, and over time, they can recall 55 percent more. You might choose to prepare a chart, show a video clip, write on the board, or distribute handouts. You might also use your computer to prepare overhead transparencies or dynamic PowerPoint presentations. As you select and use your visual aids, consider these rules of thumb:
Make visuals easy to follow. Use readable lettering, and don't crowd information. Keep the copy on each slide brief.
Explain each visual clearly.
Allow your listeners enough time to process visuals.
Proofread carefully. Mispelled words hurt your credibility as a speaker.
Maintain eye contact with your listeners while you discuss visuals. Don't turn around and address the screen.

(a) Bad example

Step 4.
Choose Your Visual Aids

- Make visuals easy to follow.
- Explain each visual clearly.
- Allow your listeners time to process visuals.
- Proofread carefully.
- Maintain eye contact with your listeners.

FIGURE 10.3 ▶

Examples of Good and Bad Presentation Slides

(b) Good example

STEP 5. PREPARE YOUR NOTES

If you are like most speakers, having an entire written copy of your speech in front of you might tempt you to read much of your presentation. Even if you can resist that temptation, your presentation could sound canned. On the other hand, your memory might fail you, so speaking without any material at all could be risky. A better strategy is to memorize only the introduction and conclusion of your speech so that you can maintain eye contact during the rest of your speech and thus build rapport with your listeners.

The best speaking aid is a minimal outline, carefully prepared, from which you can speak extemporaneously. Rehearse thoroughly in advance, and you'll be better prepared for how and when you want to present your points. Because you are speaking from brief notes, your words will be slightly different each time you give your presentation. That's okay; you'll sound prepared but natural. You might want to use some unobtrusive note cards. If so, it's not a bad idea to number them, just in case you accidentally drop the stack; this has happened to the best of speakers! When you become more comfortable with speaking, you might decide to let your visuals serve as notes. A paper copy of the PowerPoint slides can also serve as your basic outline. Eventually, you might find that you no longer need notes.

STEP 6. PRACTICE YOUR DELIVERY

As you rehearse, form a mental image of success rather than one of failure. Practice your presentation aloud several times beforehand to harness that energy-producing anxiety.

Begin a few days before your target date, and continue until you're about to present it. Rehearse aloud. Talking through your speech can help you much more than thinking through your speech. Practice before an audience— your roommate, a friend, your dog, even the mirror. Talking to something or someone helps simulate the distraction that listeners cause. Consider recording or videotaping yourself to help you pinpoint your own mistakes and to reinforce your strengths. If you ask your practice audience to critique you, you'll have some idea of what changes it might be helpful to make.

> **YOUR TURN ▶**
>
> Think about public speakers you have heard either in person or on TV. Which ones were the most effective? Why? What are some of the specific ways in which the best public speakers communicate with an audience?

Using Your Voice and Body Language

Let your hands hang comfortably at your sides, reserving them for natural, spontaneous gestures. Unless you must stay close to a fixed microphone, plan to move comfortably and casually around the room. Some experts suggest that you change positions between major points to punctuate your presentation, signaling to your audience, "I've finished with that point; let's shift topics."

Following are some other tips for using your voice and body language:

- Make eye contact with as many listeners as you can. This helps you to read their reactions, demonstrate confidence, and establish command.
- A smile helps to warm up your listeners, although you should avoid smiling excessively or inappropriately. Smiling through a presentation on world hunger would send your listeners a mixed message.

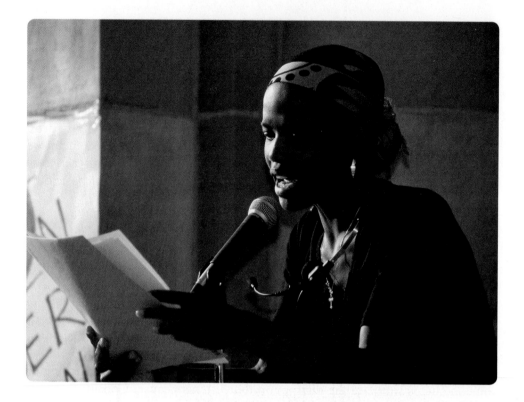

- As you practice your speech, pay attention to the pitch of your voice, your rate of speaking, and your volume. Project confidence and enthusiasm by varying your pitch. Speak at a rate that mirrors normal conversation—not too fast and not too slow. Consider varying your volume for the same reasons you vary pitch and rate: to engage your listeners and to emphasize important points.
- Pronunciation and word choice are important. A poorly articulated word (such as *gonna* for *going to*), a mispronounced word (such as *nuculer* for *nuclear*), or a misused word (such as *anecdote* for *antidote*) can quickly erode your credibility. Check meanings and pronunciations in a dictionary if you're not sure, and use a thesaurus for word variety. Fillers such as *um, uh, like,* and *you know* are distracting, too.
- Consider your appearance. Convey a look of competence, preparedness, and success by dressing professionally.

The GUIDE Checklist

Imagine you've been selected as a campus tour guide for next year's prospective first-year students and their families who are visiting your campus. Picture yourself in front of the administration building with a group of people assembled around you. You want to get and keep their attention in order to achieve your objective: increasing their interest in your school. Using the GUIDE method shown in Figure 10.4, you would do the following.

G: GET YOUR AUDIENCE'S ATTENTION

You can relate the topic to your listeners: "Let me tell you what to expect during your college years here—at the best school in the state." Or you can state the significance of the topic: "Deciding which college to attend is one of the most important decisions you'll ever make." Or you can arouse their curiosity: "Do you know the three most important factors that students and their families consider when choosing a college?"

You can also tell a joke (but only if it relates to your topic and isn't offensive or in questionable taste), startle the audience, tell a story, or ask a rhetorical question (a question that is asked to produce an effect, especially to make an assertion, rather than to elicit a reply). Regardless of which method you select, remember that a well-designed introduction must not only gain the attention of your listeners, but also develop rapport with them, motivate them to continue listening, and preview what you are going to say during the rest of your speech.

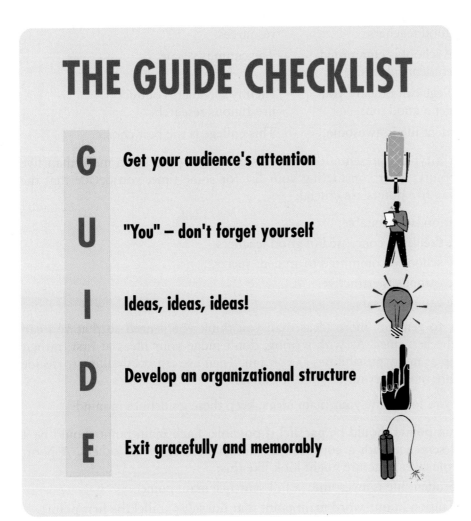

◄ FIGURE 10.4

The GUIDE Checklist

U: YOU—DON'T FORGET YOURSELF

In preparing any speech, don't exclude the most important source of your presentation: you. Even in a formal presentation, you will be most successful if you develop a comfortable style that's easy to listen to. Don't play a role. Instead, be yourself at your best, letting your wit and personality shine through.

I: IDEAS, IDEAS, IDEAS!

Create a list of all the possible points you could make. Then write them out as conclusions you want your listeners to accept. For example, imagine that on your campus tour for prospective new students and their parents, you want to make the following points:

Tuition is reasonable.	The campus is attractive.
The faculty is composed of good teachers.	The library has great resources.
The school is committed to student success.	The campus is safe.
College can prepare you to get a good job.	Faculty members conduct prestigious research.
Student life is awesome.	This college is the best choice.

For a typical presentation, most listeners can process no more than five main points. After considering your list for some time, you decide that the following five points are crucial:

- Tuition is reasonable.
- The faculty is composed of good teachers.
- The school is committed to student success.
- The campus is attractive.
- The campus is safe.

Try to generate more ideas than you think you'll need so that you can select the best ones. As with writing, don't judge your ideas at first; rather, think up as many possibilities as you can. Then use critical thinking to decide which are most relevant to your objectives.

As you formulate your main ideas, keep these guidelines in mind:

- **Main points should be parallel if possible.** Each main point should be a full sentence with a construction similar to that of the others. A poor, *nonparallel* structure might look like this:

1. Student life is awesome. (a full-sentence main point)

2. Tuition (a one-word main point that doesn't parallel the first point)

For a *parallel* second point, try instead:

2. Tuition is low. (a full-sentence main point)

- **Each main point should include a single idea.** Don't crowd main points with multiple messages, as in the following:
  1. Tuition is reasonable, and the campus is safe.
  2. Faculty members are good teachers and researchers.

Ideas rarely stand on their own merit. To ensure that your main ideas work, use a variety of supporting materials. The three most widely used forms of supporting materials are **examples, statistics,** and **testimony**.

- **Examples** include stories and illustrations, hypothetical events, and specific cases. They can be compelling ways to dramatize and clarify main ideas, but make sure they're relevant, representative, and reasonable.
- **Statistics** are widely used as evidence in speeches. Of course, numbers can be manipulated, and unscrupulous speakers sometimes mislead with statistics. If you use statistics, make sure they are clear, concise, accurate, and easy to understand.
- **Testimony** includes quoting outside experts, paraphrasing reliable sources, and emphasizing the quality of individuals who agree with your main points. When you use testimony, make sure that it is accurate, expert, and credible.

Finally, because each person in your audience is unique, you can best add interest, clarity, and credibility to your presentation by varying and combining the types of support you provide.

D: DEVELOP AN ORGANIZATIONAL STRUCTURE

For example, you might decide to use a chronological narrative approach, discussing the history of the college from its early years to the present. Or you might decide on a problem-solution format in which you describe a problem (such as choosing a school), present the pros and cons of several solutions (the strengths and weaknesses of several schools), and finally identify the best solution (your school!).

Begin with your most important ideas. Writing an outline can be the most useful way to begin organizing. List each main point and subpoint separately on a note card. Spread the cards out on a large surface (such as the floor), and arrange, rearrange, add, and delete cards until you find the most effective arrangement. Then simply number the cards, pick them up, and use them to prepare your final outline.

As you organize your presentation, remember that your overall purpose is to guide your listeners. This means you must not neglect transitions between your main points. For example:

"Now that we've looked at the library, let's move on to the gymnasium."

"The first half of my presentation has identified our recreational facilities. Now let's look at the academic hubs on campus."

"So much for the academic buildings on campus. What about the campus social scene?"

In speaking, as in writing, transitions make the difference between keeping your audience with you and losing them at an important juncture.

E: EXIT GRACEFULLY AND MEMORABLY

Plan your ending carefully, realizing that most of the suggestions for introductions also apply to conclusions.

Whatever else you do, go out with style, impact, and dignity. Don't leave your listeners asking, "So that's it?" Subtly signal that the end is in sight (without the overused "So in conclusion . . ."), briefly summarize your major points, and then conclude confidently.

Speaking on the Spot

Most of the speaking you will do in college and afterward will be on the spot. When your instructor asks your opinion of last night's reading, when another member of your study group asks for your position on an issue, or when your best friend asks you to defend your views, you have to give an impromptu speech.

When you must speak on the spot, it helps to use a framework that allows you to sound organized and competent. Suppose your instructor asks, "Do you think the world's governments are working together effectively to ensure a healthy environment?" One of the most popular ways to arrange your thoughts is through the PREP formula.[5] Short for "preparation," this plan requires the following:

P: **Point of view** Provide an overview—a clear, direct statement or generalization: "After listening to yesterday's lecture, yes, I do."

R: **Reasons** Broadly state why you hold this point of view: "I was surprised by the efforts of the United Nations General Assembly to focus on the environment."

E: **Evidence or examples** Present specific facts or data supporting your point of view: "For example, the industrialized nations have set stringent goals on air pollution and greenhouse gases for the year 2010."

P: **Point of view, restated** To make sure you are understood clearly, end with a restatement of your position: "So, yes, the world's governments seem to be concerned and working to improve the situation."

YOUR TURN ▶

Write about your experience of speaking in front of a group. Is public speaking something you enjoy or dread? Are you an anxious or a comfortable speaker? What strategies could you suggest to anyone who wants to become more comfortable when speaking in front of a group?

---

[5]Kenneth Wydro, *Think on Your Feet* (Englewood Cliffs, NJ: Prentice-Hall, 1981).

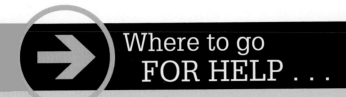

Where to go
FOR HELP . . .

ON CAMPUS ▶

Writing Center Most campuses have one. Frequently, it is found within the English department.

Learning Assistance Center In addition to help on many other topics, these centers offer help on writing.

Departments of Speech, Theater, and Communications These offer both resources and specific courses to help you develop your speaking skills.

Student Activities One of the best ways to learn and practice speaking skills is to become active in student organizations, especially those like the Student Government Association and the Debate Club.

ONLINE ▶

Writing tips: http://www.uiowa.edu/~histwrit/website/grammar%20help.htm. The University of Iowa's History Department offers help on common writing mistakes.

Plain language Have you ever been confused by government gobbledygook? Here's a guide to writing user-friendly documents for federal employees: http://www.plainlanguage.gov/howto/guidelines/reader-friendly.cfm.

Toastmasters International offers public speaking tips at http://www.toastmasters.org/pdfs/top10.pdf.

MY INSTITUTION'S RESOURCES ▶

_____
_____
_____
_____
_____
_____
_____
_____
_____
_____
_____
_____
_____
_____
_____
_____
_____
_____

Chapter
REVIEW...

One-Minute PAPER...

This chapter has information that you can use to improve your writing and speaking skills. Which strategies struck you as methods that you could or should put into practice? If your instructor could cover one area in more depth, what would you want it to be?

Applying What You've LEARNED...

Now that you have read and discussed this chapter, consider how you can apply what you've learned to your academic and personal life. The following prompts will help you reflect on chapter material and its relevance to you both now and in the future.

1. Develop a five-slide PowerPoint presentation to introduce yourself to your classmates in a new way. You might include slides that contain points about your high school years, your hobbies, your jobs, your family, and so forth. Use the effective speaking strategies in this chapter to help you outline your presentation. In addition to text, use visuals such as photos, video clips, and art to engage your audience.

2. Before reading this chapter, had you considered the differences between writing an exam response and writing a blog post or responding to someone on Facebook? Think about the online communications you've had in the last week. Can you say for certain that you knew exactly who your audience was? Did you send anything that could be misinterpreted or end up being read by someone outside your intended audience? What advice about online communications would you give to other students?

Building Your PORTFOLIO...

    ❝ According to most studies, people's number one fear is public speaking. Number two is death. Death is number two. Does that sound right? This means to the average person, if you go to a funeral, you're better off in the casket than doing the eulogy.❞

—JERRY SEINFELD (B. 1954)
American television actor and comedian

IN THE PUBLIC EYE

The media provide ample opportunities for celebrities and public figures to show off their public speaking skills. As you have probably noticed, some celebrities are much better speakers than others. However, being a good public speaker is not important just for those who are "in the public eye." Whether you want to be a movie star or a marine biologist, potential employers tend to put excellent communication skills at the top of their "must have" list.

1. Identify a public figure who, in your opinion, is a good public speaker.

2. In a Word document, explain why it is important for that person to speak well. List the specific qualities (e.g., humor, eye contact) that you think make that person a good public speaker.

3. Next, re-create the following chart. Recalling the last time you gave a presentation in front of a group and using a scale of 1 to 5 (5 being excellent), rate yourself as a public speaker using the guidelines in the chart.

Public Speaking Skills	1 Poor	2 Fair	3 Average	4 Good	5 Excellent
Level of Preparedness (well prepared and confident, last-minute technology check)					
Professional Appearance (appropriate business attire, including proper shoes)					
Effective Vocal Presentation Style (clear and persuasive, paying attention to the pitch of your voice, rate of speech, volume, and correct grammar)					
Appropriate Behavior and Speech (no chewing gum, being careful to avoid fillers such as "um," "uh," "like," and "you know")					
Natural Body Language (good eye contact with the audience, appropriate facial expressions, relaxed posture)					
Note your lowest scores as areas you need to work on as you prepare for your next presentation.					

4. Save your responses in your portfolio on your personal computer or flash drive. The next time you make a presentation, revisit the chart and spend extra time preparing in the areas in which you rated yourself less than "good."

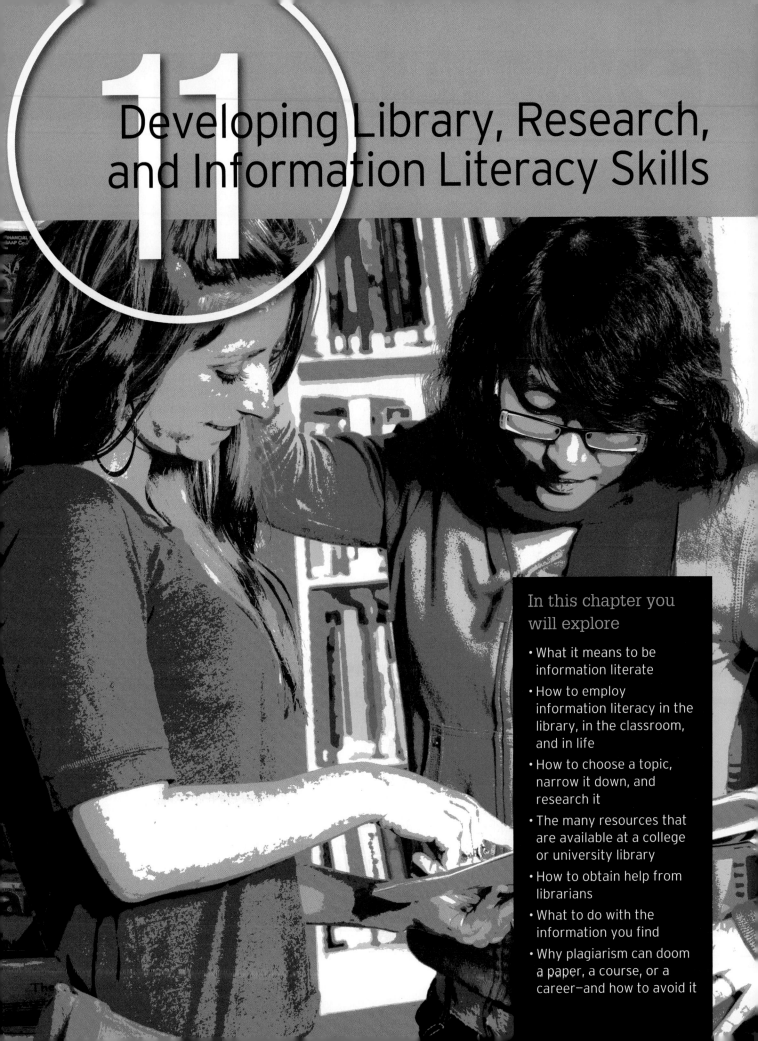

11
Developing Library, Research, and Information Literacy Skills

In this chapter you will explore

- What it means to be information literate
- How to employ information literacy in the library, in the classroom, and in life
- How to choose a topic, narrow it down, and research it
- The many resources that are available at a college or university library
- How to obtain help from librarians
- What to do with the information you find
- Why plagiarism can doom a paper, a course, or a career—and how to avoid it

JORDAN LASKOWSKI, 18
Northern Arizona University

66 You look at it and it doesn't seem that big, but when you go in there, you can get lost.99

I go to the campus library sometimes to study, but I didn't actually use it until halfway through my second semester, when I had to research an essay for my English class. It's a three-story building. It has a basement level and then two stories above ground, and it's huge. You look at it and it doesn't seem that big, but when you go in there, you can get lost.

Our library has a really good online network. They've taken all their stuff from paper and put it online, and they're connected to a bunch of libraries around the country and the Library of Congress, too. So they've got all the material in catalogs, and I just went on and entered some key words that I wanted for my topic, and it came up with hundreds of hits. I got help from a librarian, and we narrowed it down to about ten things I could look at, and then I just went through the library and picked them out—a few government documents and some books. Once I got the hang of it, it was really easy. The library is a nice, quiet, comfortable environment, and the staff are really helpful if you get lost. I think I'll probably use it more now.

Which airline or travel service offers the cheapest airfare? Is it true that certain professors always ask true/false questions? What species of poisonous serpent bit the patient, and which antivenin will work? Which is likely to be more reliable, a Subaru or a Toyota? What are the relationships between social class and mental illness? At what stress levels will bridge cables snap? How has William Faulkner's fiction influenced contemporary filmmaking? Who steals more from a chain store, customers or employees? What is the best way to shave time from the manufacture and delivery of tractors?

These questions all have something in common. Although some are academic inquiries and others are questions you might ask as part of your job or daily life, they share one important characteristic: The answers to each can be found through research. A doctor would need instant answers for the question about snakebites because a life hangs in the balance. Other situations might not be as critical, but without the ability to find and evaluate information quickly, the world as we know it would eventually fall apart. Research produces discoveries that improve our quality of life.

Developing the skills to locate, analyze, and use information will significantly enhance your ability to keep up with what is going on in the world; to participate in activities that interest you; and to succeed in college, career, and community. The research skills you learn and use as a student will serve you well as a successful professional. That holds true for whatever career path you choose. Whether you're a student of biology, engineering, business, or public relations, your task in college is to manage information for projects and presentations, both oral and written. In a few years, as a lab technician, a project coordinator, a loss prevention specialist, or a campaign manager for a gubernatorial candidate, your task will be the same: to manage and present information for your employers and clients. All colleges and many companies provide libraries for this purpose. But finding and using information involve more than operating a computer or wandering the stacks. To make sense of the vast amount of information at your fingertips in a reasonable amount of time, you'll need to develop a few key research and information literacy skills.

Information Literacy

During the Agricultural Age, most people farmed. Now only a tiny fraction of us work the land, yet edible goods continue to fill our silos and dairy transfer stations and feedlots. During the Industrial Age, we made things. We still do, of course, but automation has made it possible for more goods to be produced by fewer people. Now we live in the Information Age, a name that was created to signify the importance of information in today's economy and our lives.

Most of the global workforce is employed in one way or another in creating, managing, or transferring information. The gross national product (GNP) of the United States is substantially information based. Library science is one of the fastest-growing career opportunities around. Companies such as Google and Yahoo! have earned billions of dollars by simply offering, organizing, and selling information. Put another way, information has value: You can determine its benefits in dollars, and you can compute the cost of not having it.

The challenge is managing it all. There is more information than ever before, and it doubles at rapidly shortening intervals. Because abundance and electronic access combine to produce enormous amounts of retrievable information, people need highly developed **sorting** skills to cope. Information literacy is the premier survival skill for the modern world.

YOUR TURN ▶

Why do you think the chapter states that "Information literacy is the premier survival skill for the modern world"? Do you agree? Why or why not?

What is information literacy? Simply put, it's the ability to find, interpret, and use information to meet your needs. Information literacy has many facets, among them the following:

- **Computer literacy**: Facility with electronic tools, both for conducting inquiries and for presenting to others what you have found and analyzed.
- **Media literacy**: The ability to think critically about material distributed to a wide audience through television, film, advertising, radio, magazines, books, and the Internet.

- **Cultural literacy:** Knowing what has gone on and is going on around you. You have to understand the difference between the Civil War and the Revolutionary War, U2 and YouTube, Eminem and M&Ms, or you will not understand everyday conversation.

Information matters. It helps empower people to make good choices. The choices people make often determine their success in business, their happiness as friends and family members, and their well-being as citizens on this planet.

LEARNING TO BE INFORMATION LITERATE

People marvel at the information explosion, paper inflation, and the Internet. Many confuse mounds of information with knowledge and conclude that they are informed or can easily become informed. But most of us are unprepared for the huge number of available sources and the unsorted, unevaluated mass of information that pours over us at the press of a button. What, then, is the antidote for information overload? To become an informed and successful user of information, keep three basic goals in mind:

1. **Know how to find the information you need.** If you are sick, you need to know whose help to seek. If you lose your scholarship, you need to know where to get financial assistance. If you want to win a lawsuit, you need to know how to find the outcomes of similar cases. Once you have determined where to look for information, you'll need to ask good questions and to make educated searches of information systems, such as the Internet, libraries, and databases. You'll also want to cultivate relationships with information professionals, such as librarians, who can help you frame questions, broaden and narrow searches, and retrieve the information you need.

2. **Learn how to interpret the information you find.** It is very important to retrieve information. It is even more important to make sense of that information. What does the information mean? Have you selected a source you can understand? Is the information accurate? Is the source reliable?

3. **Have a purpose.** Even the best information won't do much good if you don't know what to do with it. True, sometimes you'll hunt down a fact simply for your own satisfaction. More often, you'll communicate what you've learned to someone else. You should know not only what form that communication will take—a research paper for a class, a proposal for your boss, a presentation at a hearing—but also what you want to accomplish. Will you use the information to make a decision, develop a new solution to a problem, influence a course of action, prove a point, or something else?

We'll be spending most of this chapter exploring ways to pursue each of these goals.

WHAT'S RESEARCH—AND WHAT'S NOT?

To discover good information that you can use for a given purpose, you'll have to conduct research. You might be working on a college research paper right now—or anxious about one that's ahead of you. As you contemplate these projects, be sure you understand what research involves.

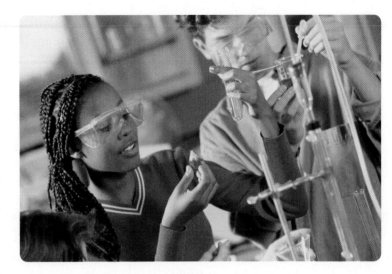

In the past, you might have completed assignments that asked you to demonstrate how to use a library's electronic book catalog, periodical index, e-mail delivery system, government documents collection, map depository, and interlibrary loan service. Or you might have been given a subject, such as ethics, and assigned to find a definition or a related book, journal article, or web page. If so, what you accomplished was retrieval. And while retrieving information is an essential element of research, it's not an end in itself.

Nor is research a matter of copying passages or finding a handful of sources and patching together bits and pieces without commentary. In fact, such behavior could easily slip into the category of **plagiarism**, a serious misstep that could result in a failing grade or worse (see p. 207). At the very least, repeating information or ideas without interpreting them puts you at risk of careless use of sources that might be new or old, useful or dangerously in error, reliable or shaky, research based or anecdotal, or objective or biased beyond credibility.

Good research, by contrast, is information literacy in action. Let's take up the ethics topic again. If you were assigned to select and report on an ethics issue, you might pick ethics in politics, accumulate a dozen sources, evaluate them, interpret them, select a few and discard a few, organize the keepers into a coherent arrangement, extract portions that hang together, write a paper or presentation that cites your sources, compose an introduction that explains what you have done, draw some conclusions of your own, and submit the results. That's research. And if you learn to do it well, you'll experience the rush that comes with discovery and the pleasure that accompanies making a statement or taking a stand. The conclusion that you compose on the basis of your research is new information!

EMPLOYING INFORMATION LITERACY SKILLS

By the time you graduate, you should have attained a level of information literacy that will carry you through your professional life. The Association of College and Research Libraries has developed the following best practices for the information-literate student. Learn how to apply them, and you'll do well no matter where your educational and career paths take you.

- **Determine the nature and extent of the information needed.** In general, this involves first defining and articulating what information you need, then identifying a variety of potential sources.
- **Access information effectively and efficiently.** Select the most appropriate research methods, use well-designed search strategies, refine those strategies along the way, and keep organized notes on what you find and where you found it.

- **Evaluate information and its sources critically.** As an information-literate person, you'll be able to apply criteria for judging the usefulness and reliability of both information and its sources. You'll also become skilled at summarizing the main ideas presented by others and comparing new information with what you already know.

- **Incorporate information into your knowledge base and value system.** To do this, you'll determine what information is new, unique, or contradictory and consider whether it has an impact on what's important to you. You'll also validate, understand, or interpret the information through talking with other people. Finally, you'll combine elements of different ideas to construct new concepts of your own making.

- **Use information effectively to accomplish a specific purpose.** You'll apply information to planning and creating a particular product or performance, revising the development process as necessary, and communicating the results to others.

- **Access and use information ethically and legally.** There are economic, legal, and social issues surrounding the retrieval and use of information. You'll need to understand and follow laws, regulations, institutional policies, and etiquette related to copyright and intellectual property. Most important, you should acknowledge the use of information from sources in everything you write, record, or broadcast.[1]

Choosing, Narrowing, and Researching a Topic

Assignments that require the use of library materials can take many forms and will come in many of your classes. There are numerous ways to search for information to complete an assignment, and we'll consider some of those later in the chapter. Before you start searching, however, you need to have an idea of what you're looking for.

Choosing a topic is often the most difficult part of a research project. Even if an instructor assigns a general topic, you'll need to narrow it down to a particular aspect that interests you enough to make worthwhile the time and energy you'll spend pursuing it. Imagine, for example, that you have been assigned to write a research paper on the topic of political ethics. What steps should you take?

Your first job is to get an overview of your topic. You can begin by looking at general and specific dictionaries and encyclopedias. To learn something about political ethics, for example, you might consult a political dictionary and the *Encyclopedia of American Political History*. Similar broad sources are available for just about any subject area, from marketing to sports psychology to colonial American literature. Check your library's reference area or consult with a librarian for leads.

Once you've acquired some basic information to guide you toward an understanding of the nature of your topic, you have a decision to make: What

---

[1]Adapted from *Information Literacy Competency Standards for Higher Education* (2000). http://www.ala.org/ala/acrl/acrlstandards/standards.pdf.

aspects of the subject will you pursue? Even if you launch the most general of inquiries, you will discover very quickly that your topic is vast and includes many related subtopics. If you look up "political ethics" in the Library of Congress Subject Headings or your library's online catalog, for instance, you will discover some choices:

Civil service, ethics	Judicial ethics
Conflict of interests	Justice
Corporations—corrupt practices	Legislative ethics
Environmental ethics	Political corruption
Ethics, modern	Political ethics
Fairness	Social ethics
Gifts to politicians	

Because the topic is broad, every one of these headings leads to books and articles on political ethics. What you want is a dozen or so focused, highly relevant hits on an aspect of the topic that you can fashion into a coherent, well-organized essay. Begin by assessing what you already know and asking what you would like to learn more about. Perhaps you know a little about the efforts of lobbyists and political action committees to influence legislation, and you're curious about recent efforts to limit what gifts politicians may accept; in that case you might decide on a three-pronged topic: gifts to politicians, political corruption, and lobbyists.

You can follow these steps to focus any topic. By simply consulting a few general sources, you'll find that you can narrow a broad topic to something that interests you and is a manageable size. From reference works and a quick search of a library catalog, periodicals database, or the Internet you will find definitions, introductory materials, some current and historical examples of your topic in action, and related information. You are now ready to launch a purposeful search.

Using the Library

Whenever you have research to do—whether for a class, your job, or your personal life—visit a library. We can't stress this enough. Although the Internet is loaded with billions of pages of information, don't be fooled into thinking it will serve all of your needs. For one thing, you'll have to sort through a lot of junk to find your way to good-quality sources online. More important, if you limit yourself to the web, you'll miss out on some of the best materials. Although we often think that everything is electronic and can be found through a computer, a great deal of valuable information is still stored in traditional formats and is most easily accessed through a library.

YOUR TURN ▶

Is the library a necessary resource for learning in college? Why or why not?

Every library has books and journals as well a great number of items in electronic databases that aren't available on public websites. Most libraries also have several other types of collections, such as government documents, microfilm, rare books, manuscripts, dissertations, fine art, photographs, historical documents, maps, and music and films, including archival and documentary productions. Remember that information has been recorded and stored in many forms over the centuries. Libraries maintain materials in whatever form they were first produced and provide access to these materials for free.

TAKING ADVANTAGE OF EVERYTHING YOUR LIBRARY HAS TO OFFER

Books and periodicals are essential, but a college or university library is far more than a document warehouse. For starters, most campus libraries have websites that offer lots of help for students. Some provide guidelines on writing research papers, conducting online searches, or navigating the stacks. And all of them provide invaluable services to students and faculty members, including virtual spaces for accessing library holdings and the web, physical spaces where you can study in quiet or meet with other students, and perhaps even social and entertainment programs.

Of course, no one library can possibly own everything you might need, so groups of libraries share their holdings with each other. If your library does not have a journal or book that looks promising for your project, the interlibrary loan department will be happy to borrow the materials for you. In most cases you can expect to receive the materials in as little as a few days, but it's always a good idea to identify and request what you might need from other libraries as far in advance as possible, in case the material is in high demand.

Are you a commuter or distance education student who cannot easily visit your college library in person? Most libraries provide proxy access to their electronic materials to students off campus. Usually, the library's home page serves as an electronic gateway to its services, which may include the following:

- A searchable catalog of the library's physical holdings
- Electronic databases, some of which let you access the full text of newspaper, magazine, and journal articles from your computer
- Interlibrary loan requests
- Course reserve readings
- Downloadable e-books
- Indexes of websites that have been carefully screened for reliability and relevance to particular subject areas
- Online chats with librarians who can help you in real time

To learn more, poke around your library's website, or e-mail or phone the reference desk.

Libraries also have a wide variety of physical spaces for students and faculty members to use. From individual study tables to private group rooms to comfortable chairs tucked in quiet corners, you should be able to find a study area that suits you and your needs. You might also discover places to eat, socialize, take in a movie or an art exhibit, check your e-mail and social networking page, search the web, type your papers, make photocopies, edit videos, give presentations, hold meetings, or take a much-needed nap.

Be sure to use the handouts and guides that are available at the reference desk or online. You will also find tutorials and virtual tours that will help you to become familiar with the collections, services, and spaces available at your library.

ASKING A LIBRARIAN

Of all the resources available in a library, the most useful—and often the least used—are the people who staff it. Librarians thrive on helping you. If you're not sure how to start a search, if you're not successful in your first attempts at retrieving information, or if you just need some ideas about what you might try as you pursue a research project, ask a librarian. Librarians are information experts who are trained to assist and guide you to the resources you need. The librarians who work in the reference area or supervise the computer stations might look busy. But they are busy helping people with projects much like yours. You are not interrupting when you ask for assistance, and with rare exceptions, any librarian will be delighted to help you.

You can contact a reference librarian in several ways. E-mail a query, and you are likely to receive a quick reply. Or call the reference desk to ask a question, such as "Do you have a copy of the report *Problems with the Presidential Gifts System*?" You can have a "live chat" online with a library staffer in real time. And of course, you can visit the reference desk in person or make an appointment for a tutorial or consultation. (Hint: You will be most successful if you bring a copy of your assignment and any written instructions you have to your meeting. Tell the librarian what you have tried—if anything.) Remember that there are no silly questions. A good librarian will treat your inquiries with respect.

The information professionals at your library are authorities on how to find information. Most important, they not only know where to find it, but also have the wonderful ability to help you use information to meet your needs, solve problems, provide explanations, open up new possibilities, and ultimately create new knowledge.

Electronic Resources

Online catalogs, periodical databases, and the World Wide Web allow you to quickly and easily locate materials in the vast universe of information. Learning how to use these resources efficiently will save you time and improve your odds of finding the information that best suits your needs.

LIBRARY CATALOGS

The card catalogs that were once common in libraries have been replaced by OPAC (online public access catalogs). These electronic catalogs tell you what books, magazines, newspapers, videos, and other materials are available in a particular library. They might also provide abstracts of the information presented in those materials, tables of contents for individual entries, and related search terms. Typically, they'll provide an identifying number that tells you where in the stacks to locate a particular document. A catalog might also inform you whether an item is already checked out and, if so, when it's due back. The catalog will also allow you to put the material on hold or give you the option of requesting it through interlibrary loan.

You can search the catalogs through terminals at the library or from your home computer or a laptop. The simplest way to search a catalog is by key word (see the guidelines for conducting an effective search on p. 214). You might also search by subject, author, title, date, or a combination of these elements. Be sure to spend a few minutes on the catalog's help or FAQ page, which will guide you through the options and demonstrate ways to customize your search terms. Each system has its own preferences.

PERIODICAL DATABASES

A library catalog helps you search for books and the titles of magazines and journals owned by a particular library. By contrast, periodical databases let you hunt down articles published in hundreds (even thousands) of newspapers, magazines, and scholarly journals. Some databases might provide a full-text copy of the article as part of the record returned from your search; other times you'll have to use the information in the record to find a physical copy in your library or request it through interlibrary loan.

Subscription services such as EBSCOHost, LexisNexis, and Gale Research compile and maintain electronic periodical databases. These are not free to the general public and must be accessed through a library. (Ask at the circulation desk for a barcode number and PIN, which will allow you to access your library's databases from remote terminals.) Most libraries subscribe to multiple databases and subdivide them by broad general categories such as Humanities, Social Sciences, Science and Technology, Business, Health and Medicine, Government Information, or by major. Under "Social Sciences," for example, you might find International Political Science Abstracts (PAIS), America: History and Life, and over twenty other databases. There are also multidisciplinary databases, such as Academic Search Premier, InfoTrac, and Reader's Guide to Periodical Literature, that provide excellent material on most topics you will encounter during your first years of college.

Databases have their own specialties and different strengths, so you'll want to select the best ones for your particular subject or topic. Check your library's subscription list for an overview of what's available, and don't hesitate to ask a librarian to make recommendations about which databases are most relevant to your needs.

Information in a database is usually stored in a single location or on a server that is owned by the subscription service company. Human beings, not computers, do the indexing, so you can be fairly sure the information in a database meets certain criteria for inclusion, such as accuracy, timeliness, and authoritativeness. And because most of the material indexed in a database originally appeared in print, you can be fairly certain that it was reviewed for quality by other scholars or an editorial staff.

THE WORLD WIDE WEB

Searching the web is a totally different story. The material retrieved by Googling is an aggregation of information, opinion, and sales pitches from the vast universe of servers around the globe. Anybody can put up a website, which means you can't be sure of the website owner's credibility and reliability.

The sources you find on the web might be written by anyone—a fifth grader, a distinguished professor, a professional society, or a biased advocate.

A recent Google search on the subject "political corruption," for instance, generated over 10 million hits. The first page yielded some interesting results:

> A collection of links on politics and political corruption
> A Libertarian Party legislative program on political corruption
> Two Amazon.com ads
> A site that offers "research" on gambling and political corruption
> A university site offering research on political corruption in Illinois

These varied results demonstrate that one must be alert when examining Internet sources. Mixed in with credible scholarship on this topic are sales promotions, some arguments against gambling, and useful links to other sources. It isn't always easy to evaluate the quality of Internet sources. Check pages 215–17 in this chapter for some helpful strategies you can use to determine whether a source is credible and authentic.

GUIDELINES FOR EFFECTIVE SEARCHES

Most searches of catalogs and databases are done by using key words. A key word is a single word that would appear in a discussion of the topic you are investigating. Other systems permit searching of phrases. A few databases and web search engines allow a natural language search, in which you can ask a question or type in a sentence that describes what you are looking for. Some databases, such as the *New York Times* Index and ERIC (Education Resources Information Center), have their own approved lists of subject terms that you should consult before searching. Be careful to choose search terms that are relevant to your investigation; this will help you retrieve material you can use. And don't forget that a librarian can help you with this.

To become a successful and savvy user of electronic resources, follow these guidelines:

- **Consult the Help or FAQs link** the first time you use any catalog, database, or search engine to learn specific searching techniques. You will get the best results if you use the tips and strategies suggested by the database provider.
- **Write out your topic or problem as a statement or question.** "Is it right for politicians to take gifts from lobbyists?" Or "The influence of lobbyists or PACs has dramatically changed American political ethics." Doing so will help you identify potentially useful key words.
- **Understand Boolean operators.** Boolean operators are the words *and*, *or*, and *not*. The Bowling Green State University Library website describes these terms this way:

    > A search for rock AND roll will locate all records containing both the word *rock* and the word *roll*. It will locate items about rock and roll music. It might also locate records that contain both words in a different context, such as "It recommends you roll the rock quickly."

    > A search for rock OR roll will locate all records containing either the word *rock* or the word *roll*—not necessarily both. It will retrieve items about bakery rolls, tumbling, rocks, music, gemstones, etc.

A search for rock NOT roll will locate records containing the word *rock* but NOT the word *roll*. It will retrieve items about rocks, gemstones, diamonds, etc.[2]

- **Write down several terms or synonyms for your topic** so that if one search does not yield any useful hits, you have some backup terms on hand. It's also a good idea to search more than one database or engine; different ones might pull up dramatically different sources.
- **Limit your search.** You can often limit a search by date, language, journal name, full text, or word(s) in title. If you still get too many hits, add more search terms.
- **Expand your search.** If you get too few hits, omit a search term. You can also truncate a word by using an asterisk to retrieve broader results. For instance, *lobby** will search for "lobby," "lobbying," "lobbyist," and "lobbyists."
- **Learn the quirks of the databases or search engines you use often.** Some yield better results from Boolean operators (e.g., "politicians AND lobbyists"); others are more attuned to natural language searches (e.g., "ethics in politics" or "gifts to politicians").
- **Check your library's electronic resources page** to see what else is available online. Most libraries have links to other commonly used electronic reference tools. These include online encyclopedias, dictionaries, almanacs, style guides, biographical and statistical resources, and news sources.

YOUR TURN ▶

Talk to a faculty member, a parent, or an older friend who went to college. Ask them how they conducted research before the Internet. Write a short review of the strategies used by former generations to access and use information.

Evaluating Sources

It's easy to assume that huge amounts of available information automatically provide knowledge. Some students might at first be excited about receiving 20,800,000 hits from a Google search on political ethics, but shock takes hold when they realize their discovery is utterly unsorted. They might respond by using only the first several hits, irrespective of quality. A more productive approach is to think critically about the usefulness of potential sources by measuring them against three important criteria: relevance, authority, and bias.

YOUR TURN ▶

How do you find sources for an important paper? Do you go to the first several hits on Google, or do you use a more deliberate process? What strategies can you use to make sure your Internet or library research results in valid information?

RELEVANCE

The first thing to consider in looking at a possible source is how well it fits your needs. That, in turn, will be affected by the nature of your research project and the kind of information you are seeking.

[2]http://www.bgsu.edu/colleges/library/infosrv/lue/boolean.html.

- **Is it introductory?** Introductory information is very basic and elementary. It neither assumes nor requires prior knowledge about the topic. Introductory sources can be useful when you're first learning about a subject. They are less useful when you're drawing conclusions about a particular aspect of the subject.
- **Is it definitional?** Definitional information provides some descriptive details about a subject. It might help you introduce a topic to others or clarify the focus of your investigation.
- **Is it analytical?** Analytical information supplies and interprets data about origins, behaviors, differences, and uses. In most cases it's the kind of information you want.
- **Is it comprehensive?** The more detail, the better. Avoid unsubstantiated opinions, and look instead for sources that consider the topic in depth and offer plenty of evidence to support their conclusions.
- **Is it current?** You should usually give preference to recent sources, although older ones can sometimes be useful (for instance, if your subject is historical or the source is still cited by others in a field).
- **Can you conclude anything from it?** Use the "so what?" test: How important is this information? Why does it matter to my project?

AUTHORITY

Once you have determined that a source is relevant to your project, check that it was created by somebody who has the qualifications to write or speak on the subject. This, too, will depend on your subject and the nature of your inquiry (a fifth grader's opinion might be exactly what you're looking for), but in most cases you'll want expert conclusions based on rigorous evidence.

Make sure you can identify the author and be ready to explain why that author is a reliable source. Good qualifications might include academic degrees, institutional affiliations, an established record of researching and publishing on a topic, or personal experience with a subject. Be wary, on the other hand, of anonymous or commercial sources or those written by someone whose credibility is questionable.

Understand, as well, whether your project calls for scholarly publications, popular magazines, or both. Do you know the difference?

You don't necessarily have to dismiss popular magazines. Many journalists and columnists are extremely well qualified, and their work might well be appropriate for your needs. But as a rule scholarly sources will be more credible.

Scholarly Journals	Popular Magazines
Long articles	Shorter articles
In-depth information on topic	Broad overview of topic
Written by academic experts	Written by journalists or reporters
Graphs, tables, and charts	Photos of people and events
Articles "refereed" or reviewed	Articles not rigidly evaluated
Formally documented	Sources credited informally

BIAS

When you are searching for sources, you should realize that there can be a heavy dose of bias or point of view in some of them. Although nothing is inherently wrong with someone's having a particular point of view, it is dangerous for a reader not to know that the bias is there. A great source for keeping you informed about potential bias is *Magazines for Libraries*,[3] which will tell you about a periodical's editorial and political leanings. *The Nation*, for instance, is generally considered liberal, while *National Review* is conservative.

Some signs of bias indicate that you should avoid using a source. If you detect overly positive or overly harsh language, hints of an agenda, or a stubborn refusal to consider other points of view, think carefully about how well you can trust the information in a document.

YOUR TURN ▶

In your opinion, what newspapers, magazines, or TV networks are biased? Does a biased point of view make you more or less likely to read or watch? Why do you think many people expose themselves only to opinions or viewpoints like their own?

A NOTE ON INTERNET SOURCES

Be especially cautious of material you find online. It is often difficult to tell where something on the Internet came from or who wrote it. The lack of this information can make it very difficult to judge the credibility of the source. And while an editorial board reviews most print matter (books, articles, and so forth) for accuracy and overall quality, it's frequently difficult to confirm that the same is true for information on a website—with some exceptions. If you are searching through an online database such as the Human Genome Database or Eldis: the Gateway to Development Information (a poverty database), it is highly likely that documents in these collections have been reviewed. Online versions of print magazines and journals, likewise, have usually been checked out by editors. And information from academic and government websites (those whose URLs end in .edu or .gov, respectively) is generally—but not always—trustworthy.

YOUR TURN ▶

One of the most frequently visited sites on the web is Wikipedia, a collaborative reference work written and maintained by hundreds of volunteers. Most of its articles can be (and have been) edited by anyone with Internet access. What are the pros and cons of using such a site as a source for a research project?

[3]Cheryl LaGuardia, Bill Katz, and Linda S. Katz, *Magazines for Libraries*, 13th ed. (New Providence, NJ: RR Bowker LC, 2004).

Making Use of What You Find

You have probably heard the saying "Knowledge is power." While knowledge can certainly contribute to power, this is true only if that knowledge is put to use. When you retrieve, sort, interpret, analyze, and synthesize sources from an information center, whether it is the library, a computer database, or the web, you can produce a product that has power.

But first, you have to decide what form that product will take and what kind of power you want it to hold. Who are you going to tell about your discoveries, and how? What do you hope to accomplish by sharing your conclusions? Remember that a major goal of information literacy is to use information effectively to accomplish a specific purpose (see p. 195). Make it a point to *do* something with the results of your research. Otherwise, why bother?

SYNTHESIZING INFORMATION AND IDEAS

Ultimately, the point of conducting research is that the process contributes to the development of new knowledge. As a researcher, you sought the answer to a question. Now is the time to formulate that answer and share it.

Many students satisfy themselves with a straightforward report that merely summarizes what they found. Sometimes, that's enough. More often, however, you'll want to apply the information to ideas of your own. To do that, first consider all of the information you found and how your sources relate to each other. What do they have in common, and where do they disagree? What conclusions can you draw from those similarities and differences? What new ideas did they spark? How can you use the information you have on hand to support your conclusions? (Refer to Chapter 5 for tips on drawing conclusions from different points of view and using evidence to construct an argument.)

Essentially, what you're doing at this stage of any research project is processing information, an activity known as **synthesis**. By accepting some ideas, rejecting others, combining related concepts, assessing the implications, and pulling it all together, you'll create new information and ideas that other people can use.

CITING YOUR SOURCES

At some point you'll present your findings. Whether they take the form of an essay, a formal research paper, a script for a presentation or broadcast, a page for a website, or something else entirely, you must give credit to your sources.

Citing your sources serves many purposes. For one thing, acknowledging the information and ideas you've borrowed from other writers shows respect for their contributions; it also distinguishes between other writers' ideas and your own. Source citations demonstrate to your audience that you have based your conclusions on thoughtful consideration of good, reliable evidence. Source citations also provide a starting place for anyone who would like more information or is curious about how you reached your conclusions. Most important, citing your sources is the simplest way to avoid plagiarism.

The particular requirements of source citation can get complicated, but it all boils down to two basic rules. As you write, just remember:

- If you use somebody else's exact words, you must give that person credit.
- If you use somebody else's ideas, even if you use your own words to express those ideas, you must give that person credit.

Your instructors will indicate their preferred method for citation: footnotes, references in parentheses included in the text of your paper, or endnotes. If you're not provided with guidelines or if you simply want to be sure that you do it right, consult a handbook or writing style manual, such as those prepared by the Modern Language Association (*MLA Handbook for Writers of Research Papers*), the American Psychological Association (*Publication Manual of the American Psychological Association*), the University of Chicago Press (*The Chicago Manual of Style*), or the Council of Science Editors (*Scientific Style and Format: The CSE Manual for Authors, Editors, and Publishers*).

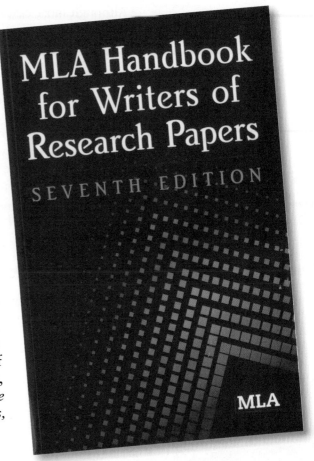

ABOUT PLAGIARISM

Several years ago, a serious candidate for the American presidency was forced to withdraw from the race when opponents discovered he had failed to give proper credit to a source he used in one of his speeches. A reporter at a top newspaper was fired for deliberately faking his sources, and a famous historian lost her peers' respect (and a portion of her royalties) when another writer noticed that the historian had included passages from her work in a book without citation.

All three writers were accused of plagiarism, but notice that only the reporter plagiarized on purpose. The political candidate and the historian were probably more guilty of poor note-taking than of outright fraud, yet the consequences were just as dire. When information or ideas are put on paper, film, screen, or tape, they become intellectual property. Using those ideas without saying where you got them—even if you do this by mistake—is a form of theft and can cost you a grade, a course, a degree, maybe even a career.

It should go without saying (but we'll say it anyway) that deliberate cheating is a bad idea on many levels. Submitting a paper you purchased from an Internet source or from an individual will cause you to miss out on the discovery and skill development that research assignments are meant to teach. Intentional plagiarism is easily detected and will almost certainly earn you a failing grade, even expulsion.

Although most cases of plagiarism are the result of misunderstanding or carelessness, be aware that "I didn't know" is not a valid excuse. Although your instructors might acknowledge that plagiarism can be an "oops!" thing, they will still expect you to avoid errors, and they will call you on it if you don't. Luckily, plagiarism is relatively easy to avoid. Most important, always cite your sources. Keep careful notes as you conduct your research, so that later on you don't inadvertently mistake someone else's words or ideas for your own. Finally, be sure to check out your own campus's definition of what constitutes plagiarism, which you will find in the student handbook or in first-year English course materials. And if you have any questions or doubts about what is and isn't acceptable, ask.

PLAGIARISM IN THE DIGITAL AGE

Since the early days of the Internet, professors have seen a rise in plagiarism. In some high schools, the concept of plagiarism is rarely explained, and students might arrive at college with an incomplete understanding of how to cite other people's work. The Internet makes it easier for students to "cut and paste" text and pass that work off as their own—a practice that is considered unethical and, at some institutions, grounds for dismissal. With the advent of new technologies, it is becoming easier to catch students who plagiarize. Some colleges and universities use a website called TurnItIn.com, where a student's paper can be uploaded. TurnItIn.com automatically checks the paper against a large database of student papers and against the web. (It's like doing a Google search on every paper ever written and on the Internet at the same time.) The website then provides instructors with an originality report for each student. The professor can then review the originality report to determine whether the student's paper was original. If TurnItIn.com finds a portion of the student's paper that matches something in its database, the portion that matches will be displayed along with the corresponding original work. Remember that most colleges, universities, and professors will not distinguish between deliberately plagiarizing and plagiarizing out of carelessness or because of a lack of understanding about what constitutes plagiarism.

Thinking Critically

Why do higher education institutions take plagiarism so seriously? What are some ways in which you can avoid plagiarizing information that you've found online? Do you think that using a service such as TurnItIn.com is a good idea? Why or why not? How would you feel if you were a faculty member who received a plagiarized paper from a student? How would you handle the situation?

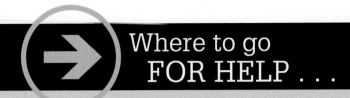

Where to go FOR HELP . . .

ON CAMPUS ▶

Your Instructor Be sure to ask your instructor for help with your information search, especially if you need to narrow your topic.

Library Libraries offer a variety of forms of help, including library orientation sessions, workshops, and, on some campuses, credit-bearing courses to develop your library search and retrieval skills.

Specialized Libraries/Collections At a large university, it is very common to find multiple librar-ies that are part of separate schools or colleges. For example, if you are a business administration major at such a university, there will probably be a separate business library that you will need to learn to use in addition to the central library. This is true for many majors.

Technology Support Centers Many campuses have units staffed by personnel who are responsible for the institution's entire technology infrastructure. These units frequently offer noncredit workshops and help sessions. In addition, many of the departments in larger universities will have their own separate technology labs and centers where you can work and get assistance. It won't surprise you to find that much of the help provided to students comes from fellow students, who are often ahead of their faculty in these skills. Some campuses also provide such assistance in residence halls, where there might even be a "comput-ing assistant" in addition to the resident assistant.

Discipline-Based Courses Many academic majors will include specialized courses in discipline-based research methods. You will find these listed in your campus catalog or bulletin. Students don't usually take these courses in their first year, but check them

out. If you are interested in credit courses dealing with technology, check out the courses in computer science.

ONLINE ▶

Research and documenting sources: http://owl .english.purdue.edu/owl/resource/584/02. Purdue University has an excellent resource on documenting sources, both print and electronic.

MY INSTITUTION'S RESOURCES ▶

_____

_____

_____

_____

_____

_____

_____

_____

_____

_____

_____

_____

_____

_____

_____

Chapter
REVIEW . . .

One-Minute PAPER . . .

Did the material in this chapter make you think about libraries and research in a new light? What did you find to be the most useful information in this chapter? What would you like to learn more about?

Applying What You've LEARNED . . .

Now that you have read and discussed this chapter, consider how you can apply what you have learned to your academic and personal life. The following prompts will help you reflect on chapter material and its relevance to you both now and in the future.

1. It is important to get comfortable with all of the resources in your campus library. Find out where your library keeps archived newspapers on microfiche. Search for a newspaper (such as the *New York Times*) that was published on the day you were born. What was the major headline that day? What movies were playing? What was happening in world news?

2. Using information literacy skills in college is a no-brainer, but think beyond your college experience. How will improving your information literacy skills help you once you are out of college? Think of a career that you are interested in, and describe how you might use those skills in that career.

Building Your PORTFOLIO . . .

“ I find that a great part of the information I have was acquired by looking something up and finding something else on the way. ”

– FRANKLIN P. ADAMS (1881–1960),
American journalist and radio personality

IN THE KNOW

Reviewing multiple sources of information can help you to get the whole story. This is especially important when using the Internet as a research tool. While the Internet is becoming a primary source of worldwide news, there is no overarching quality control system for information posted on the Internet. Regardless of where you are gathering your information, you need to read with a discerning eye to make sure the source is credible.

1. Choose a national current event.

   a. Carefully read about it on your favorite news website (e.g., http://www.cnn.com).

   b. In a traditional national newspaper (e.g., the *New York Times, Wall Street Journal, Christian Science Monitor,* or *USA Today*). Your campus library or local community library will have these national newspapers or you can find them on the Web.

2. In a Word document, compare and contrast the differences in the way the event was portrayed by the two sources.

- Is the author's name or another source provided?

- Are there clues that the author(s) are taking a biased stand in reporting? If so, describe these clues.

- Whom do you think the authors were writing for (intended audience)? For example, were they writing for any reader, or for people of a certain age or educational level?

- Were the facts presented the same way by both the Internet source and the print source? Explain your answer.

- Did one source cover more details than the other? If so, explain your answer.

- Were the writer's information sources listed? If so, what were those sources?

3. Save your responses in your portfolio on your personal computer or flash drive. Use this process as a tool to make sure you use valid resources the next time you are doing research for a project or paper.

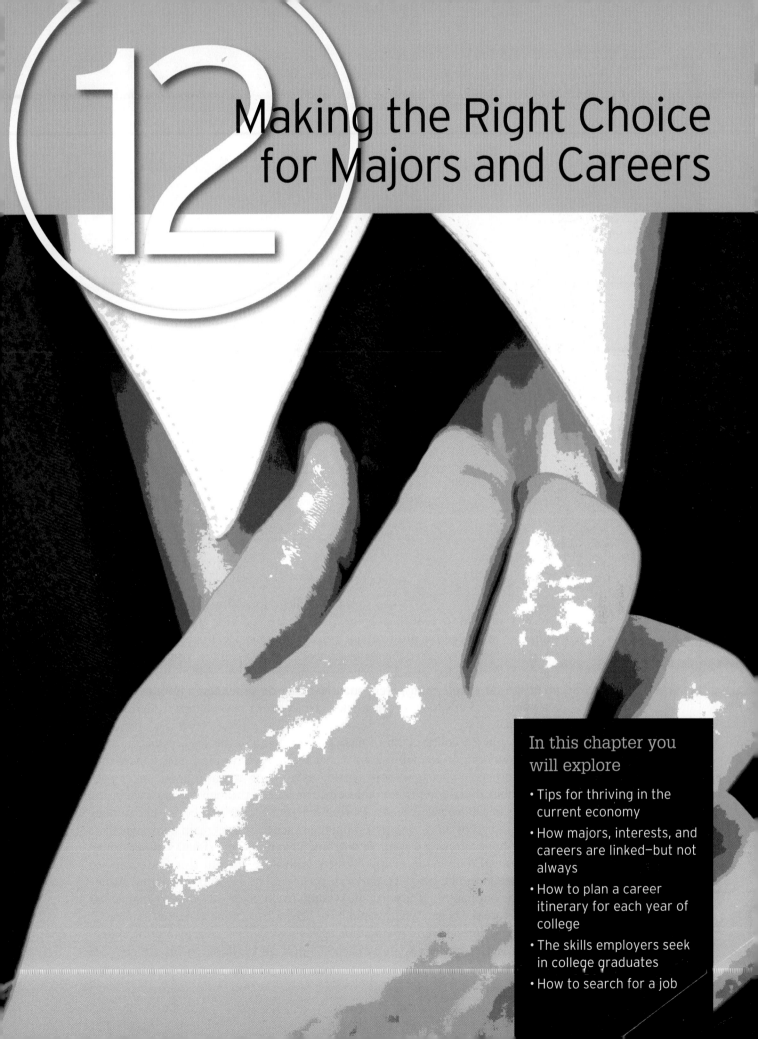

12 Making the Right Choice for Majors and Careers

In this chapter you will explore

- Tips for thriving in the current economy
- How majors, interests, and careers are linked—but not always
- How to plan a career itinerary for each year of college
- The skills employers seek in college graduates
- How to search for a job

Confessions of a
COLLEGE STUDENT . . .

BENNETT ROSSELL, 24
University of California, Riverside

66 I never talked with a counselor, and I didn't know to go to the testing center or anything like that. 99

I was really confused about choosing a major. I wasn't prepared for it. I never talked with a counselor, and I didn't know to go to the testing center or anything like that. The biggest contributing factor for me came from the people who know me best and love me most. They would suggest, "You should take a business class or an economics class. I think you're this type of person; you would do well in this; you would like it." So I looked into it, read about it, and talked to some professors, and business economics did sound like the best major for me. But up until my junior year I was really lost.

I'm still not sure what kind of career I'll go into. I've been told by a lot of people that it really doesn't matter what you get your degree in. That makes sense to me. I've heard of people getting a business degree and then going to medical school, or getting a degree in film and working for a publishing company, or getting a degree in English and becoming an attorney. People jump around from one thing to the next, so I really don't feel like it's that vital to stick with a job in my field of study. Hopefully by the time I'm deep into my career I'll have found my niche.

Students come to college for many reasons, but for the majority of them a central purpose of college is gaining the knowledge and skills they will need for future employment. Your success in your work life will often depend on whether the profession or career you think you want to pursue is really right for you. But success in the workplace also depends on your ability to do simple things well, such as being on time, being honest, and doing your best. Let's look at the work experiences of two college students, Sara and John.

Sara entered college with thoughts of majoring in the sciences because she enjoyed working in the laboratory at her hometown hospital. Her concern for helping others led her to choose nursing as a major; it was a good career path that combined her two primary interests. Sara sailed through the first two years, excelling in her science classes. During her junior year she began her nursing courses and spent more time observing the practice of nursing in her university's teaching hospital. After a summer working in various departments of her hometown hospital, Sara made an appointment with a career counselor. She confessed that she did not like being around sick people every day and wanted to change her major but had no idea what she wanted to do. Sara was wise to change her major before she began what would have been a frustrating career as a nurse.

John explored several majors during his first two years in college by choosing his elective courses with careers in mind and talking to his friends. He settled on business as a major, focusing on finance. John had high aspirations of working for a Fortune 500 company and earning a six-figure salary within five years of graduation. He performed above average in his academic work, although he was occasionally slack with assignments and frequently missed class. He interned with two prominent companies and eventually accepted a position with a Fortune 500 company. To his surprise, he was fired nine months later because he was frequently late for work and missed important deadlines on two occasions. Although John had high aspirations while he was in college, he somehow never learned, or took seriously, the basic habits of career success.

Like Sara and John, students who are planning for careers frequently encounter bumps along the way. Choosing a career is a process of discovery, involving a willingness to remain open to new ideas and experiences. Why begin thinking about your career now? Because many of the decisions you make during your first year in college will have an impact on where you end up after you graduate.

Careers and the New Economy

In your lifetime, companies have restructured to remain competitive. As a result, major changes have taken place in how we work, where we work, and the ways in which we prepare for work while in college. In many ways, the following characteristics define today's economy:

- **Global.** Increasingly, industries have become multinational, not only moving into overseas markets but also seeking cheaper labor, capital, and resources abroad. Factories around the world built to similar standards can turn out essentially the same products. Your career is bound to be affected by the global economy, even if you never leave the United States. For example, when you call an 800 number for customer service, the person who talks to you might be answering your call in Iowa, Ireland, or India. In his best-selling book *The World Is Flat*, Thomas Friedman reminds his readers that talent has become more important than geography in determining a person's opportunity in life. College graduates in the United States are now competing for jobs with others around the world who are often willing to work longer hours for less money than American workers. And this is true not only in manufacturing jobs, which are routinely being outsourced to other countries, but also in professional occupations such as medicine and accounting.

- **Unstable.** In 2008 and 2009 the world economy suffered a series of events that led to downturns in stock markets, bankruptcies, foreclosures, failing businesses, and lost jobs. Scandals within the highest ranks of major companies and constant mergers and acquisitions of companies have destabilized the workforce. Depending on how long it takes to stabilize the economy in the United States and the rest of the world, your career goals might have to be refocused. Because the global economic situation is changing continuously, it's important to keep up to date on the economic situation as it relates to your prospective major and career.

- **Innovative.** The economy depends on creativity in new products and services to generate consumer interest around the world. Especially in times of economic instability, the flexibility and responsiveness of companies to the changing economic climate will affect their ability to survive.

- **Boundaryless.** Teams of workers within an organization need to understand the missions of other teams because they most likely will have to work together. You might be an accountant and find yourself working with the public relations division of your company, or you might be a human resources manager who does training for a number of different divisions and in several different countries. You might even find yourself moved laterally to a unit that has a different function rather than being promoted to a higher position in your organization.

- **Customized.** More and more, consumers are demanding products and services tailored to their specific needs. You have probably noticed the seemingly endless varieties of a single brand of shampoo or cereal crowding store shelves. Such market segmentation requires constant adaptation of ideas to identify new products and services as new customer demands emerge.

- **Fast.** When computers became popular, people rejoiced because they believed the computer would reduce their workloads. Actually, the reverse happened. Whereas secretaries and other support workers once performed many tasks for executives, now executives design their own PowerPoint presentations and format their own documents. For better or worse, "We want it now" is the cry in the workplace, with product and service delivery time cut to a minimum (the "just-in-time" policy). Being fast requires constant thinking outside the lines to identify new approaches to designing and delivering products.

According to *Fast Company* magazine, the new economy has changed many of the rules about work. Leaders are now expected to teach and encourage others as well as to head up their divisions. Careers frequently zigzag into other areas. People who can anticipate the needs of the marketplace are in demand. Change has become the norm. Workers are being urged to continue their learning, and companies are volunteering to play a critical role in the welfare of all people through sponsorship of worthy causes. As the lines between work and the rest of life continue to blur, workers need to find healthy balance in their lives. Bringing work home might be inevitable at times, but it shouldn't be the rule.

As you work at your job, you'll be continually enhancing and expanding your skills and competencies. You can accomplish this on your own by taking evening courses or by attending conferences and workshops your employer sends you to. As you prepare for, continue, or change your career, remember the following:

- **You are, more or less, solely responsible for your career.** At one time, organizations often provided structured ladders that employees could climb in their moves to higher professional levels. In most cases such ladders have disappeared. Companies might assist you with assessments and information on available positions in the industry, but the ultimate task of creating a career path is yours.

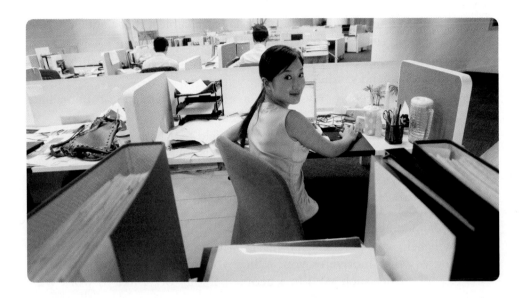

- **To advance your career, you must accept the risks that accompany employment and plan for the future.** As organizations continue to restructure, merge, and either grow or downsize in response to economic conditions, you must do your best to prepare for the unexpected. Because you can quickly find yourself unemployed, it will be wise to keep all possible options in mind.

- **A college degree does not guarantee employment.** Of course, with a degree, you'll be able to hunt for more opportunities that are rewarding, financially and otherwise, than if you did not have a degree. But just because you want to work for a certain organization or in a certain field doesn't mean that there will always be a job for you there.

- **A commitment to lifelong learning will help keep you employable.** In college you have been learning a vital skill: how to learn. *Gradus*, the Latin root of "graduation," comes from the phrase *Gradus ad Parnassum*, or "steps to Parnassus," the home of the Muses. To move toward Parnassus means moving to a higher level of knowledge. Your learning has just begun when you receive your diploma.

Now the good news: Hundreds of thousands of graduates find jobs every year, even in recessionary times. Some of them might have to work longer to get where they want to be, but persistence pays off. If you start now, you'll have time to build a portfolio of academic and **co-curricular** experiences that will begin to add substance to your career profile.

Aligning Your Sense of Purpose and Your Career

Chapter 1 in this book suggested that you think very seriously about your purpose for being in college. Here are some additional questions to ask yourself as you continue thinking about why you're at this particular college or university:

- Am I here to find out who I am and to study a subject that I am truly passionate about, regardless of whether it leads to a career?
- Am I here to engage in an academic program that provides an array of possibilities when I graduate?
- Am I here to prepare myself for a graduate program or immediate employment?
- Am I here to obtain specific training in a field that I am committed to?
- Am I here to gain specific skills for a job I already have?

Remember these six simple, one-word questions. They can help you to prepare for a career and obtain that important first job:

Why? Why do you want to be a _____ ? Knowing your goals and values will help you pursue your career with passion and an understanding of what motivates you. When you speak with an interviewer, avoid clichés such as "I'm a people person" or "I like to work with people." Sooner or later, most people have to work with people. And your interviewer has heard this much too often. Instead, be sure that you have crystallized your actual reasons for following your chosen career path. An interviewer will want to know why you are interested in the job, why it feels right for you at this time in your life, and whether you are committed to this career for the future.

Who? Who at your college or university or in your community can help you make career decisions? Network with people who can help you find out what work you want to do. Right now, those people might be instructors in your major, an academic advisor, and perhaps someone at your campus career center. Later, network with others who can help you attain your goal. Someone will almost always know someone else for you to talk to.

How? How will you develop the technical and communications skills required for working effectively? Don't be a technophobe. Learn how to do PowerPoint presentations, build web pages, and create Excel spreadsheets. Take a speech course. Work on improving your writing. Even if you think your future job doesn't require these skills, you'll be more marketable with them.

What? What opportunities are available in your preferred career fields? Be aware of the range of job options an employer presents, as well as such threats as a company's decision to **outsource** certain jobs—that is, contracting with an external organization to perform particular functions at a lower cost. Clearly understand the employment requirements for the career field you have chosen. Know what training you will need to remain and move up in your chosen profession.

Where? Where will your preferred career path take you? Will you be required to travel or live in a certain part of the country or the world? Or will job success require that you stay in one location? Although job requirements may change over the course of your lifetime, try to achieve a balance between your personal values and preferences and the predictable requirements of the career you are pursuing.

When? When will you need to start looking for your first job? Certain professions, such as teaching, tend to hire new employees at certain times of the year, generally spring or summer. Determine whether seasonal hiring is common for your preferred career.

CONNECTING YOUR MAJOR AND YOUR INTERESTS WITH YOUR CAREER

Some students are sure about their major when they enter college, but many others are at a loss. Either way, it's okay. At some point, you might ask yourself: Why am I in college? Although it sounds like an easy question to answer, it's not. Many students would immediately respond, "So I can get a good job or education for a specific career." Yet most majors do not lead to a specific career path or job. You actually can enter most career paths from any number of academic majors. Marketing, a common undergraduate business major, is a field that recruits from a wide variety of majors, including advertising, communications, and psychology. Sociology majors find jobs in law enforcement, teaching, and public service.

Today, English majors are designing web pages, philosophy majors are developing logic codes for operating systems, and history majors are sales representatives and business managers. You do not have to major in science to gain admittance to medical school. Of course, you do have to take the required science and math courses, but medical schools seek applicants with diverse backgrounds. Only a few technical or professional fields, such as accounting, nursing, and engineering, are tied to specific majors.

Exploring your interests is the best way to choose an academic major. If you're still not sure, take the advice of Patrick Combs, author of *Major in Success*, who recommends that you major in a subject about which you are really passionate. Most advisors would agree.

YOUR TURN ▶

Would you describe your major as something you're really passionate about? Why or why not? If your answer is no, why are you pursuing this particular major?

Some students will find they're not ready to select an academic major in the first year. You can use your first year and even your second year to explore your interests and find out how they might connect to various academic programs. Over time, you might make different choices than you would have during your first year.

You can major in almost anything. As this chapter emphasizes, it is how you integrate your classes with your extracurricular activities and work experience that prepares you for a successful transition to your career. Try a major you think you'll like, and see what develops. But keep an open mind, and don't pin all your hopes on finding a career in that major alone.

Your major and your career ultimately have to fit your overall life goals, purposes, values, and beliefs.

EXPLORING YOUR INTERESTS

John Holland, a psychologist at Johns Hopkins University, developed a number of tools and concepts that can help you organize the various dimensions of yourself so that you can identify potential career choices (see Table 12.1).

Holland separates people into six general categories based on differences in their interests, skills, values, and personality characteristics—in short, their preferred approaches to life. Holland's system organizes career fields into the same six categories. Career fields are grouped according to what a particular career field requires of a person (the skills and personality characteristics most commonly associated with success in those fields) and what rewards those fields provide (interests and values most commonly associated with satisfaction).

TABLE 12.1 ▶ Holland Personality and Career Types

Category	Personality Characteristics	Career Fields
Realistic (R)	These people describe themselves as concrete, down-to-earth, and practical doers. They exhibit competitive/assertive behavior and show interest in activities that require motor coordination, skill, and physical strength. They prefer situations involving action solutions rather than tasks involving verbal or interpersonal skills, and they like taking a concrete approach to problem solving rather than relying on abstract theory. They tend to be interested in scientific or mechanical areas rather than the arts.	Environmental engineer, electrical contractor, industrial arts teacher, navy officer, fitness director, package engineer, electronics technician, web designer
Investigative (I)	These people describe themselves as analytical, rational, and logical problem solvers. They value intellectual stimulation and intellectual achievement, and they prefer to think rather than to act and to organize and understand rather than to persuade. They usually have a strong interest in physical, biological, or social sciences. They are less apt to be people oriented.	Urban planner, chemical engineer, bacteriologist, flight engineer, genealogist, laboratory technician, marine scientist, nuclear medical technologist, obstetrician, quality-control technician, computer programmer, environmentalist, physician, college professor

TABLE 12.1 ▶ Holland Personality and Career Types *(Continued)*

Category	Personality Characteristics	Career Fields
Artistic (A)	These people describe themselves as creative, innovative, and independent. They value self-expression and relating with others through artistic expression and are also emotionally expressive. They dislike structure, preferring tasks involving personal or physical skills. They resemble investigative people but are more interested in the cultural or the aesthetic than the scientific.	Architect, film editor/director, actor, cartoonist, interior decorator, fashion model, graphic communications specialist, journalist, editor, orchestra leader, public relations specialist, sculptor, media specialist, librarian, reporter
Social (S)	These people describe themselves as kind, caring, helpful, and understanding of others. They value helping and making a contribution. They satisfy their needs in one-to-one or small-group interaction using strong speaking skills to teach, counsel, or advise. They are drawn to close interpersonal relationships and are less apt to engage in intellectual or extensive physical activity.	Nurse, teacher, social worker, genetic counselor, marriage counselor, rehabilitation counselor, school superintendent, geriatric specialist, insurance claims specialist, minister, travel agent, guidance counselor, convention planner
Enterprising (E)	These people describe themselves as assertive, risk taking, and persuasive. They value prestige, power, and status and are more inclined than other types to pursue it. They use verbal skills to supervise, lead, direct, and persuade rather than to support or guide. They are interested in people and in achieving organizational goals.	Banker, city manager, FBI agent, health administrator, judge, labor arbitrator, salary and wage administrator, insurance salesperson, sales engineer, lawyer, sales representative, marketing manager
Conventional (C)	These people describe themselves as neat, orderly, detail oriented, and persistent. They value order, structure, prestige, and status and possess a high degree of self-control. They are not opposed to rules and regulations. They are skilled in organizing, planning, and scheduling and are interested in data and people.	Accountant, statistician, census enumerator, data processor, hospital administrator, insurance administrator, office manager, underwriter, auditor, personnel specialist, database manager, abstractor/indexer

Source: Adapted from John L. Holland, *Self-Directed Search Manual*. Odessa, FL: Psychological Assessment Resources, 1985.

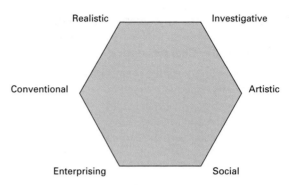

▲ **FIGURE 12.1**

Holland's Hexagonal Model of Career Fields

Your career choices ultimately will involve a complex assessment of the factors that are most important to you. To display the relationship between career fields and the potential conflicts people face as they consider them, Holland's model is commonly presented in a hexagonal shape (Figure 12.1). The closer the types, the closer the relationships among the career fields; the farther apart the types, the more conflict between the career fields. For instance, individuals with "conventional" and "realistic" characteristics will find many similar characteristics in their career fields. However, careers preferred by "investigative" individuals will have little in common with careers chosen by individuals who are "enterprising."

Holland's model can help you address the problem of career choice in two ways. First, you can begin to identify many career fields that are consistent with what you know about yourself. Once you have identified potential fields, you can use the career library at your college to get more information about those fields, such as daily activities for specific jobs, interests and abilities required, preparation required for entry, working conditions, salary and benefits, and employment outlook. Second, you can begin to identify the harmony or conflicts in your career choices. This will help you to analyze the reasons for your career decisions and be more confident as you make choices.

Never feel you have to make a decision based on the results of only one assessment. Career choices are complex and involve many factors; furthermore, these decisions are reversible. Take time to talk your interests over with a career counselor. Another helpful approach is to shadow an individual in the occupation that interests you to obtain a better understanding of what the occupation entails in terms of skills, commitment, and opportunity.

FACTORS THAT AFFECT CAREER CHOICES

Some people have a definite self-image when they enter college, but most of us are still in the process of defining (or redefining) ourselves throughout life. We can look at ourselves in several useful ways with respect to possible careers:

- **Values.** Today, more than ever, knowing your core values (your most important beliefs) will be important in shaping your career path. In a faltering and unpredictable economy, having a strong rudder will help you steer through the turbulent times.

- **Interests.** Your interests will develop from experiences and beliefs and can continue to develop and change throughout your life. You might be interested in writing for the college newspaper because you wrote for your high school paper. It's not unusual to enter Psych 101 with a great interest in psychology and realize halfway through the course that psychology is not what you imagined.
- **Skills.** The ability to do something well can usually be improved with practice.
- **Aptitudes.** Your inherent strengths, or aptitudes, are often part of your biological heritage or the result of early training. Each of us has aptitudes we can build on.
- **Personality.** Your personality makes you who you are and can't be ignored when you make career decisions. The quiet, orderly, calm, detail-oriented person will probably make a different work choice than the aggressive, outgoing, argumentative person will.
- **Life goals and work values.** Each of us defines success and satisfaction in our own way. The process is complex and very personal. Two factors influence our conclusions about success and happiness: knowing that we are achieving the life goals we've set for ourselves and finding that we gain satisfaction from what we're receiving from our work. If your values conflict with the organizational values where you work, you might be in for trouble.

YOUR TURN ▶

What kinds of jobs have you had, either for pay or as a volunteer? Which of your jobs was your favorite? Which did you dislike? What do your experiences tell you about your preferences for work in the future?

Planning for Your Career

The process of making a career choice begins with creating a career plan. A good career plan should eventually include:

- Researching possible occupations that match your skills, interests, and academic major
- Building on your strengths and developing your weaker skills
- Preparing a marketing strategy that sells you as a valued member of a professional team
- Writing a convincing résumé and cover letter

Table 12.2 on page 226 provides a guide to what you should be doing during each year of college. If you are in a two-year associate degree program, you will have to do more during your second year than this table suggests.

You might proceed through these steps at a different pace than your friends will, and that's okay. What you want is to develop your qualifications, make good choices, and take advantage of any opportunities on campus to learn more about the career search. Keep your goals in mind as you select courses and seek employment, but also keep an eye out for unique opportunities. The route you think you want to take might not be the best one for you.

TABLE 12.2 ▶ Your Career Itinerary

A. NO MATTER WHAT YEAR

- Get a job. Even a part-time job will develop your skills and might help you to make decisions about what you like—and what you don't—in a work environment. In any job, you can learn vital skills such as teamwork, communication, and interpersonal, computer, and time management skills.

- Register with your college's online job listing system to find listings for part- and full-time, internship, co-op, and seasonal employment.

- Find on-campus interviewing opportunities for internships in your early years and for full-time employment after graduation.

- Network with family, friends, instructors, friends of family, and acquaintances to find contacts in your field(s) of interest so that you can learn more about those areas.

- Volunteer! This can help you explore careers and get some experience in an area that interests you as you help others.

- Conduct occupational and industry research for your field or area of geographic interest. Look for other options within and beyond those fields.

- Explore career options through informational interviews (interviewing to find out about a career) and job shadowing (observing someone at work—with their permission).

- Prepare a draft of your résumé and have it critiqued by a career counselor and perhaps by a professional in your chosen field.

- Get involved in clubs and organizations; work toward leadership positions.

- Explore study possibilities in other countries to gain a global perspective and learn a foreign language.

- Attend career fairs to connect with employers for internships and other career-related opportunities as well as to develop a professional network.

B. FIRST YEAR OF COLLEGE

- Take the Holland Self-Directed Search or a similar interest inventory at your career center.

- Take a variety of classes to get exposure to various skill and knowledge areas.

- Attend your campus's annual career fair to see what is being offered.

- Talk to a career counselor about your skills, aptitudes, and interests. Find out what the career center offers.

C. SECOND YEAR OF COLLEGE

- Attend career fairs to learn more about employers who hire graduates in your major.

- Spend some time talking with your college advisor or career counselor to discuss your career plans.

D. THIRD YEAR OF COLLEGE

- Take an advanced computerized career assessment to discover further career options and to refine your career plans. Visit your career center.

- Take on a leadership role in a club or organization.

TABLE 12.2 ▶ Your Career Itinerary (*Continued*)

- Participate in mock interview activities to improve your interviewing skills.
- Attend workshops to learn more about résumé writing, looking for an internship, interviewing, and other job search skills.
- Explore the option of graduate school.
- Develop a top-10 list of employers of interest.

E. LAST YEAR OF COLLEGE

- Check on-campus interviewing opportunities on a daily basis, beginning in the fall term. Interview with organizations recruiting for your major.
- Conduct research on organizations of interest to you, interview with those coming to campus, and contact human resources professionals who represent organizations that won't be on campus. Find out if you can interview.
- Attend career fairs to network with employers and set up interviewing opportunities.
- If you're thinking about graduate school, request applications early in the fall, and send them out throughout the fall term.
- Target your geographic areas of interest by contacting local chambers of commerce and using local newspapers, phone books, and Internet resources.

Source: Used by permission of Career Passport, Michigan State University.

YOUR TURN ▶

What kind of "marketing strategy" could you develop to sell yourself to a potential employer? Which of your characteristics or aptitudes would you emphasize?

PLANNING FOR TWO-YEAR STUDENTS

Some students at two-year colleges pursue technical or professional degrees that prepare them for employment after two years. Others are planning to transfer to a four-year college or university. If you are a student attending a two-year college and plan to transfer to complete a four-year degree, you might find that once you get to the four-year institution, you have less time to make adjustments in your course work and career opportunities. A major stumbling block is that transfers often arrive on their new campus with enough credits to declare a major; at this point, changing your major again can be costly, because it will mean adding time, and therefore expense, before graduation.

Consider these early steps during your first three terms at your two-year college:

- Take a career interest inventory, and begin focusing on the career paths that most interest you.
- Visit with a career counselor to develop a short-term strategy to test your career interests.
- Enroll in a career decision-making class.
- Shadow a professional in the occupation(s) that you wish to enter.
- Attend a local career fair to learn about potential job opportunities.

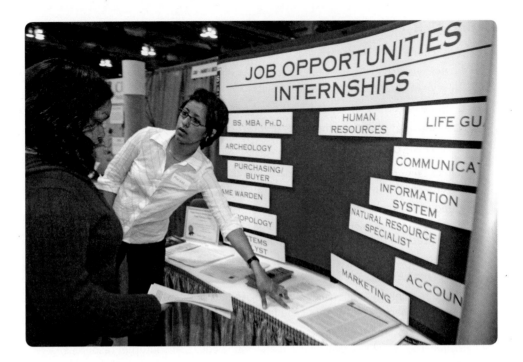

Another consideration for students at community colleges is to determine whether transferring to another institution is necessary at all. More and more community colleges are offering bachelor's degrees. Check out your opportunities for advanced education right where you are.

During your last term at your two-year college, consider these options:

- Determine what academic majors best match your occupational interests.
- Investigate whether the college or university you will attend next has the majors you need and whether there are any prerequisite requirements you will have to meet before you can enroll in your chosen major. If you find you do not have a clear career focus by the time you transfer, meet again with the college's career advisor.
- Visit the campus to which you are transferring before you register. Meet with both a career advisor and an academic advisor there as soon as possible.

> **YOUR TURN ▶**
>
> Have you explored your institution's career center? If so, what did you learn? If not, when in your college experience do you think going to the career center will be most important? Why?

GETTING EXPERIENCE

Now that you have a handle on your interests, it's time to test the waters. Your campus has a variety of activities and programs in which you can participate to confirm those interests and your values and gain valuable skills. Here are some examples:

DO'S AND DON'TS OF CAREER PLANNING

As you start examining your aspirations and interests, keep in mind these simple do's and don'ts:

Do	Don't
1. Do explore a number of career possibilities and academic majors.	1. Don't just focus on a major and blindly hope to get a career out of it. That's backward.
2. Do get involved through volunteer work, study abroad, and student organizations—especially those linked to your major.	2. Don't be motivated primarily by external stimuli, such as salary, prestige, and perks. All the money in the world won't make you happy if you hate what you're doing every day.
3. Do follow your passion. Learn what you love to do, and go for it.	3. Don't select a major just because it seems cool.
	4. Don't choose courses simply because your roommate or friend said they were easy. That's wasting your valuable time, not to mention tuition.

- **Volunteer/service learning.** Some instructors build service learning into their courses. Service learning allows you to apply academic theories and ideas to actual practice. Volunteering outside of class is also a valuable way to encounter different life situations and to gain work knowledge in areas such as teaching, health services, counseling, and tax preparation. A little time spent each week can provide immense personal and professional rewards.

- **Study abroad.** If possible, spend a term taking courses in another country so you can learn about a different culture, experience new traditions, and practice a different pace of life. Some study-abroad programs also include options for both work and service learning experiences. If this interests you, find out how financial aid applies to study abroad.

- **Internships and co-ops.** Many employers now expect these work experiences. They want to see that you have experience in the professional workplace and have gained an understanding of the skills and competencies necessary to succeed. Check with your academic department and your career center to find out what internships are available in your major. Many majors offer academic credit for internships. Remember that with an internship on your résumé, you'll be a step ahead of students who ignore this valuable experience.

- **On-campus employment.** On-campus jobs might not provide as much income as off-campus jobs, but on-campus jobs give you a chance to practice good work habits. On-campus employment also brings you into contact with faculty members and other academic professionals whom you can later consult as mentors or ask for those all-important reference letters.

- **Student projects/competitions.** In many fields, students engage in competitions based on what they have learned in the classroom. Civil engineers build concrete canoes, and marketing majors develop campaign strategies, for example. They might compete against teams from other colleges or universities. In the process, they learn teamwork, communication, and applied problem-solving skills.

- **Research.** An excellent way to extend your academic learning is to work with a faculty member on a research project. Research extends your critical thinking skills and provides insight into a subject above and beyond your books and class notes.

Skills Employers Look For

One of the many important purposes and outcomes of your college experience is the acquisition of a combination of knowledge and skills. Two types of skills are essential to employment and to life: content skills and transferable skills.

CONTENT SKILLS

Content skills, often referred to as cognitive, intellectual, or "hard" skills, are acquired as you gain mastery in your academic field. They include writing proficiency, computer literacy, and foreign language skills. Computing knowledge and ability are now perceived as core skills that are equal in importance to reading, writing, and mathematics. In fact, employers' expectations regarding computer knowledge and application continue to rise.

Content skills include specific types of information, facts, principles, and rules. For instance, perhaps you have knowledge of civil engineering related to dam construction, or you have extensive experience working with telescopes. Maybe your work in the library and study of library science have trained you in several library databases. Or you might know the most common clinical diagnoses in psychology. We often forget some of the preparation we have gained that augments our mastery of specific academic material, especially statistics, research methods, foreign language aptitude, and computer literacy. You can apply all of this specific knowledge to jobs in a particular field or occupation.

Certain types of employers will expect extensive knowledge in your academic major before they will consider hiring you; for example, to get a job in accounting, you must demonstrate knowledge of that field. However, for most college students it's sufficient to have some fundamental knowledge. You will learn more on the job as you move from entry-level jobs to more advanced positions.

TRANSFERABLE SKILLS

Transferable skills are skills that are general and apply to or transfer to a variety of settings. By category, these transferable skills are as follows:

- Communication skills that demonstrate solid oral and listening abilities in addition to a good foundation in the basic content skill of writing
- Presentation skills, including the ability to justify and persuade as well as the ability to respond to questions and serious critiques of your presentation material
- Leadership skills, or the ability to take charge or relinquish control according to the needs of the organization
- Team skills, or the ability to work collaboratively with different people while maintaining autonomous control over some assignments
- Interpersonal abilities that allow you to relate to others, inspire others to participate, or ease conflict between coworkers
- Personal traits, including showing initiative and motivation, being adaptable to change, having a work ethic, being reliable and honest, possessing integrity, knowing how to plan and organize multiple tasks, and being able to respond positively to customer concerns
- Critical thinking and problem solving, or the ability to identify problems and their solutions by integrating information from a variety of sources and effectively weighing alternatives
- A willingness to learn quickly and continuously

Transferable skills are valuable to many kinds of employers and professions. They give you flexibility in your career planning. You can gain transferable skills through a variety of activities. For example, volunteer work, study abroad, involvement in a student professional organization or club, and the pursuit of hobbies or interests can all build teamwork, leadership, interpersonal awareness, and effective communication abilities. Internships and career-related work are also valuable opportunities to practice these skills in the real world.

KEY COMPETENCIES

While employers expect skills and related work experience from today's college graduates, they also have begun to focus on additional key competencies that are critical for success in today's economy:

- **Integrity.** Your employment will depend on your being able to act in an ethical manner at work and in the community.
- **Innovation.** You should also be able to evaluate, synthesize, and create knowledge that will lead to new products and services. Employers seek individuals who are willing to take some risks and explore innovative and better ways to deliver products and services.
- **Initiative.** A great employee is able to recognize the need to take action, such as helping a team member, approaching a new client, or taking on assignments without being asked. Employers don't want employees who will wait passively for a supervisor to provide work assignments; they want people who will see what has to be done and do it.
- **Commitment.** Both employers and graduate schools look for a candidate's commitment to learning. They want you to express what you really love to study and are willing to learn on your own initiative. The best foundation for this competency is to be engaged in an academic program in which you wake up every morning eager to go to class.

Working in College

Do you hope to get a job while you are in college? Before you do, be really honest with yourself: Is this something you must do to pay for college? Is it something you want to do to maintain your lifestyle and acquire things you want? Or is it a combination of both? Most students work in paid jobs. Here are some things you should know about working in college.

Paid work can support the attainment of your college goals, provide you with the financial means to complete college, and help you structure your time so that you are a much better time manager. It can help you meet people who will later serve as important references for graduate school and/or employment. However, working too much can interfere with your college success, your ability to attend class, your homework, and your participation in many other valuable parts of college life, such as group study, foreign study and travel, and group activities. Take some time to determine how much you need to work, and stay within reasonable limits.

Stated very simply, students who work in paid jobs more than fifteen hours a week have a lower chance of success in college. Students who work on campus are more likely to graduate from college than are students who work off campus.

ON-CAMPUS JOBS

If you want or need to work, explore on-campus opportunities as soon as (or even before) you arrive at college. If you have a **work-study award,** a form of federal financial aid that covers a portion of college costs in return for on-campus employment, check with your student employment office for a listing of possible campus jobs for work-study students. Your career center can tell you how to access your college's online employment system. College employment systems generally channel all jobs collected from faculty, advisors, and career counselors into one database, so it is convenient for you to identify the sorts of jobs you are looking for.

Many campuses offer an on-campus job fair early in the fall term. Even if you might not be interested at the time, a visit to the job fair will give you a great idea of the range and type of jobs available on campus. You might be pleasantly surprised to learn that there are more opportunities than washing dishes in the cafeteria. Job fairs usually include off-campus community employers as well, in part because your institution must spend some of the work-study funds it receives in supporting off-campus work by students.

OFF-CAMPUS JOBS

The best places to start looking for off-campus jobs are your campus career center and your financial aid office. They might well have listings or websites with off-campus employment opportunities. Feel free to speak to a career counselor for suggestions. You can also use the following job-search strategies:

- Learn the names of the major employers in your college's geographic area: manufacturers, service industries, resorts, and so on. Once you know who the major employers are, check them out, visit their websites, and learn the details.

- Check out the website for the agency in your state that collects and disseminates information about available employment opportunities. Find out whether this agency has an office in the community where you are attending college.

- Visit employment agencies, particularly those that seek part-time, temporary workers. This is a convenient, low-risk (for both you and the employer) way to "shop" for a job and to obtain flexible, short-term, low-commitment employment.

- Visit online job boards, and look at the classified ads in the local newspaper, either in print or online. Don't forget the classifieds in the national press. Some national firms will have jobs that can be done part-time in your area or even from your own living space.

- Check your campus student newspaper. Employers who favor hiring college students often advertise there. Be cautious about work opportunities that seem unrealistic, such as those offering big salaries for working at home, or those that ask you to pay an up-front fee for a job.

- Be aware that many jobs are never posted. Employers find it easier to hire people who are recommended to them by current employees, friends, or the person vacating the position. Faculty members often hire students for their research labs based on performance in the classroom.

- Realize that who you know is important. Your friends who already work on campus or who have had an internship can be the best people to help you when you are ready to search for your job. In fact, nearly 50 percent of all student jobs are found through family and friends.

College students often view the choice of a career as a monumental and irreversible decision. But in its broadest sense, a career is the sum of the decisions you make over a lifetime. There is no one right occupation just waiting to be

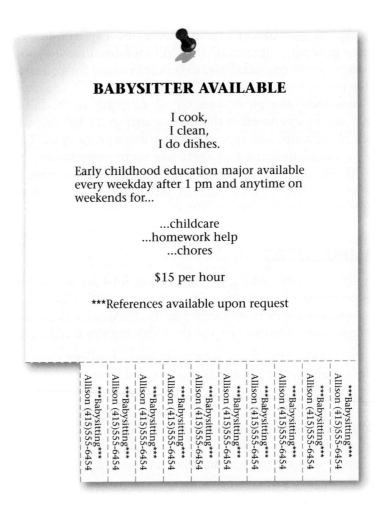

discovered. Rather, there are many career choices you might find fulfilling and satisfying. The question to consider is: What is the best choice for me now?

BUILDING A RÉSUMÉ

Before you finish college, you'll need a résumé, whether it's for a part-time job, for an internship or co-op position, or to show to a professor who agrees to write a letter of recommendation for you. Typically, there are two types of résumés; one is written in chronological format; the other is organized by skills. Generally, choose the chronological résumé if you have related job experience, and choose the skills résumé if you can group skills from a number of jobs or projects under several meaningful categories. Try for one page, but if you have a number of outstanding things to say that won't fit on a single page, add a second page.

WRITING A COVER LETTER

When sending a cover letter, heed the following suggestions:

- Find out whom to contact. It's not the same in all fields. If you were seeking a marketing position at an advertising agency, you would write to the director of account services. If you were approaching General Motors regarding a position in the engineering department, you might write either the director of human resources for the entire company or a special human resources director in charge of engineering. Your academic advisor or career counselor can help you address your letter to the right person. So can the Internet.

■ Get the most recent name and address. Advisors or career counselors can guide you to references in your campus or career library. Never write, "To whom it may concern."

■ Use the proper formats for date, address, and salutation.

INTERVIEWING

The first year of college might not seem like a time to be concerned about interviews. However, students often find themselves in interview situations soon after arriving on campus. They might be vying for positions on the student residence governing board, finding an on-campus job, competing for a second-year scholarship, applying for a residence hall assistant position, choosing a summer job opportunity, or being selected for an internship or as a research assistant. Preparing for an interview begins the moment you arrive on campus because the interview is about you and how college has changed you. Students who haven't clarified their sense of purpose or who have taken only a little time to reflect on who they are and how they have changed can feel lost in an interview.

The purpose of the interview is to exchange information. The interviewer's goal is to evaluate you on your abilities and competencies in terms of what the company is seeking. For you, the interview is an opportunity to learn more about the employer and whether the job would be a good fit with your aptitudes and preferences. Ideally, you will want to find a match between your interests and abilities and the position or experience you are seeking.

Here are some important tips as you prepare for an interview:

■ Check with a career counselor to find out whether you can attend a mock interview. Usually designed only for seniors as they prep for their on-campus interviews, mock interviews help students strategize and feel comfortable in interview situations. Even if a mock interview session is not available, the career center can offer tips on handling an interview situation. Check your career center website for sample interview questions so that you can practice before an interview.

■ Understand the nature of the **behavioral interview**. In a behavioral interview, the interviewer assumes that your past experiences are good predictors of your future abilities and performance. Interviewers want to hear stories about things you have done that can help them assess your skills and behaviors. Often, there is not a right or wrong answer. Answering a behavioral question can be hard. A method used at Michigan State University and other campuses to help students think through possible answers is the PARK method, which helps to focus on the most relevant aspects of your experience.

P: The problem or situation (What happened?)

A: The actions you took (What did you do?)

R: The results or outcomes (What was the result of the actions you took?)

K: The knowledge you gained and applied through the experience (What did you learn? How did you apply it?)

■ Dress appropriately. Dress codes vary depending on the location of the interview and the type of interview (e.g., professional, student focused). First impressions matter, so as a rule of thumb, always dress neatly and conservatively. You can be somewhat casual for some types of employers, but it is better to dress too professionally than too informally.

WILL YOUR EMPLOYER CHECK YOUR SOCIAL NETWORKING PROFILE?

In addition to checking your résumé and references, potential employers might also use online resources to learn more about you. In a national survey of college employers, slightly more than 11 percent said that they review candidates' profiles on social networking sites such as MySpace and Facebook, and more than 60 percent of employers who look at these sites said that the information they find has at least some influence on their hiring decisions. Because a user outside of your Facebook network cannot see your profile, some companies have asked their employees who are recent graduates or their college interns to research potential candidates. On profile pages, employers can find discrepancies between a candidate's résumé and his or her actual academic and work experience. Potential employers might even spot other kinds of information or see pictures that would affect their view of the candidate. When they find that a potential candidate is comfortable sharing his or her party pictures, describing personal escapades that some people might consider inappropriate, or allowing friends to post crude comments, employers are likely to seriously question that applicant's judgment.

Thinking Critically

Knowing this information, what could a potential employer find on your Facebook or MySpace site, and how might that employer react? Is there anything you would change about your Facebook and/or MySpace profile to make it more appropriate for viewing by potential employers? Check your privacy settings. Who can view your profile? Have you restricted parts of your profile to certain friends?

Now that you know what employers are looking for when they search social networking websites to research potential employees, pretend you are an employer. Pick either Facebook or MySpace, and search for your friends. What did you find? How many of your friends would you hire solely on the basis of their profile page? How many would you not hire? Why?

Where to go FOR HELP . . .

ON CAMPUS ▶

Your College Website Search your campus career resources. Larger campuses might have specialized career service centers for specific professional schools and clusters of majors. Often student professional organizations, academic advisors, and departments will provide relevant career information on their websites.

Career Center Almost every college campus has a career center where you can obtain free counseling and information on careers. A career professional will work with you to help you define your interests, interpret the results of any assessment you complete, coach you on interview techniques, and critique your résumé. It's important to schedule an appointment. By the end of your first year you should be familiar with the career center, where it is located, and the counselor who is responsible for your academic major or interests. You might also find opportunities for internships and interview practice there.

Academic Advising More and more advisors have been trained in what is known as "developmental advising," or helping you see beyond individual classes and working to help you initiate a career search. Talking to your advisor is often the best place to start. If you have not declared a major—which is true of many first-year students—your advisor might be able to help you with that decision as well.

Faculty On many campuses, faculty members take an active role in helping students connect academic interests to careers. A faculty member can recommend specific courses that relate to a particular career. Faculty members in professional curricula, such as business and other applied fields, often have direct contact with companies and serve as contacts for internships. If you have an interest in attending graduate school, faculty sponsorship is critical to admission. Developing a relationship with faculty mentor can open a number of important doors.

Library Some campuses have a separate library in the career center staffed by librarians whose job is to help you locate career-related information resources. Of course, all campuses have a main library that contains a wealth of information on careers. The reference librarian at the main desk will be glad to help you. If you are a student on a large university campus, you might find additional libraries that are specific to certain professional schools and colleges within the university, such as business, education, law, medicine, music, and engineering; these are also excellent sources for career information.

Upper-Class Students Ask whether more experienced students can help you navigate courses and find important resources. Upper-class students might also have practical experience gained from internships and volunteering. Since they have tested the waters, they can alert you to potential pitfalls or inform you of opportunities.

Student Organizations Professional student organizations that focus on specific career interests meet regularly throughout the year. Join them now. Not only will they put you in contact with upper-class students, but also their programs often include employer representatives, helpful discussions on searching for internships or jobs, and exposure to current conditions in the workplace.

ONLINE ▶

Career Center Go to your campus career center's home page, and check its resources, such as links to useful pages.

Occupational Information Network: http://www.online.onetcenter.org. This federal government site has information on occupations, skill sets, and links to professional sites for selected occupations. This is a great place to get started thinking about your interests.

Mapping Your Future: http://www.mappingyourfuture.org. This comprehensive site provides support for those who are just starting to explore careers.

The Riley Guide: http://www.rileyguide.com. One of the best sites for interviewing, job search strategies, and other critical career tips.

MY INSTITUTION'S RESOURCES ▶

_____   _____

_____   _____

_____   _____

_____   _____

_____   _____

_____   _____

One-Minute PAPER . . .

Making the right choices when it comes to picking a major and a career can be intimidating. What did you learn in this chapter that will help you prepare for declaring a major? Of the topics covered in this chapter, which would you like to learn more about?

Applying What You've LEARNED . . .

Now that you have read and discussed this chapter, consider how you can apply what you have learned to your academic and personal life. The following prompts will help you reflect on chapter material and its relevance to you both now and in the future.

1. Sometimes the best way to learn about a career is to talk to someone who is working or teaching in that field. Set up an appointment to talk with a professor who teaches in the area in which you are interested. Find out as much as possible about the education required for a specific career in the field. Ask about the skills that are necessary to succeed and the outlook for the future. Ask the professor to give you some advice for preparing for the major and the career.

2. Choosing a major is a big decision and should include consideration of your personal learning style, your personality, and your goals and values. Review what you learned about yourself in Chapter 3 ("Understanding Emotional Intelligence") and Chapter 4 ("Discovering How You Learn"). How will those insights guide your exploration of majors and careers?

Building Your PORTFOLIO . . .

66 The best career advice to give to the young is 'Find out what you like doing best and get someone to pay you for doing it.' 99

– KATHERINE WHITEHORN (b. 1926),
English writer and journalist

INVESTIGATING OCCUPATIONS

How can you select a major if you are not sure what you want to do when you graduate? College classes, out-of-class activities, and part-time jobs will help you narrow your choices and make decisions about a major and a potential career.

1. Create a Word document and list at least two majors that you are considering right now or that you would like to know more about. Why do you find these majors interesting?

2. Name two or more careers you think you might be interested in after you graduate. Explain your choice.

3. The U.S. Bureau of Labor Statistics publishes the online *Occupational Outlook Handbook*, which provides details about hundreds of jobs. You can search for a specific job, such as nursing, and learn about the training and education needed, median earnings, job prospects, roles and responsibilities on the job, and working conditions.

   a. Visit the *Occupational Outlook Handbook* online at http://www.bls.gov/oco/, and in the search field, enter one or two of the careers you listed above.

   b. Create a chart like the one below. Note the training or degree required, describe the job outlook, and list the median earnings for each career. Look through the other descriptions to learn more about the careers.

	Example	**Career 1**	**Career 2**
Occupational Outlook Handbook	Computer software engineer		
Training Required	Bachelor's degree, computer science/ software engineering		
Job Outlook	One of the fastest-growing occupations from 2004 to 2014		
Earnings	Median annual earnings: about $74,980		

4. Save your findings in your portfolio on your personal computer or flash drive. Even in your first college year it is important that you begin to think about what you are going to do after graduation. The more you investigate different types of careers, the easier it will be for you to identify a major or decide what kind of internship, part-time job, or service learning opportunity you want to experience while you are still in college. Exploring your strengths, interests, and goals will help you to find a career that you enjoy and that meets your lifestyle expectations.

13 Managing Your Money

ALANNA KEAY, 20
Salem State College

66 If I could do it over again, I would have gone to a community college my first two years and saved so much money. 99

I went to George Mason University in Virginia last year, and I loved it. I met really great friends, and honestly it was the best time of my life. But once I realized that I wasn't going to get any scholarships there, I just couldn't afford it. I didn't want to be $160,000 in debt getting out of school, so I applied to in-state schools. Because I'm a Massachusetts resident, Salem State costs about half of what I was paying at George Mason. It was all the money issue. But the whole transition has been really, really difficult.

If I don't get scholarship money, I don't know what I'm going to do. It really worries me. My parents are going to help, but most of it's on me. I've always been very independent. I have loans, and I also work twenty hours a week along with going to school full-time. It's tough. I had to get a car because I've got to get around, and I have a car payment every month. I have two store credit cards, but I'm just building up my credit with them. I have to stick to a budget. If I could do it over again, I would have gone to a community college my first two years and saved so much money. But that's the way it goes. Hopefully, it will work out.

Like it or not, we can't ignore the importance of money. Money
is often symbolically and realistically the key ingredient to independence and, some people conclude, even to a sense of freedom. You probably know of instances in which money divided a family or a relationship or seemed to drive someone's life in a direction that person would not have taken otherwise. Money can also affect your specific academic goals, causing you to select or reject certain academic majors or degree plans.

Although your primary goal in college should be a strong academic record, money or the lack of it can make it easier or more difficult to complete your degree. Educators recognize that not understanding personal finances can hinder a student's progress, and mandatory personal finance classes are now being added in high schools and are available as options at some colleges. The purpose of this chapter is to provide basic information and suggestions so that money will not be a barrier to your success in college. Think of this chapter as a summary of needed financial skills; if you want more information, consider taking a personal finance class at your college or in your community.

YOUR TURN ▶

So far, how well or poorly are you managing your money in college? Why is it difficult or easy?

Living on a Budget

Face it: College is expensive, and most students have limited financial resources. Not only is tuition a major cost, but day-to-day expenses can add up quickly. No matter what your financial situation, a budget for college is a must. While a budget might not completely eliminate debt after graduation, it can help you become realistic about your finances so that you can have a basis for future life planning.

A budget is a spending plan that tracks all sources of income (student loan disbursements, money from parents, etc.) and expenses (rent, tuition, etc.) during a set period of time (weekly, monthly, etc.). Creating and following a budget will allow you to pay your bills on time, cut costs, put some money away for emergencies, and finish college with as little debt as possible.

CREATING A BUDGET

A budget will condition you to live within your means, put money into savings, and possibly invest down the road. Here are a few tips to help you get started.

Step 1. Gather Basic Information. To create an effective budget, you need to learn more about your income and your spending behaviors.

First, determine how much money is coming in and when. Sources of income might include a job, your savings, gifts from relatives, student loans, scholarship dollars, or grants. Write them all down, making note of how often you receive each type of income (weekly paychecks, quarterly loan disbursements, one-time gifts, and so forth) and how much money you can expect each time.

To determine where your money is going and when, track your spending for a week or two (or, even better, a full month) by recording every bill you pay and every purchase you make. It might surprise you to learn how much money you spend on coffee, bagels, and other incidentals. This information will help you to better understand your spending behaviors and where you might be able to cut costs in the future.

Step 2. Build a Plan. Use the information you gathered in Step 1 to set up three columns: one for income, one for anticipated expenses, and one for actual expenses. Table 13.1 is an example of such a plan. Knowing when your money is coming in will help you decide how to structure your budget. For example, if most of your income comes in on a monthly basis, you'll want to create a monthly budget. If you are paid every other week, a biweekly budget might work better.

Be sure to recognize which expenses are fixed and which are variable. A *fixed expense* is one that will cost you the same amount every time you pay it. For example, your rent is a fixed expense because you owe your landlord the same amount each month. A variable expense is one that may change. Your textbooks are a variable expense because the number and cost of them will be different each term.

Although you will know, more or less, how much your fixed expenses will be during each budget period, you might need to estimate your variable expenses in your anticipated expenses column. Use past bills, checking

TABLE 13.1 ▶ Sample Budget

Cost Category	Expected Cost	Actual Cost
Rent	$ 500	$ 500
Electric	$ 50	$ 47
Gas (heat)	$ 75	$ 75
Cell phone	$ 45	$ 50
Water	$ 15	$ 12
Gasoline	$ 40	$ 45
Groceries	$ 150	$ 135
Dining out	$ 50	$ 40
Books	$ 200	$ 170
Miscellaneous	$ 100	$ 120
Total	$1,225	$1,194

account statements, and spending behaviors from your tracking in Step 1 to create an educated guess for your anticipated expenses in the variable categories. When you are in doubt, it is always better to overestimate your expenses to avoid shortfalls at the end of your budget period.

Step 3. Do a Test Run. Use your budget plan from Step 2 for a few weeks and see how things go, recording your actual expenses as you pay them. Don't be surprised to see differences between your anticipated and actual expense columns; budgeting is not an exact science, and you will likely never see a perfect match between these two columns. It might be wise to add a "miscellaneous" category for those unexpected and added expenses throughout the budget period.

Step 4. Make Adjustments. Although your budget might never be perfect, you can strive to improve it. Are there areas in which you spent much more or much less than expected? Do you need to reallocate funds to better meet the needs of your current situation? Be realistic and thoughtful in how you spend your money, and use your budget to help meet your goals, such as planning for a trip or getting a new pair of jeans.

Whatever you do, don't give up if your bottom line doesn't end up the way you expected it would. Budgeting is a lot like dieting; you might slip up and eat a pizza (or spend too much buying one), but all is not lost. If you stay focused and flexible, your budget can lead you to financial stability and independence.

CUTTING COSTS

Once you have put together a working budget, have tried it out, and have adjusted it, you're likely to discover that your expenses still exceed your income. Don't panic. Simply begin to look for ways to reduce those expenses. Here are some tips for saving money in college:

- **Recognize the difference between your *needs* and your *wants*.** A *need* is something you must have. For example, tuition and textbooks are considered *needs*. On the other hand, your *wants* are goods, services, or experiences that you wish to purchase but could reasonably live without. For example, concert tickets and mochas are *wants*. Your budget should always provide for your *needs* first.

- **Share expenses.** Having a roommate (or several) can be one of the easiest ways to cut costs on a regular basis. In exchange for giving up a little bit of privacy, you'll save hundreds of dollars on rent, utilities, and food. Make sure, however, that you work out a plan for sharing expenses equally and that everyone accepts his or her responsibilities. For instance, remember that if only your name is on the cable account, you (and only you) are legally responsible for that bill. You'll need to collect money from your roommates so that you can pay the bill in full and on time.

- **Consider the pros and cons of living on campus.** Depending on your school's location, off-campus housing might be less expensive than paying for a room and a meal plan on campus. However, be aware that while you might save some cash, you will give up a great deal of convenience by moving out of your campus residence. You almost certainly won't be able to roll out of bed ten minutes before class, and you will have to prepare your own meals. At the same time, living on campus makes it easier to make friends and develop a sense of connection to your college or university. Before you make the decision about where to live, weigh the advantages and disadvantages of each option, and then choose.

- **Use low-cost transportation.** If you live close to campus, consider whether or not you need to keep a car on campus. Take advantage of lower-cost options such as public transportation or biking to class to save money on gasoline and parking. If you live farther away, check to see whether your institution hosts a ride-sharing program for commuter students, or carpool with someone in your area.

- **Seek out discount entertainment options.** Take advantage of discounted or free programming through your college. Most institutions use a portion of their student fees to provide affordable entertainment options such as discounted or free tickets to concerts, movie theaters, sporting events, or other special events.

- **Embrace second-hand goods.** Use online resources such as Craigslist and thrift stores such as Goodwill to expand your wardrobe, purchase extras such as games and sports equipment, or furnish and decorate your room or apartment. You'll save money, and you won't mind as much when someone spills a drink on your "new" couch.

- **Avoid unnecessary fees.** Making late payments on credit cards and other bills can lead to expensive fees and can lower your credit score (which in turn will raise your interest rates). You might want to set up online, automatic payments to avoid making this costly mistake.

Getting Financial Aid

Very few students can pay the costs of college tuition, fees, books, room and board, bills, and random expenses without some kind of help. Luckily, several sources of financial aid, including some you might not know about, are available to help cover your costs. With a combination of research, diligence, and luck, some students even manage to enroll and succeed in college with little or no financial support from their families because of the financial aid they receive.

TYPES OF AID

Financial aid seems complex because it can come from so many different sources. Each source may have different rules about how to receive the money and how not to lose it. The financial aid staff at your college can help you find the way to get the largest amount of money that doesn't need to be repaid, the lowest interest rate on loans, and work possibilities that fit your academic program. Whether or not your family can help you pay for college, you should not overlook this valuable campus resource. The financial aid office and its website are the best places to begin looking for all types of assistance. Other organizations that can help students to find the right college and money to help them attend are located across the United States. Many of these organizations are members of the National College Access Network or participate in a national effort called Know How to Go. Check their websites at

SAVE A MINT

You might have heard the saying "You have to spend money to make money." If you were to review the pricing of online and desktop programs for tracking your budget and spending, you might conclude that this statement is true. But there are low-cost options and a few good free money management software packages. For instance, Quicken (http://www.quicken.intuit.com) offers a free website where you can track your finances and create a budget. Another highly reviewed website is Mint.com, which automatically tracks your spending and creates reports based on categories that it recognizes. You can enter the information for all of your accounts, and Mint will sift through the transactions and show you where you are spending your money. The entire process takes less than ten minutes. Mint also automatically creates a budget for you on the basis of the information that it filters from your account. You might worry about the security of your information on Mint.com; however, Mint is a read-only site that does not store your login

information. That means that in the unlikely event that someone gets into your account, they can't move money around or withdraw it. Additionally, surfing on Mint is accomplished through a secure web protocol called https (Hypertext Transfer Protocol-Secure) that encrypts the information you send and receive. Always make sure that you are using a https website and that the website security certificate is valid when you are conducting your financial affairs online.

Thinking Critically

Sign up for Mint.com, and have Mint distill your accounts to show your spending by category. What did you discover about the ways in which you spend your money? Were you surprised that you spent more (or less) on a certain category than you had guessed? Will you make any changes to the ways in which you spend your money because of what you found? If so, what changes will you make?

http://www.collegeaccess.org/accessprogramdirectory and http://www.knowhow2go.org. Very few students complete college without some type of financial assistance, and it is rare for students to cover all college expenses with only scholarships. The majority of students pay for college through a combination of various types of financial assistance: scholarships, grants, loans, and paid employment. Financial aid professionals refer to this combination as a "package."

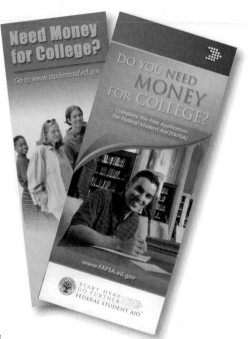

While scholarships and grants are unquestionably the best forms of aid because they do not have to be repaid, the federal government, states, and colleges offer many other forms of assistance, such as loans, work-study opportunities, and cooperative education. You might also be able to obtain funds from your employer, a local organization, or a private group.

- **Need-based scholarships** are based on both a talent and financial need. "Talent" can be past accomplishments in the arts or athletics, your potential for future accomplishments, or even where you are from. Some colleges and universities want to admit students from other states or countries. "Need" in this context means the cost of college minus a federal determination of what you and your family can afford to contribute toward those costs. Your institution might provide scholarships from its own resources or from individual donors. Donors themselves sometimes stipulate characteristics of scholarship recipients, such as age or academic major.

- **Merit scholarships** are based on talent as defined above but do not require you to demonstrate financial need. It can be challenging to match your talent with merit scholarships. Most of them come through colleges and are part of the admissions and financial aid processes, usually described on the college's website. Web-based scholarship search services are another good source to explore. Be certain the website you use is free, will keep your information confidential unless you release your name, and will send you a notice (usually through e-mail) when a new scholarship that matches your qualifications is posted. Also be sure to ask your employer, your family's employers, and social, community or religious organizations about any available scholarships.

- **Grants** are based on financial need but, like scholarships, do not have to be repaid. Grants are awarded by the federal government and state government and by institutions themselves. Students meet academic qualifications for grants by being admitted to the college and maintaining grades that are acceptable to the grant provider.

- **Work-study** jobs are reserved for students with financial need. Students receive work-study notices as part of the overall financial aid notice and then can sign up to be interviewed for work-study jobs. Although some work-study jobs can be relatively menial, the best options provide experience related to your academic studies while allowing you to earn money for college. The salary is based on the skill required for a particular position and the hours involved. Keep in mind that you will be expected to accomplish specific tasks while on duty, although some employers might permit you to study during any down-time.

- **Cooperative (co-op) education** allows you to alternate a term of study (a semester or quarter) with a term of paid work. Engineering co-op opportunities are among the most common, and the number of co-op programs in health care fields is growing. Colleges make information about co-ops available through admissions and academic departments.

QUALIFYING FOR AID

Most financial assistance requires some form of application. The application used most often is the Free Application for Federal Student Aid (FAFSA). Every student should complete the FAFSA by the earliest deadline of the colleges you are considering. Additional forms, such as the College Board's Profile form and scholarship applications, might also be required and will be listed in colleges' financial aid or admissions materials or by organizations that offer scholarships.

The following box outlines the steps you must take to qualify for most scholarships and grants, especially those sponsored by federal or state governments.

The amount of financial aid you receive will depend on the cost of your academic program and what you or your family can pay as determined by

STEPS TO QUALIFY FOR FINANCIAL AID

1. Enroll half-time or more in a certificate or degree program at one of the more than 4,500 institutions that are certified to distribute federal financial aid. A few aid programs are available for less than half-time study; check with your department or college to see what your options are.

2. Complete the FAFSA. The first FAFSA you file is intimidating, especially if you rush to complete it right before the deadline. Completing the FAFSA in subsequent years is easier because you only need to update items that have changed. To make the process easier, get your personal identification number (PIN) a few weeks before the deadline. This PIN will be the same one you'll use throughout your college career. Try to do the form in sections rather than tackling all of it at once. Most of the information is basic: name, address, driver's license number, and things you will know or have in your billfold. For most undergraduates the financial section will require your own and your parents' information from tax materials. If you are at least 24 years of age, married, or a veteran or have dependents of your own, your tax information and that for your spouse will be needed.

3. If your school or award-granting organization requires it, complete the College Board Profile form. Review your college's admission information, or ask a financial aid advisor to determine if this applies to you.

4. Identify any additional applications that are required. These are usually scholarship applications with personal statements or short essays. The organizations, including colleges, that are giving the money will provide instructions about what is required. Most have websites with complete information.

5. Follow all instructions carefully, and submit each application on time. Financial aid is awarded from a fixed pool of funds. When money has been awarded, there is usually none left for those who file late.

6. Complete the classes for which you were given financial aid with at least a minimum grade point average as defined by your academic department or college or the organization that provided you the scholarship.

FAFSA. Cost includes average expenses for tuition and fees, books and supplies, room and board, transportation, and personal expenses. The financial aid office will subtract from the cost the amount you and your family are expected to pay. In some cases that amount can be as little as zero. Financial aid is designed to make up as much of the balance or "need" as possible.

HOW TO AVOID LOSING YOUR FUNDING

If you earn average or better grades, complete your courses each term, and finish your program or degree on time, you should have no trouble maintaining your financial aid. It's a good idea to check with the financial aid office before you drop classes to make sure you will not lose any aid.

Some types of aid, especially scholarships, require that you maintain full-time enrollment and make satisfactory academic progress. Dropping or failing a class might jeopardize all or part of your financial aid unless you are enrolled in more credits than the minimum required for financial aid. Full-time financial aid is often defined as twelve credit hours per term. If you initially enrolled in fifteen credit hours and dropped one three-hour course, your aid should not change. Even so, talk with a financial aid counselor before making the decision to drop a course, just to be sure.

Remember that although the financial aid office is there to serve you, you must be your own advocate. The following tips should help:

- File for financial aid every year. Even if you don't think you will receive aid for a certain year, you must file annually in case you become eligible in the future.
- Meet all filing deadlines. Students who do not meet filing deadlines risk losing aid from one year to the next.
- Talk with a financial aid officer immediately if you or your family experiences a significant loss (such as loss of a job or death of a parent or spouse). Don't wait for the next filing period; you might be eligible for funds for the current year.
- Inquire every year about criteria-based aid. Many colleges and universities have grants and scholarships for students who meet specific criteria. These might include grants for minority students, grants for students in specific academic majors, and grants for students of single parents. Sometimes a donor will give money to the school's scholarship fund for students who meet certain other criteria, even county or state of residence. Determine whether any of these fit your circumstances.
- Inquire about campus jobs throughout the year, as these jobs are not available just at the beginning of the term. If you do not have a job and want or need to work, keep asking.
- Consider asking for a reassessment of your eligibility for aid. If you have reviewed your financial aid package and think that your circumstances deserve additional consideration, you can ask the financial aid office to reassess your eligibility. The office is not always required to do so, but the request might be worth your effort.

Achieving a Balance Between Working and Borrowing

After determining your budget, deciding what you can pay from savings (if any), and taking your scholarships and grants into consideration, you might still need additional income. Each term or year, you should decide how much you can work while maintaining good grades and how much you should borrow from student loans.

ADVANTAGES AND DISADVANTAGES OF WORKING

Paid employment while you are in college can be important for reasons other than money. Having a job in a field related to your major can help you develop a credential for graduate school and make you more employable later because it shows you have the capability to manage several priorities at the same time. Work can help you determine whether a career is what you will really want after you complete your education. And students who work a moderate amount (fifteen hours per week) typically get better grades than students who do not work at all.

On the other hand, it's almost impossible to get great grades if you work full-time while trying to be a full-time student. Some students prefer not to take a job during their first year in college while they're making adjustments to a new academic environment. You might find that you're able to work some terms while you are a student but not others. And family obligations or challenging classes can sometimes make the added burden of work impractical or impossible.

The majority of students today find that a combination of working and borrowing is the best way to gain experience, finance college, and complete their educational goals on time.

STUDENT LOANS

Although you should be careful not to borrow yourself into a lifetime of debt, avoiding loans altogether could delay your graduation and your progress up the career ladder. For most students, some level of borrowing is both necessary and prudent.

The following list provides information about the most common types of student loans. The list reflects the order in which you should apply for and accept loans to get the lowest interest rates and best repayment terms.

- **Subsidized federal student loans** are backed by the government, with interest paid on your behalf while you are enrolled in undergraduate, graduate, or professional school. These loans require at least half-time enrollment and a submitted FAFSA application (see page 248).
- **Unsubsidized federal student loans** may require that you make interest payments while you are enrolled. If not, the interest is added to the amount you owe, called "capitalization."
- **Parent Loan for Undergraduate Students (PLUS) loans** are applied for and owed by parents but disbursed directly to students. Interest is usually

higher than that on federal student loans but lower than that on private loans. Parents who apply must provide information on the FAFSA.

- **Private student loans** are offered through banks and credit unions. Private loans often have stricter credit requirements and higher interest rates than federal loans do, and interest payments on private loans begin immediately.

Student loans are a very important source of money for college, but like paid employment, loans should be considered carefully. Loans for costs such as books and tuition are good investments. Loans for a more lavish lifestyle are likely to weigh you down in the future. As one wise person put it, if by borrowing you live like a wealthy graduate while you're a student, you'll live like a student after you graduate. Student loans can be a good way to begin using credit wisely, a skill you are likely to need throughout your life.

Managing Credit Wisely

When you graduate, you will leave your institution with two significant numbers. The first is your grade point average (GPA), which represents the level of academic success you attained while in college. The second, your credit score, is a numerical representation of your fiscal responsibility. Although this second number might be less familiar to you, it could be the deciding factor that determines whether you get your dream job, regardless of your GPA. And twenty years from now, you're likely to have forgotten your GPA, while your credit score will be more important than ever.

Your credit score is derived from a credit report that contains information about accounts in your name. These accounts include credit cards, student loans, utility bills, cell phones, and car loans, to name a few. This credit score can determine whether or not you will qualify for a loan (car, home, student, etc.), what interest rates you will pay, how much your car insurance will cost, and your chances of being hired by some organizations. Even if none of these things is in your immediate future, now is the time to start thinking about your credit score.

While using credit cards responsibly is a good way to build credit, acquiring a credit card has become much more difficult for college students. In May of 2009, President Obama signed legislation that prohibits college students under the age of 21 from obtaining a credit card unless they can prove they are able to make the payments or the credit card application is co-signed by a parent or guardian.

UNDERSTANDING CREDIT

Even if you can prove you have the means to repay credit card debt, it is important for you to thoroughly understand how credit cards work and how they can both help and hurt you. Simply put, a credit card allows you to buy something now and pay for it later. Each month you will receive a statement listing all purchases you made using your credit card during the previous thirty days. The statement will request a payment toward your balance and will set a payment due date. Your payment options will vary: You can pay your entire balance, pay a specified amount of the balance, or pay only a minimum payment, which may be as low as $10.

But beware: If you make only a minimum payment, the remaining balance on your card will be charged a finance fee, or interest charge, causing your balance to increase before your next bill arrives even if you don't make any more purchases. Paying the minimum payment is almost never a good strategy and can add years to your repayment time. In fact, if you continue to pay only $10 per month toward a $500 credit card balance, it will take you more than seven years to pay it off! And assuming an 18% interest rate, you'll pay an extra $431 in interest—almost doubling the total amount you'll pay.

Avoid making late payments. Paying your bill even one day late can result in a finance charge of up to $30; it can also raise the interest rate not only on that card but also on any other credit accounts you have. If you decide to use a credit card to build credit, you might want to set up online, automatic payments to avoid incurring expensive late fees. Remember that the payment due date is the date the payment should be received by the credit card lender, not the date you send it.

> **YOUR TURN ▶**
>
> Do you have your own credit card or one that you own jointly with your parents? If not, what are your reasons for not getting one? If you do have a card, do you feel you're in control of the way you use it? Why or why not? If you don't have a card, do you think you are ready for one? Why or why not?

If you decide to apply for a credit card while you're in college, remember that credit cards should be used to build credit and for emergencies. They should not be used to fund a lifestyle you cannot otherwise afford or to buy wants (see the section on budgeting earlier in this chapter). On the other hand, if you use your credit card just once a month and pay the balance as soon as the bill arrives, you will be on your way to a strong credit score in just a few years.

FREQUENTLY ASKED QUESTIONS ABOUT CREDIT CARDS

Here are some answers to the most common questions college students have about credit cards:

- **I have a credit card with my name on it, but it is actually my parents' account number. Is this card building credit for me?** No. You are considered an authorized user on the account, but your parents are the primary account holders. To build credit, you must be the primary account holder or at least a joint account holder.

- **I choose the "credit" option every time I use my debit card. Is this building credit for me?** No. Using the credit function of your debit card is more like an electronic check because it is still taking money directly out of your checking account. Even if your debit card has a major credit card (Visa, MasterCard, etc.) logo on it, it is not building credit for you.

CREDIT CARD DO'S AND DON'TS

- **Do** use your credit card to help you build credit by making small charges and paying them off each month.
- **Don't** use your credit card to bridge the gap between the lifestyle you would like to have and the one you can actually afford.
- **Do** keep an eye on your credit report by visiting the free website www.AnnualCreditReport.com at least once a year.
- **Do** have a credit card for emergencies if possible, even if your parents co-sign for it.
- **Don't** use your credit card to pay for spring break. This is *not* an emergency!

- **I have a few store credit cards (Target, Kohl's, Best Buy, etc.). Are these accounts included on my credit report?** Yes. Although they will affect your credit score, they do not carry as much weight as major credit cards (Visa, MasterCard, etc.). It is okay to have a few store credit cards, but a major credit card will do more to help you build credit.
- **Where can I apply for a major credit card?** A good place to begin is your bank or credit union. Remember that you will have to prove your ability to make payments in order to obtain a card.
- **If one credit card will help me build credit, will several build my credit even more?** Research shows that there is no benefit to having more than two major credit cards. And even if you're able to pay the required monthly amounts, having too many accounts open can make you appear risky to the credit bureaus determining your credit score.
- **What if I forget and make a late payment? Is my credit score ruined?** Your credit report reflects at least the past seven years of activity but puts the most emphasis on the most recent two years. In other words, the farther you get from your mistakes, the less impact they will have on your credit score. There is no quick fix for improving a credit score, so beware of advertisements that say otherwise.

DEBIT CARDS

Although you might wish to use a credit card for emergencies and to establish a good credit rating, you might also look into the possibility of applying for a debit card (also called a checkcard). The big advantage of a debit card is that you don't always have to carry cash and thus don't run the risk of losing it. And since the amount of your purchases will be limited to the funds in your account, a debit card is a good form of constraint on your spending. The only real disadvantage is that a debit card provides direct access to your checking account, so it's very important that you keep your card in a safe place and away from your personal identification number (PIN). The safest way to protect your account is to commit your

PIN to memory. If you lose your debit card or credit card, notify your bank immediately.

Planning for the Future

It's never too early to begin thinking about financing your life after graduation. Here are some tips that could open future opportunities and help you avoid future problems.

- Plan now for your next step, whether that's additional education or work. Get to know faculty members by using their office hours to learn about their specific areas of study and ask their advice about your career. Faculty members mention frequently that they wish more students came to talk with them, instead of just meeting them when a problem occurs.
- Keep your address current with the registrar even when you have finished your degree or program and especially if you stop classes for a term. This is doubly important if you have student loans so you do not get a negative report on your credit rating because you missed information about your loan.
- Make a point of establishing a savings account and adding to it regularly, even if you can manage only a few dollars a month. The sooner you start, the greater your returns will be.

Your education is the most productive investment you can make for your future and that of your family. Research shows that completion of programs or degrees after high school increases earnings, opens up career options, leads to greater satisfaction in work, results in more engaged citizenship such as voting and community service, and greatly increases the probability that your children will go on to college. College is a big investment of both time and money, but it's an investment of proven worth.

Where to go
FOR HELP . . .

ON CAMPUS ▶

Your Institution's Financial Aid Office
Professionals in this office will help you understand financial aid opportunities and how to apply for scholarships.

Local United Way Office Many communities have credit counseling agencies within the local United Way.

Campus Programs Be on the lookout for special campus programs on money management. These programs are often offered in residence halls or through the division of student affairs.

Business School or College Faculty or staff members within a school or college of business or a division of continuing education sometimes offer a course in personal finance. Check your college catalog or website, or call the school, college, or division office.

Counseling Center If money problems are related to compulsive shopping or gambling, your institution's counseling center can provide help.

ONLINE ▶

Budget Wizard: http://www.cashcourse.org. The National Endowment for Financial Education (NEFE) offers this free, secure, budgeting tool.

Free Application for Federal Student Aid: http://www.fafsa.ed.gov. The online form allows you to set up an account, complete the application electronically, save your work, and monitor the progress of your application.

FastWeb: http://www.FastWeb.com. Register for this free scholarship search service and discover sources of educational funding you never knew existed.

Bankrate: http://www.bankrate.com. This free site provides unbiased information about the interest rates, fees, and penalties associated with major credit cards and private loans. It also provides calculators that let you determine the long-term costs of different kinds of borrowing.

OTHER ▶

Knox, Susan. *Financial Basics: A Money-Management Guide for Students.* Columbus: Ohio State University Press, 2004.

MY INSTITUTION'S RESOURCES ▶

_____

_____

_____

_____

_____

_____

_____

_____

_____

_____

_____

_____

_____

One-Minute PAPER . . .

This chapter covers a lot of information about financing your college experience and managing your money. Planning ahead is an important part of managing your finances. What did you find to be the most useful information in this chapter? Did anything that was covered leave you with more questions than answers? If so, what?

Applying What You've LEARNED . . .

Now that you have read and discussed this chapter, consider how you can apply what you have learned to your academic and personal life. The following prompts will help you reflect on chapter material and its relevance to you both now and in the future.

1. Sometimes it is hard to plan for the future. Why not start small? Describe at least two things you can do each week to save money. For example, using public transportation when possible can help reduce the expense of owning a car.

2. Money can be a difficult subject to talk about, and sometimes it seems easier just not to worry about it. Ask yourself some hard questions. Do you spend money without much thought? Do you have a lot of debt and not much to show for it? Describe what you want *your* financial picture to look like.

Building Your PORTFOLIO . . .

66 Life was a lot simpler when what we honored was father and mother rather than all major credit cards. 99

– ROBERT ORBEN (b. 1927),
American magician and comedy writer

CREDIT CARDS: A SLIPPERY SLOPE

Remember the saying "There is no free lunch"? That is a good maxim to keep in mind as you consider adding credit cards to your financial picture. College students are often targeted by credit card companies through an offer of a free T-shirt or other novelty if they sign up for a new card. While it might seem harmless at the time, signing up for multiple credit cards can have you in financial trouble—and fast!

A big factor in effectively managing your credit card debt is being aware of the terms and conditions that apply to each account you have.

1. If you already have credit cards (including gas cards and store credit cards such as a Gap or Sears card), find your most recent billing statements. If you do not have a credit card, use an Internet search engine to search for "credit cards for college students." You will find several Internet offers specifically for college students. Find the terms and conditions for one of the offers.

2. Next, to understand the fees associated with your credit accounts, create an Excel spreadsheet with the following headers (see example below):

- Card Issuer and Card Type
- Credit Limit
- APR (Annual Percentage Rate)
- Default APR (a default APR may be used when you fail to make the minimum payment on your credit card account or exceed your credit limit by a certain amount. The default APR is always higher than the stated APR for the credit account.)
- Due On
- Late Fee
- Over Credit Limit Fee

3. List each credit card you have and enter the associated fees.

Card Issuer & Card Type	Credit Limit	APR	Default APR	Due On	Late Fee	Over Credit Limit Fee
Example: Bank of America Student Visa	$500	18.25% variable	32.25%	28th day of each month	$29	$39
Card 1.						
Card 2.						
Card 3.						

4. Save the file to your local computer or flash drive.

5. Update the file any time you open or close a credit account.

Understanding the terms and conditions of every credit card account you have can help you avoid paying extremely high interest rates and damaging your credit history.

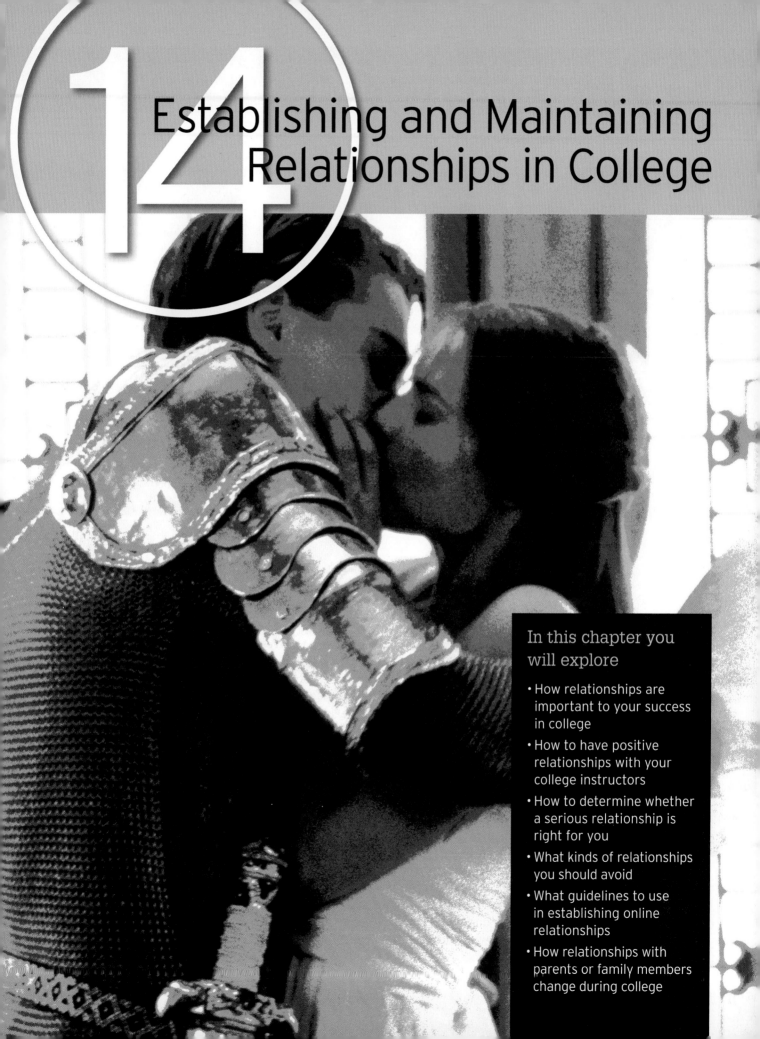

14 Establishing and Maintaining Relationships in College

In this chapter you will explore

- How relationships are important to your success in college
- How to have positive relationships with your college instructors
- How to determine whether a serious relationship is right for you
- What kinds of relationships you should avoid
- What guidelines to use in establishing online relationships
- How relationships with parents or family members change during college

ROBERT HUFFMAN, 18
Florida Atlantic University

66 In college you get to start over—decide who you want to be and who you want to hang out with. 99

It's pretty cool that in college you get to start over—decide who you want to be and who you want to hang out with. In high school your friends are the people you've been with your whole life (in fact, my closest friend here is someone from my high school). But in college you can find your own new friends. It's definitely a lot better, because there are so many people that nobody cares about the different cliques or being popular. This is a big school: twenty-five thousand undergraduates, maybe. Everybody's just friendly with everyone.

I'm in a fraternity. I just started it this semester. My main reason for joining was because I got kind of bored, and I wanted to get more involved with campus, and I thought that was a good way to do it. Some of the fraternities have a bad reputation—big partiers, stuff like that—but mine is a brand-new one that just came on campus. I like that we can create our own reputation, one that holds academic success as a value. So far, being in a fraternity has helped out a lot: I'm meeting new people and networking for jobs and different majors and finding out what my interests are. Overall, I think it's pretty good.

What does success in college have to do with relationships? As college educators, we have learned from our own experiences and the experiences of others that the quality of the relationships students develop in college can have positive or negative effects on all aspects of their success in college.

Relationships take many forms. If you live on campus, one of your primary relationships, for better or worse, will be with your roommate or suitemates. Another important set of relationships will be with your instructors. You might choose to get to know your instructors or to ignore them outside of class, but the quality and frequency of the interaction you have with them can affect how well you do academically.

Whether you live on or off campus, you will continue a relationship with your parents, spouse, children, or other family members. Sometimes the assumptions and expectations that define family interactions will change, and negotiating that change is not always easy. Parents sometimes have trouble letting go of a son or daughter, and if you are fresh out of high school, you might feel that your parents still want to control your life. If you are an adult with a spouse or partner, going to college will give you a new identity that might seem strange or threatening to your partner. If you have children, they might not understand what's going on as you try to balance your need for study time with their need for your undivided attention.

If your friends also go to college, you will have a great deal to share and compare. But if your friends are not college students, they, too, might feel threatened as you take on a new identity. And romantic relationships can support you or can create major conflict and heartbreak, depending on whether your partner shares your feelings and whether the relationship is healthy or dysfunctional.

This chapter will help you to think about all these different kinds of relationships, including those that are established and maintained online.

YOUR TURN ▶

At this point in your life, what are your three most important relationships? Write about each of those three people and what makes them special to you.

Building Relationships with College Instructors

One of the most important types of relationships you can develop in college is with your course instructors. The basis of such relationships is mutual respect. Instructors who respect students treat them fairly and are willing to help them both in and out of class. Students who respect instructors come to class regularly and take their work seriously.

WHAT YOUR INSTRUCTORS EXPECT FROM YOU

While instructors' expectations might vary depending on a particular course, most instructors will expect their students to exhibit attitudes and behaviors that are basic to student success. They will expect you to come to class, do the assigned work to the best of your ability, listen and participate, think critically about course material, and persist—that is, not give up when a concept is difficult to master. Instructors also expect honesty and candor. Many instructors will invite you to express your feelings about the course anonymously in writing through one-minute papers or other forms of class assessment.

Generally college instructors expect that you're going to be self-motivated to do your best. Your grade school and high school teachers might have spent a great deal of time thinking about how to motivate you, but college faculty will usually consider this to be your personal responsibility.

YOUR TURN ▶

Before you came to college, what had you heard about college professors? Write about what others told you and whether you have found those opinions to be accurate or inaccurate.

WHAT YOU CAN EXPECT FROM YOUR INSTRUCTORS

The expectations you have for college instructors may be based on what you have heard, both positive and negative, from friends, fellow students, and family members. But you will find that instructors vary in basic personality and in experience. You might have instructors who are in their first year of teaching, either as graduate students or as new professors. Other instructors might be seasoned professors who have taught generations of new students. Some will be introverted and difficult to approach; others will be open, friendly, and willing to talk to you and your classmates.

But no matter what their level of experience, basic personality, or skill as a lecturer, you should expect your instructors to grade you fairly and provide meaningful feedback on your papers and exams. They should be organized, prepared, and enthusiastic about their academic field. And they should be accessible. You should always be able to approach your instructors if you need assistance or if you have a personal problem that affects your academic work.

MAKING THE MOST OF THE LEARNING RELATIONSHIP

Contrary to what you might have heard, most college instructors appreciate your willingness to ask for appointments. Though it might seem a little scary, the best way to establish an appropriate relationship with an instructor is to schedule an appointment early in the term. At this meeting, introduce yourself, tell why you are taking the course (besides the fact that it's required), and what you hope to learn from it. Ask about the instructor's academic background and why he or she chose college teaching as a career. You can learn a great deal about your instructor from simply looking around the office. There will often be pictures of family members or animals or travel locations.

The relationships you develop with instructors will be valuable to you both now and in the future. People who become college faculty members do so because they have a real passion for learning about a particular subject. If you and your professor share an interest in a particular field of study, you will have the opportunity to develop a true friendship based on mutual interests. Instructors who know you well can also write that all-important letter of reference when you are applying to graduate or professional school or seeking your first job after college.

UNDERSTANDING ACADEMIC FREEDOM

Colleges and universities have promoted the advancement of knowledge by granting professors **academic freedom**—the virtually unlimited freedom of speech and inquiry as long as human lives, rights, and privacy are not violated. Such freedom is not usually possible in other professions.

Most college instructors believe in the freedom to speak out, whether in a classroom discussion about economic policy or at a political rally. Think of where education would be if instructors were required to keep their own ideas to themselves. You won't always agree with your instructors, but you will benefit by listening to what they have to say and respecting their ideas and opinions.

Academic freedom also extends to students. Within the limits of civility and respect for others you will be free to express your opinions in a way that might be different from your experience in high school or work settings.

WHEN THINGS GO WRONG BETWEEN YOU AND AN INSTRUCTOR

Although there is a potential in any environment for things to go wrong, problems between students and instructors that cannot be resolved are rare. First, ask for a meeting to discuss your problem. See whether the two of you can work things out. If the instructor refuses, go up the administrative ladder, starting at the bottom: department head to dean, and so on. If the problem is a grade, keep in mind that academic freedom includes the right of an instructor to grade you as he or she sees fit and that no one can force the instructor to change that grade. Most important, don't let a bad experience sour you on college. Even the most trying instructor will be out of your life by the end of the term. When all else fails, resolve to stick with class until the final exam is behind you. Then shop carefully for instructors for next term by asking fellow students, your academic advisor, and others whose advice you can trust.

Friendships in and Beyond College

One of the best things about going to college is meeting new people. In fact, scholars who study college students have found that you'll learn as much—or more—from other students you meet as you'll learn from professors. Although not everyone you hang out with will become a close friend, you will likely find a few relationships that are really special and might even last a lifetime.

ROOMMATES

Adjusting to a roommate is a significant transition experience. You might make a lifetime friend or end up with an exasperating acquaintance you wish you'd never known. A roommate doesn't have to be a best friend—just someone with whom you can share your living space comfortably. Furthermore, your best friend might not make the best roommate. In fact, many students have lost friends by rooming together.

With any roommate, it's important to establish your mutual rights and responsibilities in writing. Many colleges provide contract forms that you and your roommate can use. If things go wrong later, you will have something to point to.

If you have problems with your roommate, talk them out promptly. Talk directly—politely but plainly. If problems persist or if you don't know how to talk them out, ask your residence hall counselor for help; he or she is trained to help resolve roommate conflicts.

Normally, you can tolerate (and learn from) a less than ideal situation; but if things get really bad and do not improve, insist on a change. If you are on campus, talk to your resident assistant (RA) or to a professional counselor in your campus's counseling center.

SOCIAL NETWORKING

Social networking websites such as Facebook and MySpace are very popular with college students. While there are both positives and negatives associated with using social networking sites, one thing is certain: Entering college students rarely examine what they post online, the effects their online statements have on others, and the benefits and pitfalls of using social networking sites.

Social networking websites are wonderful tools to help you keep connected to your friends from high school and to your new friends in college. What you might not know is that you can also use social networking sites for more than just staying in touch with friends. Facebook can help you become more engaged in life on your campus. If you are a returning adult student, you might feel that learning how to use something like Facebook will be a daunting task. However, returning adult students, like traditional-age students, can learn a great deal about academic life and the campus community from being involved on Facebook.

You might also use Facebook to help you learn more about your instructors. When students read an instructor's Facebook profile, they might be surprised to learn that instructors are people too and engage in everyday activities such as exercising and watching movies. Learning a bit more about your professors can help you feel more comfortable participating in class discussion and asking for help.

Now for the downside: It is easy to get lost in reading profiles, status updates, notes, and checking out your friends' photos. Students often describe social networking websites as "addicting," which could interfere with your academic success and your well-being. You might have found that you spent much more time on Facebook than you expected and don't have enough time to finish your work. Some students use technology to the exclusion of other activities in their lives. If you find yourself struggling to keep up with your real-world commitments and relationships because you are spending so much time on Facebook, it might be a good idea to talk to someone at your campus counseling center.

┌─ **YOUR TURN** ▶ ──────────────────────────────

Have you met someone online whom you consider interesting? If so, describe that
person. If not, describe the kind of person you would like to meet online and why.

Getting Serious with Relationships

Not only does college present an opportunity to make lots of new friends,
it is also a place where romantic relationships flourish. Although some beginning college students are married or are already in long-term committed
relationships, others might have their first serious romance with someone
they meet on campus. If you are gay, lesbian, bisexual, or transgendered, you
might find it much easier to meet romantic partners in college than you ever
have before. Whatever your sexual orientation, you'll have many opportunities; some students will sample lots of different choices, and others will settle
in with just one person. Either way, you'll grow and learn a great deal about
yourself and those with whom you become involved. If you are seriously
thinking about marriage or a long-term commitment, consider this: Studies

Wired WINDOW

ARE YOUR FACEBOOK FRIENDS REALLY WHO THEY SAY THEY ARE?

In a recent survey, between 3 and 10 percent of college
students lied on their social networking website profiles
about their age, their gender, what they do for a living,
or their interests. The popular media frequently report
on people who use social networking websites to prey
on others. A recent article in the *Los Angeles Times*[1]
reported that MySpace identified and removed over
90,000 registered sex offenders between 2007 and
2009. Imagine how many offenders are on MySpace
and don't list their real names. Even though the
percentage of people who use social networking
websites to prey on others is small in relation to the
number of total users, it is important to consider
ways of protecting yourself online. Use commonsense
precautions (such as not giving out your location or
contact information), and adjust your privacy settings
accordingly.

The chances that people will lie about a criminal
background are greater than the chances they will lie
about their age or gender. Even if you are careful to
avoid offenders online, you can be hurt emotionally
by someone who is deceitful. You might already know
people who found that some of their MySpace or
Facebook friends weren't who they thought they were.

Think Critically

Try your own social networking website investigation.
Find either a Facebook or a MySpace profile of
someone who you think has not portrayed himself
or herself accurately. What are your reasons for
selecting this profile? Why do you think this person
is representing himself or herself in this way? Check
your privacy settings. Who can see your profile? What
privacy limits do you have on your profile? Do you post
information that is personally revealing or that can
lead someone to your room, apartment, or home?

[1]More sex offenders joined MySpace than previously acknowledged. *Los Angeles Times*. http://articles.latimes.com/2009/feb/04/business/fi-mys-
pace4.

show that the younger you are, the lower are your odds of a successful marriage. Also, a "trial marriage" or living together does not necessarily decrease your risk of later divorce. It is important not to marry before both you and your partner are certain about who you are and what you want in life. Many 18- to 20-year-olds change their outlook and life goals drastically as they get older, which can negatively affect a romantic relationship.

BREAKING UP

Breaking up is hard, but if it's time to end a relationship, do it cleanly and calmly. Explain your feelings and talk them out. If you don't get a mature reaction, take the high road; don't join someone else in the mud. If you decide to reunite after a trial separation, be sure enough time has passed for you to evaluate the situation effectively. If things fail a second time, you might need to move on.

If your partner breaks up with you, you might find yourself sad, angry, or even depressed. If your partner breaks up with you online or you learn about an imminent breakup through instant messaging, social networking websites, or blog postings, ask to discuss the matter over the phone or in person. Almost everyone has been rejected or "dumped" at one time or another. Let some time pass, be open to emotional support from your friends and your family, and, if necessary, pay a visit to your college counselor or a chaplain. These skilled professionals have assisted many students through similar experiences, and they can be there for you as well. Bookstores and your library will also have good information on the topic of surviving a breakup.

YOUR TURN ▶

On the basis of your experience or the experience of someone close to you, what advice would you give other students who are dealing with breakups?

RELATIONSHIPS YOU SHOULD AVOID

It is never wise to become romantically involved with your professor or someone who works above or for you. Many of these relationships end in a breakup. Imagine how you would feel if your ex, who might be hurt or bitter or even want you back, still had control over your grades or your job! If you date a subordinate and the relationship ends, you might find yourself being accused of sexual harassment, fired, or sued. Even dating coworkers is risky; it will be much harder to heal from a breakup if you must continue to work together.

Family Connections

Almost all first-year students, no matter what their age, are connected to other family members. Your family might be a spouse and children, a partner, or your parents and siblings. The relationships you have with family members can be a source of support throughout your college years, and it's important that you do your part to maintain those relationships.

MARRIAGE AND PARENTING DURING COLLEGE

Can marriage and parenting coexist with being a college student? The answer, of course, is yes, although linking all of these identities—student, spouse, parent—will not be easy. If you are married or in a long-term relationship, with or without children, you will need to become an expert at time management. The responsibilities of your roles might come into conflict, and you'll need to know what comes first and when. Most college instructors will be flexible with requirements if you have genuine problems with meeting a deadline because of family obligations. But it's important that you explain your situation; don't expect your instructors to be able to guess what you need. As the demands on your time increase, it is important that you and your partner share the burdens equally.

Occasionally, deciding to go to college can create conflict within a family. Partners and children can be threatened and intimidated if you take on a new identity and set of responsibilities. Financial pressures are likely to put an extra strain on your relationship, so both you and your partner will have to work hard at attending to each other's needs. Be sure to involve your family members in your decision to go to college. Bring them to campus at every opportunity, let them read your papers and other assignments, and find out whether your partner can take a course too. Finally, it's very important to carve out time for your partner and your family just as carefully as you schedule your work and your classes.

RELATIONSHIPS WITH YOUR PARENTS

Whether you live on campus or at home, your relationship with your parents will never be quite the same as it was before. You might find that your parents hover over you and try to make decisions on your behalf, such as your major, where and how much you work, and what you do on weekends. In fact, some instructors and administrators have coined the term "helicopter parents" to describe parents who exhibit these hovering behaviors. You also might find that it's hard for you to make any decisions without talking to your parents first. While communication with your parents is important, don't let them make all your decisions. Your college or university will help you draw the line between what decisions should be yours alone and what decisions your parents should help you make.

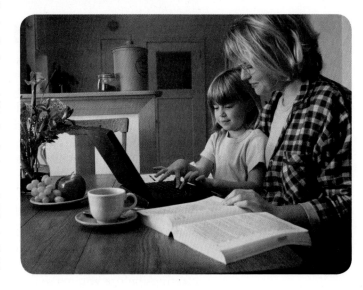

Many college students are living in blended families, so more than one set of parents is involved in their college experience. If your father or mother has remarried, you might have to negotiate with both family units.

So how can you have a good relationship with your parents during this period of transition? A first step in establishing a good relationship with them is to be aware of their concerns. Parents are often worried that you'll harm yourself in some way. They might still see you as young and innocent, and they don't want you to make the same mistakes they might have made or experience situations that have been publicized in the media. They might be concerned that your family or cultural values will change or that you'll never really come home again. For some students, this is exactly what happens.

But remember that parents generally mean well. Most of them love their children even if their love isn't always expressed well. They have genuine concerns that you will understand even better if and when you become a parent yourself. To help your parents feel more comfortable with your life in college, try setting aside regular times to update them on how things are going for you. Ask for and consider their advice. You don't have to take it, but it can be useful to think about it, along with the other factors that will help you make decisions.

Not every family is ideal. If your family is not supportive, find other people who can help you create the family you need. With your emotional needs satisfied, your reactions to your real family will be much less painful.

What should you do if your family falls apart? Divorce happens, and sometimes it happens when a son or daughter goes to college. It can be hard to proceed with life as usual when the family foundation seems to be cracking under you. But remember that your parents are adults. If your father and mother decide to go their separate ways, it's not your fault, and you should not feel responsible for their happiness.

Even if you're successful in determining appropriate boundaries between your life and your parents' lives, it's hard not to worry about what's happening at home. So seek help from your campus's counseling center or from a chaplain if you find yourself in the midst of a difficult family situation.

YOUR TURN ▶

How is your family reacting to your college experience? Are they supportive, fearful, meddling, remote? If there are problems, how are you handling them?

Getting Involved

Colleges and universities can seem to be huge and unfriendly places, especially if you went to a small high school or grew up in a small town. To feel comfortable in this new environment, it is important for you to find your comfort zone or niche. It's not hard to find the place where you belong, but it will take some initiative on your part. Consider your interests and the high school activities you enjoyed most, and choose some activities to explore. You might be interested in joining an intramural team, performing community service, running for a student government office, or getting involved in your residence hall. Or you might prefer joining a more structured campuswide club or organization.

Almost every college has numerous organizations you can join; usually, you can check them out through activity fairs, printed guides, open houses, web pages, and so on. Even better, consider attending one of the organization's meetings before you make the decision to join. Find out what the organization is like, what the expectations of time and money are, and whether you feel comfortable with the members. New students who become involved with at least one organization are more likely to survive their first year and remain in college.

Be careful not to overextend yourself when it comes to campus activities. While it is important to get involved, joining too many clubs or organizations will make it difficult to focus on any given activity and will interfere with your studies. Future employers will see a balance in academics and campus involvement as a desirable quality in prospective employees. Don't fall into the trap of thinking that more is better. In campus involvement, as in many things, quality is much more important than quantity.

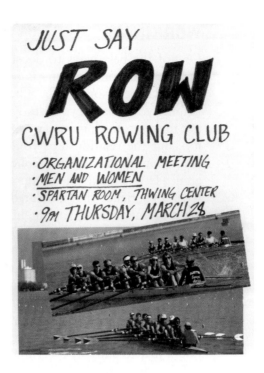

YOUR TURN ▶

Have you already become involved in campus organizations? If so, what kinds of involvement have you already experienced? If you haven't become involved, what club or organization most interests you? Explain why.

TO GREEK OR NOT TO GREEK?

Greek social organizations are not all alike, nor are their members. Fraternities and sororities can be a rich source of friends and support. Some students love them. Other students find them philosophically distasteful, too demanding of time and finances, or too constricting. Members of Greek organizations sometimes associate exclusively with other members, and this exclusivity can cause them to miss opportunities to have a more varied group of friends. Greek rush (member recruitment) on your campus might happen before you have had an opportunity to decide whether you want to go Greek or to determine which fraternity or sorority is right for you. There is nothing wrong with delaying a decision about Greek membership. In fact, we would argue that it's better to learn your way around campus and meet lots of different friends before committing to a particular organization. Fraternities and sororities are powerful social influences, so you'll definitely want to take a good look at the upper-class students who are in them. If what you see is what you want to be, consider joining. If not, steer clear.

If Greek life is not for you, consider the many other ways in which you can make close friends. Many campuses have residence halls or special floors for students with common interests or situations, such as first-year students; honors students; students in particular majors; students with strong ethnic or religious affiliations; students who do not use tobacco, alcohol, and drugs; students who are interested in protecting the environment; and so on. Check these out. Often, they provide very satisfying experiences.

WORKING

One of the best ways to develop relationships with instructors and administrators on your campus is to get an on-campus job. Generally, your on-campus supervisors will be much more flexible than off-campus employers in helping you balance your study demands and your work schedule. You might not make as much money working on campus as you would in an off-campus job, but the relationships you'll develop with influential people who really care about your success in college and who will write those all-important reference letters make on-campus employment well worth it. Consider finding a work experience that is related to your intended major. For instance, if you are a premed major, you might be able to find on-campus work in a biology or chemistry lab. That work could help you to gain knowledge and experience and to make connections with faculty experts in these fields.

If an on-campus job is not available or you don't find one that appeals to you, an off-campus job is also a good way to meet new people in the community. However, it's important that you restrict work to a reasonable number of hours per week. Although you might feel that you have to work in order to pay your tuition or living expenses, many college students work too many hours just to support a certain lifestyle. Be careful to maintain a reasonable balance between work and study. Don't fall into the trap of thinking, "I can do it all." Too many college students have found that doing it all means not doing anything well.

Many schools have **co-op programs** in which students spend some terms in regular classes and other terms in temporary paid employment in their field. Although such programs will usually prolong your education somewhat, they have many advantages. They offer an excellent preview of what work in your chosen field is actually like, thus helping you determine whether you have made the right choice. They give you valuable experience and contacts that will help you get a job when you finish school; in fact, many firms offer successful co-op students permanent jobs when they graduate.

Alternating work and school terms might be more suitable for you than eight or ten straight terms of classes, and it might help you keep your ultimate goal in mind. Co-op programs can help you pay for school too; some co-op students, especially in technical fields, make almost as much, or even more, during their co-op terms as their professors do!

COMMUNITY SERVICE

As a first-year student, you will spend much of your time on campus, either going to class, studying, or hanging out with other students. But there are also ways in which you can get involved in the surrounding community. Consider volunteering for a community service project such as helping at an animal shelter, serving the homeless at a soup kitchen, or helping to build or renovate homes for needy families. Your college might offer service opportunities as part of first-year courses (service learning), or your campus's division of student affairs might have a volunteer or community service office. You can also check Volunteer Match (http://www.volunteermatch.org/) for opportunities in your area. Simply enter your ZIP Code and, if you wish, key words to help you find volunteer work in your field of interest.

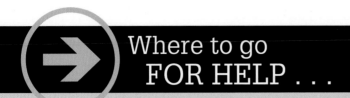

Where to go FOR HELP . . .

ON CAMPUS ▶

Counseling Center Professional college counselors help students think and talk about their relationships and then make the most appropriate decisions. It is normal to seek such assistance. It's a rare student who doesn't have some relationship challenges in college, whether with roommates, friends, family members, romantic partners, teachers, supervisors, or other individuals. This kind of counseling is strictly confidential (unless you are a threat to yourself or others) and usually is provided at no charge, which is a great fringe benefit of being in college. But unless this is an emergency, be prepared to wait for your first appointment; these centers have very heavy caseloads because so many students are experiencing stress.

Chaplains An often underrecognized resource in terms of getting help on relationships is a session (or more) with a campus chaplain. Many colleges, both public and private, have religiously affiliated chaplains, who usually have specialized training in pastoral counseling. They also organize and host group activities in campus religious centers that you might want to take advantage of. Your academic advisor might be able to refer you to an appropriate chaplain, or you can seek out the one who represents your faith. Most chaplains are happy to see students for counseling whether or not you attend their church, synagogue, or mosque.

Student Organizations The variety of student groups designed to bring together students to help them with their relationships is virtually unlimited. Everything exists—from Greek letter social fraternities and sororities to single parents with children to gay/lesbian/bisexual/transgendered student groups.

ONLINE ▶

The University of Chicago's "Student Counseling Virtual Pamphlet Collection" (http://www.counseling.uchicago.edu/resources/virtualpamphlets) takes you to dozens of websites devoted to problems in relationships. Browse among the many links to see whether any information applies to you.

Healthy Romantic Relationships during College: (http://www.utexas.edu/student/cmhc/booklets/romrelations/romrelations.html). The University of Texas Counseling Center offers an online brochure that explores the ups and downs of romantic relationships.

MY INSTITUTION'S RESOURCES ▶

_____

_____

_____

_____

_____

_____

_____

_____

_____

_____

_____

One-Minute PAPER . . .

Chapter 14 provides a lot of information about establishing and maintaining relationships in college. What did you find to be the most useful information? Was there anything in this chapter that you didn't understand or that you disagreed with?

Applying What You've LEARNED . . .

Now that you have read and discussed this chapter, consider how you can apply what you have learned to your academic and personal life. The following prompts will help you reflect on chapter material and its relevance to you both now and in the future.

1. If you are not already involved in on-campus activities and clubs, visit your campus's website or activities office to learn more about the kinds of clubs, organizations, service learning opportunities, sports teams, or volunteer work that is offered. Find at least one activity that seems interesting to you, and learn more about it. When does the group meet and how often? How many students are involved?

2. Check out some of your fellow students' profiles on a social networking site such as Facebook or MySpace. What kinds of personal information do they share? What kinds of issues are they writing about? Do they use the privacy settings that are available? Do you think it is important for college students to be careful about the kind of information they post on social networking sites? Why or why not?

Building Your PORTFOLIO . . .

> ❝ To exist is to change, to change is to mature, to mature is to go on creating oneself endlessly. ❞
>
> – HENRI BERGSON (1859-1941),
> French philosopher

A DAY IN THE LIFE

Managing family relationships while in college can sometimes be a real challenge! Whether you are attending college in your hometown or across the country, relationships with those who are close to you will change. Sometimes parents or other family members have a hard time letting go, and it is sometimes difficult for new college students to start making independent decisions.

1. In a Word document, describe some of the ways in which your life has changed since you came to college (e.g., more independence, more personal responsibility, less free time). How have you handled these changes? What has been the most difficult aspect of your new college life so far? Why?

2. Have you considered how your family's day-to-day lives might also have changed since you began college? Conduct an in-person or phone interview with one (or more) of your family members about how life has changed for them.

TIP:

- *Set up a mutually convenient time to talk.*
- *Choose a quite place, free of distractions.*

Here are a few questions to get you started:

   a. What do you feel has changed in your life since I began college?
   b. Is the family routine any different now? If so, in what way?
   c. Do you worry about me? If so, what is your biggest concern about my college experience?
   d. Do you feel that we communicate enough (by phone, e-mail, etc.)?

3. Save your responses in your portfolio on your personal computer or flash drive. Reflect on what you learned from the interviews. How can you be sensitive to your family's needs/concerns while recognizing your own changing needs?

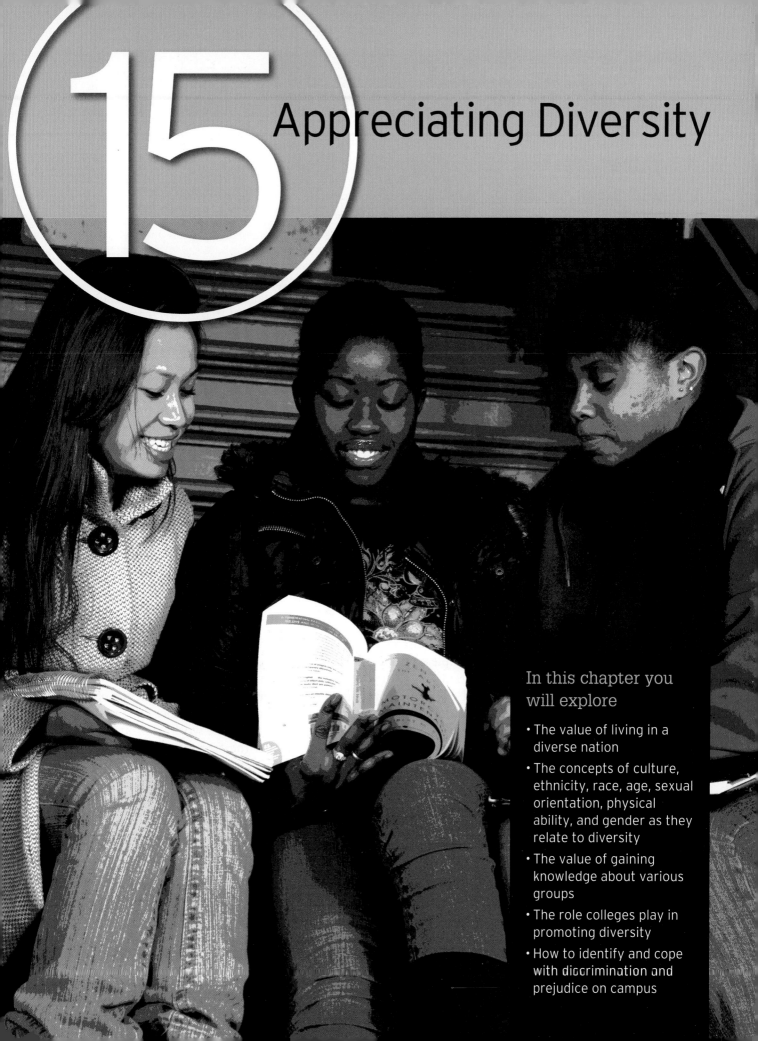

15 Appreciating Diversity

In this chapter you will explore

- The value of living in a diverse nation
- The concepts of culture, ethnicity, race, age, sexual orientation, physical ability, and gender as they relate to diversity
- The value of gaining knowledge about various groups
- The role colleges play in promoting diversity
- How to identify and cope with discrimination and prejudice on campus

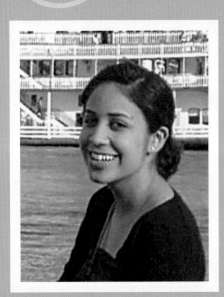

BINATA RAY, 19
New York University

> You're going to come to a place where there are people not like you at all, who have had experiences that are different from yours.

I come from a diverse background: My mom's of Russian-Jewish descent, and my dad's from India. I have an innate sense of differences, and that's helped me try new things. I think it's great to have these differences and to be able to learn about them and learn from them, because that's what makes life interesting. But as a resident assistant for first-year students, I can see the problems that arise when different kinds of people come together. A lot of people just don't realize that things they say or do could be offensive.

If there is a diversity issue where someone feels marginalized or they witness something, there are usually tons of resources on campus that can help. The biggest thing is be open-minded and truly understand that everyone is different from you. Every experience you have in college will help you be stronger in the real world and help you grow as a person. You're going to come to a place where there are people not like you at all, who have had experiences that are different from yours, and if you put up this wall and say, "Why can't they just react like I react or act like I do?," you'll be facing a lot of trouble. Keep an open mind and a willingness to get involved. No one wants to feel left out.

At the core of this country's value system is the belief that the United States of America is a place where all people are welcome. This principle has created a richly diverse society that emphasizes the importance of retaining individual cultural identity while living among others. Ethnic and cultural communities throughout the United States are preserving components of their particular heritage as they join other cultures to create a nation that is more diverse than any other in the world. Throughout our history, as this country has moved toward the Constitution's goal of achieving "a more perfect union," diversity has been both a source of conflict and a national strength. The 2008 presidential campaign marked the first time in history that a woman, Hillary Rodham Clinton, nearly became the presidential nominee of a major political party, and the first time a man with both African and American heritage, Barack Obama, was elected to be the president of the United States.

A college or university serves as a microcosm of the real world—a world that requires us all to work, live, and socialize with people from various ethnic and cultural groups. In few settings do members of ethnic and cultural groups interact in such close proximity to one another as they do on a college campus. Whether you are attending a four-year university or a community college, you will be exposed to new experiences and opportunities, all of which can enhance learning and a deeper sense of understanding.

Through self-assessment, discovery, and open-mindedness, you can begin to understand your perspectives on diversity. This work, although difficult at times, will intensify your educational experiences, personal growth, and development. Thinking critically about your personal values and belief systems will allow you to have a greater sense of belonging and to make a positive contribution to our multicultural society.

YOUR TURN ▶

If you broadly define the term *diversity* as differences in race, gender, ethnicity, religion, political preference, and the like, is your college or university more or less diverse than your high school?

Understanding Diversity and the Source of Our Beliefs

Diversity is the variation in social and cultural identities among people living together. **Multiculturalism** is the active process of acknowledging and respecting social groups, cultures, religions, races, ethnicities, attitudes, and opinions. As your journey through higher education unfolds, you will find yourself immersed in this mixture of identities. Regardless of the size of the institution, going to college brings together people who have differing backgrounds and experiences but similar goals and aspirations. Each person brings to campus a unique combination of life story, upbringing, value system, view of the world, and set of judgments. Familiarizing yourself with such differences can greatly enhance your experiences in the classes you will take, the organizations you will join, and the relationships you will cultivate. For many students college is the first time they have been exposed to so much diversity. Learning experiences and challenges await you both in and out of the classroom. College provides opportunities to learn not only about others but also about yourself.

Many of our beliefs grow out of personal experience and reinforcement. If you have had a negative experience or endured a series of incidents involving members of a particular group, you're more likely to develop **stereotypes,** or negative judgments, about people in that group. Or maybe you have heard repeatedly that everyone associated with a particular group behaves in a certain way, and you might have bought into that stereotype without even thinking about it. Children who grow up in an environment in which dislike and distrust of certain types of people are openly expressed might subscribe to those very judgments even if they have had no direct interaction with those being judged.

In college you might encounter beliefs about diversity that run counter to your basic values. When your friendships with others are affected by differing values, tolerance is generally a good goal. Talking about diversity with someone else whose beliefs seem to be in conflict with your own can be very rewarding. Your goal in this kind of discussion is not to reach agreement, but to enhance your understanding of why people see diversity differently—why some seem to flee from it and others allow experiences with diversity to enrich their college experience.

Before coming to college, you might never have coexisted with most of the groups you now see on campus. Your home community might not have been very diverse, although possibly it seemed so before you reached campus. In college you have the opportunity to learn from many kinds of people. From your roommate in the residence hall to your lab partner in your biology class to the members of your sociology study group, your college experience will be enriched if you allow yourself to be open to the possibility of learning from members of all cultural groups.

> **YOUR TURN ▶**
>
> Write about any specific lessons you learned in your family about the expectations you should have of diverse groups.

Forms of Diversity

When you think about diversity, you might first think of differences in race or ethnicity. While it is true that those are two forms of diversity, there are many other types of diversity that you will most likely experience in college and in the workplace, including age, religion, physical ability, gender, and sexual orientation.

ETHNICITY, CULTURE, RACE, AND RELIGION

Often, the terms "ethnicity" and "culture" are used interchangeably, although their definitions are quite distinct. Throughout this chapter we will use these two words together and in isolation. Before we start using the terms, it's a good idea to learn their definitions so that you're clear on what they actually mean.

Ethnicity refers to the identity that is assigned to a specific group of people who are historically connected by a common national origin or language. For example, let's look at one of the largest ethnic groups: Latinos. Latin America encompasses over thirty countries within North, Central, and South America, all of which share the Spanish language. A notable exception is Brazil. However, although the national language is Portuguese, Brazilians are considered Latinos (both Spanish and Portuguese are languages that evolved from Latin). The countries also share many traditions and beliefs, with some variations. However, we shouldn't generalize. Not every Latino who speaks Spanish is of Mexican descent, and not every Latino speaks Spanish. Acknowledging that differences exist within ethnic groups is a big step in becoming ethnically aware.

Culture is defined as those aspects of a group of people that are passed on and/or learned. Traditions, food, language, clothing styles, artistic expression, and beliefs are all part of culture. Certainly, ethnic groups are also cultural groups: They share a language, foods, traditions, art, and clothing, which are passed from one generation to the next. But numerous other, non-ethnic cultural groups can fit this concept of culture, too. Think of the hip-hop community, in which a common style of dress, specific terminology, and distinct forms of musical and artistic expression also constitute a culture but not an ethnicity.

Although we don't use the term **race** much in this chapter, it's important to understand this word as it is commonly used in everyday language. Race refers to biological characteristics that are shared by groups of people, including skin tone, hair texture and color, and facial features. Making generalizations about someone's racial group affiliation is risky. Even people who share some biological features—such as similar eye shape or dark skin—might be ethnically very distinct. For instance, people of Asian descent are not necessarily ethnically and culturally alike, since Asia is a vast region encompassing such disparate places as Mongolia, India, and Japan. Likewise, people of African descent come from very different backgrounds; the African continent is home to fifty-three countries and hundreds of different languages, and Africans are genetically very diverse. More and more individuals today, including President Obama, describe themselves as multiracial. You might meet fellow students whose families include parents, grandparents, and great-grandparents of several different racial groups.

All of us come into the world with our own unique characteristics—aspects of our physical appearance and personalities that make us who we are. But people around the world have one attribute in common: We want to be respected even if we are different from others in some ways. Whatever the color of your skin or hair, whatever your life experiences or cultural background, you will want others to treat you fairly and acknowledge and value your contribution to your communities and the world. And, of course, others will want the same from you.

Diversity of **religion** has been central to the American experience since our colonial origins. In fact, many settlers of the original thirteen colonies came to North America to escape religious persecution. Religious diversity might or might not have been obvious in your hometown or neighborhood, but unless you are attending an institution that enrolls only students of one religious sect, you will find religious diversity to be part of your college experience. Religious denominations might sponsor campus centers or organizations, and students' religious affiliations might determine their dress, attitudes, or avoidance of certain behaviors. While you are in college, your openness to religious diversity will add to your understanding of the many ways in which people are different from one another.

AGE

Although many students enter college around age 18, others choose to enter or return in their thirties and beyond. In the fall of 2006, over 37 percent of American college students were 25 years of age or older. Age diversity in the classroom gives everyone the opportunity to learn from others who have different life experiences. All kinds of factors determine when students enter higher education for the first time or stop and then reenter. Therefore there is no such thing as "the norm" in considering the age of college students. If you are attending a college that has a large number of students who are older (or younger) than you, strive to see this as an advantage for learning. A campus where younger and older students learn together can be much more interesting than a campus where everyone is the same age.

YOUR TURN ▶

Other than your grandparents, do you know people who are significantly older than you? If so, what has been the nature of your interaction and your relationship? If not, how might you meet some older people on campus or in your community?

LEARNING AND PHYSICAL ABILITIES

Although the majority of students have reasonably average learning and physical abilities, the numbers of students with physical and learning disabilities are rising on most college campuses, as are the services that are available to them. Physical disabilities can include deafness, blindness, paralysis, or a mental disorder. Also, many students have some form of learning disability (see Chapter 4) that makes college work a challenge.

People who have physical and learning disabilities want to be treated just as you would treat anyone else—with respect. If a student with a disability is in your class, treat him or her as you would any student; your overzealousness to help might be seen as an expression of pity.

If you have, or think you might have, a learning disability, consult your campus learning center for a diagnosis and advice on compensating for learning problems. Most campuses have a special office to serve students with both physical and learning disabilities.

GENDER

A basic example of diversity is gender. But other than the obvious physical differences, are men and women really that different? Or do we believe they are because of our own biases?

While you're in college, make friends with people of both genders, avoid stereotyping what is "appropriate" for one group or another, and don't limit your own interests. In today's world, there is almost no activity or profession that isn't open to everyone, regardless of gender. If your college or university has a Gender Studies department, consider taking a course in this area. Gender studies courses are generally interdisciplinary and look at the subject matter from the perspective of gender. Such a course could open up new ways of thinking about many aspects of your world.

YOUR TURN ▶

Can you remember any time in your life when you gave up a dream because you thought it was "inappropriate" for someone of your gender? Can you remember a time when you assumed you wouldn't be good at an activity, a sport, or a course because of your gender? What advice could you give to other students about not letting their gender narrow their range of life options?

SEXUAL ORIENTATION

In college you will likely meet students, staff members, and professors who are homosexual or bisexual. Because most colleges and universities openly accept gay, lesbian, bisexual, or transgendered people, many individuals who were in the closet in high school will come out in the collegiate environment. The subject of sexual orientation is highly personal and often emotionally charged, but whatever your own personal sexual orientation, it is important that you respect all individuals with whom you come in contact. Most colleges and universities have campus codes or standards of behavior that do not permit acts of harassment or discrimination based on race, ethnicity, gender, or sexual orientation.

Seeking Diversity on Campus

Acknowledging the importance of diversity to education, colleges and universities have begun to take the concepts of diversity and apply them to student learning opportunities. We see this in efforts by colleges to embrace an **inclusive curriculum**. Today, you can find courses with a diversity focus in many departments of your college or university, such as Black Studies, Asian Studies, Latino or Hispanic Studies, Women's Studies, Gay and Lesbian Studies, and Religious Studies. Many of the courses in these departments meet graduation requirements. The college setting is ideal for promoting education about diversity because it allows students and faculty of varying backgrounds to come together for the common purpose of learning and critical thinking.

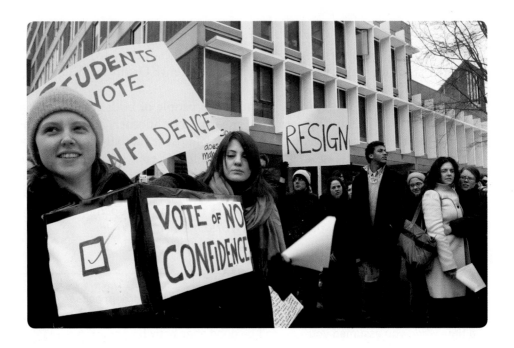

According to Gloria Ameny-Dixon, education about diversity can do the following:

- Increase problem-solving skills through different perspectives applied to reaching solutions
- Increase positive relationships through the achievement of common goals, respect, appreciation, and commitment to equality
- Decrease stereotyping and prejudice through contact and interaction with diverse individuals
- Promote the development of a more in-depth view of the world[1]

Be it religious affiliation, sexual orientation, gender, ethnicity, age, culture, or ability, your campus provides the opportunity to interact with and learn alongside a kaleidoscope of individuals.

THE CURRICULUM

College students have led the movement for a curriculum that reflects disenfranchised groups such as women, people of color, the elderly, the disabled, gays, lesbians, bisexuals, and the transgendered. By protesting, walking out of classes, and staging sit-ins at the offices of campus officials, students have demanded the hiring of more faculty members from different ethnic groups, the creation of Ethnic Studies departments, and a variety of initiatives designed to support diverse students academically and socially. These initiatives have increased academic access for students from ethnic and cultural groups and have helped them stay in school. They exist today in the form of multicultural centers, women's resource centers, enabling services, and numerous academic support programs. The movement for **multiculturalism** in education

[1]Gloria M. Ameny-Dixon, "Why Multicultural Education Is More Important in Higher Education Now Than Ever: A Global Perspective." McNeese State University (http://www .nationalforum.com).

has continued to gain momentum since it began during the civil rights era of the 1960s. By expressing their discontent over the lack of access and representation in many of society's niches, including higher education, ethnic and cultural groups have achieved acknowledgment of their presence on campus.

In almost all colleges and universities, you will be required to take some general education courses. The purpose of these courses is to expose you to a wide range of topics and issues so that you can develop and learn to express your own views. We hope you will include a course or two with a multicultural basis in your schedule. Such courses can provide you with new perspectives and an understanding of issues that affect your fellow students and community members—and affect you too, possibly in ways you had not considered. And just as your college or university campus is diverse, so, too, is the workforce you will be entering. A multicultural education can improve the quality of your entire life.

STUDENT-RUN ORGANIZATIONS

Student-run organizations can provide multiple avenues to express ideas, pursue interests, and cultivate relationships. According to our definition of culture, all student-run organizations are culturally based and provide an outlet for the promotion and celebration of a culture. Let's take, for instance, two very different student groups, a Muslim Student Union and an Animation Club, and apply the components of culture to them. Both groups promote a belief system that is common among their members: The first is based on religious beliefs, and the second is based on ideas about what constitutes animation as an art form. Both have aspects that can be taught and passed on: the teachings of the Muslim faith and the rules and techniques used in drawing. Both groups utilize language that is specific to the belief system of the group. Most campus organizations bring like-minded students together and are open to anyone who wants to become involved.

To promote learning and discovery not only inside the classroom but outside as well, colleges and universities provide programming that highlights ethnic and cultural celebrations, such as Chinese New Year and Kwanzaa; gender-related topics, such as Take Back the Night; and a broad range of entertainment, including concerts and art exhibits. These events expose you to new and exciting ideas and viewpoints, enhancing your education and challenging your current views.

Most college students, especially first-year students, are seeking their own niche and their own identity. Many have found that becoming involved in campus organizations eases the transition and helps them make connections with their fellow students.

FRATERNITIES AND SORORITIES

Fraternities and sororities provide a quick connection to a large number of individuals—a link to the social pipeline, camaraderie, and support. Fraternities and sororities differ in their philosophies and commitment to philanthropy. Some are committed to community service; others are more socially oriented. Fraternities and sororities created by and for specific ethnic groups have existed for years and were developed by students of color who felt the need for campus groups that allowed them to connect to their communities and cultures. Nu Alpha Kappa Fraternity, Alpha Rho Lambda Sorority, Omega Psi Phi Fraternity, Alpha Kappa Alpha Sorority, Lambda Phi Epsilon Fraternity, and Sigma Omicron Pi Sorority are just some of the many ethnically based fraternities and sororities that exist across the country. Such organizations have provided many students with a means to become familiar with their campus and to gain friendships and support while promoting their culture and ethnicity.

CAREER/MAJOR GROUPS

You can explore diversity through your major and career interests as well. Groups that focus on a specific field of study can be great assets as you explore your interests. Are you interested in helping minority and majority groups interact more effectively? Consider majoring in sociology or social work. Do you want to learn more about human behavior? Study psychology.

If you join a club that is affiliated with the major that interests you, not only will you find out more about the major, but you can also make contacts in the field that could lead to career options. Many of these clubs participate in challenges and contests with similar groups from other colleges and contribute to campus activities through exhibitions and events. The Psychology Club; the Math, Engineering, and Science Association; and the Association of Student Filmmakers are examples of such groups.

POLITICAL/ACTIVIST ORGANIZATIONS

Adding to the diversity mix on campuses are organizations devoted to specific political affiliations and causes. Campus Republicans, Young Democrats, Amnesty International, Native Students in Social Action, and other groups provide students with a platform to express their political views and share their causes with others. Contributing to the diversity of ideas, organizations provide debating events and forums to address current issues and events.

SPECIAL-INTEREST GROUPS

Perhaps the largest subgroup of student organizations is the special-interest category, which encompasses everything from recreational interests to hobbies. On your campus you might find special-interest clubs such as the Brazilian Jujitsu Club, the Kite Flyers' Club, the Flamenco Club, and the

Video Gamers' Society. Students can cultivate an interest in bird watching or indulge their curiosity about ballroom dance without ever leaving campus. Many of these clubs will sponsor campus events highlighting their specific interests and talents so that you can check them out. If a club for your special interest is not available, create one yourself.

Discrimination, Prejudice, and Insensitivity on College Campuses

You might feel uncomfortable when asked about your views of diversity. We all have **biases** against certain groups or value systems. Yet it is what we do with our individual beliefs that separates the average person from the racist, the bigot, and the extremist.

Unfortunately, some individuals opt not to seek education for the common good but instead respond negatively to groups that differ from their own. Documented acts of **discrimination** and **prejudice** on campuses span the country. You might be shocked to hear that these acts of violence, intimidation, and stupidity occur on campuses, when the assumption is that college students are "supposed to be above that."

RAISING AWARENESS

At a midwestern university, students arrived on campus to find racial slurs and demeaning images aimed at various ethnic groups spray-painted on the walls of the Multicultural Center. In the wake of the terrorist attack on the World Trade Center and the Pentagon in September 2001, many students of Middle Eastern descent were subjected to both violence and intimidation because of their ancestry.

While actions like these are deliberate and hateful, others occur out of a lack of common sense. Consider a campus party to celebrate Cinco de Mayo. Party organizers asked everyone to wear sombreros. On arrival, guests encountered a mock-up of a border patrol station on the front lawn and were required to crawl under or climb over a section of chain-link fencing. Student groups voiced their disapproval over such insensitivity, which resulted in campus probationary measures for the organization that had thrown the party. At a Halloween party at a large university, members of a campus organization decided to dress in Ku Klux Klan outfits while other members dressed as slaves and wore black shoe polish on their faces. The group then simulated slave hangings during the party. When photos of the events surfaced, the university suspended the group from campus, and the community demanded that the group be banned indefinitely.

For a number of years stereotypes that are used to identify school sports teams and their supporters have disturbed ethnic and cultural groups such as Native Americans. Mascots that incorporate a bow and arrow, a tomahawk, feathers, and war paint have raised awareness about the promotion and acceptance of stereotypes associated with the concept of the "savage Indian." Some schools have responded by altering the images while retaining the mascot. Other schools have changed their mascots altogether.

© Peacemonger.org (559) 799 8801   Profits benefit peaceful charities.   #S001

YOUR TURN ▶

Have you ever witnessed or been a victim of harassment because of your gender, race, regional identity, religion, or ethnic group? What can colleges and universities do to reduce the incidence of harassment?

Colleges and universities are working to ensure that a welcoming and inclusive campus environment awaits all students, both current and prospective. Campus resources and centers focus on providing acknowledgment of and support to the diverse student population. Campus administrations have established policies against any and all forms of discriminatory actions, racism, and insensitivity, and many campuses have adopted zero-tolerance policies that prohibit verbal and nonverbal harassment, intimidation, and violence. Find out what resources are available on your campus to protect you and other students from discriminatory and racist behavior and what steps your college or university takes to promote the understanding of diversity and multiculturalism. If you have been a victim of a racist, insensitive, or discriminatory act, report it to the proper authorities.

WHAT YOU CAN DO TO FIGHT HATE ON CAMPUS

Hate crimes, regardless of where they occur, should be taken very seriously. A hate crime is any prejudicial activity and can include physical assault, vandalism, and intimidation. One of the most common forms of hate crime on campus is graffiti that expresses racial, ethnic, and cultural slurs.

Whatever form these crimes might take on your campus, it is important to examine your thoughts and feelings about their occurrence. The most important question to ask yourself is: Will you do something about it, or do you think it is someone else's problem? If you or a group to which you belong is the target of the hate crime, you might feel compelled to take a stand and speak out against the incident. But what if the target is not a group you associate with? Will you feel strongly enough to express your discontent with the actions that are taken? Or will you feel that it is the problem only of the targeted group?

Many students, whether or not they were directly targeted in a hate crime, find strength in unity, forming action committees and making it clear that hate crimes will not be ignored or tolerated. In most cases, instead of dividing students, hate crimes bring students together to work toward denouncing hate. It is important not to respond to prejudice and hate crimes with violence. It is more effective to unite with fellow students, faculty, staff, campus police, and administrators to address the issue and educate the greater campus community.

How can you get involved? Work with existing campus services such as the campus police and the Multicultural Center as well as the faculty and administration to plan and host educational opportunities, such as training sessions, workshops, and symposiums centered on diversity, sensitivity, and multiculturalism. Organize an antidiscrimination event on campus in which campus and community leaders address the issues and provide solutions. Join prevention programs to come up with ideas to battle hate crimes on campus or in the community. Finally, look into the antidiscrimination measures your college is employing and decide whether you think they need updating or revising.

Just because you or your particular group has not been targeted in a hate crime doesn't mean that you should do nothing. Commit to becoming involved in making your campus a safe place for students with diverse views, lifestyles, languages, politics, religions, and interests to come together and learn. If nothing happens to make it clear that hate crimes on campus will not be tolerated, it's anyone's guess as to who will be the next target.

Wired WINDOW

USING THE WEB TO HELP EXPLORE YOUR BIASES

We all harbor biases against certain groups or value systems; however, first-year college students have rarely examined these biases. Not only is it difficult to accept that you do have biases, but it is often considered inappropriate to discuss biases openly. As you expand your knowledge about other ethnicities, cultures, and belief systems, it's a good idea to explore your own biases so that you can be more understanding and accepting of differences. Because you might not be comfortable discussing your biases in public (such as during a class or a campus discussion), you can opt to explore them on your own. One great website to help you explore biases that you might not even know that you hold is the Harvard Implicit Project (https://www.implicit.harvard.edu/implicit). Follow the link to the "Demonstration" tests. On the demonstration tests page, you can choose to

assess your implicit associations based on diversity issues such as race, sexuality, and age. Please keep in mind that you might not be consciously aware of or agree with the results. Although the Implicit Association Tests are not an absolute assessment, they are a good way to gauge your biases and to begin to explore them in a safe environment.

Thinking Critically

Pick one of the Implicit Association Tests and take it. What do you think about your results? Were you surprised? How can you continue to explore your biases now that you have this information? What is the next step you will take? Review your campus's diversity and multicultural resources. Which resource would help you enhance your awareness of your own feelings about race, ethnicity, and sexual orientation?

Challenge Yourself to Experience Diversity

During his inaugural address, President Obama reiterated the value of diversity:

> For we know that our patchwork heritage is a strength, not a weakness. We are a nation of Christians and Muslims, Jews and Hindus—and non-believers. We are shaped by every language and culture, drawn from every end of this earth; and because we have tasted the bitter swill of civil war and segregation, and emerged from that dark chapter stronger and more united, we cannot help but believe that the old hatreds shall someday pass; that the lines of tribe shall soon dissolve; that as the world grows smaller, our common humanity shall reveal itself; and that America must play its role in ushering in a new era of peace.

Diversity enriches us all. Allowing yourself to become more culturally aware and more open to differing viewpoints will help you become a truly educated person. Understanding the value of working with others and the importance of an open mind will enhance your educational and career goals and provide gratifying experiences, both on and off campus. Making the decision to become active in your multicultural education will require you to be active and sometimes to step out of your comfort zone. There are many ways to become more culturally aware, including a variety of opportunities on your campus. Look into what cultural programming is being offered throughout the school year. From concerts to films, from guest speakers to information tables, you might not have to go far to gain additional insight into the value of diversity.

Challenge yourself to learn about various groups in and around your community, at both school and home. These two settings might differ ethnically and culturally, giving you an opportunity to develop the skills you need to function in and adjust to a variety of settings. Attend events and celebrations outside of your regular groups. Whether they are in the general community or on campus, this is a good way to see and hear traditions that are specific to the groups being represented. Exposing yourself to new experiences through events and celebrations can be gratifying. You can also become active in your own learning by making time for travel. Seeing the world and its people can be an uplifting experience. Finally, when in doubt, ask. If you do this in a tactful, genuine way, most people will be happy to share information about their viewpoints, traditions, and history. It is only through allowing ourselves to grow that we really learn.

Where to go FOR HELP . . .

ON CAMPUS ▶

Most colleges and university campuses take an active role in promoting diversity. In the effort to ensure a welcoming and supportive environment for all students, institutions have established offices, centers, and resources to provide students with educational opportunities, academic guidance, and support networks. Look into the availability of the following resources on your campus, and visit one or more: Office of Student Affairs; Office of Diversity; Multicultural Centers; Women's and Men's Centers; Lesbian, Gay, Bisexual, and Transgendered Student Alliances; Centers for Students with Disabilities; and academic support programs for under represented groups

ONLINE ▶

Student Now Diversity Resources: http://www.studentnow.com/collegelist/diversity.html. A list of campus diversity resources.

Diversity Web: http://www.diversityweb.org. More resources related to diversity on campus.

Tolerance.org: http://www.tolerance.org. This website, a project of the Southern Poverty Law Center, provides numerous resources for dealing with discrimination and prejudice both on and off campus.

MY INSTITUTION'S RESOURCES ▶

_____

_____

_____

_____

_____

_____

_____

_____

_____

_____

_____

_____

_____

_____

_____

_____

One-Minute PAPER . . .

One aspect of a liberal arts education is learning about differences in cultures, races, and other groups. Were there any ideas in this chapter that influenced your personal opinions, viewpoints, or values? Was there anything that you disagreed with or found unsettling?

Applying What You've LEARNED . . .

Now that you have read and discussed this chapter, consider how you can apply what you have learned to your academic and personal life. The following prompts will help you reflect on the chapter material and its relevance to you both now and in the future.

1. Use your print or online campus course catalog to identify courses that focus on topics of multiculturalism and diversity. Why do you think academic departments have included these issues in the curriculum? How would studying diversity and multiculturalism help you prepare for different academic fields?

2. Reflecting on our personal identities and values is a step to increase self-awareness. Read and answer the following questions to the best of your ability:

   How do you identify yourself ethnically and culturally?

   How do you express yourself according to this identity?

   Are there practices or beliefs in your culture to which you have difficulty subscribing? If so, what are they? Why do you have difficulty accepting these beliefs?

   What aspects of your identity do you truly enjoy?

Building Your PORTFOLIO . . .

66 Studying abroad in Granada, Spain, was a digestive process. The world swallowed me whole. It stripped me of everything I once knew and assumed, and spit me out. The outcome wasn't a whole new person, it was an open slate in which everything I now see and hear is digested in a whole new manner that can't be explained but only experienced by traveling abroad. 99

–JULIE SANTOS, Student,
Global & International Studies Program,
University of California, Santa Barbara

IT'S A SMALL WORLD AFTER ALL!

The concepts of diversity, ethnicity, culture, and multiculturalism have been explored in this chapter. Reading about these controversial topics is one thing, but really stepping into someone else's shoes is another. Study abroad and student exchange programs are excellent (and enjoyable) ways of adding new perspectives to your college experience. What better way of learning about other parts of the world than by immersing yourself in a foreign culture, language, and people?

Consider the possibilities:

1. Visit your institution's International Programs/Study Abroad office, or, if you are at a college that does not have a study abroad program, search for study abroad opportunities on the web. *Tip:* Look for the Center for Global Education (http://www.lmu.edu/globaled/index.html), the Council on International Education Exchange (http://www.ciee.org/study.aspx), or the International Partnership for Service Learning (http://www.ispl.org).

Using a major or career that you have selected or are interested in, think about how you would like to spend a summer, semester, or year abroad to learn more about or gain experience in your major field.

2. On the basis of your research, create a PowerPoint presentation to share with your class outlining the opportunities to study abroad or participate in an exchange program.

- Describe the steps students need to take at your campus to include a study abroad trip in their college plan (e.g., whom to contact, financial aid, the best time to study abroad, how to earn course credit).
- Describe the benefits of study abroad (e.g., observing different cultures, building a good résumé).
- Include photos of the country or countries you would like to visit.
- Include information about your current or intended major and career and how a study abroad or exchange trip would fit into your plans.
- Reference web links you found useful in preparing your presentation.

3. Save your presentation in your portfolio on your personal computer or flash drive.

16 Maintaining Wellness

In this chapter you will explore

- The importance of managing stress
- Warning signs of depression
- The positive effects of exercise on your mind and body
- Strategies for better nutrition and weight management
- The many options you have for contraception and safer sex
- The realities of alcohol use on campus
- The consequences of abusing alcohol, tobacco, and drugs

Confessions of a
COLEGE STUDENT...

SHELLY SANDERS, 20
Midwestern State University

66 We would go out and eat dinner all the time. I had to learn to be careful. 99

I don't think my health affects me academically, but socially, food can be an issue. My first year in college, I didn't realize how much money I was spending on food. I have a meal plan, but I'm also in band. They were so welcoming and friendly, and we would go out and eat dinner all the time. Some of the nights I should have just said, "No, I'll eat off my meal plan," because I wasted a lot of money going out. And I am a little big. I had to learn to be careful with what I ate because we went out so much.

I do have some weight on me, but I try to be active. I exercise maybe three times a week on average, although it could be less one week and more another week. I go biking with my boyfriend, and my school has a wellness center, so I do Zumba and health classes and all that kind of stuff, and I really enjoy it. I would recommend going to those activities your school provides because they're really fun. Yes, I had a struggle with separating time between socializing and exercising and studying. As college goes on, I'm getting better at it. It took me awhile, but I've got it now.

College is a great time to explore. It's an opportunity to

exercise your mind and expand your horizons. Unfortunately, for too many students it becomes an opportunity to stop exercising their bodies and begin expanding their waistlines! Because the college environment might be new to you, you could forget to take care of yourself.

Many students can handle the transition to college easily, using various coping mechanisms. Others drink too much or smoke too much. Some overeat or develop an eating disorder such as bulimia or anorexia. Some become so stressed that their anxiety overwhelms them. Some ignore their sexual health and then have to deal with a sexually transmitted infection or an unplanned pregnancy.

This chapter explores the topic of wellness, which is a catchall term for taking care of your mind, body, and spirit. **Wellness** means making healthy choices and achieving balance. It includes reducing stress in positive ways, keeping fit, maintaining good sexual health, and taking a sensible approach to alcohol and other drugs.

Managing Stress

In the fall of 2007, according to a survey conducted by the American College Health Association, about one third of college students reported that stress had negatively affected either an exam grade or a course grade.[1] When you are stressed, your body undergoes rapid physiological, behavioral, and emotional changes. Your rate of breathing can become more rapid and shallow. Your heart rate begins to speed up, and the muscles in your shoulders and forehead, at the back of your neck, and perhaps across your chest begin to tighten. Your hands might become cold or sweaty. You might experience gastrointestinal symptoms such as an upset stomach. Your mouth and lips might feel dry and hot, and you might notice that your hands and knees begin to shake or tremble. Your voice might quiver or even go up an octave.

A number of psychological changes also occur when you are under stress. You might experience changes in your ability to think, such as confusion, trouble concentrating, inability to remember things, and poor problem solving. Emotions such as fear, anxiety, depression, irritability, anger, or frustration are common, and you might have trouble getting to sleep at night or wake up too early and not be able to go back to sleep.

YOUR TURN ▶

How do you feel, both physically and mentally, when you are stressed? What specific changes do you notice in your behavior and feelings? How does stress affect your ability to concentrate, your breathing patterns, your patience, and so on?

Stress has many sources, but two seem to be prominent: life events and daily hassles. Life events are those that represent major adversity, such as the death of a parent, spouse, partner, or friend. Researchers believe that an accumulation of stress from life events, especially if many events occur over a short period of time, can cause physical and mental health problems. Daily hassles are the minor irritants that we experience every day, such as losing your keys, having three tests on the same day, quarreling with your roommate, or worrying about money.

The College Readjustment Rating Scale is a life events scale, adapted from Holmes and Rahe's Life Events Scale and modified for traditional-age college students. Complete the scale in the box on the next page. If you find that your score is 150 or higher, you have experienced a great deal of stress over the past year. You might consider what help you need or skills you must learn to be able to cope effectively.

On this scale, each event, such as one's first term in college, is assigned a value that represents the amount of readjustment a person has to make in life as a result of change. In some studies, people with serious illnesses have been found to have high scores on similar scales. People with scores of 300 and higher have a high health risk. People who score between 150 and 300 points have about a 50-50 chance of a serious health change within two years. People who score 150 and below have a one in three chance of a serious health change.

If your score is high enough to indicate potential health problems, it would benefit you to pay special attention to the stress reduction and management techniques discussed in this chapter and to select and implement some strategies to reduce your stress.[2]

[1]http://www.acha-ncha.org/docs/ACHA-NCHA_Reference_Group_Report_Fall2007.pdf.
[2]Adapted with permission from T. H. Holmes and R. H. Rahe, "The Social Readjustment Scale," in Carol L. Otis and Roger Goldingay, *Campus Health Guide*. New York: CEEB, 1989.

WHAT IS YOUR STRESS SCORE?

To determine your stress score, circle the number of points corresponding to each event you have experienced in the past six months or are likely to experience in the next six months. Then add up the circled numbers.

Event	Points
Death of spouse	100
Pregnancy for unwed female	92
Death of parent	80
Male partner in unwed pregnancy	77
Divorce	73
Death of a close family member	70
Death of a close friend	65
Divorce between parents	63
Jail term	61
Major personal injury or illness	60
Flunked out of college	58
Marriage	55
Fired from job	50
Loss of financial support for college (scholarship)	48
Failing grade in important or required course	47
Sexual difficulties	45
Serious argument with significant other	40
Academic probation	39
Change in major	37
New love interest	36
Increased workload in college	31
Outstanding personal achievement	29
First term in college	28
Serious conflict with instructor	27
Lower grades than expected	25
Change in colleges (transfer)	24
Change in social activities	22
Change in sleeping habits	21
Change in eating habits	19
Minor violation of the law (for example, a traffic ticket)	15

My stress score is _____

The best starting point for handling stress is to be in good physical and mental shape. When your body and mind are healthy, it's like inoculating yourself against stress. This means you need to pay attention to your diet, exercise, sleep, and mental health.

DIET AND EXERCISE

There is a clear connection between what you eat and drink, your overall health and well-being, and stress. Eating a lot of junk food will add pounds to your body and reduce your energy level. And when you can't keep up with your work because you're sluggish or tired, you might experience more stress. One dietary substance that can be directly linked to higher stress levels is caffeine.

In moderate amounts (50 to 200 milligrams per day), caffeine increases alertness and reduces feelings of fatigue, but even at this low dosage it can make you perkier during part of the day and more tired later. Consumed in larger quantities, caffeine can cause nervousness, headaches, irritability, stomach irritation, and insomnia—all symptoms of stress. Many people who have heart conditions have been told to avoid caffeine, since it tends to speed up heart rates. How much caffeine do you consume? Total your caffeine on the basis of the figures in Table 16.1.

If the amount of caffeine is excessive (this will vary with individuals, so monitor such things as inability to sleep and when you are most alert

TABLE 16.1 ▶ Product Caffeine Content (milligrams per serving)

Coffee (5-oz. cup)
Regular: 65–115
Decaffeinated: 3
Tea (6-oz. cup)
Hot steeped: 36
Iced: 31
Soft drinks and energy drinks (12-oz. serving)
Coca-Cola: 46
Dr. Pepper: 61
Full Throttle (16 oz): 144
Jolt Cola: 72
Mountain Dew: 54
Pepsi-Cola: 36
Red Bull: 80
Water Joe (16.9 oz.): 115
Chocolate bar: 6–20
Caffeine gum (2 pieces): 115
Over-the-counter drugs
NoDoz (2 tablets): 200
Excedrin (2 tablets): 130
Midol (2 tablets): 65

and most tired), consider drinking water in place of caffeinated drinks, or choose decaf coffee or a caffeine-free soft drink.

Exercise is an excellent stress management technique, the best way to stay fit, and a critical element of any worthwhile weight loss program. While any kind of recreation benefits your body and spirit, aerobic exercise is the best for stress management as well as weight management. In aerobic exercise, you work until your pulse is in a "target zone" and keep it in this zone for at least thirty minutes. You can reach your target heart rate through a variety of exercises: walking, jogging, running, swimming, biking, or using a stair climber. What makes the exercise aerobic is the intensity of your activity. Choose activities that you enjoy so you will look forward to your exercise time. That way, it's more likely to become a regular part of your routine.

Besides doing wonders for your body, aerobic exercise keeps your mind healthy. When you do aerobic exercise, your body produces hormones called beta-endorphins. These natural narcotics cause feelings of contentment and happiness and help manage anxiety and depression. Your mood and general sense of competence improve with regular aerobic exercise. In fact, people who undertake aerobic exercise report more energy, less stress, better sleep, weight loss, and an improved self-image.

CALCULATING YOUR TARGET HEART RATE ZONE

1. Estimate your maximum heart rate:

   220−age = _____ (maximum heart rate)

2. Determine your lower-limit exercise heart rate by multiplying your maximum heart rate by 0.6.

   Max Heart Rate × 0.6 = _____

3. Determine your upper-limit exercise heart rate by multiplying your maximum heart rate by 0.9.

   Max Heart Rate × 0.9 = _____

4. Your Target Heart Rate Zone is the range between your lower and upper limits.

Source: *ACSM Fitness Book: A Proven Step-by-Step Program from the Experts*, 3rd edition. Indianapolis: American College of Sports Medicine, 2003.

Think about ways to combine activities and use your time efficiently. Maybe you could leave the car at home and jog to class. Try going to the gym with a friend and asking each other study questions as you work out on treadmills. Park at the far end of the lot, and walk to classes. Take the stairs whenever possible. Remember that exercise does not have to be a chore. Find something you enjoy doing, and make it part of your daily schedule. Many campuses have recreation departments that offer activities such as intramural sports, rock climbing, aerobics classes, and much more. The most important thing about exercise is that you stay active and make it part of your day-to-day life.

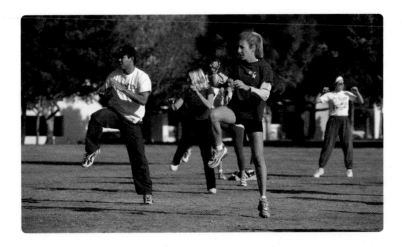

SLEEP

Getting adequate sleep is another way to protect yourself from stress. According to the National Sleep Foundation, 63 percent of American adults do not get the recommended eight hours of sleep per night. Lack of sleep can lead to anxiety, depression, and academic struggles. Researchers at Trent University in Ontario found that students who studied all week but then

Wired WINDOW

ARE YOU ADDICTED?

It's called "Internet addiction," and researchers have discovered that problems arising from Internet use have more to do with how people use the Internet than how much time they spend online. College students who use the Internet for communicating with others are less likely to be addicted than are those who use the Internet for shopping, reading news, and checking sports scores. It's a catch-22 because using the Internet has some psychological benefits. For instance, communicating via the Internet can help introverted students make friends more easily or feel more comfortable participating in class discussions (for example, by participating in course chats and realizing that it is okay to ask questions). The Internet can also help students improve their level of engagement with college friends, their studies, and campus life. However, students who use the Internet extensively tend to have less time for real-world social contacts.

Thinking Critically

How do you use the Internet? For the next week, keep a record of how much time you spend online and how much time you spend on each of the following activities: instant messaging, checking Facebook and MySpace, tweeting, sending e-mail, reading news, reading and commenting on blogs, doing research, shopping, checking sports scores, playing multiplayer games, and/or playing single-player games. How much time did you spend online? How did you spend most of your time online? If you found that you are online more for shopping, reading news, checking sports scores, and/or playing single-player games, do you have strong relationships with friends outside your online world? If you think you're spending far too much time online, you might want substitute other activities for some of your Internet time. If you can't seem to control the number of hours you spend on the Internet, it might be a good idea to talk to a counselor at your college to help you manage your Internet activities.

stayed up late partying on the weekends forgot as much as 30 percent of the material they had learned during the prior week. Try the following suggestions to establish better sleep habits:

- If you can't sleep, get up and do something boring.
- Get your clothes and school materials together before you go to bed.
- Avoid long daytime naps.
- Try reading or listening to a relaxation tape before going to bed.
- Get exercise during the day.
- Sleep in the same room and bed every night.
- Set a regular schedule for going to bed and getting up.

TAKING CONTROL

Modifying your lifestyle is yet another approach to stress management. You have the power to change your life so that it is less stressful. Teachers, supervisors, parents, friends, and even your children influence you, but ultimately, you control how you run your life. Lifestyle modification involves identifying the parts of your life that do not serve you well, making plans for change, and then carrying out the plans. For instance, if you are stressed because you are always late for classes, get up ten minutes earlier. If you get nervous before a test when you talk to a certain pessimistic classmate, avoid that person before a test. Learn test-taking skills so you can manage test anxiety better.

Relaxation techniques such as visualization and deep breathing can help you reduce stress. Learning these skills is just like learning any new skill. It takes knowledge and practice. Check your course catalog, college counseling center, health clinic, student newspaper, or fitness center for classes that teach relaxation. You'll find books as well as audiotapes and CDs that guide you through relaxation techniques.

OTHER WAYS TO RELIEVE STRESS

Your stress level plays a key role in your overall mental health. Here are several additional things you can do to improve your level of stress and your mental health:

- Reward yourself on a regular basis when you achieve small goals.
- Remember that there is a reason you are in a particular situation. Keep the payoff in mind.
- Laugh. A good laugh will almost always make you feel better.
- Get—or give—a hug.
- Pray or meditate.
- Do yoga.
- Practice a hobby.
- Get a massage.
- Practice deep breathing.

YOUR TURN ▶

Review the preceding list of ways to improve your stress level. Which of these ideas do you think makes the most sense for you? On the basis of your experience, which ideas would you suggest to other college students? Explain your choices.

Mental Health

According to the American Psychological Association, depression is one of the most common psychiatric disorders in the United States, affecting more than 15 million adults. College students are at especially high risk for depression as well as suicide.

DEPRESSION

The National Institutes of Health report that depression is diagnosed more often in women than in men. Depression is not a weakness; it is an illness that requires medical attention. You will find that many college students suffer from some form of depression. The feelings are often temporary and may be situational. A romantic breakup, a disappointing grade, or an ongoing conflict with a friend or roommate can create feelings of despair. Although most depression goes away on its own, if you or a friend have any of the following symptoms for more than two weeks, it is important to talk to a health care provider:

- Feelings of helplessness and hopelessness
- Feeling useless, inadequate, bad, or guilty
- Self-hatred, constant questioning of one's thoughts and actions
- Loss of energy and motivation
- Weight loss or gain
- Difficulty going to sleep or excessive need for sleep
- Loss of interest in sex
- Difficulty concentrating for a significant length of time

SUICIDE

The Centers for Disease Control and Prevention (CDC) report that students ages 15 to 24 are more likely than any other age group to attempt suicide. Most people who commit suicide give a warning of their intentions. The following are common indicators of someone's intent to commit suicide:

- Recent loss and a seeming inability to let go of grief
- Change in personality—sadness, withdrawal, apathy
- Expressions of self-hatred
- Change in sleep patterns

- Change in eating habits
- A direct statement about committing suicide ("I might as well end it all.")
- A preoccupation with death

If you or someone you know threatens suicide or displays any of these signs, it's time to consult a mental health professional. Most campuses have counseling centers that offer one-on-one sessions as well as support groups for their students. Finally, remember that there is no shame attached to high levels of stress, depression, anxiety, or suicidal tendencies. Unavoidable life events or physiological imbalances can cause such feelings and behaviors. Proper counseling, medical attention, and, in some cases, prescription medication can help students cope with mental health issues.

YOUR TURN ▶

Why do you think that college students are at especially high risk for depression and suicide? Is there anything that colleges and universities can do to decrease this risk, or is this all up to the students themselves?

Nutrition and Weight Management

"You are what you eat" is more than a catchphrase; it's an important reminder of the vital role diet plays in our lives. You've probably read news stories about how there are more and more obese young people than ever before in our history. The CDC reports that the rates of obesity have more than doubled in the United States since 1990: In 1990 an estimated 11.6 percent of U.S. citizens were obese; in 2007 an estimated 25.6 percent were classified as obese. One expert, Dr. James Hill, Director of Human Nutrition at the University of Colorado, predicts, "If obesity is left unchecked, almost all Americans will be obese by 2050." Many people attribute this situation to the explosion of fast-food restaurants, which place flavor and low prices before health. A Tufts University researcher found that 60 percent of college students eat too much saturated fat, which increases the risk for heart disease. Also, most of us do not consume enough fiber and whole grains. As a result, we are more likely to have long-term health problems, such as diabetes, heart disease, and cancer.

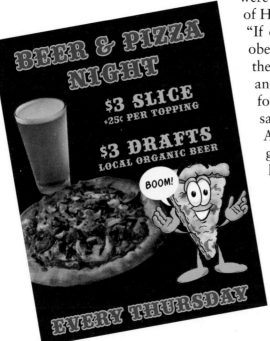

HEALTHY EATING

So what can you do about your eating habits? It's not easy at first, but if you commit to a new eating regimen, you will not only feel better, you'll be healthier and probably happier. Your campus might have a registered dietitian available to help you make healthy changes in your diet. Check with your student health center. Meanwhile, here are some suggestions:

- Restrict your intake of red meat, butter, white rice, white bread, and sweets. "White foods" are made with refined flour, which has few nutrients. Instead, go for fish, poultry, soy products, and whole wheat or multigrain breads. Remember that brown bread is not necessarily whole wheat. Check the label.

- Eat plenty of vegetables and fruits daily. These are important building blocks for a balanced diet, and they contain lots of fiber (to help fight off cancer and heart disease). Instead of fruit juices, which contain concentrated amounts of sugar, opt for the actual fruit. When you sit down to eat any meal (including breakfast), make sure you have at least one fruit or vegetable on your plate.

- Avoid fried foods—french fries, fried chicken, and so forth. Choose grilled or broiled meats instead. Avoid foods with large amounts of fat and sugar, such as doughnuts.

- Keep your room stocked with healthy snacks, such as fruit, vegetables, yogurt, pretzels, and graham crackers.

- Eat a sensible amount of nuts and all the legumes (beans) you want to round out your fiber intake.

- Watch your portion size. Avoid "super-sized" fast-food items and all-you-can-eat buffets.

- Eat breakfast! Your brain will function more efficiently if you eat a power-packed meal first thing in the morning. Eating breakfast can also jump-start your metabolism. If you are not normally a breakfast eater, try eating just a piece of fruit or half a bagel. You will notice a big difference in your energy level during your early morning classes. Avoid sugar-coated cereals. Go for healthier options that are loaded with fiber.

- Always read the government-required nutrition label on all packaged foods. Check the sodium content (sodium will make you retain fluids and increase your weight and possibly your blood pressure) and the number of grams of fat. Strive for a diet with only 20 percent fat.

Figure 16.1 shows the Healthy Eating Pyramid, designed by Walter Willett, Chairman of the Department of Nutrition at Harvard's School of Public Health. The Healthy Eating Pyramid puts exercise and weight control at the base, recommends eating whole-grain foods at most meals, and encourages eating vegetables "in abundance." This pyramid emphasizes eating lots of plant oils, such as olive, canola, and soy, and gives fish and poultry a higher profile than red meat, which you should eat sparingly.

YOUR TURN ▶

Look at the preceding list of suggestions about healthy eating. Which one of these is the most difficult for you? Which ones do you think are difficult for most college students? Do you think that college students are less likely to eat a healthy diet than the general population? Why or why not?

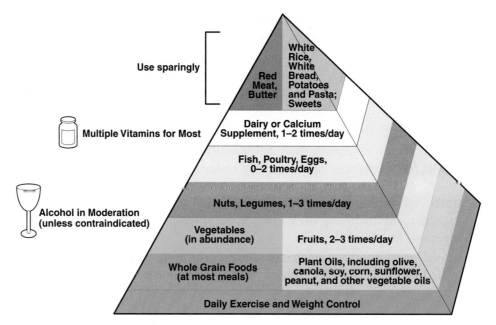

▲ FIGURE 16.1

Healthy Eating Pyramid

OBESITY

People have been joking about the "freshman 15" forever, but it's no joke that new college students tend to gain weight during their first term. Nutrition experts at Tufts University reported that the average weight gain is 6 pounds for men and about 4.5 pounds for women during the first year of college. Increased stress, lifestyle changes, new food choices, changes in physical activity, and alcohol consumption can all cause weight gain. Try eating smaller meals more often, getting regular exercise, keeping a food journal (to keep track of what you are actually consuming), and being realistic about dieting.

EATING DISORDERS

An increasing number of college students are obsessed with their bodies and food intake. This can lead to conditions such as anorexia, bulimia, or binge eating disorder, all of which affect women disproportionately more than men. Anorexia is characterized by self-induced starvation, extreme preoccupation with food, and a body weight less than 85 percent of a healthy weight. Bulimia is characterized by cycles of bingeing (eating large amounts of food) and purging by vomiting, abusing laxatives and/or diuretics, exercising excessively, and fasting. People with a binge eating disorder do not purge the calories after the binge. Individuals with binge eating disorder tend to eat secretively and are often clinically obese.

Some of the signs and symptoms of an eating disorder are as follows:

- Intense fear of gaining weight
- Restricting types of food, such as those containing any kind of fat
- Weighing less than 85 percent of recommended body weight based on height, or failure to make appropriate weight gain during a period of growth

- Stopping or never getting a monthly menstrual period
- Seeing one's body as fat, even though it is underweight
- Overexercising
- Secrecy about food and denial of a problem with eating

Anyone who is struggling with an eating disorder should seek medical attention. Eating disorders can be life-threatening if they are not treated by a health care professional. Many colleges and universities have eating disorder case management teams to help individuals on campus. Contact your student health center for more information, or contact the National Eating Disorder Association (http://www.nationaleatingdisorders.org or 1-800-931-2237) to find a professional in your area who specializes in treatment of eating disorders.

Sexual Health

Numerous studies report that about 75 percent of traditional-age college students have engaged in sexual intercourse at least once.

Whether or not you are part of this percentage, it can be helpful to explore your sexual values and to consider whether sex is right for you at this time. If it is the right time, you should choose a good birth control method and adopt some strategies for avoiding sexually transmitted infections (STIs) and unplanned pregnancies. What matters most is that you take care of yourself and your partner.

SEXUALLY TRANSMITTED INFECTIONS

The problem of STIs on college campuses has received growing attention in recent years as epidemic numbers of students have become infected. In general, STIs continue to increase faster than other illnesses on campuses today, and approximately 5 to 10 percent of visits by U.S. college students to college health services are for the diagnosis and treatment of STIs. The belief that it won't happen to you and you can't catch these sorts of infections is inaccurate and potentially more dangerous than ever before. If you choose to be sexually active, particularly with more than one partner but even if there is only one, exposure to an STI is a real possibility.

STIs are usually spread through genital contact. Sometimes, however, STIs can be transmitted through mouth-to-mouth or mouth-to-genital contact. There are more than twenty known types of STIs; Table 16.2 lists those that are most common on college campuses.

As you can see from the table, many of the STIs have similar symptoms or no symptoms at all. Many women show no symptoms and are therefore considered asymptomatic. Most health care professionals recommend that women who are sexually active be screened for all of the possible STIs during their yearly pap smear. These screenings are not part of the regular annual exam and must be specifically requested.

Not all STIs are curable. This means that medications will help alleviate the symptoms, but the virus will stay in an individual's system. Sexually transmitted infections that are left untreated can progress to pelvic inflammatory disease, which is now thought to be the leading cause of infertility in women.

TABLE 16.2 ▶ Sexually Transmitted Infections

SEXUALLY TRANSMITTED INFECTION	FEMALE SYMPTOMS	MALE SYMPTOMS	NUMBER OF NEW CASES IN THE UNITED STATES ANNUALLY	CURABLE OR TREATABLE
AIDS (Acquired immunodeficiency syndrome)	Symptoms appear several months to several years after contact with HIV; unexplained weight loss; white spots in mouth; yeast infections that do not go away	Symptoms appear several months to several years after contact with HIV; unexplained weight loss; white spots in mouth	40,000	Treatable
Chlamydia	Yellowish discharge; bleeding between periods; burning or pain during urination	Painful and frequent urination; watery, puslike discharge from penis	3 million	Curable
Genital HPV (Human Papillomavirus)	Small, bumpy warts on the sex organs and/or anus; burning or itching around sex organs	Small, bumpy warts on the sex organs and/or anus; burning or itching around sex organs	5.5 million	Treatable
Gonorrhea	Thick yellow or gray discharge; abnormal periods or bleeding between periods; cramps or pain in lower abdomen	White, milky discharge from penis; painful, burning urination; swollen or tender testicles	600,000	Curable
Hepatitis B	Symptoms appear 1-9 months after contraction; flulike feelings that go away; tiredness; dark urine	Symptoms appear 1-9 months after contraction; flulike feelings that go away; tiredness; dark urine	46,000	Treatable
Herpes	Burning sensation and redness at the site of infection; painful blister that will crust over, dry up, and disappear	Burning sensation and redness at the site of infection; painful blister that will crust over, dry up, and disappear	1 million	Treatable
Syphilis	Painless chancre; rash or white patches on skin; lymph nodes enlarge	Painless chancre; rash or white patches on skin; lymph nodes enlarge	36,000	Curable in early stages
Trichomoniasis	Yellowish, unpleasant-smelling discharge accompanied by a burning sensation during urination	Watery, white drip from the penis; burning or pain during urination; need to urinate more often	8 million	Curable

Adapted from http://www.plannedparenthood.org and www.ashastd.org and http://www.herpescounter.com.
Sources: Rebecca J. Donatelle and Larraine G. Davis, *Access To Health*, 8th ed. (San Francisco: Benjamin Cummings, 2004);
Linda L. Alexander, et al., *New Dimensions in Women's Health*, 3rd ed. (Sudbury, MA: Jones and Bartlett, 2004).

One particularly common STI is the human papillomavirus (HPV). In fact, the CDC estimates that currently 20 million people in the United States are infected with HPV. HPV is a sexually transmitted infection that is closely linked to cervical cancer. Gardasil, a vaccine that became available in 2006, provides protection against four types of HPV that cause 70 percent of cervical cancer cases. For more information about this vaccine or to receive the three injection series, contact your college or university health services or local health care provider.

NEGOTIATING FOR SAFER SEX

If you are sexually active, it's important that you talk with your partner about ways to protect against sexually transmitted infections and unwanted pregnancy.

Communicating with your partner about safer sex can be difficult and even embarrassing initially, but this communication can make your relationship stronger and more meaningful. The national organization Advocates for Youth offers these suggestions to help make this conversation easier and more effective:

- Use "I" statements when talking. For example, you might say, "I feel that abstinence is right for me at this time," or "I would feel more comfortable if we used a condom." Be assertive! Do not avoid talking about sex because you fear your partner's reaction.

- Be a good listener. Let your partner know that you hear, understand, and care about what he or she is saying and feeling.

- Be patient with your partner and remain firm in your decision that talking is important.

- Understand that success in talking does not mean getting your partner to agree to do something. It means that you both have said what you honestly think and feel and that you have both listened respectfully to one another.

- Avoid making assumptions. Ask open-ended questions to discuss relationship expectations, past and present sexual relationships, contraceptive use, and testing for STIs.

- Do not wait until you become sexually intimate to discuss safer sex with your partner. In the heat of the moment, you and your partner might be unable to talk effectively.

You can avoid STIs and unwanted pregnancies by avoiding sex entirely. Apparently, 25 percent of college students choose this option, according to national research. For many people, masturbation is a reasonable alternative to sex with a partner.

If you're in the remaining 75 percent, you'll be safer (in terms of STIs) if you have only one partner. Yet you might feel that you're at a point in your life when you would prefer to have multiple relationships simultaneously. Whether you're monogamous or not, you should always protect yourself by using a condom.

In addition to being a contraceptive, the condom can help prevent the spread of STIs, including HIV. The condom's effectiveness against disease holds true for anal, vaginal, and oral intercourse. The most current research indicates that the rate of protection provided by condoms against STIs is similar to its rate of protection against pregnancy (90 to 99 percent) when used correctly and consistently for each and every act of intercourse or oral sex. Note that only latex rubber condoms and polyurethane condoms—not lambskin or other types of "natural membrane" condoms—provide this protection. The polyurethane condom is a great alternative for individuals who have allergies to latex. Use only a water-based lubricant (such as K-Y Jelly) to keep the condom from breaking.

BIRTH CONTROL

Sexually active heterosexual students have to take steps to prevent unwanted pregnancy. Planning is the key. What is the best method of contraception? It is any method that you use correctly and consistently each time you have intercourse. Table 16.3 compares the major features of some of the most common methods of birth control. You should be aware that the actual cost of some of these methods will vary depending on where you live and the kind of medical insurance you have. The costs listed in Table 16.3 will give you a general idea of how the costs of the various methods compare.

TABLE 16.3 ▶ Methods of Contraception

METHOD	HOW EFFECTIVE IS THIS METHOD?	DOES IT PROTECT AGAINST HIV AND STIS?	AVERAGE COST	DO I NEED A PRESCRIPTION?
Abstinence	100%	Yes	Free	No
Cervical Cap	84%	No	$60-75	Yes
Contraceptive Injection	99%	No	$20-40 (visit to clinician); $35-75 (injection)	Yes
Diaphragm	94%	No	$15-75	Yes
Female Condom	95%	Yes	$4.00 per condom	No
Intrauterine Device (IUD)	99%	No	$175-500 (exam, insertion, and follow-up visit)	Yes
Male Condom	97%	Yes	$1.00; sometimes available for free	No
NuvaRing	99%	No	$15-50 monthly	Yes
Ortho Evra (The Patch)	99%	No	$15-50 monthly	Yes
Oral Contraceptive (The Pill)	99%	No	$15-50 monthly	Yes
Spermicide	94%	No	$8 per package	No
Tubal Ligation (Female Sterilization)	99%	No	$1,500-6,000	Yes
Vasectomy (Male Sterilization)	99%	No	$350-1,000	Yes

Adapted from http:// www.plannedparenthood.org.
Source: Rebecca J. Donatelle and Larraine G. Davis, *Access To Health*, 8th ed. (San Francisco: Benjamin Cummings, 2004).

Always discuss birth control with your partner so that you both feel comfortable with the option you have selected. For more information about a particular method, consult a pharmacist, your student health center, a local family planning clinic, the local health department, or your private physician. The important thing is to resolve to protect yourself and your partner each and every time you have sexual intercourse.

What if the condom breaks or you forget to take your birth control pill? Emergency contraception pills can reduce the risk of pregnancy. According to Planned Parenthood Federation of America, if the pills are taken within 72 hours of unprotected intercourse, they can reduce the risk of pregnancy by 75 to 89 percent. Most campus health centers and local health clinics are now dispensing emergency contraception to individuals in need. Emergency contraception does come with side effects, such as nausea, vomiting, and cramping. In rare cases, serious health complications can result from emergency contraception. Be sure you ask your provider what symptoms to watch for.

Substance Abuse

In this section our purpose is not to make judgments, but to warn you about irresponsible use of some substances that can have a major negative impact on your college experience and your life: alcohol, tobacco, prescription drugs, and illegal drugs. While you're in college, you will likely be exposed to the reckless use of one or more of these substances. We hope that this information will help you think twice and avoid the trouble that can come from substance abuse.

MAKING DECISIONS ABOUT ALCOHOL

Even if you don't drink, you should read this information because 50 percent of college students reported helping a drunken friend, classmate, or study partner in the past year.

A number of surveys have confirmed that your peers aren't drinking as much as you think they are, so there's no need for you to try to "catch up." Most students' estimates of how much the average college student drinks are twice as high as the actual statistics. In the final analysis, it's your decision to drink or not to drink alcoholic beverages, to drink moderately or to drink heavily, to know when to stop or to be labeled as a drunk who isn't fun to be around. Between 10 and 20 percent of people in the United States become addicted to alcohol at some point in their lives. Alcohol can turn even people who don't drink into victims, such as people who are killed by drunk drivers or family members who suffer from the behavior of an alcoholic. Over the course of one year, about 20 to 30 percent of students report serious problems related to excessive alcohol use. You might have heard news reports about college students who died or were seriously or permanently injured as a result of excessive drinking. Just one occasion of heavy or high-risk drinking can lead to problems.

How alcohol affects behavior depends on the dose of alcohol, which is best measured by blood alcohol content, or BAC (see Table 16.4). Most of the pleasurable effects of alcoholic beverages are experienced at lower BAC

TABLE 16.4 ▶ Effects of Blood Alcohol Content on Thinking, Feeling, and Behavior

BAC RANGE	EFFECTS ON BEHAVIOR AND MAJOR DANGERS
0.02–0.03	Few obvious effects; slight intensification of mood. In some states, a BAC of .02 is the legal level of intoxication for individuals under 21 years of age.
0.05–0.06	Feeling of warmth, relaxation, mild sedation; exaggeration of emotion and behavior; slight decrease in reaction time and in fine muscle coordination; impaired judgment about continued drinking.
0.07–0.09	More noticeable speech impairment and disturbance of balance; impaired motor coordination, hearing and vision; feeling of elation or depression; increased confidence; might not recognize impairment.
0.08	Legal definition of intoxication in all states for people 21 years of age and older.
0.11–0.12	Coordination and balance become difficult; distinct impairment of mental faculties and judgment.
0.14–0.15	Major impairment of mental and physical control; slurred speech, blurred vision and lack of motor skills; needs medical evaluation.
0.20	Loss of motor control; must have assistance moving about; mental confusion; needs medical assistance.
0.30	Severe intoxication; minimum conscious control of mind and body; needs hospitalization.
0.30–0.60	This level of alcohol has been measured in people who have died of alcohol intoxication.
0.40	Unconsciousness; coma; needs hospitalization.

Adapted from Brown University Health Education website: http://www.brown.edu/Student_Services/Health_Services/Health_Education/atod/alc_aayb.htm.

levels, when alcohol acts as a behavioral stimulant. For most people, the stimulant level is around one drink per hour. Usually, problems begin to emerge at doses higher than .05, when alcohol acts as a sedative and begins to slow down areas of the brain. Most people who have more than four or five drinks on one occasion feel "buzzed," show signs of impairment, and are likely to be higher risks for alcohol-related problems. However, significant impairment at lower doses can occur.

How fast you drink makes a difference, too. Your body gets rid of alcohol at a rate of about one drink an hour. Drinking more than one drink an hour might cause a rise in BAC because the body is absorbing alcohol faster than it can eliminate it.

Professionals can estimate BAC from your behavior. When someone is stopped for suspicion of drunk driving, police might videotape the person completing a series of tasks such as walking on a line and tipping his or her head back or touching the nose with the eyes closed. The degree of impairment shown in these tests can be presented as evidence in court.

At BAC levels of .025 to .05 a drinker tends to feel animated and energized. At a BAC level of around .05 a drinker can feel rowdy or boisterous. This is where most people report feeling a buzz from alcohol. At a BAC level between .05 and .08, alcohol starts to act as a depressant. So as soon as you feel that buzz, remember that you are on the brink of losing coordination, clear thinking, and judgment. Driving is measurably impaired at BAC levels lower than the legal limit of .08. In fact, an accurate safe level for most people might be half the legal limit (.04). As BAC levels climb past .08, you will become progressively less coordinated and less able to make good decisions. Most people become severely uncoordinated with BAC levels higher than .08 and might begin falling asleep, falling down, or slurring their speech.

Most people pass out or fall asleep when the BAC is above .25. Unfortunately, even after you pass out and stop drinking, your BAC can continue to rise as alcohol in your stomach is released to the intestine and absorbed into the bloodstream. Your body might try to get rid of alcohol by vomiting, but you can choke if you are unconscious, semiconscious, or severely uncoordinated.

Worse yet, at BAC levels higher than .30, most people will show signs of severe alcohol poisoning, such as an inability to wake up, slowed breathing, a fast but weak pulse, cool or damp skin, and pale or bluish skin. People exhibiting these symptoms need medical assistance immediately. If you ever find someone in such a state, remember to keep the person on his or her side with the head lower than the rest of the body. Check to see that the airway is clear, especially if the person is vomiting or if the tongue is blocking the back of the throat.

There are many home remedies (such as coffee, water, or cold showers) for helping to sober someone up, but none has been proven to work. Time is the only remedy because your liver can metabolize only one ounce of alcohol per hour. Harvard University has developed the following guidelines for helping an intoxicated friend:

- Never leave a drunk person alone.
- Keep the person from driving, biking, or going anywhere alone.
- If your friend wants to lie down, turn the person onto his or her side to prevent the inhalation of vomit.
- Don't give the person any drugs or medications to try to sober him or her up.
- You can't prevent the alcohol from being absorbed once it has been consumed, so giving a drunken person food will not prevent or reduce intoxication but can increase the risk of vomiting.
- Do not assume that a drunk person is just "sleeping it off" if he or she cannot be awakened. This person needs urgent care.

We know that many students have been subjected to what they might regard as exaggerated scare tactics by well-intentioned educators. However, there are many compelling warning indicators related to heavy drinking. Think about the following statistics and their possible application to you and your friends. The effects of heavy drinking are nothing less than a tragedy for many college students:

- 1,700 college students between the ages of 18 and 24 die each year from alcohol-related unintentional injuries, including motor vehicle crashes.

- 599,000 students between the ages of 18 and 24 are unintentionally injured each year while under the influence of alcohol.
- More than 696,000 students between the ages of 18 and 24 are assaulted each year by another student who has been drinking.[3]

Heavy, or binge, drinking is commonly defined as five or more drinks for males and four or more drinks for females on a single occasion. Presumably, for a very large person who drinks slowly over a long period of time (several hours), four or five drinks might not lead to a BAC associated with impairment. However, research suggests that in many cases the BAC of heavy drinkers exceeds the legal limit for impairment (.08).

The academic, medical, and social consequences of heavy drinking can seriously endanger a person's quality of life. Research based on surveys conducted by the Core Institute at Southern Illinois University (http://www.siuc .edu/~coreinst) provides substantial evidence that heavy drinkers have a significantly greater risk of adverse outcomes. Among other problems, the Core data identify heavy drinking with increased risk of poor test performance, missed classes, unlawful behavior, violence, memory loss, drunk driving, regretful behavior, and vandalism, compared with all drinkers and all students. At the same time, college health centers nationwide are reporting increasing occurrences of serious medical conditions—even death—resulting from excessive alcohol use:

- Alcohol poisoning causing coma and shock
- Respiratory depression, choking, and respiratory arrest
- Head trauma and brain injury
- Lacerations
- Fractures
- Unwanted or unsafe sexual activity causing STIs and pregnancies
- Bleeding intestines
- Anxiety attacks and other psychological crises
- Worsening of underlying psychiatric conditions such as depression or anxiety

If you engage in heavy drinking for so long that your body can tolerate large amounts of alcohol, you might become an alcoholic. According to the medical definition, someone is alcohol-dependent or alcoholic if he or she exhibits three of the following symptoms:

1. A significant tolerance for alcohol
2. Withdrawal symptoms such as "the shakes"
3. Overuse of alcohol
4. Unsuccessful attempts to control or cut down on use
5. Preoccupation with drinking or becoming anxious when you do not have a drink
6. Making new friends who drink and staying away from friends who do not drink or who do not drink to get drunk
7. Continued heavy drinking despite experiencing alcohol-related social, academic, legal, financial, or health problems

[3]R. Hingson et al., "Magnitude of Alcohol-Related Mortality and Morbidity among U.S. College Students Ages 18–24: Changes from 1998–2001." *Annual Review of Public Health,* 26 (2005): 259–79.

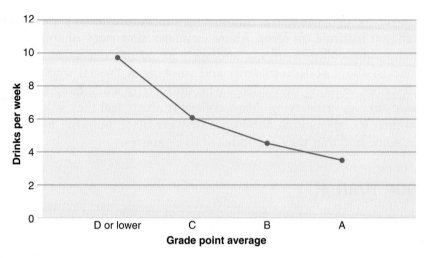

▲ FIGURE 16.2

Negative Correlation between Drinks per Week and Grade Point Average

Source: Adapted with permission from C. A. Presley, P. W. Meilman, J. R. Cashin, and R. Lyeria, *Alcohol and Drugs on American College Campuses: Use, Consequences, and Perceptions of the Campus Environment,* Volume IV: 1992-94 (Carbondale: The Core Institute, Southern Illinois University).

Through its College Alcohol Study (CAS), the Harvard School of Public Health has found that consuming alcohol at binge levels has a negative effect on academic performance, social relationships, decision making, and health. Binge drinking is also associated with risky sexual behavior such as having unplanned or unprotected sex as well as antisocial behavior such as vandalism and getting in trouble with the police.

The College Alcohol Study also finds that a student's alcohol use affects others in the immediate environment. Roommates and neighbors complain of the following:

- Disruption of sleep or study
- Property damage
- Verbal, physical, or sexual violence
- Visits from the police[4]

Since the early 1990s, surveys conducted by the Southern Illinois University Core Institute have found a consistent negative correlation between grades and the number of drinks per week—and not just for heavy drinkers. Findings are similar for two-year and four-year institutions (see Figure 16.2).

TOBACCO—THE OTHER LEGAL DRUG

Tobacco use is clearly the cause of many serious medical conditions, including heart disease, some forms of cancer, and lung ailments. Over the years, tobacco has led to the deaths of hundreds of thousands of individuals.

[4]H. Wechsler and T.F. Nelson, "What We Have Learned from the Harvard School of Public Health College Alcohol Study: Focusing Attention on College Student Alcohol Consumption and the Environmental Conditions that Promote It." *Journal of Studies on Alcohol and Drugs,* July 2008: 481–90.

The University of Michigan's Monitoring the Future Survey published by the National Institute on Drug Abuse estimates that rates of smoking have declined among college students and were at 20 percent as of 2007.[5] But one concern about college students and smoking is "social smoking." This term describes smoking by students who do so only when hanging out with friends, drinking, or partying. Most college students feel they will be able to give up their social smoking habit once they graduate, but after four years of college, some find that they are addicted to cigarettes.

> **YOUR TURN** ▶
>
> In your opinion, given the cost and the dangers of smoking, what are the reasons that some college students continue to smoke?

Although a small percentage of college students use smokeless tobacco, one "dip" delivers the same amount of nicotine as three to four cigarettes. Smokeless tobacco contains twenty-eight known cancer-causing substances and is associated with the same level of health risk as cigarette smoking.

Although smoking is more prevalent among men than among women, according to the American Lung Association,[6] the differences are narrowing, and the rates of smoking-related cancers in women are rapidly approaching or surpassing rates in men. One explanation as to why women smoke is the enormous amount of pressure on young women to stay thin. While there is some evidence that smoking increases metabolism and suppresses the appetite, the problem of being two or three pounds heavier cannot begin to compare to the dangers of smoking. It has been noted that on the average, female smokers have their first heart attack nineteen years before nonsmoking females do.

Chemicals in tobacco are highly addictive, making it hard to quit. Although young people might not worry about long-term side effects, increased numbers of respiratory infections, worsening of asthma, bad breath, stained teeth, and the huge expense should be motivations not to start smoking at all. Smoking and the use of hormonal birth control can be a deadly combination. A study conducted at Boston University School of Medicine showed that women who smoke and use hormonal birth control are nearly ten times more likely to have a heart attack than are women who don't smoke and don't use hormonal methods of birth control. A final reason for smokers to quit is the cost (see Table 16.5).

Many institutions and local hospitals offer smoking cessation programs to help individuals who are addicted to nicotine to quit smoking. Contact your campus health center for more information about taking this step toward quitting.

[5]L.D. Johnston, P.M. O'Malley, J.G. Bachman, and J.E. Schulenberg, *Monitoring the Future: National Survey Results on Drug Use, 1975–2007.* Volume II: *College Students and Adults Ages 19–45* (NIH Publication No. 08-6418B). Bethesda, MD: National Institute on Drug Abuse, 2008.
[6]American Lung Association, *Quit Smoking: Smoking and Women Fact Sheet.* http://www.lungusa.org/site/c.dvLUK9O0E/b.33572.

TABLE 16.5 ▶ The Approximate Cost of Smoking across the United States

Half-Pack-a-Day Smoker

$6.25/pack × 3.5 packs/week = $21.88/week
$21.88/week × 52 weeks/year = $1,137.76/year
$1,137.76/year × 4 years of college = $4,551.04
In 25 years you will have spent $28,444.00.

Pack-a-Day Smoker

$6.25/pack × 7 packs/week = $43.75
$43.75/week × 52 weeks/year = $2,275.00
$2,275.00/year × 4 years of college = $9,100.00
In 25 years you will have spent $56,875.00.

PRESCRIPTION DRUG ABUSE AND ADDICTION

Researchers at the University of Michigan reported in 2008 that 11.2 percent of college students have used prescription stimulants for nonmedical purposes at some point and 6.9 percent have used them in the past year. Three classes of prescription drugs are the most commonly abused: opioids, central nervous system depressants, and stimulants. Some individuals might engage in "doctor shopping" to get multiple prescriptions for the drugs they abuse.

Opioids include morphine, codeine, and such branded drugs as OxyContin, Darvon, Vicodin, Demerol, and Dilaudid. Opioids work by blocking the transmission of pain messages to the brain. Chronic use can result in addiction. Taking a large single dose of an opioid can cause a severe reduction in your breathing rate that can lead to death.

Taken under a doctor's care, central nervous system depressants, such as Valium, Librium, Xanax, and Halcion, can be useful in the treatment of anxiety and sleep disorders. The flip side is that exceeding the recommended dosage can create a drug tolerance, and the user will need larger doses to achieve the same result. If the user stops taking the drug, the brain's activity can rebound and race out of control, possibly leading to seizures and other harmful consequences.

Stimulants, such as ephedrine, Ritalin, and Dexadrine, enhance brain activity, causing an increase in alertness, attention, and energy accompanied by elevated blood pressure and increased heart rate. Legal use of stimulants to treat obesity, asthma, and other problems has dropped off as their potential for abuse and addiction has become apparent.[7]

Ritalin is prescribed for a condition called ADHD (attention deficit/hyperactivity disorder) but is gaining recognition on college campuses as a "cramming drug." This prescription drug costs only about 50¢ per tablet but sells on the street for as much as $15. College students are using Ritalin to stay awake for long periods of time to study for exams. Many students think

[7]Adapted from *Prescription Drugs: Abuse and Addiction*. Bethesda, MD: National Institute on Drug Abuse, part of the National Institutes of Health, a division of the U.S. Department of Health and Human Services, 2009.

that since it is a prescribed drug, it must be harmless. The U.S. Department of Education's Higher Education Center for Alcohol and Other Drug Abuse and Violence Prevention lists the following as possible adverse effects from abusing Ritalin: nervousness, vomiting, changes in heart rate and blood pressure, dependency, fevers, convulsions, headaches, paranoia, hallucinations, and delusions.

Another class of drugs that is of concern in the college setting is anabolic steroids. When most people think of steroids, they think about collegiate and professional athletes. But it is important for all college students to know and understand the dangers of these synthetic substances. According to the National Institute on Drug Abuse, steroids are taken orally or injected into the body in cycles that last weeks or months. Steroid abuse has many major side effects, including liver tumors, cancer, jaundice, fluid retention, high blood pressure, kidney tumors, and severe acne. Most anabolic steroid users are male and therefore have gender-specific side effects, including shrinking of the testicles, reduced sperm count, infertility, baldness, development of breasts, and increased risk for prostate cancer. Abusers also put themselves at risk for contracting HIV or other blood-borne viruses from using or sharing infected needles.

The abuse rate for steroids is fairly low among the general population. The 2007 Monitoring the Future Survey found that 1.9 percent of young adults ages 19 to 28 reported using steroids at least once during their lifetimes. Just over half a percent (0.6 percent) reported using steroids at least once in the past year, and 0.3 percent reported using steroids in the past month.[8]

Drugs that can be purchased without a prescription are generally safe when taken according to directions on the bottle or package. But never take more than the recommended dose without consulting your physician.

Drugstores and health food stores also carry many supplements in pill or liquid form that are labeled "natural." This label does not mean that the product has been tested, is safe, or is worth your money. The Food and Drug Administration (FDA) does not regulate supplements as they do food or other medication, so it is very important to do thorough research and to consult your physician before starting any over-the-counter regimen.

ILLEGAL DRUGS

Illegal recreational drugs, such as marijuana, cocaine, methamphetamine, MDMA (ecstasy), and heroin, are used by a much smaller number of college students and far less frequently than alcohol. Yet these drugs are significant public health issues for college students. The penalties associated with the possession or use of illegal drugs tend to be much more severe than those associated with underage alcohol use.

Athletic departments, potential employers, and government agencies do routine screenings for many of these illegal drugs. Future employability, athletic scholarships, and insurability could be compromised if you have a

[8] L.D. Johnston, P.M. O'Malley, J.G. Bachman, and J.E. Schulenberg, *Monitoring the Future: National Survey Results on Drug Use, 1975–2007.* Volume II: *College Students and Adults Ages 19–45* (NIH Publication No. 08-6418B). Bethesda, MD: National Institute on Drug Abuse, 2008.

positive drug test for any of these substances. A brief summary of five of the most prevalent drugs follows.

Marijuana. The effects of marijuana can linger for three to seven days, depending on the smoker and the potency of the drug. Chronic use of marijuana can lead to a lethargic state in which users might tend to forget about current responsibilities (such as going to class). Long-term use carries the same risks of lung infections and cancer that are associated with smoking tobacco.

Ecstasy. MDMA, commonly known as ecstasy, is a synthetic (human-made) drug, in contrast to drugs that are derived from plants, such as marijuana and heroin. Many young people believe that MDMA is safe and offers nothing but a pleasant high for the $25 cost of a single tablet ("How bad can it be if it's that cheap?" is one rationalization); however, the reality is far different. Taken orally, the effects of MDMA last approximately four to six hours. Many people will take a second dose when the initial dose begins to fade. Some tablets contain drugs in addition to MDMA, including amphetamine, caffeine, dextromethorphan, ephedrine, and cocaine. MDMA significantly depletes serotonin, a substance in the brain that helps regulate mood, sleep, pain, emotion, and appetite as well as other behaviors. It takes the brain time to rebuild the serotonin needed to perform important physiological and psychological functions. Of great concern is MDMA's adverse effects on the pumping efficiency of the heart. Heavy users can experience obsessive traits, anxiety, paranoia, and sleep disturbance. One study indicates that MDMA can have long-lasting effects on memory.[9]

Heroin. Numerous reports have suggested a rise in heroin use among college students. A highly addictive drug with the potential to be more damaging and fatal than other opioids, heroin is the most abused and most rapidly acting of this group. One of the most significant—and surest—effects of heroin use is addiction. The human body begins to develop tolerance to the drug on first use. Once tolerance is built up, the abuser must use more of the drug to achieve the same intensity. Within a short time, users must take the drug more and more often to alleviate the symptoms of addiction. Eventually, they don't get much of a high from the heroin but take the drug simply to avoid the discomfort of withdrawal. Heroin can be injected, smoked, or snorted. Injection is the most efficient way to administer low-purity heroin. However, the availability of high-purity heroin and the fear of infection by sharing needles have made snorting and smoking the drug more common. Some users believe that snorting or smoking heroin will not lead to addiction. They are 100 percent wrong.

Chronic users of intravenous drugs can develop collapsed veins, infection of the heart lining and valves, abscesses, and liver disease. Users are also at risk for pulmonary complications, including various types of pneumonia. In addition to the effects of the drug itself, users who inject heroin or share needles put themselves at risk of contracting HIV, hepatitis B and C, and other

---

[9]Excerpted from *Ecstasy: What We Know and Don't Know About MDMA: A Scientific Review*. Bethesda, MD: National Institute on Drug Abuse, part of the National Institutes of Health (NIH), a division of the U.S. Department of Health and Human Services, 2001.

blood-borne viruses. A heroin overdose is known to cause slow and shallow breathing, convulsions, coma, and possibly death.

Cocaine. Cocaine produces an intense experience that heightens senses. A cocaine high lasts only a short time; then the good feelings are gone. During the crash, the user might feel tired and unmotivated and find it impossible to sleep. Cocaine is highly addictive. In some instances, users have died of cardiac arrest while taking the drug. Some users are shocked into quitting when their nasal septum (the wall of cartilage separating the two nostrils) begins to develop holes caused by cocaine use.

Methamphetamine. Methamphetamine, often abbreviated to "meth," is particularly dangerous because it costs so little and is so easy to make. Much of it is produced in makeshift labs in homes or college residences, which means not only that the quality varies from batch to batch but also that it's virtually impossible to know what else is in the mixture.

The drug can initially produce euphoria, enhanced wakefulness, increased physical activity, and decreased appetite. Prolonged use can lead to binges, during which users take more meth every few hours for several days until they run out of the drug or become too disorganized to continue. Chronic abuse can lead to psychotic behavior, characterized by intense paranoia, visual and auditory hallucinations, and out-of-control rages that can be coupled with extremely violent behavior. Researchers have found that many former meth users have experienced long-term brain damage, and it is unknown whether the damage can ever be reversed.

Where to go
FOR HELP . . .

ON CAMPUS ▶

Counseling Center Professionals here will offer individual and group assistance and lots of information. Remember that their support is confidential, and you will not be judged.

Health center/infirmary: On most campuses the professionals who staff the health center are especially interested in educational outreach and practicing prevention. You should be able to receive treatment as well.

Health education and wellness programs: College campuses assume and recognize that for many students, problems and challenges with alcohol, other drugs, and sexual decision making and the consequences are part of the college universe. Student peer health educators who are trained and supervised by professionals can provide support. Taking part in such peer leadership is also a great way to develop and practice your own communication skills.

Campus support groups: Many campuses provide student support groups led by professionals for students dealing with problems related to excessive alcohol and drug use, abusive sexual relationships, and other issues.

ONLINE ▶

Advice about College Student Health Issues: http://www.goaskalice.com. This website, sponsored by Columbia University, has answers to many health questions.

Dealing with stress: http://www.stress.org. Want to combat stress? Find out how at the American Institute of Stress website.

Advice from the American Dietetic Association: http://www.eatright.org. This website provides information on healthy eating and nutrition.

How tobacco affects your health: http://www.cancer.org. To learn more about the health effects of tobacco, visit the American Cancer Society.

The Center for Young Women's Health: http://www.youngwomenshealth.org/collegehealth10.html. This website has helpful advice on sexual health as well as other issues.

National Clearinghouse for Alcohol and Drug Information: http://www.ncadi.samhsa.gov/. This organization provides up-to-date information about the effects of alcohol and drug use.

DrugHelp: http://www.drughelp.org. This is a private, nonprofit referral service for drug treatment.

Methamphetamine addiction: http://www.methamphetamineaddiction.com. Learn more about the dangers of methamphetamine at this website.

The Centers for Disease Control and Prevention: http://www.cdc.gov. This website is an excellent resource for all of the topics in this chapter.

If you have questions about suicide prevention, contact the National Suicide Prevention Lifeline at 1-800-273-TALK or on the organization's website http://www.suicidepreventionlifeline.org.

Here are some other valuable resources: National Eating Disorders Association: http://www.nationaleatingdisorders.org

U.S. Government's Nutrition Information: http://www.nutrition.gov

Shape Up America: http://www.shapeup.org

National Health Information Center: http://www.healthfinder.org

Planned Parenthood Federation of America: http://www.plannedparenthood.org

U.S. Food and Drug Administration: http//www.fda.gov

MY INSTITUTION'S RESOURCES ▶

_____

_____

_____

_____

_____

_____

_____

_____

_____

_____

_____

_____

_____

_____

One-Minute PAPER . . .

This chapter provides a lot of tips and strategies for staying mentally and physically healthy. What was the most surprising or unexpected point made in this chapter? What interesting questions remain unanswered about these topics?

Applying What You've LEARNED . . .

Now that you have read and discussed this chapter, consider how you can apply what you have learned to your academic and personal life. The following prompts will help you reflect on the chapter material and its relevance to you both now and in the future.

1. Identify one area in your life in which you need to make changes to become healthier. How do you think becoming healthier will improve your performance in college? What are the challenges you face in becoming healthier?

2. If you could make only three recommendations to an incoming first-year college student about managing stress in college, what would they be? Use your personal experience and what you have learned in this chapter to make your recommendations.

Building Your PORTFOLIO . . .

66 Imagine if every Thursday your shoes exploded if you tied them the usual way. This happens to us all the time with computers, and nobody thinks of complaining. 99

–JEF RASKIN (1943–2005),
American human-computer interface expert

ARE YOU "TECHNOSTRESSED"?

Ever-changing, ever-improving technology is a wonderful part of our modern world, but it can also be an additional stressor in our everyday lives. It seems the list of hot, new gadgets grows longer every day. How does being constantly accessible, being a multitasking marvel, having constant reminders of what you haven't done yet, and sorting an overload of information affect your stress level? Do you occasionally find yourself overwhelmed or even a bit lonely when you are face to face with your computer instead of your friends, families, or coworkers? The hurried, plugged-in life can be exhausting and nerve-racking, especially if you get an incomprehensible error message on your computer screen the night before a big paper is due!

How are you "plugged in"? Create a Word document in your portfolio and re-create the following table.

1. Describe all the ways in which your life is affected by technology. How are your health and well-being affected, both positively and negatively, by the things you list? *Tip: Think of how you use technology for entertainment and for class or work.*

My Gadgets & Gizmos	Positive Aspects	Negative Aspects
Instant Messenger	Ability to communicate anywhere in the world, in a matter of seconds, 24/7	Staying up late, talking to my friends = No sleep!

Sometimes it seems as if all of the technology that is supposed to make our lives easier actually adds to the balancing act. Here are a few tips for reducing your stress level and avoiding a "technology takeover":

- Schedule some downtime offline for yourself.
- Don't become a text message junkie.
- Don't try to multitask 24/7! Take advantage of time to exercise, eat, or just take a break without the demands of e-mail and cell phones.
- Recognize the warning signs of Internet addiction, for example:
    - Using the Internet to escape from problems or responsibilities
    - Missing class, work, or appointments to spend time online
    - Always allowing the Internet to substitute for face-to-face interaction with others

2. Save your reflections in your portfolio on your personal computer or flash drive. The next time you're feeling stressed out, revisit this activity and evaluate the role technology is playing in your life.

EPILOGUE

It Ain't Over 'Til It's Over

The great baseball player Yogi Berra is often quoted as having said, "It ain't over 'til it's over!" So here you are at the end of the course. This course is over—or is it? One thing is for sure: College isn't over for you and what you learned in this course isn't over. But finishing this course has to feel good. Because there has been so much research done on students like you, we can confidently tell you that successful completion of this course is a good predictor for overall success in college.

When you finish any of your courses in college, it is a good time to reflect, step back, and ask yourself some thoughtful questions like:

- What did I learn in this course?
- Can I apply what I learned to other courses?
- Will I use what I learned both in and out of class?
- What did I learn that I am most likely to remember?
- Do I want to stay in touch with this professor?
- Did I improve my basic skills?
- How do I feel about what I accomplished?
- Did I do better than I thought I would?
- What did I do that helped me progress, and how can I repeat those kinds of successful efforts in other courses?
- What challenges do I still face?

Whether you are finishing this course at the end of your first term in college or at the end of your first year in college, there are many success strategies that you learned in this course that will continue to help you as you move through the rest of your college experience.

SOME PARTING SUGGESTIONS

Keep in Touch with Professors We suggest that you consider keeping in touch with the professor of this course. Educators who volunteer to teach a college success course or first-year seminar really do care about students and enjoy staying in touch with them over time and noting their progress. You will also want to stay in touch with your other professors. Later in college you may need to ask them to write letters of reference for you as you seek employment or admission to graduate school. When a professor becomes part of your larger support group, this is a form of networking.

Using Campus Resources You should also keep using the campus's services and resources that you learned about in this course such as the learning center or career center. Remember, these services are most heavily utilized by the best students, and you want to be one of those. Those students continue to seek help. It's a lifelong behavioral pattern of successful people.

Practice Study Strategies in All Your Courses It's important for you to keep on practicing the success strategies that were presented in this book. Usually, you don't learn these in just one term. And, if you don't keep practicing them, you get rusty. Using these strategies is like learning anything else in life such as riding a bike. Practice is absolutely essential. But we also realize that you may not yet have been ready to attempt some of the strategies we endorsed in this book. So maybe the next term, or the next year will be a better time to revisit some of these ideas. We also suggest that you hang on to all your books so you can revisit them. We know that students like to resell their books. And if you do resell them, you could get library copies at some point in the future. But your books could be valuable resources for you when you might need to revisit course topics. There may also be friends or family members who'll be coming to college. You could share these materials with them.

Planning Your Summer We would also like to suggest that you begin thinking about what you are going to do this summer. We realize that students may have learned in high school that summer school was usually for students who slacked off during the year. But in college, nothing could be further from the truth. We now know from national research on college students' progress, that continuous enrollment is a good thing; it keeps students in the swing of things, they don't fall out of practice, and they are more likely to keep on going and going—and graduate.

An alternative to summer school is to do something in the summer that is connected to your education—or sponsored by your college, like an internship, practicum, or study abroad. Continuing your learning in summer maintains your fast pace of uninterrupted development and doesn't allow you to backtrack and get out of practice. Also, students who take the initiative to attend summer school or who have held summer jobs or internships will often be more attractive to future employers.

Planning Your Remaining Time in College As you end this course, we suggest that you once again think seriously about your major. That decision is important because eventually you have to get a degree in something. And you want to feel confident and comfortable about your major. And, even more important, your chosen major is connected to that all-important idea that we stressed in the first chapter of this book: Purpose—that is your purpose for being in this college at this time in your life. One of the ways that United States colleges are different from higher education institutions in the rest of the world is the opportunity to change majors. So this is something we encourage you to revisit now. This course may have given you some new insights into yourself and what might really motivate you now and in the future.

Now is also a good time to ask yourself about your academic advisor. Are you getting what you need from this important relationship? If not, don't hesitate to request a change.

It's possible that you haven't used the career center yet, even though you learned about it in this course. Now, as this course is coming to a close would be a great time to pay a visit to the career center to learn about possible internships, summer employment, and additional help if you haven't decided on a major.

Ending a course like this is a good time to take stock of your accomplishments this term. By all means, you should pat yourself on the back. But you also may want to take a hard look at those things that didn't go so well. Learn from your mistakes and apply what you learn to future successes.

Let's circle back to that concept of purpose. Here at the end of the term, how is the *fit* between you and this college, between you and your major? Is this campus meeting your expectations and your needs? Are you getting a clearer idea of why you are here as opposed to why some other people in your life may want you to be here? Even if you're still unsure, we hope you'll give yourself more time to get adjusted to this college thing, to get more comfortable, to find a sense of *fit*, and to accomplish some things for yourself that you can be really proud of.

We wrote this book to help students like you. Much of what we know about what students need in order to be successful, we learned from our students. Thanks for giving us the chance to help you as you began *Your College Experience*. You've already come a long way from where you started, and there are many great college experiences ahead. So practice the strategies we tried to teach you in this book and remember, if millions of students before you have made it, you can too.

Sincerely,

John N. Gardner
A. Jerome Jewler
Betsy O. Barefoot

GLOSSARY

Abstract A paragraph-length summary of the methods and major findings of an article in a scholarly journal.

Abstract conceptualization A learner's ability to integrate observations into logically sound theories; one of the four stages of the Kolb Inventory of Learning Styles.

Academic freedom The virtually unlimited freedom of speech and inquiry granted to professors to further the advancement of knowledge, as long as human lives, rights, and privacy are not violated.

Accommodators Individuals who prefer hands-on learning. They are skilled at making things happen and rely on their intuition, and might use trial and error, rather than logic, to solve problems. Accommodators often major in business. One of the learner groups of the Kolb Inventory of Learning Styles.

Active experimentation A learner's ability to make decisions, solve problems, and test what he or she has learned in new situations; one of the four stages of the Kolb Inventory of Learning Styles.

Active learning Learning by participation, such as listening critically, discussing what you are learning, and writing about it.

Adaptability The ability to adjust your thinking and behavior when faced with new or unexpected situations.

Annotate Add critical or explanatory margin notes on the page as you read.

Argument Reason and evidence brought together in logical support of a claim.

Assimilators Individuals who like to develop theories and think about abstract concepts. Assimilators often major in math, physics, or chemistry. One of the learner groups of the Kolb Inventory of Learning Styles.

Attention deficit hyperactivity disorder (ADHD) A disorder characterized by difficulty organizing tasks, completing work, and listening to and following directions.

Aural learner A person who prefers to learn by listening to information. One of the preferences described by the VARK Learning Styles Inventory.

Autonomy Self-direction or independence. College students usually have more autonomy than they did in high school.

Behavioral interview An interview in which the interviewer questions the candidate about past experiences and how it helped the candidate learn and grow. This type of interview helps assess your skills and behaviors.

Bias A leaning toward a particular point of view. Also, a negative preconceived opinion of certain peoples or value systems that can manifest either in attitude or in acts of discrimination.

Biorhythms The internal mechanisms that drive our daily patterns of physical, emotional, and mental activity.

Boolean operators The words "AND," "OR," and "NOT." They are added to specific terms when searching in databases and search engines to help yield more relevant matches.

Budget A spending plan that tracks all sources of income and expenses during a specific period of time.

Chunking A previewing method that involves making a list of terms and definitions from the reading, then dividing the terms into smaller clusters of five, seven, or nine, to more effectively learn the material.

Citation A source or author of certain material. When browsing the Internet for sources, use only material that has citations crediting the author, where it came from, and who posted it.

Co-curricular experiences Learning that occurs outside of the classroom, through on-campus clubs and groups, co-op programs, internships, or other means.

Co-op programs Programs offered at many institutions that allow students the opportunity to work in their field of study while enrolled in college. Co-op programs offer valuable experience and an excellent preview of what work in the chosen field is actually like. Also called cooperative education.

Cognitive restructuring A technique of applying positive thinking and giving oneself encouraging messages rather than self-defeating negative ones.

Concrete experience Abilities that allow learners to be receptive to others and open to their feelings and specific experiences; one of the four stages of the Kolb Inventory of Learning Styles.

Content skills Cognitive, intellectual, or "hard" skills, acquired as one gains mastery in an academic field. These include writing proficiency, computer literacy, and foreign language skills.

Convergers People who enjoy the world of ideas and theories, and are good at thinking about how to apply those theories to real-world, practical situations. Convergers tend to choose health-related and engineering majors. One of the learner groups of the Kolb Inventory of Learning Styles.

Cornell format A method for organizing notes in which one side of the notebook page is designated for note-taking during class, and the other as a "recall" column where main ideas and important details for tests are jotted down as soon after class as is feasible.

Credit score A numerical representation of your level of fiscal responsibility, derived from a credit report that contains information about all accounts in your name. This score can determine your loan qualification, interest rates, insurance rates, and sometimes employability.

Critical thinking Thoughtful consideration of the information, ideas, observations, and arguments that you encounter; in essence, a search for truth.

Culture The aspects of a group of people that are passed on and/or learned. Traditions, food, language, clothing styles, artistic expression, and beliefs are all part of culture.

Deep learning Understanding the "why" and "how" behind the details.

Discipline An area of academic study, such as sociology, anthropology, and engineering.

Discrimination The act of treating people differently because of their race, ethnicity, gender, socioeconomic class, or other identifying characteristics, rather than on their merit.

Divergers Individuals who are adept at reflecting on situations from many viewpoints. They excel at brainstorming and are imaginative and people-oriented, but sometimes have difficulty making decisions. Divergers tend to major in the humanities or social sciences. One of the learner groups of the Kolb Inventory of Learning Styles.

Diversity Variation of social and cultural identities among people living together.

Dyslexia A widespread developmental learning disorder that can affect the ability to read, spell, or write.

Emotional intelligence (EI) The ability to recognize, understand, use, and manage moods, feelings, and attitudes.

Empathy Recognition and understanding of another person's feelings, situation, or point of view.

Ethnicity An affiliation assigned to a specific group of people historically connected by a common national heritage or language.

Examples Stories, illustrations, hypothetical events, and specific cases that give support to an idea.

Explanatory writing Writing that is "published," meaning that others can read it.

Exploratory writing Writing that helps you first discover what you want to say. It is private and is used only as a series of steps toward a published work.

Extraverts Individuals who are outgoing, gregarious, and talkative. They are good communicators who are quick to act and lead. One of the personality preferences described by the Myers-Briggs Type Indicator.

Feeling types Individuals who are warm, empathetic, compassionate, and interested in the happiness of others as well as themselves. They need and value harmony and kindness. One of the personality preferences described by the Myers-Briggs Type Indicator.

Financial aid Monetary sources to help pay for college. Financial aid can come in the form of scholarships, grants, loans, work-study, and cooperative education.

Freewriting Writing that is temporarily unencumbered by mechanical processes, such as punctuation, grammar, spelling, context, and so forth.

Grade Point Average (GPA) A student's average grade, calculated by dividing the grades received by the number of credits earned. The GPA represents the level of academic success attained while in college.

Humanities Branches of knowledge that investigate human beings, their culture, and their self-expression. They include the study of philosophy, religion, literature, music, and art.

Idioms Peculiar phrases that cannot be understood from the individual meanings of the words. For example, "cost an arm and a leg," is a familiar American idiom.

Inclusive curriculum A curriculum that offers courses that introduce students to diverse people, worldviews, and approaches. Gender studies, religious studies, and ethnic and cultural studies are some areas included in an inclusive curriculum.

Information Age Our current times, characterized by the primary role of information in our economy and our lives, the need for information retrieval and information management skills, and the explosion of available information.

Information literacy The ability to find, interpret, and use information to meet your needs.

Interdisciplinary Involving two or more academic fields of study, such as history and religion. Encouraging an interdisciplinary approach to teaching can offer a better understanding of modern society.

Interpersonal Relating to the interaction between yourself and other individuals. Friendships, professional networks, and family connections are interpersonal relationships that can be mutually beneficial.

Intrapersonal Relating to how well you know and like yourself, as well as how effectively you can do the things you need to do to stay happy. Knowing yourself is necessary in order to understand others.

Introverts Individuals who like quiet and privacy and who tend to think a lot and reflect carefully about a problem before taking action. One of the personality preferences described by the Myers-Briggs Type Indicator.

Intuitive types Individuals who are fascinated by possibilities, the meaning behind the facts, and the connections between concepts. They are often original, creative, and nontraditional. One of the personality preferences described by the Myers-Briggs Type Indicator.

Judging types Individuals who approach the world in a planned, orderly, and organized way. They strive for order and control, making decisions relatively quickly and easily so they can create and implement plans. One of the personality preferences described by the Myers-Briggs Type Indicator.

Keyword A method of searching a topic by using a word related to the topic.

Kinesthetic learner A person who prefers to learn something through experience and practice, rather than by listening or reading about it. One of the preferences described by the VARK Learning Styles Inventory.

Learning disabilities Disorders, such as dyslexia, that affect people's ability to either interpret what they see and hear or to connect information across different areas of the brain.

Learning styles Particular ways of learning, unique to each individual. For example, one person prefers reading to understand how something works, another prefers being "hands-on."

Long-term memory The type of memory that is used to retain information and can be described in three ways: procedural, semantic, and episodic.

Mapping A preview strategy of drawing a wheel or branching structure to show relationships between main ideas and secondary ideas and how different concepts and terms fit together and help you make connections to what you already know about the subject.

Marking An active reading strategy of making marks in the text by underlining, highlighting, and writing margin notes or annotations.

Mind map A review sheet with words and visual elements that jog the memory to help you recall information more easily.

Mnemonics Various methods or tricks to aid memory, including acronyms, acrostics, rhymes or songs, and visualization.

Multiculturalism The active process of acknowledging and respecting the diverse social groups, cultures, religions, races, ethnicities, attitudes, and opinions within a community.

Multitasking Performing many tasks at the same time, such as eating dinner, typing a paper, and making phone calls.

Outsource To contract out jobs to an external organization in order to lower costs.

Perceiving types Individuals who are flexible and can comfortably adapt to change. They tend to delay decisions to keep their options open to gather more information. One of the personality preferences described by the Myers-Briggs Type Indicator.

Plagiarism   The act of taking another person's ideas or work and presenting them as your own. This gross academic misconduct can result in suspension or expulsion, and even the revocation of the violator's college degree.

Prejudice   A preconceived judgment or opinion of someone based not on facts or knowledge; for example, prejudging someone based entirely on his or her skin color.

Prewriting   Preparing to write by filling your mind with information from other sources; generally considered the first stage of exploratory writing.

Primary sources   The original research or documentation on a topic, usually referenced either at the end of a chapter or the back of the book.

Procrastination   Putting off doing a task or an assignment.

Race   A term that refers to biological characteristics shared by groups of people, including skin tone, hair texture and color, and facial features.

Racism   Prejudice directed at a racial group, which often stems from one group's fear of losing power and privilege to another.

Read/Write learner   A person who prefers to learn information displayed as words. One of the preferences described by the VARK Learning Styles Inventory.

Reflective observation   A learner's ability to reflect on his or her experiences from many perspectives; one of the four stages of the Kolb Inventory of Learning Styles.

Sensing types   Individuals who are practical, factual, realistic, and down-to-earth. Relatively traditional and conventional, they can be very precise, steady, patient, and effective with routine and details. One of the personality preferences described by the Myers-Briggs Type Indicator.

Service learning   Unpaid volunteer service that is embedded in courses across the curriculum.

Short-term memory   How many items you are able to perceive at one time. Memory that disappears in less than 30 seconds (sometimes faster) unless the items are moved to long-term memory.

Social responsibility   The establishment of a personal link with a group or community and cooperation with other members toward shared goals.

Sorting   Sifting through available information and selecting what is most relevant.

Statistics   Numerical data used to support ideas in a speech or written work.

Stereotype   An oversimplified set of assumptions about another person or group.

Supplemental Instruction (SI)   Classes that provide further opportunity to discuss the information presented in lectures.

Syllabus   Formal statement of course requirements and procedures or a course outline provided by instructors on the first day of class to all students.

Synthesis   The process of combining separate information and ideas to formulate a more complete understanding.

Testimony   Evidence in support of something. Quoting outside experts and paraphrasing credible sources are examples of testimony.

Thesis statement   A short statement that clearly defines the purpose of the paper.

Thinking types   Individuals who are logical, rational, and analytical. They reason well and tend to be critical and objective without being swayed by their own or other people's feelings. One of the personality preferences described by the Myers-Briggs Type Indicator.

Transferable skills   General skills that apply to or transfer to a variety of settings. Examples include solid oral and listening abilities, leadership skills, critical thinking, and problem solving.

Visual learner   A person who prefers to learn by reading words on a printed page or by looking at pictures, charts, graphs, symbols, video, and other visual means. One of the preferences described by the VARK Learning Styles Inventory.

Wellness   A catchall term for taking care of your mind, body, and spirit. This includes keeping fit, making healthy choices, achieving balance, and reducing stress in a positive way.

Work-study award   A form of federal financial aid that covers a portion of college costs in return for on-campus employment.

INDEX

Note: Figures and tables are denoted by *f* and *t*, respectively.

Opioids, 315
Optimism, 45, 46
Organization, 25–29, 64–65, 97, 98, 135, 179, 185. *See also*
    Planning
Organizations, student. *See* Campus organizations
Organizers, 25, 26*f*, 138
Outline format, in note taking, 101, 101*f*, 104*f*
Outlines
    essay question tests and, 152, 153*t*
    of lectures, 96, 105
    reading using, 117, 118, 121, 124–125
    for speeches, 179, 181, 185
    for writing, 174
Outsourcing jobs, 217, 220
Overextension, 33, 269

P

Package, financial aid, 247
PAIS (Public Affairs Information Service), 201
Paper mills, 208
Paragraph format, in note taking, 101, 102*f*
Parent Loan for Undergraduate Students (PLUS) program,
    250–251
Parenting, during college, 267
Parents
    financial assistance from, 242, 246, 247, 250–251
    relationships with, 267–268
PARK method of interviewing, 237
Participation in class. *See also* Active learning; Engagement in
    learning; Listening; Note taking; Questions
Paul, Richard, 79, 80
PDAs (personal digital assistants), 20, 25, 138
Peer review, 176
Peers
    assistance from, 35, 112
    personality differences in, 65. *See also* Diversity
    studying with (*See* Study groups)
Pelvic inflammatory disease (PID), 306*t*
Perceiving personality type, 64–65
Periodical databases, 197, 200–201
Personal attacks, 87
Personal attributes, 232. *See also* Values, personal
Personal finances. *See* Money management
Personality characteristics, 62–65, 72–73, 222, 222*t*–223*t*, 224, 224*f*
Phelps, Michael, 70
Physical abilities, and diversity, 280. *See also* Disabilities
PID (pelvic inflammatory disease), 306*t*
Pills, birth control, 308*t*, 314. *See also* Birth control
Pirsig, Robert, *Zen and the Art of Motorcycle Maintenance*, 172
Plagiarism, 162–163, 195, 207–208. *See also* Academic integrity;
    Cheating
Plain English Network, 171
Plain language, 187
Planned Parenthood Federation of America, 309, 319
Planners, 25, 26*f*, 138
Planning
    for careers, 225–227, 226*t*–227*t*, 229
    for emotional intelligence improvements, 48
    future, 7, 21, 24, 27, 29
    schedules and, 24, 25, 30, 31–32
    test preparation and, 149
PLUS (Parent Loan for Undergraduate Students) program, 250–251
Podcasts, 61
Points of view, in critical thinking, 81–92

Politics, involvement in, 8, 285
Portfolios, building
    on academic integrity, 165–166
    on careers and majors, 239–240
    on credit cards, 256–257
    on critical thinking and experiences, 92
    on diversity and study abroad, 291–292
    on family relationships, 272–273
    on learning styles, 72–73
    on memory, 144
    on presentation of notes, 113–114
    on reading strategies, 129–130
    on research, 210–211
    on self-assessment in emotional intelligence, 50–51
    on skills matrix, 15–16
    on speaking skills, 188–189
    on stress and technology, 220–221
    on time management in careers, 36–37
Positive attitude, 45
Positive thinking, 149, 160, 161
PowerPoint slides, 179, 180*f*
Practice speeches, 182
Practice tests, 156, 157, 160, 163
Preface, 121
Pregnancy, 305, 307, 308
Prejudices, 282, 286, 287, 290
PREP format, in speeches, 186
Preparation
    for classes, 96, 108
    for speaking, 178–181, 182–186
    for tests, 147–150, 147*f*, 159, 165
Prescription drugs, 315–316
Presentations. *See* Speaking
Previewing, in reading, 117–118
Prewriting, 173, 174, 176. *See also* Freewriting
Primary sources, of information, 122, 125, 126
Privacy, 24, 245, 265
Problem solving, 44, 79, 82, 123, 124, 155, 232
Procedural memory, 134
Procrastination, 21–23, 159, 164
Procrastination: Why You Do It, What to Do About It (Burka
    and Yuen), 21–22
Professional schools, 6
Professors. *See* Instructors
Profile form, College Board, 248
Progressive muscle relaxation, 161
Pronunciation, 182
Protests, student, 282
Psychological indicators, 62–65
Public affairs, 8, 285
Public Affairs Information Service (PAIS), 201
Public speaking. *See* Speaking
Publication Manual of the American Psychological Association, 207
Punctuality, 20, 34. *See also* Time management
Purdue University, 209
Purpose
    for attending college, 4, 6–7, 22–23, 221–222
    for information searches, 194

Q

Questionnaires
    emotional intelligence, 42
    VARK, 56–57

CREDITS

Chapter 1
p. 3: © Will & Deni McIntyre/Corbis; RH: Photodisc/Punchstock;
p. 5: Courtesy of The University of Texas at San Antonio;
Courtesy of St. Charles Community College; p. 6: Tetra images/
Punchstock; p. 11: © Sonda Dawes/The Image Works

Chapter 2
p. 19: Digital Vision/Getty Images; RH: Rubberball/Punchstock.
p. 21: © D. Hurst/Alamy; p. 23: Edward McDermott

Chapter 3
p. 39: Stockbyte/Punchstock; p. 39: Photodisc/Punchstock;
p. 39: © pixland/Corbis; RH: © james steidl/istockphoto;
p. 41: Corbis/Jupiter Images

Chapter 4
p. 54: purestock/Punchstock; RH: Digital Vision/Punchstock;
p. 62: © Bill Aron/PhotoEdit

Chapter 5
p. 77: © Steve Hamblin/Alamy; RH: © Vincenzo Lombardo/
age footstock; p. 82: © David Fischer/Getty Images;
p. 83: © Christina Micek; p. 88: The Advertising Archives;
p. 90: © Lisa F. Young – Fotolia.com

Chapter 6
p. 93: Jonathan Stark; RH: Schulte Productions/istockphoto
.com; p. 97: Courtesy of John Wigglesworth, Queens College,
NY; p. 107: RodneyTodt; p. 111: Begin Engaged. Jonathan
Stark

Chapter 7
p. 115: AsiaPix/Punchstock; RH: Stockxpert.com; p. 117:
Stockxpert.com; p. 119: Stockxpert.com; p. 123: © Helene
Rogers/Alamy; p. 125: © Don Smetzer/PhotoEdit

Chapter 8
p. 131: Blend Images/Punchstock; RH: Digital Vision/
Punchstock; p. 134: Courtesy of Google, Inc.; p. 135: © Digital
Vision/Getty Images; p. 141: Richard Levine

Chapter 9
p. 146: © fStop/Alamy; p. 151: Courtesy of Scantron;
p. 158: BananaStock/SuperStock; p. 161: Mark Richards/
PhotoEdit

Chapter 10
p. 169: David Young-Wolff/PhotoEdit; p. 172: Book cover from
ZEN AND THE ART OF MOTORCYCLE MAINTENANCE
by ROBERT PIRSIG COPYRIGHT © 1974 BY ROBERT M.
PIRSIG. Reprinted by permission of HarperCollins Publishers;
p. 173: © Christina Micek; p. 174: jsolie/istockphoto.com;
p. 182: Updated version of 8e pg. 184. David Young-Wolff/
Photo Edit

Chapter 11
p. 191: Jonathan Stark; RH: simple stock shots/Punchstock;
p. 194: Courtesy of Calhoun Community College;
p. 195: © PureStock/Alamy; p. 198: © Tom Holton/
SuperStock; p. 198: Courtesy of Wi-Fi Alliance. Reprinted
with permission; p. 201: This image is used with the
permission of EBSCO Publishing; p. 207: Reprinted by
permission of the Modern Language Association of America
MLA Handbook © 2009, 7th edition.

Chapter 12
p. 215: © Somos Images LLC/Alamy; RH: Photodisc/
Punchstock; p. 217 Jacket design by Dean Nicastro from THE
WORLD IS FLAT: A BRIEF HISTORY OF THE TWENTY-
FIRST CENTURY [Updated and Expanded] [Further Updated
and Expanded] by Thomas L. Friedman. Jacket design
copyright © 2007 by Dean Nicastro. Reprinted by permission
of Farrar, Straus and Giroux, LLC; p. 219: Jupiter Images;
p. 228: © Bob Daemmrich/PhotoEdit; p. 229: Courtesy of
AIFS; p. 230: Courtesy of Sumun Pendakur/USC Asian Pacific
American Student Services; p. 231: AP Photo/Dale Sparks

Chapter 13
p. 241: © RubberBall/Punchstock; RH: Stockxpert.com;
p. 253: © JUPITERIMAGES/Comstock Images/Alamy

Chapter 14
p. 259: Twentieth Century Fox Film/Photofest; RH:
Stockxpert; p. 262: © Jupiter Images; p. 267: Scott T. Baxter/
Photodisc/Getty Images; p. 269: Courtesy of the Spartan
Alumni Rowing Association

Chapter 15
p. 275: Jonathan Stark; RH: Stockxpert.com; p. 278: Andersen
Ross/Blend Images/Punchstock; p. 282: © John Hilton/Getty
Images; p. 283: © Bettmann/Corbis; p. 284: Courtesy of
Takebackthenight.org; p. 285: © Telepool GmbH/Courtesy
Everett Collection and Stanford Amnesty International; p. 287:
carryabigsticker.com; p. 289: Joe Raedle/Getty Images

Chapter 16
p. 293: Steve Casimiro/Getty Images; RH: © CSLD/Alamy;
p. 297: Richard Levine; p. 299: David Young-Wolff/Photo Edit;
p. 302: courtesy of www.ethosvegankitchen.com